ART AS SPECTACLE

Images of the Entertainer since Romanticism

NAOMI RITTER

University of Missouri Press
Columbia and London

Copyright © 1989 by
The Curators of the University of Missouri
University of Missouri Press, Columbia, Missouri 65211
Printed and bound in the United States of America
All rights reserved

93 92 91 90 89   5 4 3 2 1

Library of Congress Cataloging-in-Publication Data
Ritter, Naomi.
  Art as spectacle : images of the entertainer since romanticism / Naomi Ritter.
  p.   cm.
  Bibliography: p.
  Includes index.
  ISBN 0-8262-0719-7 (alk. paper)
  1. Entertainers in art. 2. Arts, Modern—19th century. 3. Arts, Modern—20th
century. I. Title.
NX652.E56R58   1989   89-4844
700—cd20   CIP

∞™ This paper meets the minimum requirements of
the American National Standard for Permanence of Paper
for Printed Library Materials, Z39.48, 1984.

Permission granted by New Directions to reprint "Constantly Risking
Absurdity," from *A Coney Island of the Mind.* Copyright © 1958 by
Lawrence Ferlinghetti.

For
(alphabetically)
ROSS CHAMBERS
JEAN STAROBINSKI
ROBERT STOREY

CONTENTS

> It is not so much what you say in a book that constitutes its value . . .
> but all you would like to say, which nourishes it secretly.
> **—André Gide**

PREFACE

A gestation of more than twenty years for this book has involved many debts. Unlike Rimbaud, I alone do *not* have the key to this savage spectacle. In the early sixties, Neil Harris and Robert Spaethling first nurtured my folly. Not only did they already glimpse more in the circus theme than I did, but they also detected a lurking identity between me and the topic. Manfred Durzak, Leonard Forster, and Robert A. Jones offered support when I needed it most. My exhilaration in reading *Portrait de l'Artiste en Saltimbanque* was matched only by meeting Jean Starobinski, who expressed the most gracious interest in my dabbling. Other great minds reacted with an appreciation that amazed me: Willard Bohn, Norbert Fuerst, Henri Peyre, Theodore Reff, Walter Strauss.

Some of my primary readers dealt with more than one chapter, which I consider cruel and *unusual* punishment for any colleague. For this trench work I specially thank Ross Chambers, that savant of the histrionic, whose collegial kindness has no equal. Ursula Franklin never failed to boost my confidence with her enthusiasm; Lilian Furst encouraged my efforts generally and gave specific good advice on German texts; and the astute comments of Donald Haase improved several chapters. Robert Storey, mentor extraordinary, gave the whole manuscript his usual perceptive scrutiny. Unwittingly, my last three chapters seem to answer his call for scholars to decipher the material beyond literature. "Perhaps the illustrations I have included will someday encourage one or two other *amis de Pierrot* to supply us, not only with his pictorial history, but with an equally welcome chronicle of his life in dance, music and film" (Storey, *Pierrot: A Critical History of a Mask*, xv).

As an interloper in art history, I benefited from the aid of Patricia Crown, Adelheid Gealt, and Janice McCullagh. Michael Ossar, Audrone Willeke, and Theodore Ziolkowski sparred admirably with me on German texts; John Swan did likewise on *Commedia* matters; and Anya Royce, defying all adjectives, has served for years as adept midwife. Stephen Archer and Carla Waal gave much time and energy to my thespian department. Katerina Clark, Murlin Croucher, James Curtis, Marjorie Hoover, and James Peters helped to expand my grasp of Russian Modernism. In the French area, I relied on Scott Bates, Anne Greet, Benjamin Honeycutt, Bernadette Murphy, Vivienne Rubin, Emile Snyder, and James Wallace. Robert Barth, Julia and Peter Bondanella, Adrian Del Caro, Harry Geduld, Charlotte Ghurye, and Harry Zohn supplied much information on—respectively—Christclowns, Fellini, Nietzsche, Chaplin, Böll, and the Austrian decadence.

On the technical side, I thank the Indiana University Honors Division, especially Warner Chapman and James Ackerman, for the space and equipment they provided. As for resources, this book owes most to the Indiana University Main Library, my home at home. Its specialists—notably Patricia Riesenman and Anthony Shipps—gave invaluable help. The support of the University of Missouri Research Council has also been indispensable. In particular, I am grateful to John McCormick, Robert Sattelmeyer, Judson Sheridan, and Richard Wallace. My colleagues Eugene Barabtarlo, Roger Cook, and Melissa Poole patiently guided me through the computer labyrinth. Finally, I thank that trio who have given constant support of many kinds: Eileen Gargill, Jon Ritter, and Orlando Katz.

Parts of chapters 3 and 5 have already appeared in *Franz Grillparzer's Der arme Spielmann* and the *Yearbook of Comparative and General Literature*. I thank the genial Clifford Bernd and Henry Remak for allowing me to reprint this material. Economic constraints have forced me to omit quotations in original languages. My apologies to all comparatists for this lack! English translations are my own, unless otherwise noted.

Art as Spectacle

1 INTRODUCTION
Why the Spectacle?

If one asks why the author does not print at the beginning of his book some handsome literary theory, he will be forced to answer that . . . Polichinelle hides from the curious crowd the string that activates his arm.

—Aloysius Bertrand

This book began as a question: why do circus figures abound in modern literature? My first gropings through German texts dealt only with clowns, aerialists, wild animals—and, of course, Kafka's unique hunger-artist. But as my focus necessarily expanded to include first French players, then the *Commedia dell'Arte* and the Russian fools, this study became broadly comparative. Finally, embracing also the graphic arts and film, the book covers the whole troupe of modern European performers. Naturally, such older personnel as the medieval jester or antique slave comedian drew my attention. So I hope to have adequately grazed the import of these forebears for later artistes. But only one chapter deals in detail with pre-Romantic works. In the visual arts, we must start with Callot; as a comparison of my frontispiece and figure 34 suggests, even recent clowns echo his symmetrical pairings. Nor can we neglect Watteau's baffling *Commedia* figures, who seem to anticipate the "difficult" players of our own time.

The unity among these intertextual essays lies in their subject: the recurring imagery of the entertainer. As the chapter titles suggest, my method has a thematic focus. Each chapter treats a cluster of problems posed by the artiste. However, I do not neglect history either, since the players are "the abstracts and brief chronicles of the time."[1] Accordingly, five of my seven chapters present their themes chronologically.

Chapter 2 discusses two major texts by Baudelaire that I view as a genetic chord for the following century of clowns. Chapter 3 delves back into Kleist as one source for the post-Romantic dualities found in Baudelaire. Here I analyze what writers mean in rendering the player as problematic. ("I haven't been a human being, I've been a *performer!*" says André in Wallace Shawn's *My Dinner with André*.) Part of the struggle to define creativity lies in the ambiguous moral status of art, a dilemma as old as Plato. I discuss it from Goethe onward in chapter 4. Next, in chapter 5, I treat one

1. *Hamlet* II, ii, l. 553.

theme synchronically, through the comparative lens of a triptych: two poems and a painting. Chapter 6 studies one ballet in detailed context; the next chapter traces two developing primary themes in the visual arts. The last chapter compares relevant films by two directors strongly tied to the circus aesthetic. Hence the book has a basic symmetry: three chapters on literature, one synchronic chapter on poetry and painting, three chapters on the other arts.

This wealth of material yields answers to my initial question in three areas. First, all the artists considered here identify personally with their performing alter egos. Implicit in this link lies the notion of art as spectacle and artist as entertainer. I discuss the many reasons for these equations, trying to explain their significance. In 1842 Gautier proclaimed, "The era of purely visual spectacles has arrived!" He spoke specifically of drama in his own time; yet this perception also applies to the arts since then.

The ties between creator and popular player have a clear historical basis. For the declassed artist of the nineteenth century, the legitimate actor had less appeal than the showman, who occupied a lower professional level. The recent end of patronage explains part of this kinship, for the unsponsored writer or painter now finds a brother in poverty, the buffoon. But we must go beyond the sociopolitical level to see the lowly status of artists in general. What Jonas Barish calls "the antitheatrical prejudice" extends beyond the stage to anyone who must use his talent to amuse an audience. Nomadic players arouse particular distaste among the landed middle class. For many creators, actual or virtual exile creates the same homelessness; they share with artistes the status of vagrants.

The view of such outsiders as disreputable marks not only modernity, though Cesar Graña demonstrates that the Second Empire brewed a relatively acute antagonism between player and public. As for the past, no one in Roman society enjoyed less repute than the slave comedian. His medieval successor, the ambulant minstrel, always complained of his lot at the courts he entertained. Villon expressed in his life and poetry the plight of the eternal outcast. Even the elevated Walther von der Vogelweide often assumed the tone of the reviled servant. Art and society seem to have always shared a mutual hostility. The Italian Renaissance offers a striking exception to this rule.

Beyond social and historical links, the artist also perceives professional ties to the entertainer. Both must forego ordinary pleasures for the sake of constant discipline. Both depend on talent and skill to survive. Both their pursuits create illusion. Moreover, artists often identify with the daring of aerialists and animal trainers in actually risking their lives. On the aesthetic level, artists think their own vulnerability to critical and financial failure demands the courage of all "risktakers and laughmakers."[2] Fellini defines film-making as a daredevil pursuit; Picasso likens painting to walking a tightrope.

Jean Starobinski proposes that the modern artist, seeing himself as a buffoon, denigrates his own art. Like almost everyone writing in this field, I consider Starobinski's work a virtual Bible; yet I must take issue with this particular point. Naturally, I heed the complex of sociopolitical factors that have cast much of our culture in a starkly negative light. However, despite such pessimism, I find in this material too much of my second item of explanation, transcendence, to settle for an ultimate degrading of art.

By transcendence I mean the elevating of players—clowns, fools, mimes, jesters, musicians, puppets, dwarves, aerialists—above the status of ordinary mortals. From Baudelaire's ruined *saltimbanque* (1861) to Fellini's spiritual clown-waif Gelsomina (1954), even the lowliest performer bespeaks an art "grounded in a sacramental view of the universe."[3] As a logical result of such transcendence, artists persistently make the player a superior being. "Sure they have families, go to church and do a lot of the things that everyone does, but I truly believe that circus folks are a superior people. They're a cut above the man on the street. Theirs is a way of life where they have to face unusual hardship, adversity and danger, but they have some superhuman drive and strength that keeps them going."[4]

Echoing his physical superiority, such spiritual elevation appears throughout works devoted to the aerialist. From this soaring symbol of the circus, writers since Banville have created a vertical metaphor for their own aspirations. The acrobat's lofty perfection translates readily into a divine grace shared by the verbally agile poet. Ferlinghetti gives perhaps the most familiar recent eulogy to the acrobat-poet in *A Coney Island of the Mind* (1955).

> Constantly risking absurdity
> and death
> whenever he performs
> above the heads
> of his audience
> the poet like an acrobat
> climbs on rime
> to a high wire of his own making
> and balancing on eyebeams
> above a sea of faces

2. Dean Jensen, *Center Ring: The Artist,* 15.
3. Suzanne Budgen, *Fellini,* 8.
4. F. Beverly Kelley, quoted in Jensen, *Center Ring,* 11.

                    paces his way
                              to the other side of day
              performing entrechats
                              and sleight-of-foot tricks
        and other high theatrics
                              and all without mistaking
                    any thing
                              for what it may not be
              For he's the super realist
                              who must perforce perceive
                    taut truth
                              before the taking of each stance or step
        in his supposed advance
                              toward that still higher perch
        where Beauty stands and waits
                              with gravity
                              to start her death-defying leap
              And he
                a little charleychaplin man
                              who may or may not catch
                    her fair eternal form
                              spreadeagled in the empty air
                    of existence

For a contrasting deflation, see John Steinbeck. "In the United States, writers are considered just below acrobats and just above seals."[5]

Like the adored ballerina, the soaring aerialist embodies that image of freedom craved by disillusioned artists of the post-revolutionary generation. In Banville specifically, that liberty has a negative basis, his need to escape the philistine bourgeois. Nietzsche transforms the Parnassian rejection of literal and figurative gravity into a new idealism. His first Superman, the rope-dancer, has the positive effect of molding a vitalist philosophy in Zarathustra. But Wedekind's aerialists reflect the failure of art to connect with humanity. The abstractions of his windy idealists signal the end of *l'art pour l'art*.

Not only the lofty acrobat but also his absurd counterpart, the clown, transcends mere entertainment. The inept fool mocks the adept vaulter, yet he too bears a special blessing: laughter. Since its advent in archaic rites, the mockery both invited and inflicted by the clown serves to dispel death. As

5. Lawrence Ferlinghetti, *A Coney Island of the Mind,* 30; Steinbeck quoted in Cesar Graña, *Bohemian versus Bourgeois,* 42. See also the rhapsodic treatment of the acrobat in e. e. cummings's farce *Him* (1927).

pagan scapegoat he carries death away with him; as Christian savior he redeems mankind. Such sacramental functions have not escaped modern artists. Ever since Baudelaire likened the smell of the carnival to incense at a feast, writers have created holy fools.

Generally also, the stylized acts of the circus recall sacred rites. Hence artists suggest a mediating role for all players. Heinz Politzer speaks of the circus as a *Zwischenreich* (a world between); Gerhard Neumann calls vaudeville a *Halbwelt* (an only half-human realm). Apollinaire said of Picasso's tumblers, "They are celebrating silent rites with a difficult agility."[6] Mallarmé's *pitre*-poet-priest, Rouault's grieving martyr-fools, Bergman's crucified clown in *The Naked Night:* all merge mimetic and sacral functions, and all mediate between life and death.

Perhaps the most arresting aspect of the vertical metaphor is the elevation of the clown from clod to Christ. We see this ascent most clearly in the complex figure of Petrushka, who sums up a trend noticeable since the midnineteenth century. Its secularizing climate formed this syllogism: clown = Christ; artist = clown; artist = Christ. Seeing themselves as martyred clowns, poets and painters also gained divine blessing. Hugo considers all artists mediating fools, for he calls them "prêtres du rire" (high priests of laughter).[7] Hence we find the many incarnations of the player as suffering victim, who represents the artist sacrificed to social alienation.

This pervasively negative relation of creator to audience produces what Starobinski calls "sacrificial art." "Just as Christ lost his divinity and became human, and, as a man, was cast out, abandoned, and driven into final isolation, it had to happen that poets, and among them just those who felt misunderstood and rejected, as martyrs to their time and their society, saw him not as the son of God or the savior of mankind, but as a sublime symbol of their own suffering."[8]

The identification of artists with transcendent players comes from more than the secularizing process. Indeed, its roots lie deep in the primitivist retreat from rationality that began with the Romantics. This controversial aspect of the latter nineteenth century goes far to explain the affinity our artists felt for all theater of ritual, mask, and gesture. Claudel, defining Rimbaud as "a mystic in the savage state," captures just this primal mystery that artists perceived in such performances.[9] Hence "primitivism" forms the

6. Heinz Politzer, *Franz Kafka der Künstler,* 146; Gerhard Neumann, "Identifikation in der Gesellschaft," in *Kafka-Handbuch in Zwei Bänden,* ed. Hartmut Binder, 333; L. C. Breunig, ed., *Apollinaire on Art,* 30.

7. Victor Brombert, *Victor Hugo and the Visionary Novel,* 189.

8. Bernhard Blume, *Existenz und Dichtung,* ed. Egon Schwarz, 130.

9. Arthur Rimbaud, *Oeuvres,* ed. Paterne Berrichon, 3.

third part of my account for the ubiquity of showmen. I use quotation marks as William Rubin does, albeit grudgingly, in his incisive catalogue for a recent major exhibit. Apparently no one can improve on the disputed term.

Anthropologists now largely agree that the idea of the primitive expresses more about the condition of Europe in the waning Romantic era than about "tribal" cultures themselves. (Even that seemingly neutral term needs quotation marks, for the societies it denotes elude a single definition; some, like Egypt, were courtly.) "Conscious primitivism represents a failure of romantic aspiration."[10] Like the "japonisme" of the 1860s, the later urge for the exotic marks a disillusion with over-refined Western art. Unfortunately, such early enthusiasts as Gauguin and Nolde confused the animism of African and Oceanic art, its forceful expressive energy, with naiveté. Generations of artists and their critics, influenced by ethnocentric Darwinists, thought they saw mere innocence in reduction, simplicity, and sincerity. This "primitivism" resulted from outdated ideas of evolution.

However, the term may someday lose its pejorative edge. We remember that the labels *Gothic, Baroque,* and *Impressionist* first implied a negative reaction. In any case, we must find some way to discuss the specifically nonrational traits of the popular stage that fascinated our artists. Within the limits of this book, Kleist was the first to hail the "primitive" lack of consciousness in the marionette. His idea of pre-lapsarian paradise stems from Rousseau, and his disciples extend to the present. Not only Nietzsche glorifies vital instinct over crippling intellect; so do Wedekind and Böll. These authors, like their Surrealist, Dada, and Absurdist kin, want to wipe clean the soiled slate of European consciousness. They seek a "simple" art that harks back to emotive origins. In our time, Susan Sontag echoes such urges in calling for "an erotics of art."[11]

Accordingly, these writers relate closely to the most "simple" artist, the child. I trace to Schiller the view of art as imaginative play; Baudelaire extends this idea by deeming the creator "childhood regained at will."[12] The Romantic stress on fantasy and freedom from conventional adult norms makes the child-artist inevitable. We find a related motif in the recurring nostalgia aroused by popular drama. Most obviously, a love of the circus expresses a longing for childhood innocence. In this light we may understand the enthusiasms of artists from Gautier through Fellini: almost all of them adored the ring and its personnel, who often became close friends.

But beyond the emotional pull of the show associated with youth, we

10. William Rubin, *"Primitivism" in Twentieth Century Art,* 1:61.
11. *A Susan Sontag Reader,* ed. Elisabeth Hardwick, 104.
12. Baudelaire, *Oeuvres,* 2:690.

find a more conceptual longing for past traditions. Tiepolo enshrined the national folk comedian Punchinello in protest against encroaching Napoleonic rule; *Petrushka* evolved as a memorial to the recently banned puppet shows; *Les Enfants du Paradis* (*The Children of Paradise*) paid homage to the *Funambules* and the broader spirit of the French theater; Fellini tried to capture the great European clowns before the circus vanished. The creators of all these works share a "primitivizing" motive, for they all seek to immortalize the mythic imagination that they see endangered by a crass materialism.

Perhaps mime is the most noticeable nonrational trait in our examples. To be sure, presenting an idea by movement and gesture alone demands close logical analysis. Yet the mute message reaches the viewer not through reason but through pure perception. The attraction of post-Romantics to the whole nonverbal repertoire—masks, dance, silence itself—bespeaks their complex problems with their own medium, language. Simple, direct contact with an audience offers an envied escape from the inadequacies of speech felt by many writers. Among our graphic artists, the "pre-primitivist" Callot, Watteau, and Tiepolo use the *Commedia* mask to connote that mysterious world beyond words. The moderns, from Daumier through Beckmann, suggest in the haunting mime of their players the truly primitive symbolism of the most basic and universal human gesture.

Artists beat an ultimate retreat from intellectual culture in focusing on the nonhuman and the animal. Like the swan-woman of the ballet, the mythic figures of puppets, marionettes, ghosts, and sprites raise questions about how human beings relate to other creatures. Wedekind makes Lulu both snake and tiger, powerful metaphors for the *femme fatale*. His human animal makes no oxymoron, for he both deflates mind and idealizes nature. The actual trained wild animal poses the crucial problem of defining man in Mallarmé, Kafka, Aichinger, and Bergman.

My thesis, then, has three parts. To put it contextually, these chapters juggle three large balls. In each work discussed, the artist identifies with an entertainer whom he sees as somehow transcendent. The most apt examples integrate all three elements: Picasso's *Les Saltimbanques,* an emblem for this book, shows us Picasso-Harlequin amid his troupe of other-worldly players (see figure 3).

A word on my title *entertainer:* here it signifies the best English approximation of the French *artiste* or German *Artist*. These words connote more skilled technique than art, more craft than creativity. Picasso is an artist, Gypsy Rose Lee an artiste. Nietzsche, claiming himself and Heine as the supreme *Artisten* of the German language, saw their style itself as a feat. Of course, in some examples art and skill overlap. Chaplin amuses millions, yet he transcends the merely popular level of most clowns, who mainly vary vintage routines. Most of my examples enjoy a major ambiguity: the metaphor of artiste as artist. Hence identification of the creator with the player forms my most obvious category. Purists may object that I discuss the actual artists of Thomas Mann, Tonio Kröger and Aschenbach. Naturally, I do not regard these cerebral types as vulgar showmen. But their ultimate, dreadful self-perception—as "gypsies in a green wagon"—demands my attention. In fact, Aschenbach eventually becomes the garish fool he has always loathed.

Finally, I offer some definition of the scope and aims of the thematic approach. All those carping voices in my head ask: how can one justify the seeming fragmentation of works, authors, and periods in focusing on mere clowns? Most obviously, a theme serves as a manageable handle for grasping that complex entity, the history of literature and the other arts. Goethe suggests the importance of motifs in calling them constantly repeated expressions of the human spirit.[13] This idea of a constant in culture may underlie Rilke's plea for a history of the color blue: a task only partly fulfilled by William Gass's genial study of the erotic shade, *On Being Blue.* Mircea Eliade, speaking of "the paradise of archetypes and repetitions," may recall what Kierkegaard saw in recurrence itself.[14] "Hope is an alluring fruit which does not satisfy, recollection is a miserable pittance which does not satisfy, but repetition is the daily bread which satisfies with benediction."[15] (Note the satisfying repetition in this statement.)

Heeding H. O. Burger's call for a literary history based on the comparative interpretation of imagery, thematic scholars have discussed motifs as "seismographs of the historical process," as "the indices of humanity, the ideal forms of the tragic destiny, the human condition."[16] Less grandly and more sensibly, Harry Levin calls them "an avenue for a progression of ideas, whose entrance into literature it invites and facilitates. . . . [Themes] . . . are polysemous: that is, they can be endowed with different meanings in the face of different situations. That is what makes an inquiry into their permutations an adventure into the history of ideas.[17] Theodore Ziolkowski stresses the ability of thematic work to reveal what surrounds literature. "Themes, motifs and images constitute an important link between the liter-

13. Johann Wolfgang Goethe, *Werke,* 12:495.
14. Brombert, *Victor Hugo,* 236.
15. Sören Kierkegaard, *Repetition,* ed. Walter Lowrie, 34.
16. Manfred Frank, *Die Unendliche Fahrt;* Raymond Trousson, *Un Problème de littérature comparée,* 7.
17. Harry Levin, "Thematics and Criticism," in *The Disciplines of Criticism,* ed. Peter Demetz et al., 140, 144.

ary work and the social, cultural and historical contexts in which a post-formalist age now again insists on apprehending the work of art."[18]

In my own simple view, thematics best unveils the myths that nourish literature. Hence I hope to transcend a mere catalogue of comparable images. The developing history of artists' perceptions of the player forms only the surface here. Beyond that descriptive layer lies the denser substance of the conditioning culture. My antic troupe reveals some major facets of the time: the end of romantic aspiration in political disillusion; decadence, death, and rebirth; commercialism; the social alienation of the artist, who becomes both child and narcissist; the escape into "subversive" popular theater; a retreat from analysis, language, rationality.

Some may wonder how we can derive such breadth from a selective thematic focus. My reply concerns the choice of theme. Because my subject lies at the intersection of art and society, this study delineates their crucial relation. In exploring the nature of this link, we touch the essence of the time. Put specifically, my discussion of only one aspect of an oeuvre should reveal the characteristic vision of an artist. I treat only two Fellini films, and even these works from only one angle. However, since his idea of the clown unlocks the essential Fellini, what I say may telescope his general import. In this sense, my book may profile the arts in post-Romantic Europe.

18. Theodore Ziolkowski, *Varieties of Literary Thematics,* ix.

2 ARTISTE, AUDIENCE, AND AUTHOR
A Triangular Relation

Art is not a healthy activity. It is instead a
sublime pantomime at the edge of the grave.
—Jean Starobinski

Baudelaire implies a triangle in two of his most famous images of performance. In the prose poems "Le Vieux Saltimbanque" ("The Old Clown") (1861) and "Une Mort Héroique" ("A Heroic Death") (1863), a tragic drama unfolds through the interaction of the player, his audience, and a narrator who feels emotionally involved in the event. Indeed, this narrator plays the most complex role, for he ambiguously shares in both aspects of the show represented by the player and his public. As narrator he belongs to the audience; as artist he identifies with the performer.

Distinguished critics have already devoted detailed studies to these works. These two prose poems from *Le Spleen de Paris* (*The Spleen of Paris*) have inspired a small school of interpretation focusing on the *saltimbanque* as alter ego for the poet. Jean Starobinski has both engendered this line of criticism with his "Note sur le Bouffon Romantique" ("Note on the Romantic Buffoon") (1966) and given it a decisive climax in *Portrait de l'Artiste en Saltimbanque* (*Portrait of the Artist as Saltimbanque*) (1970).[1] Starobinski's thesis specifies the negative aspect of artists' identification with performers. In the two pieces I discuss, he interprets the narrator's involvement as based on pity and fear. Finding an alter ego in the buffoon particularly, Baudelaire constructs a "mythic representation of the artist" that is both "spectacular and travestied." Moreover, "The writer projects his social decline and his isolation into the abject pariah of the spirit who is the buffoon."[2] Starobinski explores this derogatory self-image of the artist in

---

1. See also the extensive notes in the Baudelaire editions of Robert Kopp and Henri Lemaitre. Ursula Franklin, "The Saltimbanque in the Prose Poems of Baudelaire, Mallarmé and Rilke"; Russell King, "The Poet as Clown: Variations on a Theme"; and Henri Leyreloup, "Baudelaire: Portrait du Poète en Saltimbanque" also make basic contributions to this area of research.

2. Jean Starobinski, "Sur Quelques Répondants Allégoriques du Poète," 402.

many works of modern art. He concludes that this condition reveals a debasement of art itself that characterizes the post-Romantic era.

In *Der Dichter als Dandy* (*The Poet as Dandy*), Sebastian Neumeister discusses one determining aspect of this pessimistic view of art that Starobinski only implies. Neumeister highlights the pervasive venality of the public shown by Baudelaire and his contemporaries. In their era, which Walter Benjamin calls "high capitalism," the artist appears increasingly as a martyr to the commercialization of art. Naturally, the showman, making a commercial spectacle, offers a compelling image of the creator who must beg his living from a consumer society.

While heartily applauding the perceptive analyses of Starobinski and Neumeister, I cannot accept all their conclusions. Here I shall discuss one crucial factor in the artist's conception of the performer that precludes the idea of art as wholly debased and/or commercialized. Namely, the player somehow transcends his wretched condition. Indeed, this transcendence that artists attach to various participants in the popular show—clowns, aerialists, mimes, even the sensitive spectator himself—marks the works I discuss throughout this book. Let us begin to examine this idea in Baudelaire.

POET AND CLOWN

The triangle postulated by Starobinski defines the essential structure of "Le Vieux Saltimbanque." The piece begins with the narrator's visit to an annual Parisian fair. This scene has considerable meaning for him; indeed, he devotes about half the piece to a detailed account of the spectacle. He visits the fair "as a true Parisian," to enjoy its carefree mood. Yet the festival does not attract him solely as a man among peers. On the contrary, he introduces himself into the scene as part of two classes that stand outside and above the working people. "The man of the world himself and the intellectual can hardly escape the allure of this popular festival. They absorb, unwittingly, their part of this carefree atmosphere. And I, . . . as a true Parisian, never miss examining all the booths displayed at these solemn events."[3] Hence, though feeling like part of the crowd, the writer also represents its antithesis. The fair allows him to mingle with the people who normally form only his subject matter, not his companions. The spectacle unites separate classes: a function of significant social import since ancient times.

Moreover, this third paragraph suggests a transcendent union between poet and people. The word *spirituel* for a man of intellect recalls the earlier

3. Charles Baudelaire, *Oeuvres Complètes*, ed. Claude Pichois, 1:295.

description of the fair itself as a *solennité*. This word, echoed here by "époques solennelles" (solemn events), establishes right away the aura of ritual celebration that the fair connotes. Accordingly, the narrator elevates the personnel of this show to classic status, comparing the clowns' act— "solid and heavy"—to Molière's comedy. A hint of fairy-tale magic appears in the dancers, who resemble fairies or princesses. At the end of the first part of the piece, Baudelaire again stresses the transcendence of the scene. "And everywhere, dominating all the odors, a scent of frying, which was like *the incense of this feast*." Both this phrase and "solemn events" occur emphatically at the end of a paragraph.[4]

The second part of the prose poem brings us directly to the old clown. In total contrast to the hectic interplay of performers and public around him, this miserable figure—"emaciated, decrepit, a ruin of a man"—stands alone in his wretched shack. One could hardly imagine a greater contrast to the glittering fair. Yet the old man still belongs to this world, if only through the past. In referring to his former supremacy, Baudelaire uses one word, *abdiqué*, which immediately relates the man to the fairy-tale world of the carnival. Such implied past mastery links the old clown to both the other-worldly dancers and the herculean strongmen. Thus the man represents decadence.

Like his opposite number in age and sex, the subject of "A Une Jeune Saltimbanque" ("To a Young *Saltimbanque*") (1845), the old clown is also a fallen angel. "But fallen now, there you are, my poor angel."[5] Furthermore, one symbol shows that he still shares the transcendence of the fair. Two stubs of candle illumine not only the darkness of his hovel, but also his identity as part of a special communion. Like the solemnity and the incense above, these smoking bits of candle again punctuate the end of a paragraph with an image suggesting ritual ceremony.

In the final part of the prose poem, the poet returns to his own perceptions. Indeed, his focus shifts sharply from the old man to himself, as he discovers what this figure means for him. His first reaction gives the sensation of choking and repressed tears. "I felt my throat gripped by the terrible hand of hysteria, and it seemed that my vision was blocked by those rebellious tears that refuse to fall." This sentence recalls the similar inward tears of "La Muse Vénale" ("The Venal Muse") (1857). But there the choked emotion belongs to the performer, not the spectator. The poet, expressing his anxieties, envisions himself as a "starving player," entertaining the mob with his "laughter soaked in invisible tears."[6]

4. Ibid., 1:296; italics mine.
5. Ibid., 1:221.
6. Ibid., 1:296, 1:15.

Hugo gives perhaps the earliest Romantic model for such invisible tears, forcibly masked by laughter, in *Le Roi S'Amuse* (*The King at Play*) (1832). Triboulet expresses the impotent anger of one compelled to hide his pain in playing the jester.

> If I want for a moment to withdraw
> and calm my heart, which weeps bitterly,
> my master intrudes, my joyous master,
> who, all-powerful, beloved of women, happy in life . . .
> kicks me into the shadows where I moan,
> and says with a yawn: Buffoon! Make me laugh![7]

The operatic progeny of Triboulet, Verdi's Rigoletto (1851), was first called Triboletto.[8] However, his final name reminds us of his trade: laughter. And his tragic fate also involves the repressing of tears. He too lives out the bitter irony of personal misery varnished with public mirth.

> O torture, being a cripple!
> O torture, wearing a foolscap!
> Night and day I must laugh,
> Shamming hilarity!
> I'm denied man's relief in sorrow,
> Consoling tears!
> There is my noble master,
> Youthful and carefree, Always happy, handsome,
> Who commands when he pleases:
> Come, my fool, and amuse me![9]

Hugo explores more of this ambiguity of tearful laughter in *L'Homme Qui Rit* (*The Man Who Laughs*) (1869). The face of the freak hero, Gwynplaine, has been disfigured into a frozen smile, so he too must always laugh. He says "I laugh: which means: I cry." Gwynplaine's petrified laugh-

7. Victor Hugo, *Théâtre Complet*, ed. J.-J. Thierry and Josette Mélèze, 1:1380.
8. See Anni Ubersfeld, *Le Roi et le Bouffon*, 102, on the ultimate source for Triboulet in Rabelais. Her quotation from the *Tiers Livre* (1546) shows that Shakespeare was not the first to suggest role reversal as the essential relation of king and fool. "Mathematicians say that kings and fools are born under the same star." With convincing evidence, Ubersfeld accepts the link of *Le Roi S'Amuse* to *Pantagruel*. In any case, we must note Rabelais' presence in the theory and practice of the grotesque that looms so large for Hugo. The detailed discussion of Hugo and Bakhtin by Ubersfeld also necessarily involves Rabelais. See chapter 5 here for further links of carnivalization with the modern grotesque.
9. *The Authentic Librettos of the Italian Operas*, 5.

ing face may recall the Greek mask of comedy. "The 'sepulchral immobility' of the sneering face becomes an emblem of eternal punishment."[10]

The most familiar example of the tearful jester appears in Leoncavallo's *Pagliacci* (1892). In his aria "Vesti la giubba," Canio invokes this same pathos of the clown's laughter.

> To act, with my heart saddened with sorrow.
> I know not what I'm saying or doing.
> Yet I must face it. Courage, my heart!
> Thou art not a man; thou art but a jester!
> On with the motley, the paint and the powder,
> The people pay thee, and want their laugh, you know.
> If Harlequin thy Colombine has stolen,
> Laugh, Punchinello! The world will cry "Bravo!"
> Go hide with laughter thy tears and thy sorrow,
> Sing and be merry, playing thy part,
> Laugh, Punchinello, for the love that is ended,
> Laugh for the sorrow that is eating thy heart.[11]

This juxtaposition of tears and laughter recalls Beaumarchais' classic formulation, "I must laugh, for fear of having to weep," or Byron's, "And if I laugh at any mortal thing, / This that I may not weep." In the operas, however, the authors sharpen the paradox of laughter masking tears by linking both reactions to the clown. Beaumarchais and Byron note a general psychological response; Baudelaire attributes this reaction to the fool's profession. Again in "Le Fou et la Vénus" ("The Fool and Venus") (1862), the jester, symbol of mirth, cries out to the goddess, "with eyes full of tears."[12] The poet associates all his clown figures—in both these poems and in the two prose poems "Le Vieux Saltimbanque" and "Une Mort Héroïque"— with that particular pathos resulting from the mixture of laughter and tears.[13]

Despite his tears, the poet in "Le Vieux Saltimbanque" cannot identify the exact import of the old clown until after he has left him. As he is about to leave the man some money, the crowd pushes past, carrying him far away. Finally, still "obsessed with this vision," the poet realizes he has seen his own alter ego: "the image of the old man of letters who has outlived his generation, for whom he was the brilliant entertainer; of the old poet with-

10. Victor Brombert, *Victor Hugo and the Visionary Novel*, 188, 179.
11. *Authentic Librettos*, 378.
12. Baudelaire, *Oeuvres*, 1:284.
13. For a thorough study of this dialectic of tearful laughter in Hugo, see Brombert, *Victor Hugo.* Pauline Newman-Gordon explores the problem in *Le Rire en Pleurs: Corbière, Laforgue, Apollinaire.*

out friends, without family, without children, degraded by his misery and by public ingratitude, and into whose shack the fickle audience no longer wants to venture."[14]

An unusual and neglected interpretation of "Le Vieux Saltimbanque" depends specifically on these last lines. Robert Füglister sees in the old clown Baudelaire's image of Daumier, whom the journal Le Charivari had abruptly dismissed in 1860. In "Gaukler und Akrobat als Alter Ego des Künstlers" ("Buffoon and Acrobat as Alter Ego of the Artist"), Füglister argues that since Baudelaire published his prose poem only five weeks after the appearance of an article criticizing Daumier, the work served to eulogize the artist Baudelaire revered. In February 1860, Daumier was fired; on 11 March 1860, Baudelaire wrote to Poulet-Malassis that Charivari had thrown Daumier out with a mere half-month's pay. On 21 September 1861, the founder of Le Charivari, Charles Philipon, published his article "Abdication de Daumier I" in Le Journal Amusant. The essay title alone suggests the hostility of Philipon, also a caricaturist, to his famous rival. Accordingly, Philipon claims that the master of amusement had lately disappointed his following. "This man, having been the brilliant entertainer of the public for thirty years, has finally bored the readers, rather than diverting them."[15]

On 1 November 1861, Baudelaire published "Le Vieux Saltimbanque" in La Revue Fantaisiste. Füglister identifies the old clown as an image of Daumier because of this close dating of the critical article by Philipon and the portrait of the rejected artist by Baudelaire. And we find further proof of a close relation between the text and Daumier in the publication of his last series of Saltimbanques pictures in 1867, shortly after Baudelaire's death.

Here we might compare the similar treatment of Daumier by Baudelaire in "Quelques Caricaturistes Français" ("Some French Caricaturists") (1857): "A man who, each morning, diverts the Parisian public, who satisfies its need for amusement and supplies its food. The bourgeois, the man of affairs, the

14. Baudelaire, Oeuvres, 1:297. The word baraque also appears in a similar context in Mallarmé's "La Déclaration Foraine" (1887): "Strange and purple, a heart-gripping spectacle detained us: a shanty, apparently empty, repudiated by the many-colored frame or the inscription in capital letters" (Ursula Franklin, trans., An Anatomy of Poesis, 238). Here again a tawdry shack houses symbols of sanctity, connoting even the ultimate mysteries of "the arcane." Comparable to the candle stubs in "Le Vieux Saltimbanque" suggesting ritual communion, here a "tattered mattress" ironically symbolizes a sumptuous theater curtain or a veil over holy objects. Franklin specifies in admirable detail how Mallarmé "confers on the sideshow the spirituality of a ritual performance" (124). Just as Baudelaire evokes the image of his decrepit showman by means of the things surrounding him, so does Mallarmé characterize the old trouper by an object. Indeed, the tattered mattress stands for the man himself, who, typically for Mallarmé, does not appear.

15. Charles Baudelaire, Petits Poèmes en Prose, ed. Robert Kopp, 2:236. For an alternate view of Daumier's dismissal, see Howard Vincent, Daumier and his World, 172.

urchin, the woman: they all laugh and go on, the ingrates, without even noticing his name. Up to now, only some artists have seen something serious here, which is truly *material for a study*."[16] The italics are mine, to suggest that this project became "Le Vieux Saltimbanque."

However, I find an even stronger tie between the old clown and Daumier in two textual links that we can hardly ignore. First we note the title of the essay by Philipon, "Abdication de Daumier I." Baudelaire clearly echoes this title in "He had renounced, he had abdicated." What Philipon meant ironically now becomes a serious tribute to a former king. Here we may catch an allusion to the ironic relation of king and jester. Baudelaire seems to say that Daumier, as caricaturist, played buffoon to his two monarchs: Louis-Philippe and Louis-Napoleon. As in the literary tradition of Shakespeare, the traditional roles are reversed; the supposed jester becomes the sage, the king a true fool. Second, Baudelaire calls his clown "le brillant amuseur," the same epithet used by Philipon. The exact repetition of this phrase makes it likely that Baudelaire used his piece to reply to Daumier's critics.

"THE PEOPLE"

So much for the relation of artist to artiste, which depends on identification. As for the third part of our triangle, the audience, Baudelaire portrays it ambiguously. In fact, his attitude to the people almost splits the prose poem in half. We may read the first part, up to the presentation of the old clown, as a eulogy to the fair itself. Here Baudelaire gives us one of his most evocative treatments of Parisian public life, a principal subject of the book *Le Spleen de Paris*. We may see here a prime example of what Mikhail Bakhtin calls "carnivalisation." In his renowned books on Dostoevsky and Rabelais, Bakhtin investigates many modern examples of this process, which he traces to Menippean satire.

Carnivalization involves subverting conventional social order through an integration of normally conflicting elements. The carnival attitude produces a free interrelationship among people and things usually separated by many hierarchies: the poor from the rich, the lowly from the lofty, the sacred from the profane, even the living from the dead. Hence we see the easy mixing of social types at the fair, not only among the audience but also among this varied public and performers. A supreme example of carnivalization appears in the film by Carné and Prévert *Les Enfants du Paradis* (1944). All social elements mix in a climactic carnival: actors, criminals,

16. Baudelaire, *Oeuvres*, 2:549.

aristocrats, children, beggars. In "Le Vieux Saltimbanque," this mixture achieves total reciprocity. "All was light, dust, cries, joy, tumult; some spent while others gained, all equally joyous." Therefore the phrase "incense of this feast" a few lines later implies a communion among celebrants in a rite.[17]

Adding to his idealization of the scene, Baudelaire refers to the audience repeatedly as "the people." Three times he uses the phrase; he also calls the fair "this popular jubilee." Considering the importance of each word in the prose poems, the reader must note the difference between "spectators," or simply "the public," and the repeated "the people." No other concept gets such insistent reiteration here.

Already in 1832, Jules Janin had glorified the mime theater of the *Funambules* as the home of proletarian art. In his biography of the famous clown Jean-Gaspard Deburau, Janin specified Deburau's genius in creating the first Pierrot of the people.

How he is Pierrot I cannot say. . . . The fact is that he has made a revolution in his craft. . . . He is the actor of the people, the friend of the people, a gossip, a gourmand, a man of the streets, a rogue, invulnerable, revolutionary like the people. . . . Gilles is not such and such a man with a proper name and a definite social position; Gilles *is* the people . . . always poor, like the people; it is the people that Deburau represents in all his dramas; above all he has the sensibility of the people.[18]

Janin was probably the first writer, and certainly the most insistent one, to forge this link between the mime artist and his lower-class audience. Of course, we find irony in the fact that such supposedly proletarian theater, and especially Deburau himself, became the darling of the literati, who only fancied their kinship with "the people." However, problematic though this relationship was, it remained a dominant factor in subsequent images of players such as Baudelaire's old clown.

To take just one example of this democratic, even revolutionary, aspect of the clown figure, consider the character of Deburau in the film *Les Enfants du Paradis*. In an early scene of the film, Baptiste drinks wine with his new colleague, Frédérick Lemaitre. As the mime describes his kind of acting, he

---

17. Ibid., 1:296. Compare Apollinaire's reaction to Picasso's painting "Les Saltimbanques" (1905): "One cannot confuse these saltimbanques with actors. The spectator must be pious, for they are celebrating silent rites with a difficult agility" (*La Plume,* 15 June 1905, in L. C. Breunig, ed., *Apollinaire on Art,* trans. Susan Suleiman, 16). Here too we sense a binding community of performers and public.

18. Quoted in Paula Harper, *Daumier's Clowns,* 69.

shows right away that it depends on his identification with the popular audience.

Baptiste: Yes, [the gallery-gods] understand everything. They are poor people, but I am like them. I love them, I know them well. Their lives are small, but they have big dreams. And I don't only want to make them laugh, I want to frighten them, to move them, to make them cry.[19]

Lemaitre, who represents the most grandiose style of "legitimate" acting, had just revealed *his* identification with the heroes he plays.

Frédérick: . . . tonight you have been drinking with Julius Caesar! Julius Caesar or somebody else! Charles the Bold . . . Attila . . . Henry IV . . . Ravillac . . . Yes, I'm sure of it, my destiny is to bring to life again the great men of the world. . . . They played their role, now it's my turn! . . . Julius Caesar, arise! It's Frédérick who calls you! I shall shake out his dust . . . and drag his ghost onto the stage flooded with light . . . and he will be alive again . . . and he will astonish the world because of me.[20]

The contrast between these two speeches characterizes the two figures with admirable economy. Here we find in nuce the opposition between "serious" and popular drama that became a significant conflict in the latter part of the nineteenth century. Think of Dumas versus Labiche, Schnitzler versus Nestroy, Shaw versus Barrie. On another level, we may also see the dualistic play of Harlequin against Pierrot. In personal terms, the heroic self-inflation of Harlequin-Frédérick appears comic, whereas the modesty of Pierrot-Baptiste attracts our sympathy. Indeed, these few lines of the mime pay tribute to that same proletarian ideal proclaimed by Janin.

We need not wonder long why Baudelaire first idealizes the democratic aspect of the fair. For as soon as the miserable old clown appears, he presents a complete contrast to his carnival surroundings. There we find "everywhere joy, gain, debauch; . . . here absolute misery." In Bakhtin's terms, the first half of the piece depicts carnivalization; the second half shows alienation. Accordingly, the joyous communion of the people turns to ostracism and exile of the unfit. "The people" becomes simply "the forgetful world." After showing us the positive aspect of a spiritual community, Baudelaire reveals its cruelty as a crowd of hedonists. This negative side of the public remains our final view of it, since the poet's last image of the

19. Jacques Prévert, *Children of Paradise,* trans. Dinah Brooke, 61.
20. Ibid., 60.

crowd is its pushing past him and the old clown. Hence they effectively abort his act of sympathy for the spurned artiste.

Such antipathy of the poet toward his public had already emerged in "La Muse Vénale." There again, the parting words evoke a lasting hostility for the audience.

> In order to earn your daily bread,
> you will have to be like a choir-boy, swinging the censor
> and chanting the *Te Deums* that you hardly believe in.
>
> Or you will be a mountebank, using all your arts,
> plus your laughter steeped in invisible tears,
> to entertain the boorish public.[21]

As in "Le Vieux Saltimbanque," Baudelaire leaves us with a bitterly negative image of the audience. Indeed, one can hardly imagine a greater contrast to the ideal relation between actor and public that Baptiste describes in *Les Enfants du Paradis*.

This mutual harmony between the artist and his audience has no historical basis. Contemporary sources show that Deburau had more complex relations with his public. The climax of his troubles came when he hit and unwittingly murdered a man who had insulted him. Such actual incidents lend credence to the overwhelmingly negative view of the relation between artiste and spectator in the work of Baudelaire and his peers. His fellow Parnassians, for instance, though idealizing the player himself, show the audience as philistine at best, hateful at worst. In "Le Saut du Tremplin" ("The Spring in the Air") (1857) Banville has his clown soar from his springboard into the sky to escape "the bespectacled bankers, the critics, the young ladies and the passionate realists."[22]

In Banville's *Pauvres Saltimbanques* (*Poor Saltimbanques*) (1853) the audience again treats the artistes as little better than beggars. When a street crowd assembles to watch a performance, some prosperous men attempt to drive off this public. "Suddenly, four or five bearded men in elegant capes started hitting the crowd with blows to the stomach and elbow, and then withdrew, crying 'It's a scandal! How can the police tolerate such things?' 'Indeed,' said the citizen, who always represents the Greek chorus, 'it is bizarre that the police tolerates them.'"[23]

Perhaps the most malign vision of the crowd emerges from one of Le-

---

21. Baudelaire, *Oeuvres*, 1:15.
22. Théodore de Banville, *Oeuvres*, 290.
23. Théodore de Banville, *Pauvres Saltimbanques, 7*.

conte de Lisle's *Poèmes Barbares* (*Poems on the Barbarians*), "Les Mon-
treurs" ("The Showmen") (1862).

> Even if it meant burying myself in some eternal anonymity,
> in my stoical pride and from the depths of my unknown grave,
> I would not sell my secret ecstasy or my disillusion to you.
> I refuse to expose my private life
> to the cries and the clamor of the general public.
> And I will not dance on your indiscriminate stage
> with your clowns and your prostitutes.[24]

The language of commerce—"deliver," "sell," "prostitute"—makes explicit
what Baudelaire only implies in "Le Vieux Saltimbanque." By juxtaposing,
hence equating, *histrions* and *prostituées*, the author specifies the performer's social and moral degradation. Baudelaire concentrates this link in
himself as poet-whore in an early poem.

> My mistress is no modish beauty;
> the ugly one gets all her luster from my love.
> Invisible to all the mocking world,
> her beauty flowers only in my sad heart.
>
> In order to have slippers, she has sold her soul;
> but dear God would laugh if, beside this tramp
> I played heroic and aped nobility,
> I who sell my thoughts and call myself author.[25]

Both Leconte de Lisle and Baudelaire associate the poet with the prostitute.
But they differ basically in their attitudes toward this link. Leconte haughtily
declares himself superior to those who sell their wares, either artistic or
sexual; Baudelaire, compassionate to all forms of suffering, finds a sister in
the woman who sells herself. Walter Benjamin compares this poem to "La
Muse Vénale" of the same period. He suggests that poet and prostitute
belong together as peers in a commercial culture. "The final strophe, beginning 'This vagabond, she is everything to me,' readily includes this creature
in the community of Bohemians. Baudelaire knew how it really was with
the man of letters: as a *flâneur* he mingles among the public. He claims to
thereby study it, but actually he is looking for a buyer."[26]

24: Robert Denommé, trans., *Leconte de Lisle*, 90.
25. Baudelaire, *Oeuvres*, 1:203.
26. Walter Benjamin, *Das Paris des Second Empire*, ed. Rosemarie Heise, 60.

In a more general statement, Benjamin shows the inevitable ties among Baudelaire, prostitution, and the big city. "For the work of Baudelaire, a decisive problem lies in the changing face of prostitution when the big cities were evolving. Baudelaire expresses this change, it is one of the great subjects of his poetry. Prostitution acquires new arcana through the labyrinthine quality of the city itself. Like the *flâneur*, the prostitute becomes part of the labyrinth at the mythic heart of the great city."[27]

The whore, though comparable to the artist, does not offer enough professional parallels to constitute a true alter ego. The *saltimbanque*, however, that lowliest of street players, is just such a brother to the alienated poet of the Second Empire. First of all, this man had already suffered a loss of class with the end of patronage. Now he had to sell his wares like any common hawker. Second, his increasingly outspoken hostility to the Philistine regime conferred a dubious political status. Like the reviled *saltimbanque*, this rebel feared harassment by the police. Third, the rise of commercialism in this era helps to explain why writers and artists identified with entertainers at the lowest social level. In the fragile subsistence of such players, artists saw their own economic marginality in a materialistic society.

These ties between performer and worker take us back to that vivid evocation of the time, *Les Enfants du Paradis*. The connection between players at the *Funambules* and their proletarian audience gives one of the most basic concepts of the film. The title itself, as Prévert explained, refers to both sides of the footlights.

Interviewer: To begin with, this paradise, what is it?
Prévert: It is the Gods! . . . the cheapest seats in the theater, the worst, the furthest
    away from the stage, for the "people," that is why it was called Paradise
    in those days . . . the days of the Boulevard du Crime . . .
Interviewer: And the children, the children of Paradise?
Prévert: They are the actors . . . and the audience too, the good-natured, working-
    class audience.[28]

Ironically, those furthest from the stage share an identity with the actors.

27. Walter Benjamin, *Schriften*, 1:688. Karl Kraus also takes up the parallel of writer and whore. "Hunger can make any man into a journalist, but not any woman into a whore" (quoted in Hans Mayer, *Outsiders*, trans. Dennis Sweet, 111). Here the woman seems morally superior to the man. In a famous epigram, Kraus treats language as impure goods. "With hungry heart and burning brain, / Night after night I sought her. / As a brazen whore I caught her, / And made her a virgin again" (Harry Zohn, *Karl Kraus*, 58).
   28. Prévert, *Children*, 9.

The gallery gods, the peanut gallery, belong just as much to the metaphorical paradise of innocence as the "blessed" artistes themselves.

Accordingly, Prévert often shows us determining aspects of this kinship between players and audience. One scene in particular evokes summarily the interdependence of the two groups: the first encounter between Baptiste and his beloved, Garance. While she watches his performance, he spies her companion, Lacenaire, robbing the man between them. He then rescues her from the police because only he, onstage, saw what actually happened. Their subsequent love affair exemplifies the intermingling of artistes and their public. Furthermore, Garance does not give up her proletarian status by briefly starring at the *Funambules;* she merely joins the troupe. She had been working as a bathtub Venus in the first scene of the film, where we see a typical sidewalk *parade.* Such shows gave enticing previews of what the theater provided; this scene highlights the close, even bodily, contact between hawkers and spectators.[29]

For this job, Garance needed only to sit, seemingly naked, in a tub that the public could inspect. Here she is no artiste, only a woman on display. The revelation of this beauty by a *montreur* at the start of the film recalls a similar show in the first of Mallarmé's collected prose poems in *Divagations,* "Le Phénomène Futur" ("The Future Marvel") (1864). In both the film and the prose poem a hawker proclaims a great marvel he will show. The woman they reveal, called "La Verité" in the film and "A Woman of Old" in the text, symbolizes the work of art she initiates. Here we see "the prophetic character" of Mallarmé's Birth of Venus, which announces "in a blinding vision his own poetry."[30]

Similarly, we may view the immersed Venus in the first scene of the film as a vision of two chief entities it will depict: the magical personality of Garance, the woman who both activates and ends the plot, and the commercial spectacle of the *Funambules.* Mallarmé's Ideal Woman signifies redemption through art; so does Garance intimate that same paradise of the film's title. Here too the film provides a parallel for Mallarmé, who shows the decadence of the world framing his Future Marvel. In the film, Paris appears at both the beginning and end as a riotous carnival. However, the story this city holds unveils the pervasive corruption and suffering, even death, that lie beneath its glittering surface.

When Baptiste finally convinces Garance to work inside the theater, she

29. Ibid., 34–38. For a familiar painting of this subject, see Seurat's *La Parade* (1887) (Metropolitan Museum of Art). The ballet *Parade* by Cocteau, Satie, Picasso, and Massine (1917) also immortalizes this sidewalk preview, whose commercialism links it to the carnival (see chapter 7, note 32).

30. Franklin, *Anatomy of Poesis,* 18.

actually performs. Hence she embodies the easy transition from proletarian to actor. Her life as artiste does not differ much from what it was before; she still earns a meager living and has no home. The accidents of fortune still determine her fate, for she must continue to live by her wits alone in a world of daily uncertainty. Indeed, the film brilliantly evokes the magical ambience of Paris in the 1830s, when the lives of people like Baptiste and Garance could change literally overnight.

Another scene shows the essential relation of the "gallery gods" to the stage as negative, even hostile. When chaos ensues onstage from the eruption of a vendetta among two warring families of players, the balcony patrons demand their money back. Their taunts enrage the greedy director, since they threaten his reputation, not to mention his financial survival. This view of the crowd recalls what Baudelaire shows us in "Le Vieux Saltimbanque." The film depicts the same reckless hedonism in the angry mob that the prose poem suggests in its final image of the carnival mob sweeping the poet away from the old clown. In both scenes we have striking views of "public ingratitude," which suddenly polarizes the previously intermingled actors and audience. As in the first part of the prose poem, where "the people" and the players share their reciprocal carnival joy, so in the *parade* scene of the film do spectators mingle happily with performers. But now the crowd turns against the entertainer who no longer meets their need for amusement. Both the film and the prose poem show the audience as demanding consumers.

Critics have long recognized that artistic images of the crowd grow increasingly ominous as the nineteenth century progresses. Benjamin, for instance, sees alarming portents in the new power of the masses. "Fear, revulsion and horror were the emotions which the big-city crowd aroused in those who first observed it. For Poe it has something barbaric; discipline just barely manages to tame it. Later, James Ensor tirelessly confronted its discipline with its wildness; he liked to put military groups in his carnival mobs, and both get along splendidly—as the prototype of totalitarian states, in which the police make common cause with the looters."[31]

Benjamin anticipates one of the first books to treat crowd behavior in anthropological detail: *Masse und Macht* (*Crowds and Power*), by Elias Canetti (1960). We may compare what Canetti says of man in primitive societies to what Benjamin shows of Baudelaire in the age of capitalism. The essay "Some Motifs in Baudelaire" relates the poet to his culture specifically through his perceptions of the Parisian masses. "This crowd, of whose existence Baudelaire is always aware, has not served as the model for any of

31. Walter Benjamin, *Charles Baudelaire: Lyric Poet in the Era of High Capitalism,* 131.

his works, but it is imprinted on his creativity as a hidden figure. . . . To endow this crowd with a soul is the very special purpose of the *flâneur*. His encounters with it are the experience that he does not tire of telling about. Certain reflexes of this illusion are an integral part of Baudelaire's work."[32]

Beyond these statements, Benjamin does not specify the nature of the relation between *flâneur* and crowd. He does not, for instance, explicate the complex dialectic of "Les Foules." However, he does imply that the "universal communion" of the one with the many belongs to the new European experience of a purely optical relation to masses of people. As Georg Simmel notes in his *Soziologie,* "Interpersonal relations in big cities are distinguished by a marked preponderance of the activity of the eye over the activity of the ear."[33] Baudelaire develops the at first bewildering, then alienating effect of this urban silence in "Le Peintre de la Vie Moderne," inspired partly by *The Man of the Crowd* by Poe. This man, who lives through his eyes only, is not only a "solitary stroller"; he becomes, in extreme form, a convalescent. Considering the title of this essay, we must conclude that Baudelaire perceived such a passive experience of life as characteristic of his time.

Both Benjamin and Naomi Schor (in her *Zola's Crowds*) cite Hugo as the first writer to address the problem of the crowd. One need only think of his titles—*Les Misérables, Les Travailleurs de la Mer*—to feel the weight of the people in his consciousness. Hugo senses the power of nature in the urban mass. Zola inherited from Hugo not only his republican empathy for the people, but also the master's idea of the writer himself as "leader of the crowd."[34] One does not sense this positive self-image in the poet-narrator of "Le Vieux Saltimbanque," for he separates himself sharply from the mob. Indeed, we may consider this text one of the clearest statements of the writer's hostility to the crowd. Accordingly, the text glorifies the artist, whose relation to the public amounts to martyrdom.

THE HEROIC ARTIST

In "Une Mort Héroique," instead of a contemporary fair and an aging clown, we have a Renaissance prince, his court, and his jester. Although this setting and personnel differ considerably from those in "Le Vieux Saltimbanque," the two pieces still relate closely. Again a poet-narrator mediates between the player and his public. And both the prince-impresario and

32. Ibid., 120.
33. Ibid., 38.
34. Naomi Schor, *Zola's Crowds,* 43. See also Benjamin, "Die Menge bei Hugo und Baudelaire," "Der Mann der Menge," and "Die Menge als Schleier," in *Das Paris.*

his nobles parallel the crowd in the earlier piece, for all three parties represent the audience/antagonist for the performer. Moreover, both milieux convey a political meaning. The tragic old clown rejected by his own carnival suggests the artist's alienation from his public in the Second Empire. In "Une Mort Héroique," the cast of characters alone—prince, nobles, and jester—highlights immediately the power structure of feudal despotism.

In "Le Vieux Saltimbanque," the clown does not appear until about halfway through the piece. Here, by contrast, Baudelaire immediately gives us his image of the performer. And the problematic status of this man emerges just as promptly. Fancioulle, the first word in the piece, is "almost one of the friends of the Prince." With this disturbing "almost," Baudelaire introduces a note of conflict that he intensifies with the word *fatal* in the next sentence. In fact, by means of a general remark on psychology, the narrator implies his mime's tragic fate. "But for those dedicated by temperament to comedy, serious matters have a fatal attraction, and although it may appear bizarre that ideas of liberty should arise in the mind of a buffoon, Fancioulle did one day join a conspiracy formed by some malcontent nobles."[35]

Our next subject of scrutiny, the prince, relates reciprocally to Fancioulle. Not only does the ruler represent a frustrated artist, plagued by ennui, but Fancioulle also imitates the sadistic role of the prince, whom he conspires to kill. The ruler envies the mime his artistry, whereas Fancioulle has a "fatal attraction" to political power. Indeed, he dies from shock when a hiss of disapproval threatens the climax of his act. So we see that both figures need to wield power over a public.

The polar relation of these two characters recalls the interdependence of the Shakespearean king and jester. One thinks of Hamlet, who sees in Yorick an alter ego. Hamlet also puts on "an antic disposition" in seeking to expose the present king. Indeed, he vacillates, characteristically, between the roles of prince and jester. More specifically, Lear and his Fool relate through paradoxes and ambiguities that resemble the ironic reciprocity of the prince and Fancioulle. "Lear's tragedy is the investing of the King with motley; it is also the crowning and the apotheosis of the Fool."[36] Similarly, Fancioulle's betrayal constitutes a dethroning of the prince, whose attempt at vengeance is thwarted by the mime's heroic death and posterity. Fancioulle does not resemble the other Renaissance buffoons Triboulet and Rigoletto, for his story does not focus on the moral questions posed by these malevolent men.[37] Hugo creates a dialectic of laughter and power;

35. Baudelaire, *Oeuvres*, 1:319.

36. Enid Welsford, *The Fool*, 271.

37. If we compare Triboulet to Quasimodo, for instance, we see the difference between basic corruption and basic goodness. Despite some similarities between the two hunch-

Baudelaire evokes the dilemma of autonomous art. Nor does Fancioulle resemble Poe's Hop-Frog (1849), in whom some critics see his source. Although vengeance again forms a major theme here, Hop-Frog is no artist.

Despite these differences, Triboulet does represent an important forebear for Fancioulle: he embodies the first tragic buffoon. Even the Fool, in *King Lear*, though bearing significant pathos, does not have tragic stature. Indicatively, he does not die but merely vanishes, well before the end of the play. We might conclude that the unresolved ambiguities of the figure precluded a clear fate for him. In treating the history of buffoons in French literature, Vivienne Rubin shows that Hugo's own kinfolk for Triboulet—the four fools in *Cromwell* and L'Angely in *Marion de Lorme*—have none of his moral breadth.

Thus we may see Triboulet as the model for Fancioulle's tragic side; another forebear appears between these two as the buffoon-artist. Musset's Fantasio (1833), the first Romantic fool, brings some important new traits to the traditional role reversal of ruler and jester. Although he too derives from the Shakespearean models of Touchstone and Feste, Fantasio adds to their ironic wit the modern melancholy of ennui. Several other traits mark this man as a Romantic artist type: ambivalence, homelessness, a lack of professional identity. Indeed, we may see in him a prototype of the tormented modern artist and of "difficult" art itself. The closely following figure of Valerio in Büchner's *Leonce und Lena* (1836) shows how quickly this Romantic type began to populate the European stage. Finally, we must note that the court fool as tragic artist goes well beyond Romanticism. In *König Nicolo* (1901), Wedekind creates the ultimate role-reversal in making his jester a king. And a prophet-jester delivers the key political message in Max Frisch's farce *Die Chinesische Mauer* (*The Chinese Wall*) (1947).

Fancioulle occupies a special place among these fools, for only he performs for nobles on a stage. In this new function we see his ambivalent position between two institutions: the court and the theater. The court symbolizes the Renaissance and its feudal basis, whereas the theater implies the different, more complex relations in industrial culture. One cause for Fancioulle's downfall may lie in this very bridging of two historical forms. That is, his conspiracy against the prince belongs to the era of revolution, not to his own epoch of hierarchical order.

---

backs, their characters differ in essence. (See John Porter Houston, *Victor Hugo*, 55, and Ubersfeld, *Le Roi*, 101.) Triboulet facilitates the pleasures, usually destructive, of the prince. As the buffoon says of the court, he too is "prostituted to evil." Triboulet invites the curse of St. Vallier by his mockery of the grieving father, exactly what he himself will later become. Quasimodo, on the other hand, attempts to rescue Esmeralda, thereby becoming what Jean Starobinski calls a "buffoon-savior" ("Note sur le Bouffon Romantique," 274). But Triboulet cannot save his daughter; indeed, he helps to kill her.

Hence Fancioulle determines his own death, which we may interpret in any case as a suicide merely provoked by the prince. Furthermore, Fancioulle's public performance presages those of the many kinds of artistes who follow him onto the stage of post-Romantic writing. His triangular relation to both the prince/audience and the narrator represents something new in the tradition of the court jester in literature. For all the buffoons before him, the dual relation of intimacy with the ruler prevails. After Fancioulle, the patronless clown both enjoys the freedom and suffers the jeopardy of the artist who sells his wares publicly.

Critics have seen in the courtly pair of ruler and buffoon something deeper than the classic irony of inverted roles. Starobinski speaks of "a mythic relation" that goes beyond politics. "In a complementary and symmetrical way, the buffoon is tied to the Prince, to whom he replies. Also, while the fool has only the power of the spirit, the Prince has only earthly power."[38] Lescek Kolakowski analyzes this dynamic relation in his introduction to *Marxism and Beyond*. In "The Priest and the Jester," he claims that any healthy society needs a polar tension between the forces maintaining order and those questioning it. "The priest is the guardian of the absolute; he sustains the cult of the final and the obvious as acknowledged by and contained in tradition. The jester is he who moves in good society without belonging to it, and treats it with impertinence; he who doubts all that appears self-evident. . . . In every era, the jester's philosophy exposes as doubtful what seems most unshakeable, reveals the contradictions in what appears . . . incontrovertible, derides common sense and reads sense into the absurd."[39]

Hence the jester's opposition to the regime is universal and timeless. This view of the comedian recalls what Cornford, Welsford, and others have said about the earliest fools of ritual celebrations. Ancient societies chose a scapegoat from their midst to carry away their sins. Before killing the victim, the celebrants reveled in a Dionysian abandon of all societal restrictions: the birth of carnival. The resurrection of the slain fool insured the cyclical return of such necessary festivals. As these rites developed into mimetic art, the revelry of the fool, mocking all foundations of ordered society, became the hallmark of comedy. Clowns thus defy convention, giving catharsis to "the impulses we must daily repress."[40]

38. Starobinski, "Note," 274.
39. Lescek Kolakowski, *Marxism and Beyond*, 53.
40. Freud, quoted in Wylie Sypher, ed., *Comedy*, 221. Compare Gerald Mast: "Great comedy is always impolite" (*The Comic Mind*, 301). Both Hobbes and Bergson interpret the laughter thus released as aggressive. Psychoanalysts of the circus experience continue

The jester Fancioulle as conspirator against his despotic prince represents just this link of comedy with rebellion. Perhaps our oldest example of this tie comes from the *Symposium,* where "the goat-faced Socrates, the philosopher-clown" mocks the sober sophistry of Alcibiades.[41] Goethe's Mephistopheles has this same antagonistic character of the archetypal jester. Of him God says, "Of all the negating spirits, the devil bothers me least." Later on, the devil confirms his identity as a naysayer in calling himself "the spirit that always negates."[42] Mephisto defines himself largely in contrast to Faust, who represents the opposite archetype of heroic striving. That the two characters also constitute two halves of the same self in no way contradicts their polar opposition. Indeed, we see the same phenomenon of the "split self" in the prince and Fancioulle. Don Quixote and Sancho Panza, Don Giovanni and Leporello, and Tamino and Papageno make similar pairs of the Ideal and its comic inversion.

SUPERIORITY AND TRANSCENDENCE

The third key character in "Une Mort Héroique," the poet-narrator, intrudes again quite early in the poem. Like the "I, . . . as a true Parisian" of "Le Vieux Saltimbanque," this writer also locates himself right inside the given setting, as a witness deeply involved in the event. He calls our attention to both his presence and his insight by analyzing the prince in psychological detail. Through his superior awareness, the poet distinguishes himself from the others at the court, who mistake the prince's actual sadism for seeming forgiveness. "But for those who, like me, had been able to perceive more deeply that strange, sick heart, it was infinitely more probable that the Prince wanted to test the acting ability of a man condemned to death."[43]

The narrator intrudes again when he describes Fancioulle's supreme performance. Here, indeed, we have the climax of the work, whose ultimate subject is the triumph of art over death.

This buffoon moved, laughed, cried with an indestructible halo over his head, a halo invisible to all but *me.* In it were strangely merged the splendor of Art with the glory of the Martyr. Fancioulle introduced, by some special grace, the divine and supernatural into the most outlandish buffooneries. *My* pen trembles and

---

that line of interpretation. Compare Sidney Tarachow: "The clown grimace is an aggression, related to the compulsive grimacing of certain compulsive neurotics and to the grimacing of children" ("Circuses and Clowns," in *Psychoanalysis and the Social Sciences,* ed. Geza Roheim, 184). However, more recent theorists of comedy see the views of Bergson and Freud as unduly limiting (see Edith Kern, *The Absolute Comic*).

41. Sypher, *Comedy,* 214.
42. Johann Wolfgang Goethe, *Werke,* ed. Erich Trunz, 3:18, 47.
43. Baudelaire, *Oeuvres,* 1:320.

tears of an emotion still present come to *my* eyes as *I* try to describe this unforget-table evening. Fancioulle convinced *me*, beyond any doubt, that the ecstasy of art, better than any other means, can veil the terrors of the abyss; that genius can play its comedy at the edge of the tomb with a joy that prevents it from seeing death; for it is lost in a paradise beyond any idea of dying or destruction.[44]

My italics show that the narrator refers to himself three times in this cli-mactic passage. First he asserts, once again, that he sees more than the other spectators; Fancioulle's halo appears only to him. Second, he reveals his intense emotion by saying that his pen trembles and that tears well up as he writes. Finally, he specifies the meaning of this scene for him. Namely, Fan-cioulle shows him, and presumably *only* him, that art can triumph over death. Indeed, one can hardly imagine a greater transcendence for the mime, whose artistry transports him into a paradise beyond the grave.

Let us closely examine the narrator's three intrusions, for they contain some essential ideas in the work. The author's superiority reminds us of the narrator in "Le Vieux Saltimbanque," who also saw more in the old clown than anyone else. The evidence of special perception appears in the second self-reference: the trembling hand and the tears of the narrator. This poet, like the earlier man of letters, is suddenly transported beyond his usual role of objective, distanced observer. His trembling and tears show that he is deeply moved by the actor, who surpasses even his own superlative art when faced with death.

The writer shows these signs of passion because of his own identity as an artist. Again as in "Le Vieux Saltimbanque," the player touches the author far more deeply than anyone else. Although the audience acclaims the per-former, only the narrator feels tears. Identification, based on pity and fear, must lie at the root of such emotion. Again, as in the earlier work, the artist perceives his alter ego. His superior awareness parallels the mime's superb performance.

The artist of this era finds another alter ego, comparably superior, in the dandy. As his title *Der Dichter als Dandy* shows, Sebastian Neumeister considers the dandy a determining figure. He quotes Baudelaire to justify the claim of heroism: "Dandyism is the last gasp of the heroic in the era of decadence."[45] More concretely, Benjamin sees the dandy, like the clown, as a fitting mask for the poet. Otto Mann finds in the dandy a bourgeois substitute for the court jester. Like his feudal forebear, the dandy "satisfies the need for mirth in a society bored by strict conventions."[46]

44. Ibid., 1:323, italics mine.
45. Sebastian Neumeister, *Der Dichter als Dandy*, 67.
46. Ibid., 57.

The dandy depends more than the clown on a sense of superiority, for he must "épater le bourgeois." However, both figures have a problematic relation to society: both are outsiders, living in isolation. They express their nature by protesting against convention. In psychoanalytical terms, both have locked themselves in the world of childhood. Moreover, the dandy, like any performer, expects to be observed. In this showmanship we find the roots of the blatant exhibitionism in much of modern art. Andy Warhol exemplifies the dandy-clown in our time.

Dandy, fool, poet: this complex of types congregates as critics of the Second Empire. Wolf Lepenies adds a fourth, less expectable member to this group, the *flâneur*. Baudelaire assumes this new mask for the court fool. Both figures banish boredom; the jester did so for the court, now the *flâneur* must conquer his own ennui. Moreover, this man feels just as alone in a street crowd as the fool was at court. He rebels against prevailing norms, just as the jester upset the feudal hierarchy. And, like the dandy, he counters the trend surrounding him with his own dissonant style. The dandy flaunts his frivolity in a gravely purposeful society; the *flâneur* cultivates nonchalance to defy the speed of industrial production.[47] This man of the street has inherited the sense of superiority underlying such behavior from all three forebears.

A similarly superior *flâneur* narrates the prose poem "Parade," in Rimbaud's *Illuminations* (1886). Two of his lines link this man to the narrator of "Une Mort Héroique": "I alone have the key to this savage side-show," and "O the most violent Paradise of the furious grimace!" The former line, ending the work, captures the same egotistic artist who tells the story of Baudelaire. The paradise he sees on the street recalls the immortality that Fancioulle creates for himself (see chapter 7, note 30).

Returning to the kinship of poet and player, we see that it proceeds from both negative and positive traits. Whereas the writer identifies with the social debasement of the artiste, he also sees him as a brother in transcendence. Here lies the heroism of both poet and performer, a glorification of art over the ordinary that enters our context of popular performance with Banville. This poet did not tire of equating the artist and the clown, usually in the tone of eulogy.

The clown! The poet! For whoever sees superficially, there is no resemblance; but for whoever can see truly, who can detach himself from mere appearance, they are one and the same person. . . . The same character, the same words, the same definitions apply to both, for there is a rhymer in every acrobat, and there is in

47. Benjamin, *Schriften*, 679; Wolf Lepenies, *Melancholie und Gesellschaft*, 94.

every facile scribbler an acrobat. . . . To plunge with agility and certainty through space, above the abyss, from one point to another: that is the supreme science of the clown, and I think it is also the only science of the poet.[48]

In the first of his *Odes Funambulesques,* "La Corde Roide" ("The Tight-rope"), Banville asserts the superiority of the *saltimbanque* over the acclaimed artist. Here, as in *Pauvres Saltimbanques,* he not only maligns his hypocritical established colleagues; he also proposes "the tightrope" as the proper locus for true art. Characteristically, he locates his ideal creator high above the crowd. Thus this first poem refers, through its vertical imagery, to the closing piece of the collection, "Le Saut du Tremplin."[49]

In these two odes, Banville transfers Baudelaire's imagery in "Plaintes d'un Icare" ("Lament of Icarus") and "Élévation" ("Elevation") from the poet to the artiste. Published in the same year as Banville's *Odes Funambules-ques,* 1857, "Élévation" tells the poet's spirit to fly from the earth, just as Banville's *sauteur* does.

> Fly far from this morbid place!
> Go purify yourself in better air,
> And drink the clear flame, that divine nectar,
> That fills the cloudless space.
>
> Beyond the ennui and deep despair
> That weigh down our earthly life,
> He is happy whose mighty wings
> Can soar into a region bright and calm![50]

The poem preceding "Élévation" in *Les Fleurs du Mal,* "L'Albatros" ("The Albatross") gives the opposite, negative image of this ideal flight: the paralysis of the captured bird who cannot even walk.

> The poet resembles the prince of the clouds,
> who rides the storm and mocks the hunter;

48. Banville quoted in Robert Füglister, "Gaukler und Akrobat als Alter Ego des Künstlers."

49. Barbey d'Aurevilly claims a similar superiority for the aerialist in a review of the Goncourts' *Les Frères Zemgannos* (1879). "If we writers could write the way those people move, if we had in our style the inexhaustible resources of their vigor, their almost fluid suppleness, their flowing grace, their mathematical precision . . . we would be great writers. . . . I am convinced that, for anyone who has a sense for analogies and the power of mysterious assimilations, to watch them is to learn how to write" (*Le Constitutionnel,* 12 May 1879, in Helen Trudgian, *Les Idées Esthétiques de J. K. Huysmans,* 120–21).

50. Baudelaire, *Oeuvres,* 1:10.

> exiled on earth among the jeering mob,
> his giant wings prevent him from moving.[51]

Ascent characterizes Romantic writing. Indicatively, Maurice Shroder entitles his study of the French Romantic writer *Icarus*. Susan Sontag echoes this focus in calling Romantic art "a species of heroism, a breaking through or going beyond."[52] In *L'Air et les Songes* (1959), Gaston Bachelard treats the Icarian motif as part of the development of European literatures since the Middle Ages (see chapter 4). We must credit Banville with introducing the logical and evocative metaphor of the aerialist into the Icarian tradition. And we cannot ignore his influence. Even the gloomy poet in Mallarmé's "L'Azur" (1864), who only glimpses the heights, owes something to Banville's striving language. The closing line—"I am *haunted*. The heavens! The heavens! The heavens!"—closely echoes "Le Saut du Tremplin": "Higher! Further! Air! Sky! Wings! Wings!"[53]

Gautier used the same exclamation in describing the youthful Romantics. "The fate of Icarus frightened no one. 'Wings! Wings! Wings!' they cried on all sides, even at the risk of falling into the sea. In order to fall from the sky, one must climb up, if only for a moment, and that is more beautiful than spending one's whole life earth-bound."[54] The essay containing this quotation, "Reprise de Chatterton," appeared in December 1857; Banville published his *Odes* in February of that year, but they had already appeared separately in various journals. So we may assume that the phrase originated with him.

Through such romantic idealizing, the buffoon articulates the artist's own longing for flight. In thus elevating the clown, as Banville does, the artist also heroizes himself. However, in identifying with the vulgar player specifically, the poet also creates that tension between the great and the small that marks this period. The generation that had grown up with the ideals of the Revolution, with Napoleon and Werther as its heroes, tended naturally to disillusion, hence the unheroic attitudes embodied in figures such as Julien Sorel, Pechorin, Woyzeck. In this regard, Edith Kern quotes the Goncourts: "Everything goes to the people and deserts the kings. Even literature descends from royal misfortunes. From Priam to Birotteau!"[55]

The prologue to Adalbert Stifter's *Bunte Steine* (*Bright Stones*) (1853) contains a famous eulogy to the "gentle" forces of nature, which prevail

51. Ibid.
52. Susan Sontag, *A Susan Sontag Reader*, ed. Elisabeth Hardwick, 403.
53. Banville, *Oeuvres*, 290.
54. Théophile Gautier, *Histoire du Romantisme*, 153.
55. Edith Kern, "The Modern Hero: Phoenix or Ashes?" in *The Hero in Literature*, ed. Victor Brombert, 267.

over the mere moments of violence. Similarly, in Franz Grillparzer's story of a poor fiddler, "Der arme Spielmann" (1847), the narrator claims that we cannot grasp the heroic without knowing its opposite. "We cannot understand the great heroes unless we have sensed the feelings of the humble. An invisible but unbroken thread connects the brawling of drunken porters to the warring sons of the gods; within every young servant-girl, reluctantly following her insistent lover away from the throng of dancers, there lies in embryo Juliet, Dido or Medea." Like Stifter's prologue, this passage elevates what we usually consider trivial to a new importance. Traditional ideas of great and small are becoming increasingly relative.[56]

In our specific context of the popular player, the tension between these two poles bears some paradox. Embedded in the striving of Banville's *sauteur*, who escapes the petit-bourgeois world, we have the irony of his identity as a lowly buffoon. Indeed, any such performer "sells" himself, so he does not differ in economic terms from the bourgeois. Here *l'art pour l'art* is undercut by the populism implicit in the spectacle. We find a similar ambiguity in carnival transcendence in Mallarmé's prose poems. In "Un Spectacle Interrompu" ("An Interrupted Spectacle"), for instance, he speaks of the poet's longing to become merely one of the crowd. "To enjoy like the crowd the myth enclosed in every banality, what a relaxation for the mind and, without neighbors to whom to pour out reflections, to behold the ordinary and splendid vigil found at the footlights by my search appeased with imaginings or symbols."[57]

In that he unearths a myth in the vulgarity of the fair, Mallarmé transcends the elitism of *l'art pour l'art*. Indeed, a principal idea of the prose poems in *Divagations* lies in just this broadening of "high" art to include the crowd. Naturally, the poet of these pieces must constantly struggle with his love/hate for the brute public. But the artist resolves this tension in "Conflit" ("Conflict"), the culmination of the cycle, by a return to Nature. As Ursula Franklin shows, for art to become religion again, it needs a priest as

56. Franz Grillparzer, *Sämtliche Werke,* 3:148. The trend away from all heroism intensifies in the latter half of the century. For a discussion of a principal anti-hero in our era, Petrushka, see chapter 6. Harry Levin charts the progress from the most heroic to the least heroic values, as the journey "from the battlefield of Waterloo to the sickroom of Proust." "The epoch from Flaubert to Joyce transposed the revolt of the individual against society into a personal quarrel between the artist and the bourgeoisie. . . . Underground man, the shuddering protagonist of Kafka, is the absolute negation of the heroic" ("From Priam to Birotteau," 80, 82). See also Cesar Graña, *Bohemian versus Bourgeois.* And now we have, from the self-proclaimed heir to Kafka, Milan Kundera, the current form of the anti-hero: the worker-victim of the totalitarian state. In *The Book of Laughter and Forgetting,* the characters no longer struggle, as Kafka's K. did, to understand or accommodate the power that dominates them; heroes exist only in the mythology of the Party.

57. *Oeuvres Complètes,* 276; trans. Ursula Franklin, *Anatomy,* 230.

well as a poet. And the priest serves as mediator for man—for Mankind. "Poet and poetry are inextricably linked: while his poetry at the beginning alienated the persona from the crowd, it now leads him to serve it; like the priest, the poet must first leave that humanity to which he returns later as its servant."[58]

In this development we may find a paradigm for what follows Mallarmé. The task of many later artists lay in a similar return from the hermetic to humanity. Perhaps the first such echo of Mallarmé resounds in Nietzsche's essential book *Also Sprach Zarathustra* (*Thus Spake Zarathustra*) (1884). One can readily see in the prologue biography of Zarathustra a profile of the artist in our century, emerging from the lonely mountain retreat of Romanticism into a new integration with the public. Zarathustra finds one follower in Hofmannsthal, who early renounced the "elite" genre of lyric poetry for the more publicly accessible form of drama. The writer Aschenbach in Thomas Mann's *Der Tod in Venedig* (*Death in Venice*) (1912) represents a staunchly moral rejection of *l'art pour l'art*. Apollinaire's poetry also moves toward "moral synthesis," uniting "the poetic, creative spirit in all men."[59]

As for Baudelaire's two players, both the old clown and Fancioulle symbolize the superiority of art; yet otherwise they differ significantly. The vicarious image of the artist in "Le Vieux Saltimbanque" has mainly negative overtones, for it implies the decline of art in a commercial culture. This man, once "the brilliant entertainer," now faces a miserable death. In following the natural law of aging, he must endure exile from the wholly unnatural world of the fair. In "Une Mort Héroique," however, the creator appears most positively, for he has the power to transcend death itself. Indeed, art brings salvation here, in a literal sense.

The narrator sees a halo crowning Fancioulle, which mixes "the radiance of Art" with "the glory of the Martyr." Hence the artist appears as a Christ figure. The old clown, whose smoking candles illumine his misery, also recalls Christ, but only as a suffering martyr. For him, salvation is impossible, since the wretched conditions of his life condemn him to an ignoble death. In particular, the rejection he suffers from his callous audience precludes any transcendence of his actual state.

Starobinski speaks of both these figures in terms recalling Christ, as "men of sorrows," and "allegorical representations of a sacrificial concept of art."[60] However, this view of the artist predominates only in "Le Vieux Sal-

---

58. Franklin, *Anatomy,* 205.
59. Margaret Davies, "Poetry as the Reconciliation of Opposites," in *Order and Adventure in Post-Romantic Poetry,* ed. E. M. Beaumont et al., 182.
60. Starobinski, "Répondants," 406.

timbanque." Although Fancioulle does die horribly, sacrificed to the prince's murderous sadism, his final performance has taken him beyond life and death. The buffoon moves "into a paradise without death or destruction." And the last paragraph of the prose poem, describing the inferiority of his successors, shows that Fancioulle survives in a glowing posterity at the court.[61] Hofmannsthal's 1897 elegy for the revered actor Mitterwurzer evokes the same magical aura that surrounds Fancioulle's death.

> Then we knew who had left us:
> The magician, the great, great artist!
> And we came out of our houses,
> And began to speak of who he was.
> But who was he really, and who was he not?[62]

The final italicized word in "Une Mort Héroique," *faveur,* pertains to more than the favor the mime enjoyed with his earthly ruler; it also connotes his unique artistic gift. The passage quoted above specifies this "special grace" as something divine and supernatural. So we understand this last word as characterizing his condition, *faveur,* as a blessing from God. However, considering the political context of the piece, we must also note the typically Baudelairean irony of this *faveur.* Beyond the actual privilege Fancioulle enjoyed, it connotes the "favor" the prince shows in the death sentence. He thus provokes from the mime a performance surpassing even his usual excellence. With this ironic sense of princely favor, Baudelaire suggests that political suppression helps to produce the greatest art.

MIME

The specific nature of Fancioulle's art helps to explain its power. "Fancioulle excelled above all in mute roles or those with few words, that are often the major ones in those fables which represent symbolically the mystery of life."[63] This last suggestive phrase gains resonance in the context of the words *mysterious* and *solemnity* in the paragraph above. This "true solemnity," recalling the same transcendent word for the fair in "Le Vieux Saltim-

---

61. This interpretation does not ignore the persuasive view of Ross Chambers, who wisely stresses the mythology of failure ("scenarios d'échec") that Baudelaire wills to *his* posterity ("L'Art Sublime du Comédien," 200). Although I agree wholeheartedly with Chambers, I still cannot downplay the transcendence of Fancioulle. So perhaps I must take an aptly dualistic position and call his art a transcendent failure.

62. Hugo von Hofmannsthal, *Gesammelte Werke: Gedichte und Lyrische Dramen,* ed. Herbert Steiner, 47.

63. Baudelaire, *Oeuvres,* 1:322.

banque," refers to Fancioulle's command performance. A special moral quality attaches to this solemn spectacle, namely the sight of an artist playing for his life. By thus echoing the idea of the mysterious, the author associates "the value of the dramatic talent of a man condemned to death" with the mime's art, which symbolizes "the mystery of life." Hence this mystery of life that the actor evokes must relate to death.

In the next paragraph we learn just how Fancioulle manifests this mysterious, even paradoxical, link of acting and stasis, life and death. "If an actor succeeded in being, relative to the role he plays, what the best statues of antiquity would be—miraculously animated, living, walking, seeing—in relation to the general and confused idea of Beauty: that would be a truly singular case, utterly unheard of. That night Fancioulle was just such a perfect idealisation, which it was impossible not to consider absolutely real."[64] Like a Greek statue amazingly brought to life, the mime also animates an ideal image of life. The actor transforms something static and abstract— namely, the role he plays—into tangible reality. In superbly miming his own "mystery of life," this hero acquired "the divine and the supernatural." This likening of the ideal actor to a classic statue reflects the longing for a sacred art. Beyond the tragic death of the divine Fancioulle lies the plight of the resolutely profane poet yearning for transcendence.[65] Accordingly, we marvel at the mime's ability to live on in heroic posterity.

We must also note the actual means of this transcendence: pantomime. Baudelaire, a devoted fan of Deburau and the *Funambules,* did not just happen to make Fancioulle a mime. The old clown in "Le Vieux Saltimbanque" also does not speak; appearance and gaze alone register his significance. Indeed, the "profound, unforgettable gaze" of this man has a power beyond words to express his misery. In repeating the word *gaze,* Baudelaire stresses that both men are observers. By saying "my sight was blocked by those rebellious tears that refuse to fall," he links the narrator-poet with the clown through the pathos of what they both see. Similarly, the poet in "Une Mort Héroique" also relates to the mime through observation alone. So does the prince, another spectator-artist.[66]

The old man's pathetic gaze evokes a primary image in Baudelaire. "In . . . the clown, as with so many of Baudelaire's old men, life is concentrated mysteriously in the eyes alone, for it has deserted the rest of the body. Here

64. Ibid., 1:321
65. Chambers, "L'Art Sublime," 249.
66. Baudelaire recalls the superior secrecy of this observing prince-artist in "Le Peintre de la Vie Moderne" ("The Painter of Modern Life"). "The observer is a prince enjoying his incognito" (*Writings on Art and Artists,* trans. and ed. P. E. Charvet, 400).

is another contrast: the life of his gaze, isolated as it is, makes the irremedi-
able inertia of the old man all the more tragic."[67] Preceded by nine rhyth-
mically emphatic negative phrases, the rendering of the man's unforgettable
gaze implies paralysis. "He did not laugh, the wretch! He did not cry, he did
not dance, nor gesticulate, nor cry out: he sang no song, neither gay nor sad,
he did not implore. . . . But what a profound gaze, unforgettable. . . ."[68]

In this man's stasis we perceive the prelude to death. Alive only through
his eyes, he exists in a silent prison. Such a description bears a haunting
likeness to Baudelaire in his last year, silenced by aphasia. So we may see in
the old clown a prophetic link to the poet's own death. It seems fitting that
this supreme observer finally had to live without speech.[69]

We can hardly exaggerate the import of observation in *Le Spleen de
Paris*. For the most part, the narrator of these pieces, the archetypal *flâneur*,
relays his experience of urban life as he sees it. Characteristically, he takes
no part in the action but only conveys the thoughts and feelings provoked
by the sight of myriad intersecting lives in the metropolis. Charles Mauron
notes that the participant narrator of *Les Fleurs du Mal* becomes a passive
spectator in *Spleen;* Claude Pichois sees in this visual quality the realism
that contrasts with the Romanticism of the earlier collection.

Not only the narrative attitude but also the subjects of the prose poems
bespeak the primacy of the visual. Think of the titles alone: "The Eyes of the
Poor," "The Windows," "The Mirror," "The Evil Glazier." Both this last piece
and its stimulus, "The Song of the Glazier" by Arsène Houssaye, owe much
to the linking of eyes and fantasy by E.T.A. Hoffmann. In particular, the final
outcry recalls the deceptive mirrors and eyeglasses of several Hoffmann
characters. "What? You have no colored glass? Red glass, blue glass, magic
glass, the glass of paradise? You scoundrel! How dare you venture into the
slums without glass that makes life beautiful?"[70] Knowing what follows
Baudelaire, we may readily see in these late works a presage of Symbolism.
One thinks of the famous passage from *Fusées:* "In certain, almost supernatural states of the soul, the profundity of life reveals itself entirely in the
sight, however ordinary it may be, of what one experiences. That sight
becomes the symbol of the experience."[71]

Like the mime of Fancioulle, revealing "the mystery of life," the specta-

67. Starobinski, "Répondants," 410.
68. Baudelaire, *Oeuvres,* 1:296.
69. Compare the parallel drawn by Benjamin between the mime and Baudelaire. "He
had something of the mime about him, who must play the role of the poet on stage, for a society that no longer needs the true poet and gives him space only as a mime" (*Schriften,* 662).
70. Baudelaire, *Oeuvres,* 1:287.
71. Ibid., 1:659.

cles in our two texts visualize symbolic relations. Such ties of the performer to his audience appear complex, for they mix several conflicting emotions: identification, awe, incredulity, fright. Hence the symbols through which one sees the event—costume, fairground, candles—contain more than they show to the eye. Here lies the dual character of symbols, their ability to transport us beyond physical appearance into the realm of imagination. Mallarmé fulfills the promise of this transcendence in his mystical view of things. Rejecting the purely external vision of Impressionism, Mallarmé cares more about what the physical world conceals than what it reveals. For him, the inner eye takes poetic precedence over mere physical perception. Only the inward vision yields the true import of experience.

For Baudelaire, however, the external world still has significant power to convey meaning. A primacy of visual symbols characterizes *Le Spleen de Paris,* which depends on the manifold tensions that relate the spectator to his physical surroundings. In this regard Baudelaire exemplifies what Simmel says of the purely optical life of the new urban masses. Critics have noted that this predominance of the visual stresses the nonverbal experience. Indeed, silent relations abound, not only in *Le Spleen* but also in much writing of the latter nineteenth century. Here lies an intriguing paradox, for literature necessarily demands words.

The title "Shroud of Silence" reveals how darkly Oskar Seidlin interprets this problem in German literature. More broadly, George Steiner discusses "the retreat from the word" in *Language and Silence.* His examples confirm my claim that the search for nonverbal means starts after Baudelaire: he cites Rimbaud, Lautréamont, Mallarmé, Rilke, and Maeterlinck. Steiner places his "best hope for the renascence of the word" among the Anglo-Americans. Joyce, Faulkner, Stevens, and Durrell may "restore literacy." Echoing Seidlin's pessimism, Steiner ends on a typically apocalyptic note, concluding that our society may undergo "a new Dark Ages," it may even "perish by silence."[72]

Other critics transcend such gloom, for they perceive the liberation offered by nonverbal language. In *Das Geschehen und das Schweigen* (*Happening and Silence*) (1969), Hans Mayer justifies the necessity of new means of expression for the interiority in our "late period of human development." Susan Sontag probes many expressions of the urge to get rid of speech, from medieval mystics to Rilke. She concludes that this need stems from attributing "certain absolute and ineffable qualities to the art object." Hence our contemporary silences still appear as signs of post-Romantic

72. Steiner, *Language,* 12–35.

aesthetics. Walter Strauss also links "the paradoxical attempt of language to express silence" to the last century. "Mallarmé's blank page, Webern's silences, Mondrian's empty canvases: are they not testimonials to a quest for Orphic purity in a world that is no longer open to . . . orphic transformation? They are an end, but also, perhaps, a beginning." Ihab Hassan, echoing this hopeful note, sees that "the end . . . heralds a new beginning—negative transcendence, as we call it today, is a form of transcendence nonetheless. And therefore silence in literature does not necessarily augur the death of the spirit."[73]

In the texts discussed here and in later chapters, the paradox of silence appears in the identification of the poet, a verbal artist, with the mute player. Not only clowns and mimes but also aerialists, equestriennes, jugglers, animal trainers—in short, the whole personnel of the popular show—perform without words. Here lies one reason the modern artist finds an alter ego in such players: he envies their muteness. The starkly commercial values of his newly bourgeois public alienate them from his art. Hence he perceives in pantomime a better means of communication than language. The nonverbal medium attracts him by its simple, direct way of creating rapport with an audience. In mime he sees an escape from the intellectual distancing of speech in a populist culture.

Our two Baudelaire texts suggest a logical connection between mime, the drama of symbol, and the retreat from rational discourse that marks modern French drama.

The traditional concept of a literary theater has been under serious attack during the twentieth century. The Surrealist cult of the subconscious has helped to undermine the traditional notions of coherent characterisation and dialogue, substituting the arbitrary incoherence of random experience for the ordered logic of a work of art; while the determined efforts of Artaud and other influential

---

73. Mayer, *Outsiders,* 34; Sontag, *Reader,* 202; Walter Strauss, "The Reconciliation of Opposites in Orphic Poetry: Rilke and Mallarmé," 236; Ihab Hassan, *The Literature of Silence,* 4. Hassan continues: "The myth of Orpheus may be a parable of the artist at certain times. The powers of Dionysos, which civilisation must repress, threaten at these times to erupt with a vengeance. In the process, energy may overwhelm order; language may turn into a howl, a cackle, a terrible silence; form may be mangled as ruthlessly as the poor body of Orpheus was. Yet the haunting question remains, now as on that wild day in the hills of Thrace: must not the head of the poet be severed in order that he may continue to sing? . . . Must not *life overwhelm art* periodically to insure the health, the prevalence of man? Must not words aspire to stillness?" (18, italics mine). In the idea of life overwhelming art, I find a contemporary counterweight to the hegemony of *l'art pour l'art.* Hassan thus explains our need for anti-art. See also John Stark, *the literature of exhaustion,* for an analysis of Sontag, Steiner, and Hassan in relation to current literary trends.

theorists to play down the role of language in the theater and to stress the importance of gesture, mime and spectacle have had the effect . . . of devaluing the role
of the creative writer vis-à-vis that of the producer, and of radically altering the
relationship between the spectator and what he sees on the stage.[74]

In 1842, Gautier wrote, "The time of purely visual spectacles has arrived!"[75] Since then the speechless show has fascinated both writers and
visual artists. Gautier's proclamation bears particularly rich meaning for our
topic, the purely optical experience of mime.

In 1806 only eight of forty-five Parisian theaters had the license for speaking. This statistic not only shows the prevalence of mime but also suggests
that the regime was trying to literally silence opposition. Not until 1864 did
it grant the freedom of mere physical speech on the stage. This context
recalls the historically accurate image of the *Funambules* in *Les Enfants du
Paradis*. There the director imposes a three-franc fine on any actor, even his
daughter Natalie, who breaks the rules by speaking.[76]

Caricature and mime, both purely visual, emerged as determining forces
in the mid-century. Both forms depend on that essential post-Romantic figure, the viewer. Both Deburau and Baudelaire —not to mention Daumier—
depict what the urban spectator sees; they intensify that vision by its
silence. Not only the obvious Balzac but also other writers characterize
their figures by codes of physiognomy and gesture conveyed publicly in
newspapers and mime theaters. "The pantomime is the real human comedy, and though it doesn't employ 2000 characters like Balzac, it is not less
complete: with four or five types it manages everything."[77] Externals had to
rule perception at this time of radical and constant social change. The era
saw four revolutions (1789, 1830, 1848, and 1870), a four-fold increase in
population, and the physical transformation of Paris from a medieval to a
modern city.

People faced with what seem irreversible, destined changes in their lives can
believe, out of resignation if nothing else, that the meaning will eventually come
clear. But the citizens of Paris and London in the mid-nineteenth century had no
such comfort that society in the fullness of time would reveal its grand design.
There thus arose a hunger in the lives of these people to impose order, to fix
meaning, to arbitrate in the midst of chaos. Caricature and stylized gesture . . .
were such codes of arbitration.[78]

74. W. D. Howarth, *Sublime and Grotesque: A Study of French Romantic Drama*, 407.
75. Théophile Gautier, *Histoire de l'Art Dramatique en France depuis 25 Ans*, 175.
76. Prévert, *Children*, 98.
77. Gautier, quoted in Judith Wechsler, *A Human Comedy*, 42.
78. Richard Sennett, quoted in ibid., 8.

We have already noted the democratic aspect of nonverbal theater that Janin glorified. A "legitimate" actor such as Frédérick Lemaitre could not represent "the people" as Deburau's Pierrot did, for language can never appeal to such a broad public as do movement and gesture alone. Hofmannsthal, the Austrian poet fascinated by "the silent arts," spoke of words as individual and gesture as universal. Indeed, a prime reason for the long life of the mime tradition inherited from antiquity lies in its use of the most common gestural communication. Mime, then, has its roots in universal experience. It relates to the audience in direct physical terms, without verbal mediation. Using the most basic human images, the mime forces the viewer to identify with him. We have a poignant example of this immediate empathy in the early scene of *Les Enfants du Paradis* where Baptiste first appears in the *parade*. The sudden hush of the raucous sidewalk crowd aptly demonstrates this mime's power.[79]

In this crucial scene, the remarkable mimed performance has several functions. Most obviously, it depicts the daily routine of the actors, showing their dependence on the proletarian crowd. However, an idea more essential to the film emerges when the pickpocket incident inspires Baptiste to use his professional skill to help Garance. He thus puts his art to work for an actual life. Suddenly he transforms a mere commercial show into drama as a distilled, stylized form of reality. Here lie the roots of mimesis. By miming the actual event, Baptiste persuades the crowd more effectively than he could ever have done in words. Indeed, the words of the accusing victim have already expressed a lie. Mime, lacking the deceptive quality of language, evokes the truth of pure movement. As dancers know, the body cannot lie.

DUALISM

Returning to our two texts, we must distinguish between the two audiences. Unlike the fickle public in "Le Vieux Saltimbanque," the court in "Une Mort Héroique" acclaims the mime. Such homage is especially surprising in view of the usual indifference of these people, "blasé and frivolous." Therefore this work conveys not the negative effect of a hostile reception but rather the transcendence of the spectacle itself. The two titles themselves imply this difference. "Le Vieux Saltimbanque" spotlights the man alone, while "Une Mort Héroique" points to the genius of the performer.

The clown's decline represents the tragedy of art in a decadent culture;

79. Barrault claims that he needed "three full days and nights to work out the little pantomime of the stolen watch" (quoted in Toby Cole, ed., *Actors on Acting,* 230).

the mime triumphs over mere mortality. Death looms inevitably for both players, but one has the power to transcend the tomb. So the two pieces give opposing conclusions about the condition of art. In one case, the commercial ethic dooms the artist. In the other case, even a cruel death cannot stifle the artist's fame, which flourishes in posterity. Of these two contrasting views of art, we might well ask, in Baudelaire's own words, "Laquelle est la Vraie?" (Which is the real one?) The dualism of this title characterizes not only our two texts but also most of *Le Spleen de Paris*. As Mauron shows, the conflicts with "the significant Other" represent the narrator's passionate confrontations with other aspects of himself. Our two texts typify such primal relations between the poet and the antagonist within.

Neumeister sums up one of the most haunting dualisms in Baudelaire's world. "The gates of paradise open only at the edge of the abyss."[80] Starobinski gives the classic formulation of "antithetical values" in our context of popular players. "Baudelaire, poet of two simultaneous assertions, bestowed on the artist, in the figure of the buffoon and the *saltimbanque,* the contradictory vocation of flight and fall, of the heights and the abyss, of beauty and of misfortune."[81]

Most of the critics point to similar dualities in Baudelaire. Henri Lemaitre speaks of "La Chambre Double" ("The Double Room") (1862) as an "auto-biographical synthesis of the Baudelairean dialectic of the ideal and the real, a new revelation of the 'double postulation.'" Chambers sees in him the opposite tendencies of the myth of the poet: both glorified, as one who seeks to live poetically, and condemned, as a charlatan and panderer, whose art can only play out stories of defeat. Other interpreters quote lines from the most revelatory poems, such as "I am the victim and the knife!" Or they discuss the critical writings that reflect the same wish for a dual existence. "To be outside oneself, yet also to be everywhere oneself; to see the world, to be at the center of it and yet to stay hidden from it, such are some of the slightest pleasures of those spirits who are independent, passionate, individual."[82]

The "psychocritics" delve deeper into the subconscious for the roots of such dualism. Mauron calls the poet's self-projection onto other lives "defenses against anxiety." Leo Bersani analyzes this process of identification in Freudian terms. "Considered in the light of passages from Freud's 1924 essay on narcissism, the narrator's sentimental identifications with unhappy, persecuted figures . . . dramatize his inability to love himself." Com-

80. Neumeister, *Der Dichter,* 57.
81. Jean Starobinski, *Portrait de l'Artiste en Saltimbanque,* 83.
82. Charles Baudelaire, *Petits Poèmes en Prose,* ed. Henri Lemaitre, 22; Chambers, "L'Art Sublime," 200; Baudelaire, *Writings on Art,* 400.

menting specifically on our two prose poems, Bersani speaks of "a narcissistic pity for a maimed part of the narrator's self." This "crippled form of self-love" "sets him afloat between the cool, ironic observer and the doomed poet-histrion."[83]

Baudelaire claims that any artist must have such a "split self." In "De l'Essence du rire" ("The Essence of Laughter") (1855) he calls a character comic "in that he is ignorant of his own nature." But the artist himself, conversely, is an artist only "on condition that he is a dual being, and that he ignore no aspect of his double nature."[84] From this thought we may conclude that the artist must be tragic. Full consciousness would not alone make him so; but his divided nature precludes any resolution of the conflicts he constantly perceives. Like Faust, the creator has two souls within, which he cannot unite. We see here not only a portrait of Baudelaire but also of many modern artists. I find no accident in their projection of ambivalence onto popular players.[85] Hence the haunting openness of these figures, who represent the perils of uncertainty. And, as Marjorie Perloff shows, the aesthetics of our age still expresses indecision. Baudelaire's dualism appears as one crucial strand in the dense fabric of modern art.

83. Charles Mauron, *Le Dernier Baudelaire,* 65; Leo Bersani, *Baudelaire and Freud,* 143–44.

84. Baudelaire, *Oeuvres,* 2:543.

85. One example from the visual arts: the *homo duplex* that George Mauner finds in Manet's *Le Vieux Musicien* (*The Old Musician*) (1862). In chapter 7 I discuss the close link of this picture to "Le Vieux Saltimbanque" (1861).

3 THE PERFORMER AS PROBLEM
What Is Art?

No problem in the world is more tormenting than the nature of the artist and its effect on humanity.

—**Thomas Mann, "Tonio Kröger"**

KLEIST: "ÜBER DAS MARIONETTENTHEATER" ("ON THE MARIONETTE-THEATER") (1810)

We may trace the dualities in Baudelaire to earlier Romantic notions of art. Not only Musset, the Parnassians, and Hugo contributed to his view of the artist as ambivalent by nature; this idea harks back to developments in the eighteenth century. Kleist, drawing unique conclusions from Kant's revolutionary cognitive theory, posits a new kind of consciousness through the metaphor of the puppet. The human counterpart of the puppet, the dancer, exemplifies for Kleist the fallen human condition of lost innocence. Since he no longer exists in the paradise of oneness with his Creator, the dancer has a split identity. He is still an animal in movement, yet his awareness of that movement burdens him with human awkwardness.

Here, then, lies an early root of the ambivalence we find in Baudelaire. In this chapter I shall discuss this and other important aspects of the problematic Kleistian artist in the works of Eichendorff, Grillparzer, Hofmannsthal, Kafka, and Grass. We shall see that the self-awareness Kleist highlights intensifies into self-parody. Let us first look closely at "Über das Marionettentheater," for it contains several clues for understanding the popular players who follow it. Indeed, many recent critics—Barthes, Sartre, Sontag—hail this early piece as a landmark in Modernist aesthetics.

In this essay, the narrator discusses marionettes with a star dancer. This man claims, paradoxically, that a puppet on strings displays more grace than the human dancer. The mechanical being moves in perfect accord with the puppeteer's hand movements. The dancer, no longer attached to his creator, cannot attain that harmony, for it depends on a lack of self-awareness. Kleist exemplifies the dilemma of such consciousness with four kinds of movement. The dancer represents the systematized technique of ballet, evolved over centuries of refining movement; he in turn glorifies the marionette, an ancient effigy of the human body in motion. In contrast to this ideal of innocence, the speaker decries the affectation of his fellow dancers, whose awareness of their own bodies makes them awkward.

The dancer cites another instance of lost beauty in a young swimmer. He also turns clumsy after comparing his own innocently graceful gesture to a famous Greek statue, the Boy Removing a Thorn. The last example, a deftly fencing bear, represents the natural and ideal state of unconscious grace. All these types demonstrate their condition dynamically, thus all are dancers. For Kleist, the dancer presents a metaphor for the modern human plight of lost innocence, of self-awareness.[1]

Ever since the sequential appearance of this dialogue in the *Berliner Abendblätter,* readers have hotly debated its ideas. We may measure the range of this criticism by the two notable books by Walter Silz (1961) and Ilse Graham (1977). Silz devotes a whole chapter to debunking not only the voluminous literature on the essay but also the work itself. Richard Daunicht also denigrates the massive criticism on the essay, but only to lend appeal to his substitute reading of it as satire. He sees Kleist as attacking the Berlin National Theater, Iffland in particular. Graham, ignoring such earlier work, bases her whole interpretation of Kleist on what Silz calls this mere "genial belles-lettres."[2]

To my mind, Silz errs in taking all too literally what Kleist intends as metaphor. Indicatively, Silz cites the obtuse estimate of the essay by Max von Boehn, author of a history of marionettes. Max von Boehn rightly observes that the work does not really concern the puppet theater; but he sees no other value in it. Silz also seems to denigrate the essay because it does not discuss the actual workings of puppets. Chiding Kleist for a lack of logic, Silz sounds both pedantic and blind to the deepest intent of the essay. Graham, on the other hand, portrays Kleist as a deft metaphysician. Although neither estimate is wholly suitable, Graham does offer the best analysis to date for Kleist's reading of Genesis 3, which lies at the root of his work.

Most of the critics stress either the negative attitude of the essay toward consciousness or its contrary positive aspect, which offers a hopeful future solution to the present human dilemma. I believe we may sensibly reconcile these divisive interpretations in acknowledging the equal weight of both these poles. Primarily, of course, Kleist expresses his despair, following

---

1. By now it has become axiomatic that self-consciousness connotes a loss. See Johan Huizinga, *Homo Ludens,* 202: "It was a blessing for art to be largely unconscious of its high purpose and the beauty it creates. When art becomes self-conscious, that is conscious of its own grace, it is apt to lose something of its eternal childlike innocence."

2. Walter Silz, *Heinrich von Kleist,* 71.

his Kant-crisis, of fulfilling his earlier ideals of enlightenment. This search for truth, inspired by his revered classical models Goethe and Schiller, now became impossible, for Kleist understood Kant to say that true knowledge lies beyond our grasp. Accordingly, we may read the essay as *Dekadenz-dichtung* (the expression of decadence), for it shows mankind as fallen. Its perceptions of the human condition echo Schiller in his famous essay "Über Naive and Sentimentalische Dichtung" ("On Naive and Sentimen-tive Poetry") (1795). In Schiller's essay we have the same duality between nature and mind, being and consciousness, that Kleist assumes. Graham quotes at length from another, less famous essay by Schiller, which makes the same observations that Kleist does but draws a different, Schillerian conclusion: since man has forever lost his innocence, he must become a moral being.

Kleist introduces the image of the marionette into a statement of modern dualistic decadence. By 1810, the puppet-figure already traditionally con-veyed a pessimistic image of man. Rudolf Majut gives a detailed catalogue of literary examples ranging from Goethe through most of the Romantics. Werther's familiar remark sums up the lifeless determinism that the puppet represents for Enlightenment authors: "I stand there as if before a dumb-show, and watch the figures dancing around, and often ask myself if it isn't an optical trick. I play along, or rather I am pulled like a marionette, and sometimes grasp my neighbor by the wooden hand and tremble."[3]

Majut notes the radical change from this perception of the mechanical being to that of Kleist. "Faust, the son of a dying rationalism, at least tried to be godlike; Kleist, the son of the beginning nineteenth century, glorifies, albeit with concealed melancholy irony, the lot of a puppet." Lieselotte Sauer states the case more simply. "The inflated value of the marionette is linked necessarily with the reciprocal denigration of man." As the image of man deteriorated in the nineteenth century, that of the puppet improved. Like Majut, Sauer traces this seesaw movement in Tieck, Hoffmann, and Büchner.[4]

The positive aspect of Kleist's essay emerges mainly from his concept of an expanded consciousness, which man may yet attain. The dancer assures the narrator that we may never regain the innocence of paradise. Yet we may, in "the last chapter of world history," return through a back door. "Par-adise is locked and the Cherub is behind us; we must make a trip around the world, to see if a back door is open anywhere."[5] Kleist takes leave of more

3. Johann Wolfgang Goethe, *Werke,* ed. Erich Trunz, 6:65.

4. Rudolf Majut, *Lebensbühne und Marionette,* 95; Lieselotte Sauer, *Marionetten, Mas-chinen, Automaten,* 216.

5. Heinrich von Kleist, *Werke in einem Band,* ed. Helmut Sembdner, 804.

reactionary Romantics, who glorified the irrational and decried the self-awareness demanded by civilization. For them, the essence of humanity lay in the preconscious, which they took as a sign of God in nature. But Kleist does not reject awareness; in fact he envisions a better, higher level of it. Instead of denying human consciousness, Kleist seeks to extend it as far as possible—indeed, to transcend it.

By getting beyond our present limited perception, we will attain grace. "When awareness has gone through infinity, grace will likewise return to us."[6] The means for thus uniting mind and nature lies in art, represented by the puppeteer. Some critics try to explain the puppet itself as a symbol of art. But such attempts founder on the one indispensable ingredient of art that the doll lacks: the mind.[7] The rational artist, creating grace through the marionette, reconciles the Kleistian demands for both rationality and innocence. Only art allows man to transcend consciousness and return to grace. This concept of a special blessing through art recalls the italicized *faveur* of the mime Fancioulle in "Une Mort Héroique."

Kleist claims that the puppeteer, in directing his puppet's act, himself dances. "The puppeteer transposes himself into the marionette's center of gravity, or, in other words, he *dances*."[8] Vicariously, then, the artist gains the grace of his own creation. Thus the essay treats the utopian idea of striving for infinite, divine awareness through art. Manfred Durzak notes that, in this view, creativity reaches beyond ordinary thinking. "Of course art has a rational basis, born of consciousness, but its realization, its aesthetic effect, which Kleist describes through the dance of the doll, transcends all rational structure." Hence the total image of the marionette and its creator expresses the unity that art makes possible. Moreover, "just as the puppeteer regains, through his puppet's dance, an inkling of paradisical grace, so can poetry overcome history for Kleist and bring the momentary utopia of paradise regained."[9]

This interpretation of the essay, beyond making sense of the text, also resolves one aspect of the Kant-crisis. It does not matter that Kleist never managed, in his own life, to replace his classical ideal of knowledge with this pursuit of truth through the transcendence of art. For our purpose in understanding the image of the artist since Romanticism, the essay still forms a landmark. Like Rousseau and Schiller, Kleist builds a bridge from

6. Ibid., 807.
7. See the essays by Paul Böckmann and Clemens Heselhaus in *Kleists Aufsatz über das Marionettentheater*, ed. Helmut Sembdner.
8. Kleist, *Werke*, 803.
9. Manfred Durzak, "Über das Marionettentheater von Heinrich von Kleist," *Jahrbuch des Freien Deutschen Hochstifts*, 325, 326.

the eighteenth century into a new time. Indeed, this essay especially unearths Kleist's roots in the earlier period. He proceeds from a Rousseauistic
concept of civilized man as decadent; accordingly, Kleist completes Rousseau in the realm of art. That is, he claims that an expanded consciousness
may return us to nature on a higher level.

Kleist intensifies Schiller's belief that art overcomes human dualism
through symbolic activity. In his essay "Über die Aesthetische Erziehung
des Menschengeschlechts" ("On the Aesthetic Education of Mankind")
(1795), Schiller advocates the unifying of mind with nature through artistic
play. He claims that we must extend the innocence of the child into the only
adult pursuit that allows, even demands, the free reign of fantasy. Similarly,
Kleist sees the salvation of wholeness in the merging of intellect and spon-
taneity in the work of art.

Here he partakes of that sweeping drive toward unity that characterizes
German writing from Hamann onward. Indeed, we may see all nineteenth-
century art as seeking a lost prerevolutionary unity. As for Kleist's forebears,
not only Goethe and Schiller but also many lesser lights—Wieland, Klinger,
Lenz, Schlegel—idealize *Ganzheit,* oneness. Like Faust, most protagonists
in early-nineteenth-century literature suffer from the two souls they hold
within. Their creators invent a number of resolutions in wholeness. For
Schiller, the "schöne Seele" (beautiful soul) represents the harmonizing of
all human conflict. Kleist approaches the same ideal with his notion of the
center of gravity within the marionette. This unifying force directs the
seemingly spontaneous dance of the limbs. So the Kleistian dualistic image
of man, torn between instinct and awareness, contains the possibility of
resolution. Combined with the superior consciousness of the artist, the central certainty of the human being may permit him to regain grace.

What, then, does this figure tell us about the image of the artist since
Romanticism? Most important, perhaps, he performs. All four protagonists
in the essay execute some kind of dance: the marionette, the swimmer, the
bear, and the dancer-narrator. Even the puppeteer, we have seen, dances
mentally, through the movement of his doll. Art, then, requires both a
player and an observing audience. No longer can the writer, supported by a
patron, isolate himself from the public in an ivory tower. We have already
seen, in chapter 2, some aspects of this change in the artistic mentality.
Accordingly, all the artist figures I survey after Kleist perform for an audience. Taugenichts and Jakob play fiddles, the *Hungerkünstler* starves publicly, and Kafka's other troupers appear in circus or burlesque. Oskar Matzerath performs amazing histrionic feats in his childhood: breaking glass by
screams, disrupting demonstrations. Later he becomes a renowned jazz
musician.

Naturally, the performer expects to be observed. Kleist shows the conse-
quence of this aspect of self-consciousness in the swimmer. Once aware of
his graceful movement, this man cannot stop rehearsing it in front of a mirror. This latter-day Narcissus, again linked with water, prefigures the self-
obsessed modern artist. The writer's concern with the life of art intensifies
throughout the nineteenth century, producing many *Künstlerromane* (novels about artists). In this century, such stories express the decadent human
condition through the artist as protagonist. Think only of some famous
examples: *A Portrait of the Artist as a Young Man, Death in Venice, The
Diaries of Malte Laurids Brigge, The Counterfeiters.* Recent works, though
surpassing mere decadence, still echo the questions posed by Kleist, Flaubert, Mallarmé, Rilke, Kafka, Joyce: What is art? Who is the artist?

Philip Roth's latest anti-hero, Zuckerman, suffers the agonies of the self-
obsessed writer through three volumes. By-products of this narcissism,
such as the exhibitionism of the dandy, appear in the other arts too. Picasso,
whose showmanship surfaced in clowning and masquerade, set a pattern
for recent artists. Christo shows a similar capacity in his genius for self-
publicity. Perhaps we have reached the ultimate stage of narcissism in Norman Mailer's title *Advertisements for Myself.* Yet the self-inflating artist goes
on, turning to increasingly outspoken buffoonery. Think of Warhol, Johns,
Cage.

The problem of the modern artist also proceeds from the Kleistian view
of man as both dual and seeking unity. For all the figures I discuss here,
human ideals conflict with lowlier, more animal drives. Their striving takes
some artistic form, or a parody of it; the demands of ordinary existence
undercut and eventually destroy their hopes. Only Taugenichts gains the
final unity he has sought throughout his wanderings, in the love of Aurelie.
Jakob, his tragic brother, also seeks love in Barbara, but his only fulfillment
comes in a saintly death. Kafka's figures cannot resolve the split between
their desires and the reality of their miserable lives. Yet they continue to
blindly seek an unknown ideal. One thinks of what their author himself
said: "There is a goal, but no way to it."[10] Such a statement characterizes the
helpless lot of the artist figures discussed here. Grass goes yet further than
Kafka in showing the impossibility of the modern artist in his Oskar. For the
eternal dwarf-child, withdrawing to an insane asylum, even a goal makes
no sense. Of course, Oskar has managed to write an imposing monument
to his times, no mean feat for any artist. Perhaps, then, only art can confer
wholeness on its practitioner. We seem to have landed right where Kleist
left us, long ago.

10. Franz Kafka, *Hochzeitsvorbereitungen auf dem Lande,* 42.

EICHENDORFF: "AUS DEM LEBEN EINES TAUGENICHTS" ("FROM THE LIFE OF A GOOD-FOR-NOTHING") (1826)

This late Romantic work starts when the hero's father throws him out. Such an inauspicious opening recalls the Kleistian idea of man as fallen, for Taugenichts represents, above all, the son of God. Accordingly, in terms of Kleist, the story allows him to regain the grace he loses when expelled from the paradise of childhood. This young man's world, like that which Kleist describes, has a circular form. He must journey to Rome in order to return home on a higher level of consciousness. Here we see what Kleist means by "the ring-like world."

Critics have already spilt much ink over Taugenichts' identity. For our purpose, tracing the development of the artist through his popular guises in the nineteenth century, we need only grant the artistic aspect of this enigmatic hero. From start to finish, Taugenichts functions as a musician. His fiddle lies always close to hand; he readily plays it while singing the songs that punctuate his pilgrimage. At some points, he even relates to his fiddle in ways transcending the merely instrumental. When Taugenichts first sets out, he takes no baggage except the violin. He needs only his music, it seems, to survive a lonely wandering. The fiddle belongs to him as part of his identity. Characteristically, as soon as he reaches an open field, the musician plays and sings. Already, on the first page of his story, we associate the man with music.

Taugenichts reveals his attachment to the fiddle most tellingly at the end of the second chapter, when he decides to leave the castle and resume his travels. "My fiddle, that I had almost forgotten, hung on the wall, covered with dust. But a ray of morning sun from the window opposite suddenly hit the strings. That struck quite a chord in my heart. 'Come here, you trusty instrument,' I said, 'Our realm is not of this world!' "[11] Here we note the transcendent mystery implied by the flash of sun illuminating the strings. This startling image produces music in Taugenichts' heart, a note of his harmony with the heavenly spheres. He interprets this sanctified vision and the sound he feels within as a message: both he and his instrument must move onward. Taugenichts addresses the fiddle as a dear friend, even a beloved. Finally, leaving no doubt as to the significance of man and fiddle combined, Eichendorff ends the paragraph with the transposed words of Christ: "My kingdom is not of this world" (John 18:36).

Surprisingly, few commentators explicate this idea of music and the musician as sanctified. Thomas Mann and others take the line quite naively,

---

11. Joseph von Eichendorff, *Werke in einem Band,* ed. Wolfdietrich Rasch, 1080.

as a sign of Taugenichts as "an artist and a genius."[12] Since all the critics see Taugenichts as a spiritual pilgrim, a holy fool, one wonders why they do not note the inclusion of music as essential to his sanctity.

The lengthy critical discussion of Taugenichts' artistic nature depends, of course, on the definition of art. Benno von Wiese speaks of a "poetic relation to the world." Wolfgang Paulsen stresses the freedom of Taugenichts, who shows no responsibility to anything or anyone. Although he emerges from the rococo Austrian tradition of the servant musician, he also anticipates the new bourgeois figure of the "free" artist.[13] We see in this man an early sign of the *Künstlerproblematik* that dominated the second half of the nineteenth century. Loneliness appears as the hallmark of the artist's plight. From now on we find the creator forced to live on the edge of the bourgeois world. But I date this aloneness earlier: think of Tasso, of Werther.

Taugenichts may show his artistic side most clearly in opposing the philistine. Regardless of his considerable lack of imagination and insight, this man still transcends the limits of the materialistic world around him. His brief career as tollkeeper immediately reveals that his temperament can tolerate no such regulated life. In the terms of Robert Mühlher, his poet's mantle fits far better than the tollkeeper's dressing gown. Yet the Bohemians he meets in Rome suit him just as little as the old gateman at the castle. Moreover, Taugenichts shows nothing of the driven, demonic artist enshrined by many Romantic writers. His innocence precludes any such tendencies to excess. He understands little of worldly matters, for he lives mainly within his own spirit. Besides, his childish faith in divine guidance protects him from the various forms of corruption that cross his path.

This last trait, innocence, relates Taugenichts to the Kleistian ideal of prelapsarian grace. Paulsen goes back much further, finding a prototype of childish simplicity in Parzival. The medieval fool also loses and finally regains divine grace. In our next example, Grillparzer's poor fiddler, innocence bears a new and threatening dimension. Between 1826 and 1847, the world surrounding the childlike musician has become so corrupt that he cannot survive. Imagination can no longer bridge the gap between his ideal world and what actually surrounds him. In contrast to Taugenichts' happy end, Jakob must die. Eichendorff's wandering poet, worthy or not, could find his place among the bourgeois; but society finds his younger brother, the saintly fool Jakob, truly worthless.

12. Thomas Mann, *Betrachtungen eines Unpolitischen,* 377.
13. Benno von Wiese, *Die Deutsche Novelle,* 1:83; Wolfgang Paulsen, *Eichendorff und sein Taugenichts,* 16.

GRILLPARZER: "DER ARME SPIELMANN" ("THE POOR FIDDLER") (1847, BEGUN 1831)

Not only innocence links Jakob with Taugenichts. The fiddle belongs to Jakob's identity too, although, like all else in his life, it brings grave problems. Singing also has crucial, almost magical meaning for Jakob. And here too the father expels the son. After he deems both Latin and violin studies a failure, the *Hofrat* no longer speaks to his son. Then he banishes him to a tiny back room and sends him to eat in cheap restaurants. So here also, the ejection by the father activates the son's development.

In the terms of Kleist, this loss of divine grace has tragic consequences for Jakob, whereas for Taugenichts it offers freedom. Yet both figures retain their innocence, they do not represent a fallen condition. We see part of their innocence in the way both figures take themselves seriously. Taugenichts tells us right away that he plays his fiddle very well; when complimented on his music, he says it is a gift from God. Jakob intensifies this pride to a point approaching madness, for he believes in his cacophonous playing as a form of prayer. Both men, associating their music with God, make it an expression of their own worth. We shall see below the secularized version of this blind belief in an insane art in the *Hungerkünstler.*

Furthermore, what several critics note of Taugenichts applies equally well to Jakob: he poetizes his world. To be sure, this musician does not compose and sing verses to express his feelings about life; but he perceives the environment with a similar childlike optimism. His story celebrates the inner life, regardless of its apparent poverty. The plain Barbara looks beautiful to Jakob, just as his pathetic scratching sounds like heaven to him. But poetizing here also has negative meaning, for it involves ignoring the gross cruelties that almost everyone inflicts on the hapless innocent. In repeatedly calling his tyrannical father "a good man—only violent and ambitious," Jakob appears as a saintly fool. We see the same compulsive respect for authority, masked as love, in Gregor Samsa.

The beginning of this story bears a striking resemblance to "Le Vieux Saltimbanque." Critics have not yet noted the many likenesses between both the carnival settings and the two wretched artist figures they frame. First of all, each first-person narrator participates in an urban fair, which draws his initial interest. As we saw in chapter 2, Baudelaire devotes about half of his piece to this explosion of free spirits, which he also characterizes as a solemn rite. Grillparzer's fair celebrates an actual religious holiday, St. Bridget's Day, which he precisely dates in the first sentence. Here too, the narrator highlights the transcendent aspect of the event. Both he and Baudelaire's poet see the popular festival as a "solemn event." Indeed, the inflated prose of Grillparzer's narrator makes explicit the religious aura that Baudelaire only implies. "As a lover of mankind, I say, especially when they forget their individual goals and feel as one in the mass, wherein lies, ultimately, *the divine*—as such a man every folk festival is to me a festival of the soul, a pilgrimage, an act of worship."[14]

Clearly, then, both narrators evoke something like what Mallarmé, in "Un Spectacle Interrompu," calls "rejoicing, like the crowd, in the myth contained in all banality." The myth that the poet finds in the banal fair concerns its communal identity. With the magic words "parts of the whole," Grillparzer pinpoints the major problem of the mid-nineteenth century that I discuss in chapter 2 in relation to Baudelaire's "Les Foules" and the crowds in Hugo, Benjamin, and Canetti. Already in the 1830s, Grillparzer felt the ambivalent power of the crowd. On the one hand, as both he and Baudelaire note at the start of their stories, the holiday crowd has a positive, even uplifting, sense of mutual pleasure. But on the other hand, the initially benevolent crowd later becomes a threatening herd of animals, driven by instinct. "Le Vieux Saltimbanque" closes with the ruthless impulsion of the hedonist crowd, pushing the narrator away from the clown. (We shall see the same crowd movement in Kafka's "Ein Hungerkünstler.")

In "Der arme Spielmann" the final mob does not contrast with the initial crowd at the fair. Indeed, it realizes the image of overpowering force suggested in the first scene. "Two streams flow, the old Danube and the more swollen wave of the people, one crossing under the other: the Danube rushes toward its ancient bed, the river of people, once undammed, is a wide, tossing lake, submerging itself in a flood that covers everything." At the end of the story, the metaphor of the crowd as a rushing river becomes the reality of a mass of people, fleeing from an actual flood. The power of their former joy shrinks to helplessness before the ultimate force of nature. "The area had become a lake. On all sides crying and bells tolling, mothers searching and children lost."[15] The people, who once overflowed the Danube bridge, are now themselves flooded.

While the mob in Baudelaire seeks amusement, this crowd must save their lives. We see both masses as equally driven, equally threatening in potential. But Grillparzer adopts a more dramatic, even melodramatic, tone, for he speaks of actual death. Baudelaire suggests more than he specifies; he treats spiritual rather than actual death. Accordingly, the pathos of the old clown, with his vestiges of grandeur, has more subtle expressive

14. Franz Grillparzer, *Sämtliche Werke*, 3:148, italics mine.
15. Ibid., 3:184.

power than does that of the pitiful old fiddler, whose whole life bespeaks misery.

Grillparzer's narrator tends to intrude on his material. First he tells us that he loves mankind; later he repeats the claim while making *his* perception the subject of the sentence. Like the poet-narrator in "Une Mort Héroique," this man cannot stop reminding us of his presence. And, as we shall see, despite his supposed warmth, he too feels superior to others. He claims to frequent the fair out of a "passionate love of people," yet he also shows that the spectacle furnishes material for his work.

To illustrate this putative love for the crowd, the narrator claims that the response of an overflowing audience for a play means more to him than the judgment of a cool critic. Naturally! He prefers the material success symbolized by such a crowd to the risk of critical appraisal. But he goes on in populist vein, championing the unsung over the famous, the humble over the heroic. On first reading, such laudable sentiments seem honest enough; but his later behavior shows his self-delusion. In particular, the sentiments reveal the posturing behind the rhetorical monstrosity of a ninety-five-word sentence.

As for the narrator in "Le Vieux Saltimbanque," let us compare his modest mention, in three suggestive sentences, of his reason for visiting the fair. In contrast to the page of voluminous remarks made by Grillparzer's narrator, Baudelaire simply says that the intellectual also absorbs the carefree feeling of the place. His only claim to populism lies in the intriguing phrase "I, as a true Parisian. . . ." Although this poet is deluded in thus labeling himself a mere Parisian, he has already recognized his status as outsider. He never abandons his self-awareness as the man of intellect.

To compare the Baudelaire and Grillparzer texts in their fullest context, we must first consider a famous literary forebear: "Das römische Karneval," in Goethe's *Italienische Reise* (1789).[16] In this account, both later writers have a detailed model of the poet as witness to a ritual event of deep social meaning. We do not know if Grillparzer thought of this popular festival in writing his introductory scene. But in any case, he paraphrases two essential ideas from Goethe: autonomy and classlessness.

Goethe: The Roman Carnival is a festival that is not given the people; they give it
          to themselves.

16. Among the critics, only Paulsen briefly refers to Goethe as a possible source for Grillparzer. Four prose poems by Mallarmé also treat the poet at the fair. In particular, "Le Phénomène Futur" (1864), "Un Spectacle Interrompu" (1875), and "La Déclaration Foraine" (1887) show the wealth of perceptions aroused in the writer by the spectacle. Taken together, these pieces constitute a virtual dialectic on the problem of art as elite or popular. I discuss the related "Réminiscence" (1888) in chapter 5.

Grillparzer: The people participate in the fair that they give themselves.
Goethe: The gap between the classes seems bridged for a moment: everyone
    comes close, each one easily accepts whatever confronts him, and the
    mutual daring and freedom is held in check by the general good spirits.
Grillparzer: Class distinctions have disappeared.[17]

Another sentence in Goethe lends two words to Grillparzer that characterize the spectacle: "This carnival of *abandon,* this modern *Saturnalia*
ends with a general stupor." I italicize the words that Grillparzer reiterates:
"Long awaited, the *saturnalian feast* finally arrives. . . . It is . . . total *abandon.*"[18]

Of these three references to Goethe, the idea of temporary equality
among classes has the most importance. Both writers depict what Bakhtin
calls carnivalization, the free intermingling of people normally kept apart.
Here lies the "revolutionary" aspect of the festival that Grillparzer aptly
suggests in 1847. Furthermore Goethe, suggesting what the later poet specifies, starts his story with a scene of carnival rebirth and ends it with communal death. The Roman Carnival celebrates the overcoming of winter, of
death, by the power of spring reborn. Modern man rejoices in his fertility as
much as the ancient world did; indeed, Catholicism has added to the jubila-
tion by supplying the strict order for the carnival to overthrow.

The link of carnival with death has more than ritual significance. Goethe
devotes some thirty pages to the myriad hilarities of the Roman festival,
ending with Ash Wednesday. In the final entry for this day, he symbolizes
this lengthy outburst of pleasure with the phallic Pulcinella. The images of
love that such figures arouse prompt Goethe to think of "die letzte Feier-
lichkeit" (the last ritual). Indeed, he sees the carnival as an allegory of life,
whose greatest delights remind us of our evanescence. Grillparzer recalls
this view of the celebration in his summary statement of the crescendo and
end of the *Volksfest.* "Music and dance, wine and merriment, shadow-
plays and aerialists, lights and fireworks . . . unite in a land of plenty, an El
Dorado, a fool's paradise, which, happily or not, depending on how you
look at it, lasts only a couple of days, and then disappears, like the dream of
a summer's night, and remains only as a hopeful memory."[19]

Robert Browning sees in this carnival experience "a regression or rebirth
. . . into a dreamy, womblike utopia of equality perhaps, of irresponsibility
and license certainly."[20] Just as certainly does death finally appear for this

17. Goethe, *Werke,* 11:484, 485; Grillparzer, *Werke,* 3:146.
18. Goethe, *Werke,* 11:514; Grillparzer, *Werke,* 3:146; italics mine.
19. Grillparzer, *Werke,* 3:147.
20. Robert Browning, "Language and the Fall from Grace in Grillparzer's *Der arme
Spielmann,*" 217.

mass of celebrants. And the *Spielmann,* although he has stood apart from the mob, dies with them. Indeed, he sacrifices himself to their material values, for he makes his last exertion in rescuing his landlord's paltry savings. Baudelaire leaves his old clown alive, but the hedonist crowd that has rejected him has clearly killed his spirit. Carnival, it seems, leads to death. Below, in chapter 5, we shall see the same link in the work of Apollinaire and Picasso. The ballet *Petrushka,* the subject of chapter 6, even echoes the structure of Grillparzer and Baudelaire in starting with carnival and ending with death.

Baudelaire does not locate his fair specifically, since all his prose poems transcend the quotidian. Although his language does not betray an allegorizing intent as clearly as Goethe's does, each tableau conveys an experience of larger emotional meaning. Grillparzer, often called a Realist, sets his carnival on an actual bridge over the Danube, which connects the inner Vienna with its proletarian suburbs. Hence the narrator must leave his own quarter to cross the bridge. He reminds us of this separation each time he "crosses over" to visit the *Spielmann* in his workers' quarter. This trip signifies not only his confrontation with the lower class, but also a new and moving experience. In this respect, his story stands very close to "Le Vieux Saltimbanque"; there too the essential idea is this assault on the narrator's feelings. Martin Swales, the only critic to note a link between Grillparzer and Baudelaire, speaks of "the role of shock meetings" for both authors.[21]

We find a clear echo of the experience of Grillparzer's narrator in Hofmannsthal's "Das Erlebnis des Marschalls von Bassompierre" (1900). Again, an upper-class narrator crosses a bridge, the newly built *Pont Neuf,* and inside the poor section confronts his magical shopwoman. Like our modern poets, the baroque cavalier is overwhelmed by this meeting with "the other half." And he too has crossed over, from his external life of decorum into the internal area of his own heart. In this revelation lies the greatest threat to his existence: the contamination of the plague. On a less literal level, all these narrators undergo the danger of confronting their inmost being. What constitutes a brief but poignant love affair for the marshal is for them the shocking experience of the alter ego. The stories these three men write bear lasting witness to the passion involved in the encounter.

Both Baudelaire and Grillparzer, like Goethe, begin their pieces with seeming objectivity. Yet each description of an arresting old man soon reveals more than mere curiosity. In "Le Vieux Saltimbanque," the poet suddenly sees in the old clown his future self; this shock of recognition

---

21. Martin Swales, *The German Novelle,* 130.

stuns him. Only later can he articulate the meaning of this crucial confrontation. Grillparzer's narrator, struck by the oddity of a begging musician who speaks Latin, determines to know his story. This writer also finds in the desolate fiddler the reverse image of his own success. Jakob belongs by birth to the upper bourgeoisie, and only his miserable history has brought him so low. The narrator thus relates to him through class.

Baudelaire's old clown has also "abdicated" from former glory, but his fall results mainly from the natural process of aging. Hence the poet relates to him professionally; in this ruined player he foresees his own decline. For both narrators, what first appears as merely a fascinating case of decadence becomes a prophetic *Schreckbild* (warning image) of the perils of art. Starobinski highlights the further effect of this process. "The poet-witness captures the image of an agony, in the strict sense of the word, in order to apply it, symbolically and prophetically, to himself."[22]

Grillparzer's narrator feels more horror than sympathy for the old man. Baudelaire, by contrast, shows only compassion. One senses that, in the Freudian terms of Leo Bersani, the old clown represents a deeply loved self, estranged by the cruel realities of the poet's life. But Grillparzer's narrator, whose attraction to the fiddler is always ambivalent, seems cold at best. At both their meetings, the narrator tries to give Jakob money. Yet the beggar proudly refuses the gift, for he thinks he has earned nothing. The narrator, blind to the man's understandable attempt at dignity, continues to offer money as a reward for his story. Such a motive, like his later bid to buy the dead man's fiddle, shows that he values Jakob as a commodity for sale. Indeed, the narrator sees only the commercial value of all around him. By contrast, Baudelaire's narrator seeks simply to leave, unnoticed, some coins on the old clown's table.

Grillparzer's narrator repeatedly shows his sense of superiority over both Jakob and the carnival crowd. Despite his frequent claims to populist feeling, he spurns the common and reveres status. Jakob arouses his interest only when he mutters a Latin phrase, a sure sign of his elevated background. Unlike the narrator in Baudelaire, this man could not make spiritual contact with an ordinary player; he must sense a kinship in class. Yet he needs to feel superior to Jakob too, for he renders the musician as an inept failure. Baudelaire's narrator also has a marked sense of superiority, but only toward the insensitive crowd rejecting the clown. Only he can notice the suffering that the fair contains; only he can weep for the old man. The narrator in "Une Mort Héroique" shows the same distinction from the court: only he sees the halo crowning Fancioulle.

22. Jean Starobinski, *Portrait de l'Artiste en Saltimbanque*, 99.

Hence, despite the "revolutionary" carnivalization at the start of these pieces, the poet-narrator's superiority alienates him from the people. Moreover, his alter ego, the miserable old artist, also stands apart from the crowd. In the first scene, the narrator stresses the contrast that Jakob offers to the mob framing him. Here we see hectic movement versus stillness, the raucous versus the dignified. The fiddler also distances himself from the other begging players, and he leaves the fair when the crowd swells to its evening peak. Going homeward, he symbolizes his lot, struggling against the stream of people moving in the opposite direction. Later on, Jakob reveals the ultimate symbol of his condition as outsider: the chalk line drawn on the floor of his room to separate him from two messy roommates. This line best expresses his self-imposed apartness.

Like Baudelaire, Grillparzer clearly structures the separations among his narrator, the player, and the crowd in a triangle. Each element in the triangle, though interdependent, also opposes the others. Hertha Krotkoff implies this structure in speaking of the three religious worlds of the story. "There are the people, still in the grip of a now decadent Baroque piety, . . . the narrator, with his secularized religion of humanity, and . . . the pure filial relation to the divine of Jakob."[23] Since some critics lump Jakob with the working people around him, it is important to distinguish not only these three separate realms but also their mutual antagonism. For both Baudelaire and Grillparzer, the player suffers from his public. The mob scorns the old *saltimbanque;* it ignores or ridicules the fiddler. At best, the people show indifference to art.

Let us now examine Jakob's music, since it conveys his essential character as an artist figure. From the title of the story onward, this man represents a special kind of player. Like "Le Vieux Saltimbanque," "Der arme Spielmann" enshrines a specific profession in the performing arts. Baudelaire's figure, no simply generic clown, belongs to a class of urban *histrions;* the very name *saltimbanque* summons up images of lower-class theater. Similarly, in using the word *Spielmann* instead of *Geiger* or *Musikant,* Grillparzer draws on revered associations for the title. A whole literary tradition grew up around the late-medieval minstrel, wandering from court to court. This very mode of life of the singer-poet expresses the outsider. Grillparzer injects into his title the first note of the irony pervading his story, for no one considers Jakob's "crazy" music as the true art of a *Spielmann.*

Critics have applied a wide range of mostly negative labels to the sound Jakob produces. Only August Sauer naively romanticizes it as embodying

23. Hertha Krotkoff, "Über den Rahmen in Franz Grillparzer's Novelle 'Der arme Spielmann,'" 364.

the dying musical spirit of Vienna. Perhaps the worst reaction comes from the narrator himself, who calls this performance a "hellish concert." Several readers take this verdict at face value, calling Jakob incompetent, self-deceived, a bungler. More sympathetically, Heinz Politzer refers to "mystical music," and Robert Browning finds in these weird notes "a theodicy without evil."[24] This striking formulation makes dissonance a metaphor for evil; the essential madness of this music lies in its total ban on conflicting chords.

Any discussion of Jakob's "crazy" playing must refer to his contemporaries, the truly mad musicians of E.T.A. Hoffmann. The Baron von B. also thinks his own cacophonous sounds are wonderful. Indeed, unlike Jakob, he seeks to transcend his insane private aesthetics and gain recognition. With his wild fiddling the Baron thinks he reveals innovations to a jaded musical public. Madly enough, he sees himself as revolutionary. Such pretensions lie well beyond Jakob's modest vanities.

Moreover, the *Spielmann* can correctly play Barbara's song. Hence, unlike the Baron, Jakob escapes total subjectivity through his involvement with another person. Ritter Gluck, whom another writer-narrator meets mysteriously, also expresses his delusions through music. But Hoffmann portrays a musician of uncanny talent, an artist deranged yet fully in control of his life. Jakob has none of these attributes. In comparing him to the Baron, Ritter Gluck, and Rat Krespel, we cannot call him mad at all, for he lacks the demonic dimension of their inner world. We may say of them, more emphatically than of Taugenichts, that their realm is not of this world. But whatever his practical failings, Jakob participates in ordinary reality, something which these insane men cannot do. He resembles a child more than a madman. In addition, Krespel's destructive violence distinguishes him from the passive Jakob.[25]

A less familiar musician of the period again reminds us of Jakob: the *Rentherr* in Stifter's "Turmalin" (1853). This man from the upper class has also descended to begging with his flute. And his playing sounds just as chaotic as Jakob's fiddling. We may understand his music also as an expression of his painful life, for the *Rentherr* has lost his wife and hidden his

24. W. E. Yates, Walter Silz, and Günther Jungbluth noted in Browning, "Fall from Grace," 223–24; Heinz Politzer, *Franz Grillparzer, oder das Abgründige Biedermeier,* 373.

25. Another significant musician of the period, the Black Fiddler in Keller's *Romeo und Julia auf dem Dorfe* (1856), exemplifies a range of traits associated with the demonic. His music seduces the lovers into the underworld of outcasts; his homelessness symbolizes the only fate on earth imaginable for the bourgeois victims of a forbidden love. For them, the manic playing of the sinister man expresses all the terror of that declassing at the heart of their ruin.

daughter in a cave. He seems mad indeed, and harmful, thus differing in character from the benevolent Jakob. But a loss of class and the attendant mad music link the two figures. Moreover, the background of both stories goes beyond *Standesverfall* (loss of class) to *Familienverfall* (decay of the family). This social problem, intensifying in the latter nineteenth century, culminates in German literature with *Buddenbrooks*.

Comparing Taugenichts' normal music with what Jakob produces, we see a new kind of art indeed. Most obviously, people like listening to Taugenichts, whereas they can hardly stand to hear the *Spielmann*. Taugenichts plays mainly to sing and provide dance music for others. Although Jakob seems to perform for a mendicant living, he really plays only for himself. The *Rentherr* does the same thing, which causes the narrator in his story to speculate on the strange life behind such tortured sounds. Jakob himself gives the best account of what his music means for him. "They play Mozart and Bach, but no one plays dear God."[26] Music means prayer for the saintly man, whose survival depends on transcending his miserable history through art. Yet for us, of course, the weird sounds evoke only a private world, unfathomable to our ears. Jakob's "hellish concert" signifies an unbridgeable gap between artist and audience.

Accordingly, the story gives us what Browning calls "a parable of the expressive dilemma of the artist."[27] I believe this phrase refers to the inevitably narcissistic need for self-expression in the creator since Romanticism. Browning's view of Jakob as "pre-lapsarian man," incomprehensible to the rest of us fallen creatures, does not diminish Jakob's self-awareness. To be sure, Jakob remains innocent in the theological sense; for him, unlike his progeny in Kafka and Grass, the corruption of irony is unthinkable. Yet art provides an outlet for his personal drama, which distinguishes his innocence from that of Taugenichts. For that less self-conscious artist, music may reflect mood, but it cannot evoke the pathos of the outsider, since Taugenichts lacks Jakob's emotive depth. In short, Taugenichts embodies the Kleistian puppet, while Jakob is a complex human being.

The last scene of the story symbolically relates the narcissistic artist to his transcendence. When the narrator finally visits Barbara and her family, he sees Jakob's fiddle, hanging on a wall with a mirror and a crucifix. This telling composition, with the cross and the violin framing the mirror, immortalizes Jakob in his three major aspects. The Christian stands "with a sort of symmetry" beside the artist; yet the center of this dual person lies in

---

26. Grillparzer, *Werke*, 3:163.
27. Browning, "Fall from Grace," 232.

the mirror.[28] This suggestion of Narcissus refers to the egocentric musician who plays only for himself. We see in Jakob the presage of the artist to come, since his reverence for his own work prefigures the full-blown egotism of his progeny. In retrospect, it seems only a short step from the artist's worship of "dear God" in his art to self-worship. Especially in the secular age that Grillparzer anticipates, the artist becomes his own god.

Our summary evaluation of Jakob depends largely on how we understand Grillparzer's irony. On the simplest level, we note right away that the begging musician cuts a comic figure. Only his fervor matches his incompetence. Paulsen finds not only Jakob but his whole milieu the subject of pervasive satire. His father, for instance, resembles the tyrants in Wedekind and Hasenclever, vehicles of the attack on bourgeois society itself. As for Jakob, he shows two determining bourgeois traits: the pedantic chalk line separating his order from the chaos of the working class, and his ironic final sacrifice to money.

The deeper level of irony in the story concerns Jakob's identity as holy fool. The world scorns him, but only the backward beggar saves others. He represents the clown as Christ, even the poet as God. As a "secularized martyr," Jakob belongs among Baudelaire's artistes, for he too embodies "sacrificial art". Politzer traces the process suggested by Starobinski. "The essence of Jakob is the mystery of art, just as it is for artists from Goethe's Tasso to Kafka's Hunger Artist; but the reality, which this wonder transcends, has always treated the artist with either blows or a much more humiliating pity, depending on its mood. So the world classifies the artist as a masochist, tracing the miracle he has experienced in his ecstasy to the wounds it has inflicted. In this way the artist has become a secularized martyr."[29]

Looking at Jakob most positively, we may conclude that he has successfully transcended a bitter reality through his emotions. Soul has triumphed over matter, according to a persistent belief in "German inwardness." Tacitus notes that the Germanic tribes tended to settle apart from each other; more-recent cultural historians have developed this remark into a virtual school of interpretation. According to it, German writers tend to stress individuality and isolation. As for Jakob, he fits into the tradition of "the little man," seen as typical of more than German literature since the mid-nineteenth century.

28. Grillparzer, *Werke,* 3:186.
29. Politzer, *Biedermeier,* 381.

More often than not, the protagonists of Austrian stories have been variations on the theme first played by the poor fiddler on his cracked violin. A veritable procession of complex-ridden, indecisive anti-heroes, "superfluous men" (well-known to the readers of the Russian novel), failures in practical life but pure of heart, people the Austrian novel and stage to this very day. They are usually presented with . . . a psychological insight such that even those works conceived well before Freud may strike one as being positively "Freudian."[30]

This insight shows that we cannot simplify "the little man" into a hero. On the contrary, by the universally popular criterion of success, Jakob is at best pathetic. He makes a uselessly spiritual response to the age of pragmatism. Indeed, even beyond the socioeconomic reality, Jakob fails in the Darwinian context of survival of the fittest. To be sure, the story predates the German translation of *The Origin of Species* (1859). Yet the idea of natural selection was already in the air; Hegel and others held that success determines survival.[31] Although we cannot attribute such a crass naturalism to Grillparzer, a tinge of Darwinism does contribute to his critique of Jakob's innocence.

However, we cannot consider the fiddler a failure when we look at the opposite figure of success here, the narrator. In this man, most of the recent critics see pretense, egotism, coldness. He recalls Nietzsche's sweeping condemnation of worldly power: "Success was always the greatest liar."[32] Among the critics, John Ellis gives the narrator the worst marks; indeed, his deprecation of the man seems overstated, for Swales and Browning evince some psychological grounds to justify the behavior Ellis decries.

The narrator feels compulsively drawn to Jakob. Their first encounter makes the declassed beggar irresistible, and the writer insists on a later visit. When he arrives he must hear the man's story; finally the flood draws him back to the workers' quarter, specifically to know how Jakob has fared. Beyond all these obvious signs of attraction by the opposite, the narrator's remarks and gestures often bespeak his susceptibility to Jakob.

Like Barbara, this man reveals a hidden link to his antagonist. Both he and the "barbaric" girl represent the world of commercial success that opposes Jakob, yet they both have a weakness for him. When she bids farewell to him, Barbara gives a clue to both her character and its natural sympathy for the musician. "Now I must go out among the common folk, against which I have struggled so long."[33] The narrator also has mixed feel-

30. Ivar Ivask, introduction to *The Poor Fiddler,* 11.
31. Karl Löwith, *From Hegel to Nietzsche,* trans. David Green, 218.
32. Friedrich Nietzsche, *Werke: Jenseits von Gut und Böse,* ed. Alfred Baeumler, 216.
33. Grillparzer, *Werke,* 3:181.

ings about the people; he alternates between rhetorical flourishes of populism and outspoken distaste for humanity. Hence his "affair" with the *Spielmann,* like Barbara's, may have a secretly cathartic purpose.

Intent on demolishing the biographical approach, John Ellis gives short shrift to the interpretation of Jakob and the narrator as Grillparzer's "split self." Critics have long favored this view because it stems from the author himself. "Two fully separate beings live within me. A poet with the most overwhelming imagination, and a rationalist of the coldest and toughest kind." Grillparzer also spoke of himself as both spectator and play.[34] This simultaneous dualism reminds us again of Baudelaire: "I am the the victim and the knife!" Both poets seem compelled to live inside and outside themselves, in that place that Baudelaire calls "hors de chez soi" (outside the self).

Ellis does more than anyone else to show that "Der arme Spielmann" transcends a self-portrait of Grillparzer. However, his conclusions do not vitiate the more general view of the story as a dualistic picture of the modern artist. With both figures, Grillparzer renders the perils of art in a world torn between the "barbaric" pragmatism of the narrator and the Christian suffering of Jakob. Baudelaire also puts himself into both his protagonists, and his tears express a debased self-love. Indeed, we may see him in all three elements of the show in "Une Mort Héroique": the prince, the player, and the court.

Apparently we cannot get rid of the author as easily as Ellis imagines. Although the New Criticism underlying his attitude has helped to open up vast areas of interpretation, it tends to ignore the crucial role played by the writer's personality. In his link of the artist with Narcissus, Wallace Fowlie captures not only the creator in general but also our two authors specifically. "The hero created by the artist is always the artist himself, and the artist is all men of his age. . . . All men are mirrored in the artist, . . . as the mythical adolescent was mirrored in the clear fountain."[35]

Baudelaire's compassionate poet contrasts sharply with Grillparzer's cold playwright. This man recalls what Flaubert's mother supposedly said of him: "Your mania for phrases has dried up your heart."[36] Such a common critique of the intellectual may add credence to the view of Grillparzer's narrator as self-criticism. But we may also understand his harsh character as a reflection of the bitterness born of the Metternich era. Richard Brinkmann and Politzer find signs here of Grillparzer's ambivalent hope and fear of

34. Grillparzer, *Werke,* 3:204, 4:88.
35. Wallace Fowlie, *Love in Literature,* 127.
36. Flaubert quoted in Maurice Shroder, *Icarus,* 165.

revolution. As we have seen above, the rushing mob of the first scene portends both the freedom and the danger of social upheaval.

This comparison of "Le Vieux Saltimbanque" and "Der arme Spielmann" is not meant to show Grillparzer's influence on Baudelaire. It is unlikely that the French poet knew of the Austrian dramatist at all, though Byron had already proclaimed his merits in 1821. "Grillparzer—a devil of a name . . . for posterity, but they *must* learn to pronounce it."[37] In any case, I find a putative link between the two writers less interesting than the textual relations between these two works.

These likenesses show that the despairing image of the artist varies little from the Second Empire to the Metternich era of the Hapsburg monarchy. But how can this be so? We assume that poets are products of their cultures; yet these two countries differ basically in political background. The modern Austrian Empire, uniting diverse nationalities in an unbroken baroque Catholic tradition, had no history of republican opposition. Indeed, some critics think that Austria still awaits its Bastille Day. Ulrich Greiner shows the hopelessness of Austrian liberals under Metternich: "Whoever fought for bourgeois rights fought against the monarchy. The German situation was the opposite: such opponents understood themselves as fighting for Germany. In Austria one could not be both a patriot and a revolutionary."[38] We think of the German tradition of social protest among poets from Büchner onwards: Heine, Heinrich Mann, Brecht, Tucholsky. In Austria, except for Karl Kraus, writers continued to enshrine the paternal tyranny and decadent bureaucracy that we find in "Der arme Spielmann." Hofmannsthal, Rilke, Musil, and Roth do not interrupt what Greiner calls "the hymn to sweet passivity."

Both the Baudelaire texts treated above, "Le Vieux Saltimbanque" and "Une Mort Héroique," bespeak the depoliticized disillusion of French intellectuals in the 1860s. Therefore we might speak of a moment in French history akin to centuries of apolitical passivity in Austria. But still, the quietism of the French Second Empire resulted from a sobered defeat; at least Baudelaire had known the hectic activism of 1848. And he had some revered models of patriotic protest in Lamartine and Hugo. Hence his tone has the pathos of true decadence, a lost liberation, a dead idealism. Grillparzer had no such memories and no such forebears in literature. His models, Goethe and Schiller, convey an honorary liberalism at best. Thus the similarities of these texts show that the plight of modern art transcends deep

37. Byron quoted in Politzer, *Biedermeier*, 7.
38. Ulrich Greiner, *Der Tod des Nachsommers*, 14.

cultural differences. Regardless of their separate traditions, post-Romantic poets see themselves as an endangered species.

HOFMANNSTHAL: *DER SCHWIERIGE*
(THE DIFFICULT MAN) (1918)

Jakob, like all the artist figures discussed here, performs for a living. Accordingly, his art depends as much on a pantomime of movement as it does on actual music. Indeed, like Taugenichts, he best expresses himself nonverbally—and not only when he plays. Browning bases much of his interpretation on Jakob's suggestive remark, "Words ruin the music."[39] The title of Browning's article, "Language and the Fall from Grace in Grillparzer's *Der arme Spielmann*," recalls Kleist. Although the essay on the puppet theater does not refer specifically to speech as part of the fall of modern man, that idea seems implicit. For Kleist generally, language tends to create misunderstanding. In chapter 2, we saw one result of the problem that modern writers have with their own medium: an attraction to mime. As Majut shows, Kleist gives a climactic turning point in the devaluation of man and the corresponding affirmation of the nonhuman. We may also see him as crucial in the related denigration of language. For beyond the alienation from language lies the larger event of a widespread doubt about the basic values of Western culture.

The problem of language in a decadent culture, already implied by Kleist and Grillparzer, becomes a dominant theme in the work of another Austrian dramatist, Hofmannsthal. Like Rimbaud, who abandoned literature at nineteen, the prodigy Hofmannsthal gave up lyric poetry at twenty-one. His crisis, discussed in the "Brief des Lord Chandos" (1901), concerns the viability of language. This verbal means of abstraction cannot serve human life, which defies such conventions. The author's reverence for everything in creation prevents him from generalizing. He cannot see things with the simplifying eye of convention, for that reduction seems to him deceptive and hence dangerous. Lord Chandos refuses to abstract life, to disregard the details that only seem trivial.

One dramatic character best represents these values: the clown Furlani in the comedy *Der Schwierige*. This *dummer August* embodies the central idea of the play. Specifically, Furlani provides a mute alter ego for the problematic hero of the title, Hans Karl. At the crucial midpoint of the work, he gives his impressions of a circus act he has just seen. Beyond the clown's

39. Grillparzer, *Werke*, 3:162.

evident grace and effortless charm, Hans Karl envies his seeming aimlessness. Unlike the society satirized here, the player shows no calculating aims; he pays no heed to his audience; he performs out of pure excitement and delight. Hans Karl admires above all the elegant nonchalance of this performer, whom he finds more entertaining than anyone imaginable. In fact, claims Kari, all circus acts demand more intellect than do the social graces.

Like Chandos, Furlani respects every smallest detail. Kari echoes this precision of the artist morally in his scrupulous respect for all people. For him, "speech is based on an indecent self-inflation."[40] Only silence offers the safety of remaining humble. So Kari identifies with the clown's silent and aimless art as an ideal of behavior. Therein lies much of his social difficulty. The witty confusions in the circus ring, when transferred to the drawing room, cause deep misunderstandings. Although Hofmannsthal focuses on the comic aspect of such chaotic relations, his play still implies the tragic moral view of the *Chandos* letter. Ultimately, for all three figures, the only solution to the cultural dilemma of language lies in a mystical escape from reality. In such a state, "the language would perhaps be given, in which I would not only write but also think, . . . a language of whose words I know not a one, . . . a language in which the mute things speak to me, and in which I will one day answer to an unknown judge."[41]

This mystical state of oneness with all creation characterizes Furlani too. In his silence Kari finds an envied salvation from the endless, egoistic conversation of those around him. Furlani embodies a fully asocial ideal, an escape from the rational goals of daily life into pure style. Indeed, Kari even elevates him above the other circus artistes, who pursue their aims as relentlessly as the Viennese aristocracy. Just as Furlani's detachment mocks the aerial feats of his colleagues, so does Kari's coolness ridicule the ambitious social games of his friends. Both men show the paradoxical power of nonchalance.

Of course, the clown as artist only seems aimless; in fact his art demands constant calculation. However, such self-awareness escapes Kari, who feels only the strong appeal of the clown's childlike harmlessness and illusion of disinterest. Moreover, Kari himself stands close to childhood. Not only does he often refer to his youth, but also other figures characterize his seeming

40. Hugo von Hofmannsthal, *Gesammelte Werke: Lustspiele,* ed. Herbert Steiner, 2:389. Compare Beckett's Molloy, who considers speaking "merely complying with the convention that demands you either lie or hold your peace" (*Molloy* [New York: Grove Press, 1955], 119). Beckett, like Harold Pinter, assumes the "indecency" of speech that haunted Hofmannsthal. For a perceptive treatment of silence in contemporary drama, see John Lahr, "The Language of Silence"—an essay inspired by Susan Sontag—in his *Up Against the Fourth Wall.*

41. Hugo von Hofmannsthal, *Gesammelte Werke: Prosa,* ed. Herbert Steiner, 2:22.

unawareness as childlike. Furlani signifies a rebirth of the child in Kari, for he speaks of the clown as "a true re-creation."[42]

Furlani thus exemplifies the innocence that can purify a life corrupted by the falseness of society. Only the clown gives this possibility of redemption. Here Hofmannsthal touches Kleist, who also implies that the artist can recapture that grace denied to fallen man. Henri Vermorel speaks of something similar in Mallarmé: "the search for the lost paradise of which all poetry sings."[43] Even for Kari, the non-artist, Furlani offers a model of the aesthetic life. Hofmannsthal reveals through Helene, the voice of moderation in the play, his only objection to art as a guide for behavior. When Kari acclaims the clown's act, she notes its fragility, even its dangers for others.

Hans Kar. He is so fascinated by every tiny thing that happens: when he balances
  a flower-pot on his nose, he does so out of politeness, so to speak.
Helene. But he lets it fall anyway?
Kar.   But the way he lets it fall, that's the thing! He drops it from pure delight
  that he can balance it so beautifully! . . .
Helene. (to herself): And the flower-pot usually can't stand that and falls.[44]

The restraint of this remark, like the veiled skepticism of the happy ending for the play, expresses Hofmannsthal's equivocal attitude. Although he clearly delineates the problem of dying Austrian culture, he cannot propose a solution for it. Nonetheless, his "difficult" play makes a strong plea for the silent grace that Furlani represents. At least such an aesthetic program has a positive moral intent: to avoid the "indecency" of speech. Moreover, it offers a counterforce to any culture that distances man from instinct.

In Furlani, Hofmannsthal created his most concise symbol of the mute performance. All his works document what the poet called "a desperate love for all the non-verbal arts: music, dance, and all the skills of acrobats and clowns."[45] In this statement of 1895, Hofmannsthal joins many of his peers in turning to pantomime and the popular stage as a source of renewal for the arts. Even before the *Chandos* letter, he reacted against the barren rationalism he found in language. Like many other writers of the time, Hofmannsthal rebelled against the prevailing tendencies of the *fin de siècle:* Naturalism, a surfeit of psychology, the abstractions of *l'art pour l'art,* mimesis itself. Maeterlinck, Craig, Schnitzler, Blok, Jarry, Wedekind: all, despite some basic differences, resemble Hofmannsthal in this respect. They all seek to vivify a cerebrally sterile world through immediate feeling.

42. Hofmannsthal, *Lustspiele,* 2:342.
43. Quoted in Robert Storey, *Pierrots on the Stage of Desire,* 278.
44. Hofmannsthal, *Lustspiele,* 2:345.
45. Hofmannsthal, *Prosa,* 1:265.

KAFKA

"Ein Hungerkünstler" ("A Hunger-Artist") (1924)

An unbridgeable gap lies between the ideal artist Furlani and the hunger-artist. Hofmannsthal at least tries to combat the inevitable decline of art with his graceful clown. Indeed, Furlani stands closer to Kleist than to our other figures. Both Taugenichts and Jakob, though essentially *Gotteskinder* (children of God), are too ambiguous to offer any lasting salvation from the hostilities of bourgeois society. Accordingly, we must view Furlani as a fleetingly hopeful image of the artiste. He forms part of what Stefan George calls "der farbenvolle Untergang" (the brilliant dying), which Hofmannsthal felt as both his own and the Austrian tragedy.[46] In Kafka, his contemporary in the Austrian Empire, we find none of this nostalgia. Yet Kafka makes an essential link with our earlier Viennese dramatist, Grillparzer. Bracketing Furlani, we may trace a direct line from the poor fiddler to the hunger-artist.

What Politzer says of Gregor Samsa in "Die Verwandlung des armen Spielmanns" goes also for the starver: "Jakob's music gets distilled into that 'unknown nourishment,' of whose lack Gregor Samsa dies."[47] Indeed, the idea of a mysterious, unattainable food for the soul forms the center of this story of the starving artist. To be sure, "Ein Hungerkünstler" is missing one parallel to "Der arme Spielmann" in family decline, seen through the victimizing of the son. But it shares with that story the crucial protagonist that "Die Verwandlung" lacks: the performer as metaphor for the artist. In this ultimate work, Kafka reduces his subject to pure abstraction.

As we shall see below, the art of his other players has some actuality. The ape performs in a burlesque, the aerialist and the equestrienne work in a circus, and Josephine sings for her mouse-audience. But the starver practices no tangible art. He merely demonstrates the most basic fact of animal existence. Showing only that man finally dies without food, this "art" is actually mere endurance. At best, it signifies only a literal version of art as sacrifice. At worst, it is a futile display of utter asceticism. This "man of sorrows" embodies the opposite of grace, which we have regarded, until recently, as the hallmark of art. Instead of free movement, this "scurrilous perversion of the artist," this "caricature," shows us paralysis.[48]

Jakob, the saintly musician, dies because he cannot survive in a mate-

46. Stefan George, *Werke,* 214.
47. Politzer, *Biedermeier,* 392.
48. Jean Starobinski, "Sur Quelques Répondants Allégoriques du Poète," 406; Hermann Pongs, *Franz Kafka, Dichter des Labyrinths,* 87; von Wiese, *Deutsche Novelle,* 1:331.

rialistic world; the hunger-artist dies because he cannot find food that appeals to him. He too cannot live in this world, but not because of its brutality. He simply cannot eat normally, he cannot fill the most basic need of life. In short, he rejects the human condition. Hence his starving represents an art wholly divorced from life. Kafka wept while reading the proofs for this story on his deathbed, so we know it had tragic meaning for him. We cannot ignore its autobiographical content.

But the comic aspect of the piece, often slighted by critics, has equal importance. Literally, the starver is deadly serious about his "art." Such an intensifying of the vain pride that we already noted in Taugenichts and Jakob seems ludicrous. So does the ritual scene of his periodic halt to the fast, a mock pietà with two reluctant virgins. The art of starving thus distills Jakob's crazy music into parody. Jakob separated himself from the rest of the world by his unfathomable sounds; this man severs his link to life itself. The empty, nihilistic "art" of this man mocks the very notion of art as ideal. The comic martyr becomes a fully parodied "Spielmann."

All Kafka's artiste stories create images of the player by means of three interrelated elements: the art produced, the nature of the performer, and his relation to the audience. Let us first consider the art of the hunger-artist, starvation. The problem of starving pervades Kafka's stories. Not only Samsa dies by refusing food; the dog in "Forschungen eines Hundes" also fasts, and the beast in "Der Bau" frets constantly about nourishment. In his final moments of life, Georg Bendemann in "Das Urteil" grasps the railing of a bridge "as a hungry one grasps food."[49] Like the hunger-artist, Georg hungers for a normal life, yet his father has condemned him to the total isolation of death. Indeed, we may see both textual and biographical parallels between Georg's suicide and the starver's self-destruction. Georg's death constitutes Kafka's famous "breakthrough," and the hunger-artist, the ultimate symbol of suicide, emerges in the last year of the author's life.

We might also compare the burly leopard, who replaces the hunger-artist, and the healthy body of Grete Samsa, whose promise of posterity replaces Gregor. A similar parallel for both these stories exists in "Der arme Spielmann": Barbara's vigorous butcher husband replaces the weak Jakob. And another symbol of healthy life, the guards of the hunger-artist, are again butchers. However, we cannot equate the starvation of Gregor with that of the later figure. Gregor's starving signifies regression, in contrast to the transcendence of hunger for the hunger-artist. Gregor returns to an animal origin, whereas his counterpart, the starver, aspires to transcend human life itself.[50]

49. Franz Kafka, *Sämtliche Erzählungen*, 37.
50. Ingeborg Henel, "Ein Hungerkünstler," 231.

One thinks of the similar spiritualizing hunger that sublimates earthly needs in Mallarmé's figures. As I show in chapter 5, the urchins in "Pauvre Enfant Pâle" (1866) and "Réminiscence" (1888) anticipate the obsessive emotional fasting of the hunger-artist. Moreover, we may see the same urge in Mallarmé himself, who constantly sought to purify and to elevate his art above its individual human character. He expresses this idealism specifically as hunger: "I think the only occupation of a self-respecting man is to gaze at the heavens while dying of hunger." "Mallarmé . . . sacrificed the man in himself for the sake of the poet. One of his . . . primary structural tensions is that fundamental one of Life and Death, . . . the dying of a man and the becoming of a Poet." For the starver, fasting allows just this kind of escape from the physical self. Once freed from appetite, the purely spiritual being can triumph.[51]

What, then, does this ideal goal of starvation mean? We may trace the theme of hunger to its roots in the mystical asceticism born of Romantic guilt. Only through the self-purification of fasting can the fallen soul approach the ultimate mystical union with all Being. "The obsession with sin joins with a thirst for renunciation of earthly things, with a desire for freedom from all human bonds, which are tainted in the eyes of the severe internal judge."[52] Starting with Baudelaire, scornful of the whole human condition, this expiatory refusal of life develops throughout the century. Flaubert, Mallarmé, Kafka, Eliot, and Benn express a mounting revulsion for all earthly life.

Claude Vigée illumines several forebears for the hunger-artist: Flaubert's St. Antoine and Mallarmé's Hérodiade give striking examples of earlier souls "closed in on themselves, . . . paralyzed in their inhuman purity."[53] We see an obvious autobiographical link to Kafka. For him, the emotional starvation of art represents the opposite of human fulfillment in paternity. Rebelling against the patriarchal Jewish heritage embodied by his hefty father, Kafka developed the ascetic habits of celibacy and vegetarian diet. In his inability to marry, he saw a refusal to procreate. Unable to get beyond his own consciousness, Kafka shows the reverse of the Baudelairean ideal of transcending the self, "être hors de chez soi" (going outside the self). Kafka believed that instead of founding a family he should commit himself to literature. For him, posterity could come only from writing.

The rejection of marriage as debilitating for artists goes back to Goethe at least. But there is more than professional ambition in the idea of literature as

51. Stéphane Mallarmé, *Correspondance,* ed. Henri Mondor, 118; Ursula Franklin, *An Anatomy of Poesis,* 15; see also Leo Bersani, *The Death of Stéphane Mallarmé.*
52. Claude Vigée, "Les Artistes de la Faim," 97.
53. Ibid., 108.

a denial of life itself. Like Thomas Mann, Tonio Kröger, and Aschenbach, Kafka sees the artist as permanently excluded from normal living. His starver gives several metaphors for art, but perhaps the most basic is this one, of art as utterly apart from the human community. The artist's work denies ordinary needs; it demands that the artist transcend nature. Such asceticism recalls Kröger's view that artists are simply not human. But, of course, the idea of the artist as inhuman goes back much further. Think of the radical attitude of Flaubert, a spiritual brother to Kafka: "The artist, in my opinion, is a monstrosity, something outside nature. All the misfortunes that Providence loads upon him come from his stubborn denial of that axiom."[54]

The artist, then, acknowledging his monstrosity, lives in constant protest against the normal world he can never enter. He becomes a "man of refusal," whose self-denial can lead only to self-destruction. In this protesting suicide, the starver demonstrates his superiority. Baudelaire attributed a deeper sensitivity to his narrators, as we saw in chapter 2; Kafka gives the sense of superiority to his artistes. The hunger-artist claims that no one can fast as he does, a remark recalling what Jakob says of his crazy playing. Others can play Bach and Mozart, but only he plays dear God. Again, we note parody: Jakob's faintly comic vanity becomes blatant caricature in this artiste.

Beyond the metaphors of art as exclusion and art as denial, "Ein Hungerkünstler" gives us art as extremism. Kafka told Gustav Janouch that extreme states of being fascinated him. Accordingly, many of his protagonists become fanatics of some kind: Josef K., K., Josefine. The hunger-artist offers a climactic version of the obsessive character, for he makes his physical need to fast into the goal of his life.

Walter Sokel traces this inhuman craving to "a deep wound of existence" that forces the man to make himself rigid. We cannot know what has injured the starver, but we do see that the wound has paralyzed him in self-obsession. Indeed, toward the end of his story, deserted by the public, the artiste has only himself as observer. His cage appears as the perfect symbol for such self-imprisonment. For the spectacles staged to celebrate the end of the forty-day fast, the hunger-artist unwillingly leaves his cage, to appear as the triumphant Christ of starvation. In his hatred for this exposure, we note his fear of life beyond the bars. Imprisonment offers him the safety of the purest narcissistic isolation. This state, perhaps the one closest to death, recalls Sartre's statement: "There are many ways to lock a man up. The best way is to make him lock himself up."[55]

54. Quoted in Shroder, *Icarus*, 163.

55. Walter Sokel, *Franz Kafka: Tragik und Ironie*, 432; Jean-Paul Sartre, *Les Séquestrés d'Altona*, 33.

The obsession with self offers a fourth metaphor for art. The hunger-artist goes beyond the ambition and vanity we have already seen in Jakob and Taugenichts, for he exhibits only himself. And the self of this artiste seems empty indeed. "The self, formerly exalted by the Cartesian and Romantic traditions, becomes for Kafka an interchangeable, anonymous and suffering subject. It fragments into a scrap, lost in a universe of scraps, of impotence and of waste."[56] Perhaps because he perceives his own emptiness, this artiste claims just the opposite. Declaring his own freakish nature to be art, he exhibits himself publicly. With this absurd demonstration of nature as art, the hunger-artist again exaggerates what Jakob does. That player also finds the highest artistic merit in his display of unskilled self-expression. Jakob's mad music, a symbol of his disturbed nature, almost matches the fasting of the starver in worthlessness. The difference between these two kinds of "art" concerns sincerity. Jakob believes in his music, while the hunger-artist finally admits he is a fraud.

The starver demanded recognition, not for art but for a lie. Thus he never earned the acclaim he sought, for his starving fulfilled only a freakish necessity. Like many of Kafka's protagonists, this man deserves no trust; the audience, like the reader, must not believe him. Kafka's last works typically depict such devious, deceptive characters. Consciously or not, they conceal and even distort the true situation. Either their demise reveals what they have hidden, or it remains mysterious, as in *The Castle*.

The lie of the starver, a key theme in his story, results in misunderstanding between him and the audience. Such confusion characterizes the third principal element in our image of the artiste: his relation to the public. In this negative tie to the crowd we may compare him to Baudelaire's old clown. L. W. Michaelson sees a similar pathos in the description of the degenerate buffoon and the last moments of the hunger-artist.[57] However, this comparison seems strained, for Kafka's narrator evokes none of the palpable sympathy for the figure that Baudelaire does. On the contrary, the cool, even amused, tone of Kafka's narrator suggests that his subject appeals to him only as an eccentric. Michaelson makes a more convincing argument for a link relating the public in "Le Vieux Saltimbanque," at both beginning and end, to the leopard in "Ein Hungerkünstler." Both the leopard and the hectic crowd make emphatic contrasts to the wretched player. And both symbols of vitality end the story with the worldly triumph of amoral, animal power.

In Kafka the crowd determines, less than in Baudelaire, the fate of the

---

56. Vigée, "Les Artistes," 107.
57. L. W. Michaelson, "Kafka's Hunger-Artist and Baudelaire's Old Clown," 293.

nameless artiste. In "Le Vieux Saltimbanque," a hostile public drives the aging clown to indigence. But the starver, despite desertion by his audience, continues to fast anyway. He does decline for lack of observers, as he must abandon his own show for a circus. There he becomes less an artiste and more a freak. But this man chooses his plight as outcast, whereas the public imposes that fate on the old buffoon. The old clown becomes the victim of his audience, but the starver victimizes both them and himself. Accordingly, the social reality implied in the condition of the old clown has no relevance for the hunger-artist. Like much of Kafka's work, this story exists outside any definable historical context. Indeed, it often evokes the whimsical quality of a dream.

Ultimately, Baudelaire and Kafka make different conclusions about their miserable artist figures. The old clown suggests the death of art in a world hostile to imagination; the starver commits the suicide of art that divorces itself from the human condition. Both works bear a "derisive epiphany of art," and both create "a self-critique of the aesthetic vocation itself."[58] Yet Kafka shows mainly the artist as the ultimate, absurd embodiment of l'art pour l'art. Baudelaire shows the cause of this radical aesthetics as an inevitably disturbed relation of art in his time to its public. In short, we have here the tragedy of modern art (Baudelaire) versus the tragedy of the artist creating it (Kafka).

Beyond the lie that the hunger-artist perpetrates on his audience, his "art" also depends on a paradox. Despite his denial of humanity, he refuses to live without it. On the contrary, he persistently demands recognition from the very world he scorns. Like Kafka's other late figures, this man struggles for an impossible acceptance. In expecting acclaim from those he repudiates, the starver recalls the plea of Molière's misanthrope, Alceste: "I want people to honor me!" In this context we also recall the mixed love and hate for the crowd felt by Mallarmé's player in "La Déclaration Foraine." Wedekind gives us yet another such conflicted performer in the "abstract-sublime" idealist of "Zirkusgedanken" (1887) (see chapter 4). This man perishes in falling from the heights far above humanity, which constitutes his audience. We may see Wedekind's Karl Hetmann, who symbolizes just this peril of idealism, as a type of hunger-artist also.[59]

The paradox of a person demanding recognition from those he actually

---

58. Starobinski, *Portrait*, 11.

59. Among Kafka's critics, only Harry Steinhauer notes Wilhelm Raabe's *Der Hungerpastor* (1864) as a possible source for Kafka's starver. This figure hungers for knowledge and for the normal life he mainly observes. He may even represent a kind of artist in his own struggle to write. But here hunger seems actual rather than metaphorical; it does not express a revulsion for the human condition.

scorns exemplifies the typical Kafka figure in conflict. Most critics agree that such a basic contradiction expresses the essential Kafka. Probably the first statement of this interpretation came from Charles Neider in 1946. "[All Kafka's work] confirms his neurotic insistence on irresolvable conflict." More specifically, Henel ties the hunger-artist to this characteristic theme. "[K.'s problem] is the conflict inherent in life, the impossibility of living without lying, of living by starving, or, as Kafka himself put it, the impossibility of living." Sokel gives the superlative formulation of this view, tracing the theme to Kafka's earliest work. "From the first line of his work to the last, from 'Beschreibung eines Kampfes' to 'Josefine,' twenty years later, Kafka's work was the description of a struggle between the self and the world. He says 'In the struggle between you and the world, side with the world.' His whole work is the constantly varied and developing depiction of this sentence."[60]

This focus on conflict may well remind us of the dualism in Baudelaire, discussed in chapter 2. Indeed, Kafka himself suggests this tie of essential paradox in his own reference to the French poet. "Poetry is disease. Yet one does not get well by suppressing the fever. On the contrary! Its heat purifies and illuminates." "Ein Hungerkünstler" offers us the ultimate view of the sick artist. Here lies perhaps the closest of several links to Baudelaire, that primary witness of art as affliction.[61]

"Erstes Leid" ("First Sorrow") (1917)

Kafka's other tales that contain artistes belong to either the *Hungerkünstler* or the *Landarzt* collection. Although only the starver represents a parody of art, elements in the other stories relate essentially to that complex idea. So it seems helpful to investigate the contribution of these relevant players to the ultimate one in "Ein Hungerkünstler." "Erstes Leid," the story of an aerialist who begins to feel an insatiable ambition, contains the seeds of the later story. Just as Tonio Kröger anticipates the fully problematic artist, Aschenbach, so does this man prefigure the doomed hunger-artist. In his demand for two trapezes instead of one, we see the same urge to intensify a skill that the hunger-artist drives to absurdity. Like this compulsion to fast forever, the trapeze-artist's drive to double his exertion points toward infinity. Accordingly, the death that brings the starver his fulfillment lies implicit in the manic striving of the aerialist.

60. Charles Neider, "Two Notes on Kafka," 95; Henel, "Hungerkünstler," 246; Sokel, *Tragik*, 530.

61. Quoted in Gustav Janouch, *Gespräche mit Kafka*, 133. Compare Karl Kraus: "Today's literature: prescriptions written by patients" (quoted in Harry Zohn, *Karl Kraus*, 161).

Several critics have likened this "first sorrow" of the artiste to the loss of natural grace that accompanies the first moment of awareness in Kleist's "Über das Marionettentheater." According to this view, the artiste has now lost the innocence of mere perfectionism and has gained a threatening neurosis. Yet I doubt that we can convincingly compare the aerialist, even at the start of his story, to a creature unconscious of his freedom. After all, this performer has always perfected his art compulsively; presumably he lost any instinctual grace he had long ago. We may even wonder if he ever had the kind of gift Kleist means, a sort of divine blessing. For we never read of extraordinary skill or beauty in his act. And he himself seems to get no pleasure from it. All we really learn of his performance is its fanatic motivation.

However, we cannot ignore the transcendental meaning of the aerial performance. The French tradition has already shown us that this spectacle can represent a superhuman striving. Of all the circus personnel, the trapeze-artist works closest to heaven; he occupies a truly transcendent spot. In fact, Kafka's artiste refuses to descend from his trapeze. Due to "a habit turned tyrannical," he must practice constantly. Compulsively clinging to his heights, he has food sent up, and colleagues from below ascend for visits. When traveling, he stays in the luggage net above the train seats, a rare touch of outspoken Kafkan humor. Completing this elaborate celestial metaphor, the aerialist craves the divine quality of perfection.

This artiste embodies the absolute aloneness of a god among men. But the godly image contains no blessing. What for Banville and Mallarmé expressed ideal aspiration becomes for Kafka only the threat of the insatiable. To be sure, Banville's clown must die in freeing himself from bourgeois, philistine surroundings; yet his immortality brings glory. Beyond merely dying, he joins the stars. Here, however, the escalation of the aerialist's act connotes only a fatal flight from humanity. Like the hunger-artist, this man shows the tragic end of *l'art pour l'art*. As his impresario puts it, the cravings of superhuman ambition threaten life itself. "Once such thoughts began to plague him, could they ever stop completely? Mustn't they always intensify? Wouldn't they menace his very existence?" Moreover, the compulsive condition cannot reverse itself. "The solution to such mania lies not in an escape to humanity, but rather in the absurd doubling of the desperate exertion."[62]

In "Erstes Leid," as in "Ein Hungerkünstler," the manic art produced expresses the performer's disturbed character. In both cases, the obsessive

62. Kafka, *Sämtliche Erzählungen*, 177; Norbert Fuerst, *Die Offenen Geheimtüren Franz Kafkas*, 78.

performers have little or no relation to an audience; this missing link helps to explain their estrangement from the human condition. Both figures have only one actual relationship, with their managers. And oddly enough, these men seem specially devoted to their eccentric clients. In "Erstes Leid," the management takes care to satisfy the whims of the aerialist. The impresario in "Ein Hungerkünstler" humors the starver like a child. Nowhere else does Kafka give us players so coddled by others. In "Josefine," the last artiste story, they have a starkly opposite effect.

"Josefine, die Sängerin, oder das Volk der Mäuse" ("Josephine the Mouse-Singer, or the Mouse Folk") (1924)

Here the title immediately tells us that the audience has as much importance as the artiste. In fact, Kafka told Max Brod that the revised "or-title" should suggest a balance.[63] We may see in this supposedly equal relation between art and its public Kafka's final attempt to resolve one of those eternal conflicts that typify his work. Yet the world wins out here as usual; although Josefine gives the most imposing image of the artist, she loses her struggle for artistic autonomy. Denied her demand not to work, she first pouts, then malingers, and finally disappears. Accordingly, although the narrator deems her a hero of her people, they will forget her.

In conveying this thought, the final sentence of the story exemplifies Kafka's famous style of prevarication: "But Josefine, released from her earthly misery, which she believes inevitable for the chosen few, will happily lose herself in the *countless throng of heroes* of our people. And, since we write no history, she will be forgotten, like all her brothers, in *heightened redemption*." Critics make much of the possible autobiographical element here, for these words were literally among the last that Kafka wrote. As with most of the autobiographical interpretations, this putative link helps us little in understanding the story. More relevantly, some readers discuss the paradox of "heightened redemption." Logically, redemption signifies an absolute condition; it can neither grow nor shrink. In this absurd phrase, Politzer sees a metaphor for the balance of the title. "By granting Josefine an oblivion she will share with the rest of her brothers, Kafka establishes the equilibrium of the balance, the image with which he chooses to describe this tale. It is the equilibrium of a perfect paradox."[64]

Similarly, one cannot speak of "countless hordes of heroes," since heroism connotes a special state reserved for the very few. In both these phrases,

---

63. Elisabeth Rajec, *Namen und ihre Bedeutungen in Werke Franz Kafkas*, 91.
64. Kafka, *Sämtliche Erzählungen*, 209, italics mine; Heinz Politzer, *Franz Kafka: Parable and Paradox*, 318.

Kafka gives final expression to his constant theme of contradiction. More-over, how can a people forget its heroes? And finally, if this people has no history, what is the present story anyway? As in most of his work, Kafka leaves such logical questions open.

For Josefine, then, posterity remains an unresolved problem. Her death has dignity, unlike that of the hunger-artist, who absurdly believes he will go on fasting. Yet her only lasting monument is this story, which tells us the people will forget her. Not only in this questionable ending but throughout the work, Josefine relates to her public ambiguously. They appreciate and protect her, but she behaves like a child when denied her wishes. They acclaim her concerts, finding ecstasy in her singing; yet they cannot grant her the special status of work exemption.

This mutual conflict stems mainly from the political function of the art depicted here. Josefine's recitals are "not so much a concert as an assembly of the people." Indeed, several scenes suggest that the singer has all the power of a political leader. The people gather suddenly when she wants to sing, like an army mobilizing at the behest of a general. Josefine uses the slightest disturbance at her concerts as a political tool, "to awaken the crowd, to teach them not understanding but awed respect."[65]

The narrator's various confusions about the nature and function of art suggest that he and his peers glean little from the music itself. By contrast, he specifices convincingly the mystical communion that occurs at these concerts. Josefine's singing, though "nothing extraordinary," still unites the audience, both to her and to themselves, in her magical transcendence of ordinary piping. The narrator expresses his skepticism toward the artiste in one tortuously convoluted paragraph on this subject. However, even he finally admits that she indeed creates a remarkable communal experience.

In his repeated and futile attempts to define the nature of Josefine's sing-ing, the narrator at least confirms that it is no true art. Indeed, art seems meaningless for these people. "Josefine asserts herself, this nothing of a voice, this nothing of accomplishment, and communicates with us, it is good to think of that. A real singer, if one should appear among us, would be unbearable; we would all reject the senselessness of such a perform-ance."[66]

Despite the struggle of some critics to do so, no one can adequately define Josefine's music. At best we can say it lies somewhere between the piping that comes naturally to all mice—their "characteristic expression of life"—and the art of singing. Again, as in "Ein Hungerkünstler," Kafka treats

65. Kafka, *Sämtliche Erzählungen,* 200, 197.
66. Ibid., 200.

the difficult relation of art to nature. That story reveals that what the artiste claims as art is in fact only his strange nature. Josefine's singing, however, blurs the lines. Her art recalls Nietzsche's definition: "Art is not an imitation of nature but its metaphysical supplement, raised up beside it in order to overcome it."[67]

Since Josefine's piping-song is based on the mouse sounds it transcends, she shares with her audience their own state. Indeed, she gives voice to the mouse condition itself, which provides her art with its universal appeal. In his play *Josephine: The Mouse-Singer* (1978), Michael McClure makes this point particularly clear.

> Each of you can feel it.
> Feel what I feel.
> from your paws nail
> to your ear tips.
> Everyone can know
> the transcendence
> that I feel
> when I'm singing.
> It is within
> the reach
> of all of you.[68]

The people can recognize themselves in this music; they identify with it. Such art lies within them all, yet only Josefine expresses it.

We may infer that the artiste makes this primal connection with her public through the profound psychic effect she creates. "Most of the crowd has withdrawn into themselves, that is clear to see. In these brief pauses between battles, the people dream: it is as if each one freed his limbs, *as if the restless one could for once stretch himself out in the great warm bed of the people*. . . . There is something of our poor little childhood in that, something of that lost happiness that we can never regain."[69] This passage evokes not only a powerful sense of social unity but also the regressive infantile pleasure that art induces. The narrator shows that art fulfills the need for both these elements, society and childhood, in one particular phrase: the image of the troubled adult finding release through the dream of

67. See Sabina Kienlechner's brave attempt to define Josefine's music in *Negativität der Erkenntnis im Werk Franz Kafkas*, 139–47; Friedrich Nietzsche, *Werke: Geburt der Tragödie*, ed. Alfred Baeumler, 186.
    68. Michael McClure, *Josephine: The Mouse-Singer*, 20.
    69. Kafka, *Sämtliche Erzählungen*, 203, italics mine.

freedom in the great communal bed. Hence Josefine connects with the inmost being of the listener, with his longing for the paradisical oneness of childhood.

Kafka often relates music to the child. Gregor Samsa, hearing Grete play her violin, reverts to the simple sensuality that he, as alienated adult, could no longer enjoy. We again recall Jakob, whose infantile music also soothes his adult pain. For Josefine's audience, the memory of childhood that the song invokes has crucial importance. The mice lead such a traumatic life, filled with the constant fear of destruction, that they lack a truly carefree youth. Undoubtedly this problem relates to the narrator's claim that they also have no history. Both factors may influence their skeptical attitude to art. In any case, the deprivation of full childlike freedom helps to account for the intense pleasure the mice feel when Josefine sings.

Sokel, calling this music Dionysian in effect, traces the idea of it to Nietzsche. For both him and Kafka, as for the Romantics, art ultimately points to the origins of man, to nature. And Kafka equates nature with child-hood. The mouse-audience, united with their youth by Josefine's song, dream of a Dionysian return to their source. Such abandon displays the Nietzschean spirit of music. The experience of song dissolves the battle among individuals into the harmony of all in union. "The Dionysian dithyramb expresses something unheard of . . . , the oneness of nature. . . . And this is the effect of Dionysian tragedy, that the cleft between men yields to an overpowering sense of unity, which leads back to the heart of na-ture. . . . The metaphysical consolation appears in bodily clarity as the satyr-chorus, as the chorus of natural beings, which lives indestructibly behind all civilisations." Kafka shows elsewhere that he "sides with the world" in saying that the individual lies, only the chorus may hold some truth.[70]

In this opposition of the united crowd toward the single Josefine lies a basic idea of the story. The individual artist can never attain that Dionysian oneness that his work makes possible for the public. He stands outside that unity, but not because of his bizarre art, as in "Ein Hungerkünstler," or his superhuman ambition, as in "Erstes Leid," or his split identity, as in "Ein Bericht für eine Akademie," or his brutal exploitation, as in "Auf der Galerie." Here the performer's aloneness causes her exclusion. To be sure, Josefine intensifies her isolation by demanding special status. Yet her char-acter as an artiste, a "loner," has already determined her place apart from the society she serves.

70. Sokel, *Tragik,* 515; Nietzsche, *Geburt,* 56, 80–81; Kafka, *Hochzeitsvorbereitungen,* 44, 343.

Having assessed both Josefine's music and her relation to the public, we now come to our third major item, her personality. Elisabeth Rajec gives a good account of the unconvincing attempts to link her to biblical forebears. More plausibly, her name relates her to Josef K., who also seeks satisfaction from the authorities. Her sex may relate to Kafka's association of music with the female, as in "Die Verwandlung." As for Josefine's other traits, we may dismiss the various claims to a specific identity. Several critics extend the thoroughly "Jewish" reading of the story by Brod, interpreting Josefine as a Yiddish singer, a Zionist, a cantor, or a new Jeremiah. Accordingly, the mouse-folk represent the Jews, plucky despite their persecution. As we might expect in such views, the Jewish Kafka stands behind the meager curtain of his creation. "Josefine has apparently struggled, like Kafka, for a job with a single shift, leaving her free for art after two in the afternoon." From the author we then jump to universals. "As the songstress subtilizes from the Yiddish stage singer to the universal artist, the audience expands to the citizenry of the twentieth century."[71]

Such whimsical excursions have simply no basis in the text. They have as little justification as does, for instance, the identification of the hunger-artist with actual starvers in circuses. The many attempts to label the enigma underlying Kafka's figures assume that a hidden meaning will thereby yield its mysteries to the desperate interpreter. Hence some critics pedantically name what Kafka has carefully left vague: the giant insect Samsa becomes a cockroach or beetle; the beast in "Der Bau" is a badger. Similarly, the trained ape in "Ein Bericht" represents a converted Jew, offering "the ape-mask of Kafka." William Rubenstein even equates the impresario and guards in "Ein Hungerkünstler" with critics and publishers.[72]

Of course, we cannot ignore the fact that Kafka always makes various ciphers for himself; yet the writer's identity transcends mere self-reflection. Instead of interpreting the books through the life, we should do the opposite. "Kafka's life imitates his writing because his work documents the life that has not yet penetrated consciousness, has not yet become fact." Hence we may see in Josefine not a literal version of the author but a psychic mirror of his last months.[73]

Josefine differs from Kafka's other artistes in working free-lance. All the

71. Carl Woodring, "Josephine the Singer," in *Franz Kafka Today*, ed. Angel Flores, 74.

72. Meno Spann, "Franz Kafka's Leopard," 101; William Rubenstein, "Ein Bericht für eine Akademie," in *Franz Kafka Today*, ed. Angel Flores; Karl-Heinz Fingerhut, *Die Funktion der Tierfiguren in Werke Franz Kafkas*, 254; William Rubenstein, "Franz Kafka: A Hunger-Artist," 14.

73. Sokel, *Tragik*, 565. Kafka himself said something similar about Picasso's art. "He notes the distortions that have not yet entered our consciousness. Art is a mirror, which sometimes goes fast, like a clock" (quoted in Janouch, *Kafka*, 195).

others have managers, impresarios, or some structure—fair, circus, or burlesque—to cushion their relation to the audience. But Josefine confronts the people directly; she gives the starkest metaphor of the modern artist without a patron. Accordingly, her ego has grown to preposterous size, for the narrator speaks of her as blinded by her self-awareness. Her massive egotism compares to that of the hunger-artist, who also demands public acclaim for what he considers great art.

Both of them exemplify the Faustian ego of Kafka's last figures, who have achieved the self-confidence lacking in his earlier types. Like K. in *Das Schloss* and the beast in "Der Bau," both Josefine and the starver believe fanatically in their power to fulfill their self-imposed mission. Indeed, the self-deception of these characters brings their ruin. As for Josefine, she seeks the impossible goal of unprecedented and permanent acclaim. "She strives for clear public recognition of her art, which will last forever and transcend by far all fame known until now."[74]

Like the hunger-artist, Josefine wants to be an absolute exception. But the very nature of her art, rooted in the mouse character, essentially links her to the others. Her blind egotism denies this tie and even alienates her from her own singing. Here lies a major irony in the story: her boundless ego, which creates her music, also conflicts with it. Instead of concentrating on her song, Josefine must constantly try to feed her ambition. In short, the ego triumphs over the creative self.

Josefine loses her battle for work exemption because the authorities find her singing unworthy of such special status. For them, art does not constitute work. In their attitude to the artist, dominating the last part of the story, we see again the problem of childhood that concerned Kafka from his earliest writing onward. These mice not only have a traumatic tie to their own youth, they also treat Josefine as a father does a child. Those in power protect her; they even humor her vanity somewhat. Their fatherly concern reminds us of the managers in both "Ein Hungerkünstler" and "Erstes Leid," who humor the eccentric player. Yet Josefine's people ultimately refuse to indulge her whims. They turn a deaf ear to her demands, just as a parent does when a child acts unreasonably.

Hence Josefine struggles in vain against the power of the public. Despite her supreme contribution to culture, she must finally bow to the others' determination of her status. The outlandish demands of her ego represent the pure subjectivity of art, which always yields to the objectivity of life. Inevitably, the artist refuses to accept the norms of society; his position must be problematic. This story raises the most fundamental questions about the

74. Kafka, *Sämtliche Erzählungen*, 205.

nature of art: What does it do? Is it work? Who determines its value? Kafka gives only two clear answers to such problems. First, in the struggle between the public and the individual artist, society always wins. Second, we cannot accept the claims of the self-deluded artist about his work.

However, the world opposing the artist must not have the last word either. Posterity must consider the balance between these two factors. Although Josefine loses her battle for autonomy, she still has achieved the greatest artistic good. Uniting her people in the ecstasy of art, she ranks unquestionably as a hero. None of Kafka's other artistes attain such a status. Yet the haunting ambiguity of the last sentence in the story, juxtaposing "heightened redemption" to the forgetting of Josefine, precludes any triumph of art. Sokel and others see this artist as a redeemer of society, but the text contradicts such a positive reading.

In evaluating the people's relation to Josefine, we must take note of the narrator. This person, "half in sympathy with her opponents," represents a middle ground between the two factors. Hence we see the player through the eyes of her public. In this respect the story differs from Kafka's other tales of artistes: "Ein Bericht" has a first-person narrator, and the others unfold in the third person. Despite Roy Pascal's belabored attempt to identify the narrator of "Ein Hungerkünstler," he still matters little in that story. Pascal corrects the claim of several critics that we understand the work through the eyes of the starver himself. But his strained argument for a showman-narrator does not add perceptibly to our image of the artiste.[75]

Surprisingly, Pascal does not focus on "Josefine," where the narrator bulks larger than anywhere else. Here he has the crucial function of mediating, for he fulfills the promise of the title by creating a balance of voices. Moreover, the narrator thus imparts irony, since only he can distance himself from both society and the artiste. We see Josefine more clearly than the starver because we can filter what we learn of her through the specific personality of the narrator. The unidentified voice in "Ein Hungerkünstler" forces us to concentrate on the subject of the piece. In "Josefine," however, the mouse-narrator shows us the spectrum of perceptions that compose the experience of art.

"Ein Bericht für eine Akademie" ("A Report for an Academy") (1917)

Like Josefine, the virtuoso ape is a performing animal. Indeed, this double identity defines the main problem of the story: the loss of animal innocence in a creature that imitates men. Critics readily refer to Kleist's essay as a

75. Ibid., 196; Roy Pascal, *Kafka's Narrators*, 243.

source for this portrait of the artist alienated from his natural self. Yet the ape has a more complex condition. First of all, he has willfully abandoned his ape nature to enter the human world. Once captured, he perceives the necessity of becoming a mock human being. Here lies his only escape from a caged existence. Second, his art of imitation represents merely the lowest level of consciousness. Even as a metaphor for primitivist art, the burlesque entertainments of the ape relate only distantly to the implied creativity of the Kleistian artist.

Since this tale deals less with art than with the problematic hybrid of the ape-man, I find its major idea in anti-Darwinism. Despite his bravura, the ape often intimates a pervasive sadness at his condition. Particularly at the end of the report, he reveals the loneliness of the ape who belongs neither with his kind, the half-trained chimpanzee, nor among men. He only entertains society, he can never be part of it. "When I come home at night from banquets, from scientific meetings, from congenial company, a little half-trained chimpanzee awaits me, and I divert myself with her, as apes do. By day I don't want to see her; for she has the madness of the confused trained animal in her look; only I perceive that, and I cannot bear it." It seems that evolution, though inevitable, has its deceptive side. In reaching "the level of an average educated European," the ape makes a hollow achievement indeed. His "humanity" consists in purely external mimicry. So one can hardly speak of "a successful battle with alienation." Rotpeter will always remain an outsider.[76]

Unlike the other stories in the *Landarzt* volume, "Ein Bericht" describes a humanizing process. The ape contrasts, for instance, with Gregor Samsa, who turns from human to animal. But both figures feel deep alienation from the normal human beings around them. Moreover, Rotpeter's resigned tone gives his story the aura of Clemens Heselhaus' "anti-fairy tale." The critics point to several models for the social satire we find here: Cervantes, Hoffmann, and Bulgakov created the best-known talking dogs.[77] Of course, the ape closely relates to Kafka's philosophizing dog in "Forschungen eines Hundes." However, although the report involves as much social criticism as do the investigations, Rotpeter interests us mainly for his attitude to the performing life.

Among all the works surveyed in this book, "Ein Bericht" stands quite alone in evoking the ambiguities of the animal act. At the simplest level, Kafka suggests the oxymoron implicit in the trained animal. Many circus-

76. Kafka, *Sämtliche Erzählungen,* 174; Pascal, *Narrators,* 198.
77. Hartmut Binder, *Motiv und Gestaltung bei Franz Kafka,* 161–66; Theodore Ziolkowski, *Varieties of Literary Thematics*; Ross Chambers, "The Artist as Performing Dog."

goers speak of the haunting discomfort they feel when viewing such acts: the tiger as pussycat, bears as hockey players, and the ape as all-too-human make us both laugh and cry. Much of this poignant mixture of feeling may stem from seeing the beast harnessed for commercial ends. Yet the animal routine challenges more than the idealism of the naturalist. On a less conscious level, it also implies some of our deepest qualms about the human condition. Particularly in the circus context, in which men and women perform beside the beasts, we must ask ourselves: What is human, what is animal? How do the performances of these different creatures relate? And what do we derive from the entertainment of their juxtaposed acts? Such questions raise basic moral issues. "This is the purpose of animal metamorphoses: to lay bare human flaws and shortcomings by juxtaposing and intermixing human and animal qualities. Through an ambiguous presentation of the human/animal relationship, we see especially clearly what the human animal is and what he should be."[78]

The ape begins to probe this relation by denying that men, unlike beasts, have freedom. Recalling Freud's conclusions in *Civilization and Its Discontents,* Rotpeter claims that we enjoy only an illusion of autonomy. "And just as freedom belongs among the most sublime feelings, so also does the illusion of it. In the burlesque shows, before my routine, I have often seen trapeze artists practicing aloft. They swung each other, they rocked back and forth, they jumped, they hung in each other's arms, one held the other by the hair in his teeth. 'So that is human freedom,' I thought, 'autonomous movement.' O mockery of holy nature! No structure could withstand the laughter of the ape world at this sight."[79]

Only the wild creature knows true freedom: a thought close to Wedekind (see chapter 4). Naturally, the ape feels superior to man, whose habits indeed disgust him. He disdains not only the boozing sailors he first meets but also his gullible, childish audience. Moreover, this artiste has achieved his remarkable level of development by a unique act of will. He has become a replica of the average educated European through an effort unprecedented on earth. Both the sense of superiority in the outsider-artist and his complementary distaste for humanity recall the hunger-artist.

Perhaps parody offers the closest link between these two figures. We have already seen the starver as a parody of the artist. Rotpeter's mimicry itself pillories the human. However, beyond this similarity, the two players show sharp contrasts. Consider first the cage: whereas the ape makes the

---

78. D.B.D. Asker, "Vixens and Values: The Modern Metamorphoses of Garnett and Vercors," 191.
79. Kafka, *Sämtliche Erzählungen,* 169.

utmost exertion to escape his prison, the starver wills just as strenuously to stay caged. Accordingly, their observers react in opposite ways to their liberation. When Rotpeter leaves his cage, the people rejoice at his freedom. But they feel horror on seeing the emaciated hunger-artist after forty days of starvation. The two figures contrast also in their treatment of the self. Rotpeter overcomes his identity, while the starver intensifies his essential being. The ape feels proud of the scar he has grown over the wound his captors inflicted. But the hunger-artist leaves his psychic wound open. This man finds a "way out" from humanity in the inhuman act of fasting; the ape makes his *Ausweg* from captivity by seeming human.

These two figures also display contrasting aesthetics. Rotpeter, a classic Aristotelian artist, depends on the technical skill of imitating nature. The hunger-artist, exaggerating Romantic values, expresses only himself. The ape entertains an amused public, while the starver shocks his horrified observers. He struggles endlessly for recognition by a hostile power; Rotpeter seeks approval through adaptation to power. Finally, the starver dies because he cannot accept the limits of the human condition. Rotpeter survives because he has successfully repressed his need for animal freedom. According to this scheme, Josefine also represents a Romantic artist, for she too refuses to sublimate her ego to social norms. Among these three figures, only Rotpeter shows the possibility of a compromised survival. The other two loudly express their nature and die, while he continues an unsatisfying life.

"Auf der Galerie" ("Up in the Gallery") (1917)

The consumptive, victimized equestrienne in this piece gives the image of greatest pathos among Kafka's players. To be sure, the hunger-artist offers a more extreme version of deprivation. Yet he has imposed his inhuman condition on himself, something this artiste has not done. Literally driven by a cruel ringmaster, she suffers further exploitation by an audience of crass hedonists. Neumeister stresses the brutality of commerce that the circus enshrines in its woman on display; Starobinski likens her to the trained beasts performing in the same arena.

The exploitation of the artiste, a key theme here, recalls Baudelaire's "Le Vieux Saltimbanque." Like Baudelaire and the Parnassians, Kafka blames the public for the performer's wretched condition. Yet, we must note, he does so only here. In all his other works we have considered, he blames the artiste. We have seen other examples of hostility between the player and the public, notably in "Taugenichts" and "Der arme Spielmann." In the former, the hero's very name indicates his uselessness to society. Jakob exemplifies the artistic mentality wholly destroyed by its materialistic environment. In the next chapter we will meet Wedekind's victimized artist figure, Karl Hetmann, who sells his soul to the capitalists. In surveying these metaphoric treatments of art in mass society, we see that Eichendorff first formulated this Romantic problem. Thus we might go further back than Neumeister does in tracing to Baudelaire what Kafka brought to a climax. "Baudelaire experienced, two generations before Kafka, the origins of modern mass society. . . . Its hostility to art made failure the mark of true worth, and the misunderstanding of the public the first condition of immortality."[80]

Not only exploitation but also many other traits of "Auf der Galerie" recall "Le Vieux Saltimbanque." In both pieces, a triangular sentence expresses the determining relations among performer, public, and narrator. As for the audience, Baudelaire shows us their scorn for the old man who had once amused them. Kafka creates the worse image of a dehumanized current public. Even in her prime, the equestrienne hears only the applause of "banging steam-hammers."[81] Moreover, her misery seems endless, for she must constantly circle the ring, impelled by both the demonic master and that insatiable applause.

Another similarity to the prose poem lies in the pervasive dualities. Baudelaire makes some essential contrasts: the brilliant world of the fair against the misery of the old clown, the suave man of letters against the rejected buffoon, the sympathy of one artist for another against the indifference of the crowd. The Kafka work depends on just such basic oppositions in its dual structure. The first paragraph-long sentence describes one scene; the second one gives its exact opposite. One can hardly imagine a more effective rendering of dualism in the perceived world. Hartmut Binder takes the sensible view that the first sentence shows truth, the second one reality.[82] However, most of the many commentaries involve tortuous ontological arguments.

In its opposed views of one woman, "Auf der Galerie" recalls another prose poem by Baudelaire, "Laquelle est la Vraie?" ("Which Is the Real One?") (1863). Here again a woman presents two opposing faces to the bewildered male narrator. The ideally virtuous Benedicta becomes, when buried, a violent, vengeful slut. But the devoted narrator, like Kafka's observer, clings desperately to his primary perception of her. Indeed, his fanatic insistence on "his" Benedicta seems fatal, for he sinks with it, "perhaps forever, into the grave of the ideal."

80. Sebastian Neumeister, *Der Dichter als Dandy,* 43, 59.
81. Kafka, *Sämtliche Erzählungen,* 145.
82. Binder, *Motiv,* 193.

So much in this piece relates to "Auf der Galerie" that its title might well serve as a subtitle for Kafka. Consider first the woman herself, Benedicta: "this miraculous girl was too beautiful to live long." The equestrienne also appears in Kafka's second sentence as magically beautiful, and in the first sentence we learn that she has tuberculosis. Lemaitre sees in Benedicta a typical version of Baudelaire's always ambiguous female. But on a deeper level, we might also say of the man's relation to her what Starobinski notes of the link between the narrator and the old clown in "Le Vieux Saltimban-que": the "significant Other" represents an alter ego, another aspect of him-self. The passionate confrontation with that hidden self constitutes the essential subject of the work.[83] In "Auf der Galerie," we find a similar situa-tion. The narrator shows his deep involvement with the artiste by his unwept tears, which also tie him to the narrators of both "Le Vieux Saltim-banque" and "Une Mort Héroique."

In all four texts, the man projects himself so fully into the person per-ceived that he merges with that identity. In the case of Benedicta, the man also sinks into the grave; in that of the old clown, the narrator sees himself as just such a wretch. The narrator of "Une Mort Héroique" feels tears in describing Fancioulle because he too perceives the mime as part of himself. As for the gallery observer, he weeps inwardly for his own self, which he sees martyred in the arena. And he, like the man in "Laquelle est la Vraie?," passionately rebels against the apparent denial, by the rest of the audience, of his own perceived reality. However, his passive impotence turns this rebellion inward, into unconscious tears.

We may explain the similar dualisms in two such different writers as Kafka and Baudelaire quite simply: conflict dominates their visions of the human condition. Both deeply ambiguous authors polarize the actual world that they transform into fictions of irresolvable discord. Charles Bernheimer sees the dualism in Kafka as a sign of the urge for deepening unity that Freud calls "characteristic of Eros." In this light, Kafka's work and, presumably, Baudelaire's, show a "narcissistic urge" for primal union.[84]

83. Charles Baudelaire, *Oeuvres Complètes,* ed. Claude Pichois, 1:342; idem, *Petits Poèmes en Prose,* ed. Henri Lemaitre, 181; Starobinski, "Répondants," 410.

84. Charles Bernheimer, *Flaubert and Kafka,* 233. Compare John Barth: "In myth, twins signified whatever dualisms a culture entertained: mortal/immortal, good/evil, creation/destruction. . . . In Western literature since the Romantic period, twins (and doubles, shadows, mirrors) usually signify the "divided self," our secret sharer or inner adversary—even the schizophrenia some Freudians claim lies near the heart of writing. Aristophanes, in Plato's *Symposium,* declares we are all twins, indeed a kind of Siamese twins, who have lost and eternally seek our missing half: the loss accounts for alienation, our felt distance from man and god. The search accounts for both erotic love and the mystic's goal of divine atonement" (*New York Times Book Review,* 9 May 1982, p. 3).

Despite the structural importance of the double portrait of the artiste in "Auf der Galerie," she is not its essential subject. Recently, some critics have focused less on the two versions of the spectacle and more on what actually happens "up in the gallery." As I have claimed elsewhere, the action of the piece lies in the crisis of the balcony observer. First of all, this man has an identity split by his unique position as part of both the audience and the artiste. This alienation from his peers forms his first conflict. Second, only he perceives the two blatantly clashing realities presented by the show. And most important, only he wants to stop the cruel scene depicted in the first sentence. Like the narrator in "Le Vieux Saltimbanque," this last moral person in a corrupt world gives the only humane reaction to a brutal display.

Herein lies his superiority, a quality often found in Kafka's protagonists. Rotpeter, the hunger-artist, and Josefine, as we saw, think themselves better than those around them. But in the latter two, such superiority is mainly imagined and deceptive. The man in the balcony does transcend his peers, both literally and metaphorically. Inwardly, only he has enough sensitivity to feel moral outrage. Physically, he sits higher than most, indeed closest to heaven. For a discussion of various intimations of paradise in this balcony location, see my essay "Up in the Gallery: Kafka and Prévert."[85]

Hence Kafka's transcendent spectator parallels Baudelaire's transcendent performer. For Baudelaire, the player rises above his misery by the special grace of his talent. For Kafka, the superior observer bonds with the superior artiste. So despite the viewer's lack of catharsis, he also goes beyond his own pain. The past glory of the *saltimbanque* mitigates his present misery; so also the spontaneous sympathy of this man redeems his passive impotence.

The demonic ringmaster, dominating the second sentence, represents the tyranny of social forces confronting the artist. Specifically he symbolizes the commercial exploitation of modern art. Alternatively, Freudian critics see in this man the terrible father, an evil God. With this figure Kafka depicts even more clearly than Baudelaire does the martyrdom of the performer. Here again we find "sacrificial art."

A symbolic use of the ring as an infinite circle conveys acute hopelessness. Not only for the driven equestrienne but also for her impotent observer, the suffering in this arena can never cease. The idea of infinity occurs often in Kafka's typically extremist characters: think of the starver, trying to fast forever, or Josefine, demanding permanent, unique fame. But

85. See also Jürgen Kobs, *Kafka*; Friedrich Nemec, *Kafka-Kritik*; Gerhard Neumann, "Identifikation in der Gesellschaft," in Hartmut Binder, ed., *Kafka-Handbuch*, 2:320; and Klaus Peter Philippi, *Reflexion und Wirklichkeit*.

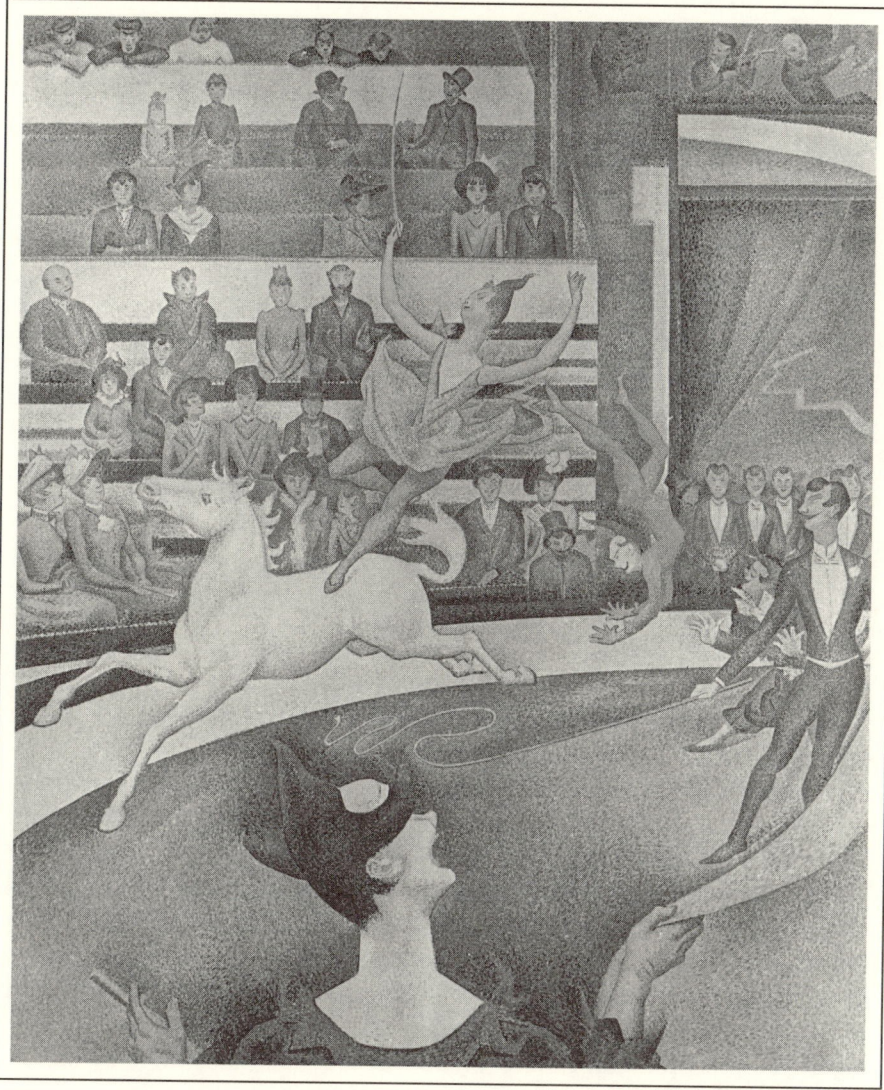

Figure 1. Georges Seurat, *Le Cirque* (1900). Courtesy of Musées Nationaux de France, Orsay and Louvre.

in "Auf der Galerie," the artiste's ceaseless circling around the ring conveys her despair with visual effect. Heinz Ladendorf was the first to compare this piece with Seurat's painting *Le Cirque* (1890–1891). The circular composition works even more forcefully in the painting that inspired Seurat, *Le Cirque Fernando* by Toulouse-Lautrec (1888). And here the ringmaster seems especially menacing to the resisting equestrienne (see figures 1 and 2).

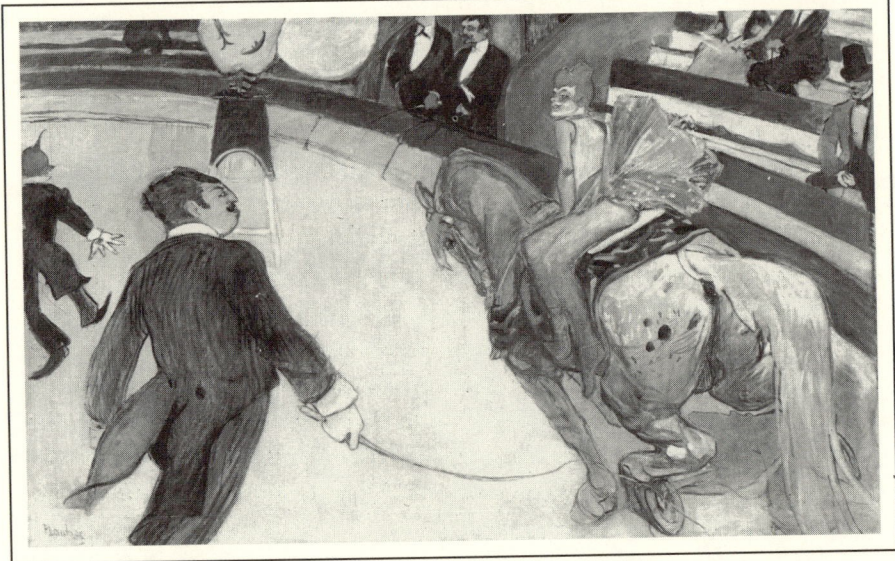

Figure 2. Henri de Toulouse-Lautrec, *Le Cirque Fernando* (1888). Courtesy of the Art Institute of Chicago.

For this woman, like Kafka's other artistes, the life of art leads to death. More inevitably than in Baudelaire, the artist must suffer from a hostile public. In "Auf der Galerie," the sensitive observer unmasks the false glitter of the spectacle, showing us its ultimate horror. "Pretense and suffering, beauty and crass kitsch are so tightly intertwined here as to make an impenetrable, inescapable lie." A. P. Foulkes likens this dualistic "portrayal of reality" to the medieval image of *frô welt*. This "lady world," sculpted on the portals of many Gothic cathedrals, appears beautiful in front but hideously worm-eaten in back. Her meaning emerges clearly in the words of Walther von der Vogelweide: "The world is beautiful outside, / white, green and red, / but inside it is black, / dark like death."[86] Kafka may well have chosen a woman as his protagonist here, one of very few in his work, to evoke this female Janus figure of *frô welt*.

GRASS: *DIE BLECHTROMMEL (THE TIN DRUM)* (1959)

The parody of art, resulting from the problematic self-awareness of the Kleistian artist, begins to develop in "Der arme Spielmann." The starver intensifies the idea of art as a mockery of ideals. Oskar Matzerath gives a

86. Heinz Ladendorf, "Kafka und die Kunstgeschichte," 304; A. P. Foulkes, "Auf der Galerie: Some Remarks Concerning Kafka's Concept and Portrayal of Reality," 35.

climactic example of the artist as total parody. Indeed, he attains self-parody, the logical end of artistic self-consciousness. We may view both Jakob and the hunger-artist as forebears of Oskar, for both these men are as crippled spiritually as he is physically. All three represent artists of hunger in that their "art" proceeds from a lack, a missing link to humanity. Moreover, Oskar's compulsion to withdraw from society, the self-enclosure of the complete outsider, recalls the starver. But Grass makes a comic masterpiece of his freak, who depends on many literary traditions besides that of the popular player. For our context, Oskar plays mainly the supreme clown: "satirist, parodist, negator."[87]

The first link between Oskar and the hunger-artist lies in Oskar's willful creation of his midget condition. Just as Kafka's artiste escapes the human world by fasting, so does Oskar stop normal growth by throwing himself down the cellar stairs at age three. The starver clearly disdains any ordinary life; Oskar repudiates the mores of both Fascist Germany and the postwar years. The drum becomes his instrument of protest against the whole era, just as the hunger-artist makes fasting his weapon against all physical life.

Oskar also owes something to the ape in "Ein Bericht." Both the ape-man and the boy-dwarf relate to their society through mimicry. Imitating human adults, they pose hauntingly ironic questions on the nature of humanity: Does the animal differ significantly from the man? Does stunted physical growth block the mind? In short, what borderlines can we draw between animal and human, sick and normal? Furthermore, both Rotpeter and Oskar see mainly the underside of their worlds, both literally and metaphorically. This uniquely Swiftian satiric view affords extraordinary perceptions, which make them paradoxically superior. Oskar feels not only the ape's disgust for life around him; in addition his self-importance becomes a mad megalomania. This sense of superiority in the abnormal person belongs to the German idea of the artist since Goethe's Tasso at least. Thus Oskar's titanism gives a climax to this tradition. Compared to our other comically vain artistes—Taugenichts, Jakob, the hunger-artist, and Josefine—Oskar represents the ultimate self-inflator.

We first notice this trait in Oskar's identity as multiple narrator. Indeed, the reader may feel overwhelmed by his many parodied personae: the picaro, the medieval jester, Mephisto, the Shandian satirist, Dionysos, Wilhelm Meister, Rasputin, Parzival, Christ and anti-Christ, the *Übermensch*. This profusion of narrative masks calls immediate attention to the telling of the story itself.

Apart from his many narrative voices, Oskar as dwarf embodies the gro-

---

87. Ann Mason, *The Skeptical Muse: A Study of Günter Grass' Conception of the Artist,* 45.

tesque. Comparing him to Jakob, we might say that Oskar's distorted form, a parody of the human male, makes visible the grotesque sounds of the beggar, a mockery of conventional music. As Leslie Fiedler and Wolfgang Promies show, the dwarf as a clown, representing the artist, has a venerable history in literature and art. Since the eighteenth century in particular, artists have created freakish fools as a symbol of irrational forces.

We may see the profusion of such grotesques in our century as a sign of the ultimate eccentricity of the artist figure. To truly represent our time, any artist must appear both crippled and childlike. In chapter 4 we will meet Karl Hetmann, the "giant dwarf" played by his author, Wedekind, and Mann's hunchbacks Friedemann and Cipolla. Grass stresses the scurrilous aspect of the professional dwarf-artist in Bebra. This parody of the guide figure in the classical *Bildungsroman* presages the political crisis, which he later uses to his own advantage. Although Gordon Cunliffe labels this man as Goebbels, we may see in him any opportunistic artist who participated in both the war and its aftermath.

Oskar, though infatuated with Bebra's charismatic success, lacks his essentially demonic nature. To be sure, Oskar destroys much as a child: his shattering of glass extends from eyeglasses to the State Theater. But this way of dominating the normal world ceases with the end of the war. Abandoning his drum-identity at Matzerath's grave, Oskar attempts to integrate himself into postwar society. Of course, this traditional behavior of the *Bildungsheld* cannot work for him, so Oskar must resume drumming. Yet then he becomes a serious and successful jazz artist. Only at the end of the novel does his certified madness bring out the demon—specifically, the Black Witch—that has governed Oskar's life.

Grass has another source of burlesque in the Romantic tradition of the insane artist. As a fool, Oskar unlocks our subconscious, our world of childhood and dream. His fantastic narration fascinates us accordingly. Vladimir Nabokov's madly literate clown Humbert Humbert in *Lolita* (1955) has a similar effect. He too, an alleged criminal, writes his story from a mental ward.[88]

While Bebra embodies the demonic side of the infantile, Oskar reveals more of its fantastic aspect. His magical effects recall Freud's concept of the artist as both childlike and primitive. In *Totem and Taboo* and *The Interpretation of Dreams,* Freud works out this conjunction of traits that creates the work of art. Johan Huizinga expands on this idea in *Homo Ludens:* "In the sphere of sacred play, the child and the poet are at home

88. Nabokov best displays this affinity for the clown of fantasy in his memoir *Look at the Harlequins!* The title refers to a command of his great-aunt when the child seemed bored. "What harlequins? Where?" "Oh, everywhere, all around you. Trees are harlequins, words are harlequins. So are situations and sums. Put two things together—jokes, images—and you get a triple harlequin. Come on! Play! Invent the world! Invent reality!" (8).

with the savage." Alan Bance sees the fantasy of Oskar as a Schillerian *Spieltrieb* (play-urge), which determines both his behavior and the spirit of his book. The child within the artist that Schiller presents in his *Aesthetic Education of Mankind* (1793) survives in Baudelaire. For him, the artist evokes "the green paradise of childhood loves." But the inner child signifies more: "But genius is only *childhood regained* at will, childhood now supplied with the mature means of self-expression, and with the analytical mind that enables it to bring order to random experience."[89]

Grass follows Baudelaire, not only in making his artist a child for life but also in having this child-artist, like the page in "Une Mort Héroique," serve evil ends. Baudelaire's page utters the hiss, ordered by the prince, that fells Fancioulle. Both boys bespeak "the spirit of evil that is 'the essence of laughter.'" However, the child-Oskar also has a positive side, for he identifies with the Christ-child. From his first confrontation with the church statue to his final statement in Paris—"I am Jesus"—Oskar persistently parodies the Savior. Grass develops a clear parallel to what Jung and Kerényi explore as the myth of the Divine Child.[90]

The identity of Oskar as artist depends on an essential childishness. Even as an adult, he achieves the peak of his musical career by invoking both his own infantile spirit and that of his audience. The chapter "In the Onion Cellar" climaxes in the greatest outburst known at that nightclub: Oskar's wild drumming turns the audience into kindergartners, literally unable to contain themselves. In perfect self-abandon, they follow the Pied Piper Oskar into the night, pick daisies, and wet their pants. Like Kafka's Josefine, Oskar induces a rapturous return to infancy. Both authors not only show us the artist as a child but also suggest that we experience art as an infantile pleasure.

This idea of the magical artist, allowing us to regress to childhood, stems partly from German Romanticism. We have already noted above the positively infantile aspect of the *artiste* in *Der Schwierige*. The clown Furlani, alter ego for the childlike Kari Bühl, represents the same idea of art that Grass gives us in Oskar. In the next chapter, we will see a similar link between the ideal child figure and the innocent mime in Böll's *Ansichten eines Clowns*.[91]

Naturally, since the child bulks so large in this novel, his fathers do too.

89. Huizinga, *Homo Ludens,* 26; Alan Bance, *The German Novel, 1945–1960,* 140; Baudelaire, *Oeuvres,* 1:64, 2:690.

90. Ross Chambers, "L'Art Sublime du Comédien," 250; Erhard Friedrichsmeyer, "Aspects of Myth, Parody and Obscenity in Günter Grass' *Blechtrommel* and *Katz und Maus,*" 241.

91. The "infantile system" of all mimesis features exhibitionism, voyeurism, and identification, all essential components of childhood. "The pleasure of acting and looking on at a theatrical performance is a very narcissistic one, through regression to the early childhood stage of magic world creation" (Eric Bentley, *The Life of the Drama,* 163).

Again our previous context offers parallels. Starting with Kleist's puppeteer-God, we see that most of the protagonists discussed here have a crucial and problematic relation to the father. Taugenichts' story depends on his expulsion from the paternal paradise; the ruthless *Hofrat* determines both character and fate for the diminished Jakob; the ringmaster in "Auf der Galerie" embodies the menacing God who condemns his progeny to suffering and death. Even the graceful comedy of *Der Schwierige* reveals Kari as a man repressed by aristocratic culture, by what Carl Schorske calls "the world of the father." And in the next chapter we will see other victims of paternal tyranny in the artist figures of Mann and Böll. By contrast, fathers and daughters usually relate in positive ways. Lulu and her first "father," Schigolch, understand and accept each other, and King Nicolo and Alma give deep mutual love, as do Vater Knie and Katharina.

These examples of the son's trauma of authority may arise more from the condition of the capitalist family than from the problematic nature of the artist. Yet the two phenomena, products of industrial society, are intricately linked. "The great complex called Father," inevitably devoted to profit, has an inimical effect on art.[92] Kafka gives perhaps the best evidence for this relationship. In the early works, the enemy of art resides clearly in a father figure; later it takes the larger shape of society. Compare the father of Georg Bendemann and the anonymous authorities in "Josefine." The collective replaces the individual.

Some of this enmity persists in Oskar's relation to Matzerath, yet Grass shows a broader concern with the problem of paternity. As in many of his later works, legitimacy itself remains questionable: we never know whether Matzerath or Jan Bronski actually fathered Oskar. And Kurt, whom Oskar claims as his own son, may also have Matzerath as father. Both Oskar and Kurt defy paternal authority in rejecting the ways of the father. Kurt despises the drum, just as Oskar despises the grocery store. The Nazi background summarizes this problem of authority in a particularly ironic way. The *Kleinbürger* (lower middle class), whom Grass displays in a colorful variety of forms, created the Third Reich, but they also became its victims. The attraction of the small by the large plays a determining role in this political drama. Like Barbara in "Der arme Spielmann," forcing herself out of the grocery world of her father, Matzerath's generation strove to transcend its class.

The instrument of transcendence for Oskar, his drum, bears many meanings. First of all, the title of the book refers to it, not to Oskar. We have already seen musical instruments as an expression of the artist's identity: the violins of Taugenichts and Jakob. Oskar abandons his drum only when

92. Barbara Beutner, *Musik und Einsamkeit bei Grillparzer, Kafka, del Castillo*, 37.

he gives up childhood at the end of the war. He best summarizes the unifying role of this symbol in saying he has "two souls in one drum." Here, as elsewhere, he invokes both Faust and Rasputin in one version of his many complementary pairs of identities.[93]

The many critical readings of the drum tend toward either the psycho-analytical or the political. In the former group, the phallic view seems suitable. According to Jung, the blocked libido "regresses to infantile rhythmic activities." Hence the drumming Oskar expresses his blocked sexual development. As for the political slant, the drum functions most clearly as protest. But the drummed outrage of the dwarf has deeply ambiguous import; we cannot equate it with resistance, for several reasons. First of all, the drum itself creates a dictatorship. "A tyranny of the drum is needed, to exorcize the demon-possessed spirit" of Germany. Several critics link not only Oskar's manners to Hitler but also his red-and-white drum to the red-and-white Nazi flag. Indeed, Hitler himself accepted, as a compliment, the damning epithet "the drummer."[94]

The implied complicity of the drum emerges also from Oskar's function as the anti-Christ. To be sure, he also identifies with Christ, as we see when Oskar offers the drum to his double, the statue of the infant Jesus. When Christ refuses to drum, Oskar assumes that he alone must save mankind. "Either he drums or he is no real Jesus, then Oskar is a more real Jesus than he is." After the war, when the same statue does miraculously drum, Oskar becomes furious with jealousy. In this climactic rage, Grass suggests that Christ has lost his chance for compassion; now it is too late to save anyone. Denouncing Jesus "and all his hocus-pocus," the adult Oskar acquires his own disciples, the delinquent Dusters.[95]

Oskar's link to both Hitler and the anti-Christ raises the question of his guilt. Indeed, most of the critics focus on this problem. Does Oskar lack all compassion; is he finally brutish, perverse, monstrous? Or does he retain a moral conscience, as "the only sane element in a crippled society?" John Reddick, finding Oskar profoundly human, calls him "a desperate Victim," and Wilfried van der Will even includes him among his "worldly saints." However, most readers settle for ultimate ambivalence. Mason thinks Oskar symbolizes all of Nazi Germany; he both exemplifies and parodies

93. Günter Grass, *Die Blechtrommel*, 110.
94. David Roberts, "Aspects of Psychology and Mythology in *Die Blechtrommel*," in *Grass: Kritik, Thesen, Analysen*, ed. Manfred Jürgensen, 50; Kurt Tank, *Günter Grass*, 69; Gordon Cunliffe, *Günter Grass*, 53. In Harold Pinter's *The Birthday Party* (1960), another childlike and repressed musician receives a drum as a birthday gift. Stanley also drums in an "erratic, uncontrolled" way. His drumbeats, "savage and possessed," recall Oskar's drumming (New York: Grove Press, 1961, p. 36).
95. Grass, *Blechtrommel*, 169, 444.

"the Nazi mythology of art and society." Others see both Oskar and fascism as symptoms of the same disease. "Oskar can offer effective resistance to the Nazis because he taps the same sources of irrational power."[96]

To my mind, the essential irony of the figure precludes our moral condemnation. Oskar, the blue-eyed dwarf, is both the perfect Aryan and the monster eliminated by the Nazis. Therefore he cannot belong to their camp. Besides, despite actual crimes and a pervasive guilt, Oskar shows a unique compassion for suffering. For Völker Schlöndorff, the essence of Oskar lies in his "withdrawal and protest." And Grass says he "embodies the lust for revenge and the anarchic megalomania of the lower middle class." Neither of these views of the dwarf implies major immorality. Referring to his "premeditated Fall [down the stairs] to eternal innocence," David Miles suggests that Oskar, though far from guiltless, still retains a childlike goodness. Finally, seeing Oskar as both product and victim, I find his guilt irrelevant.[97]

Like our previous artistes, Oskar is a nonverbal performer. He writes a superbly articulate memoir; yet ironically, in his own story he characteristically lacks words. The same irony emerges from Böll's clown, a professional mime who writes like a Nobel Prize winner, as does Felix Krull, who also works best silently (see chapter 4). Schlöndorff's film *Die Blechtrommel* perfectly captures the mute quality of Oskar; David Bennent creates him mainly with his eyes, gestures, and movements. Aptly enough, Schlöndorff claims both the puppet theater and Jackie Coogan's *The Kid* as forebears for Oskar.

Like Krull, Oskar learns his trade from staged examples. Both children attend spectacles that offer impressive histrionic models. For Oskar, Tom Thumb has obvious appeal; *The Flying Dutchman* inspires his first grandiose disruption of a public event; and a circus brings the crucial alter ego, Bebra. These three performances anticipate the climactic Nazi rally that Oskar destroys. Hamlet, another man with a father problem, provides a later model for the adult Oskar. While installing a gravestone Oskar comes upon the mutilated corpse of a woman, whose severed finger evokes a parody of Hamlet and Yorick à la Gründgens. Suddenly the hideous industrial landscape becomes Denmark, the corpse Hamlet, and Oskar Yorick. "The fields were Denmark's fields, the Erft was my Belt, what rotted here was the rot of Denmark."[98] On one level, this moment satirizes the self-

---

96. Manfred Durzak, *Der deutsche Roman der Gegenwart,* 149; John Reddick, *The Danzig Trilogy of Günter Grass,* 6; Mason, *Skeptical Muse,* 47; Cunliffe, *Grass,* 63.
97. Völker Schlöndorff, *Die Blechtrommel: Tagebuch einer Verfilmung,* 38, 39; David Miles, "Kafka's Hapless Pilgrims and Grass' Scurrilous Dwarves," 344.
98. Grass, *Blechtrommel,* 569.

aggrandizing tone of the theater in postwar Germany. Grass attacks not only the posturing of the Fascist actor Gründgens but also the falseness of his whole establishment.

On the deeper level of Oskar's psyche, this episode changes his life. Invoking Shakespeare, Oskar actually compares his own condition to that of Germany. Just as the rottenness of Denmark expresses the corruption of its court, so does the division of Germany parallel Oskar's post as the hunchback Yorick. Despairing of unification, he must now don the jester's mask and probe the meaning of life. Accordingly, he answers the question "To marry or not to marry?" in the affirmative, hoping to become "a bourgeois Yorick." But when Maria refuses him, Oskar must become only a foolish Hamlet.

Later on, costumed as a dwarf jester after Velasquez, he again invokes the shade of Yorick. "Now you are Yorick the fool, Oskar. But where is a king for you to play fool to?"[99] This line recalls Grass's essay "Vom mangelnden Selbstvertrauen der schreibenden Hofnarren unter Berücksichtigung nicht vorhandener Höfe" ("On the lack of self-confidence in literate court fools when there are no courts"). Grass explores the political impotence of the literary fool, the writer, when the contemporary world offers no true king, no viable court.

Oskar's total self-consciousness, his identity as *Kunstfigur* (artifice, construct), distinguishes him from two contemporary "blood-brothers": Felix Krull and Hans Schnier.[100] In the decade between 1954 and 1963, major German writers created three supreme clowns, three parodic inversions of the classic *Bildungsroman,* three acutely eccentric images of the anti-hero artist. All three protagonists raise the primal postwar issue of guilt; Krull and Oskar emerge as amoral beings, beyond good and evil. Far from being monstrous, all three reveal deeply human traits. As to form, the three write in the unreliable first person, forcing the reader to evaluate both them and the history they personalize.

Such figures represent the end of the positive Kleistian artist. They have no possibility of achieving a higher awareness through art, for they have already reached the ultimate self-consciousness in self-parody. Oskar especially dwells wholly in this realm of complete satire. Hence he transcends

---

99. Ibid., 580.

100. Hans Mayer draws many parallels between Oskar and Krull in *Steppenwolf and Everyman,* trans. Jack Zipes, 196. He does not consider one essential difference: recent history plays no role in *Krull.* Both Grass and Böll focus on "Vergangenheitsbewältigung" (overcoming the past); Mann ignores it (see chapter 4). Recently, however, critics have linked Oskar with the Mann figure who does struggle with the war, Leverkühn. Both mad musicians give us the "twentieth century successors" to Faust (Roberts, "Psychology and Mythology," 71; Judith Ryan, *The Uncompleted Past,* 61).

the Kleistian duality of being and consciousness. Oskar does not suffer from conflict with his creator, since he has created himself. His answer to the question "What is art?" concerns self-transcendence. Indeed, Oskar's madness proves that he has no identity of his own. Once fully unmasked, he appears as an empty being. This mad dwarf-child renders a stunning portrait of the German artist: a being crippled by his lack of a viable self.

Referring that madness to the times, Grass reveals the moral intention of the satirist. Indeed, *Die Blechtrommel* has the ethical aim of all fool literature: to hold up the mirror to human folly. Oskar lets us see our history and laugh at it. His art of total parody gives the only response that Grass finds possible in our grotesque era.

4 HEIRS OF ZARATHUSTRA
The Morality of the Show

We have art lest we perish from the truth.
—Nietzsche

THE ROPE-DANCER

The ultimately moral attitude of *Die Blechtrommel* does not stem solely from the horror of Germany since 1933. The roots of conscience in Grass lie deep in classical soil, for the aesthetics of both Goethe and Schiller have a strongly didactic streak. In the modern era, Nietzsche propounded the idea that the creator has a moral task. In *Also Sprach Zarathustra* (1884), we find such values symbolized in the rope-dancer, his abstract counterpart the *Übermensch,* and Zarathustra himself. This aerialist represents the final stage of what Banville developed: an image of the impossible ideal of human flight. Again, as in the *Odes Funambulesques,* the familiar man above the crowd symbolizes heroic mastery over human limitations, over nature itself.

But the transcendence of this aerialist connotes more than the Banvillian liberation of the superior artist from meager earth. Nietzsche means far more with his artiste than his forebear did with his aerialists. In this chapter I shall first explore the significance of the artist as *Übermensch* and then show how later authors transformed this idealistic image of the performer. All the writers treated here—Wedekind, Zuckmayer, Mann, Böll—retain essential Nietzschean values, but each introduces conflicts crucial enough to gradually vitiate the heroic ideal of Nietzsche.

Zarathustra's rope-dancer is not the first one to appear in German literature. We find two important forebears in Goethe's Narziss and Landrinette, the artistes whom Wilhelm Meister eulogizes in the second book, fourth chapter of *Wilhelm Meisters Lehrjahre* (*Wilhelm Meisters Apprenticeship*) (1795). Here the aerial act, described as a superlative technical feat, has nothing to do with the Romantic heroism of freedom gained through a triumph over nature. However, these figures do display a different sort of heroism for Meister; their performance morally benefits a grateful public. In this regard they indeed have exemplary value, for Wilhelm claims that actual artists must envy the effect they have.

What actor, what writer, indeed what person would not feel at the height of his capacities if he could create such a great effect through a noble word or a good deed? What a precious feeling it must be to arouse noble emotions worthy of mankind as quickly as an electric shock, to excite such joy among the people as these people do with their physical skill! It is as if one could give the crowd a sense of community with all of mankind, as if one could enflame and thrill them with an image of joy and misery, of wisdom and folly, even of nonsense and stupidity. Then one could set their stumbling spirit free in pure and lively movement![1]

Again we note the theme of superiority treated in chapter 2. Banville and Barbey d'Aurevilly made similar comparisons between aerialists and writers. Moreover, Wilhelm implies that the legitimate stage could not achieve the inspiring results that this passage indicates. Indeed, he leaves no doubt that these troupers—specifically *not* actors or writers—fulfill the most intense desire of his youth, namely "to embody the good, the noble, the great through acting."

Such sentiments recall Schiller, whose own idealistic vision of the theater pervades Wilhelm's thinking. For both Goethe and Schiller, the actor possesses a virtually political power, for he can unite mankind in "the empathy of all humanity." In contrast to the Romantics, who focus on the individuality of the artist, these writers portray him as the servant of culture. For them, the primary value of art lies in its effect on the public. For the Romantics, the public is indifferent, even hostile, to the outcast onstage. Think of the change from Tasso to Triboulet: both men embody the conflicts created by the artist who stands apart from the court, yet only Tasso shows any possibility of integration into that world. In the age of reaction, the writer seldom sees his work as welcome. Accordingly, his artist figures relate to society in the problematic ways treated in chapter 2.

Clearly, then, Nietzsche's rope-dancer bespeaks a reaction against the social idealism of Goethe. What he essentially represents derives from "the vertical metaphor" created by Banville and company. Nietzsche subsumes the link of agile acrobat and daring poet that these writers forged. To this equation he adds a crucial new focus: danger. Indicatively, the rope-dancer falls to his death. Indeed, Nietzsche claims that he, like all Supermen, *must* fall. *Untergang* is a notion pervading this book written as a protest against decadence. Accordingly, the true transcendence it preaches must start with

---

1. Johann Wolfgang Goethe, *Werke*, ed. Erich Trunz, 7:106.

descent. The work begins when Zarathustra goes down from his mountain, abandoning ten years of solitude to rejoin mankind.

On the clearest level of relationship, the aerialist serves as the model of the *Übermensch* for Zarathustra. Nietzsche links the two figures in part three of the prologue, when Zarathustra enters the town where the rope-dancer will perform. Here we find, within two lines of each other, the juxtaposed words *Seiltänzer* (rope-dancer) and *Übermensch* (Superman): "for it had been announced that a tightrope-walker would appear. And Zarathustra spoke thus to the people: *I teach you the Superman*."[2] Zarathustra's ensuing sermon serves as a prelude to the promised aerial act, which does not occur until the sixth part of the prologue. And even here we do not see the man perform, for the *Possenreisser* follows him immediately onto the tightrope. As a result of this jester's taunting, the rope-dancer falls and dies. Hence this artiste exists not to perform, but to fall.

Nietzsche first speaks of the rope-dancer in a disarmingly simple yet vatic statement: "Man is a rope, stretched between beast and Superman, a rope over an abyss." He then interprets this image more clearly: "What is great in man is that he is a bridge, not a goal: what one can love in man is that he is a transition and a descent. . . . I love those who can live only as the condemned, for they are the ones who cross the abyss."[3]

Before this interpretation, Zarathustra extracts from his initial image of rope and abyss its essential import. With his four-fold repetition of the word *dangerous,* he defines the life of those like the rope-dancer: "A dangerous crossing, a dangerous life enroute, a dangerous look backward, a dangerous shuddering and paralysis." Such extreme peril surpasses the risk taken by the Romantic artist figure, for it concerns not only the achievement of art but a whole way of life. Such constant danger, transcending the metaphysical, connotes an existential state. For the rope-dancer, the ultimate danger lies not in his death-defying profession but in the taunts of his detractor, the buffoon. The aerialist sees in this figure the devil, but we may also view him as any rival force. We need not speculate on the jester's motivation, as Nietzsche purposely omits such analysis. But we must see the jester's effect on the aerialist, whose resultant loss of confidence causes his fall.

On another level, we may see in the *Possenreisser* the other half of the rope-dancer himself. One recalls the dialectic implied in the two selves of Faust and Mephisto and the other pairs noted in chapter 2. Critics have

2. Friedrich Nietzsche, *Werke: Also Sprach Zarathustra,* ed. Alfred Baeumler, 8.
3. Ibid., 11.

described the conflict in *Zarathustra* as progress versus destruction, enlightenment versus irrationality, even Apollonian versus Dionysian. Marion Faber calls this artist Apollonian, "a self-conscious creator, . . . manipulating movement in space, concerned with form."[4]

The description may well recall a dancer, that creator of visual forms through movement in space. Indeed, the *Tänzer* in the word *Seiltänzer* means just as much to Nietzsche as does the word's other half, *Seil* (tightrope). Considering the disdain he expressed for some artists, we realize how positively Nietzsche felt about dance. In "Vom Probleme des Schauspielers" ("On the Problem of the Actor"), for instance, he speaks of the actor as "jester, liar, buffoon, fool, clown." Acting is simply "falseness with a good conscience, a joy in the power of disguise."[5] Hence the author cannot show authenticity, one of Nietzsche's highest ideals. The dancer, however, must exhibit the inevitable truth of the body. Moreover, dancing naturally expresses the Nietzschean value of transcendence, for it overcomes the deadly *Geist der Schwere*. In "Das Tanzlied" Zarathustra sings about this spirit of gravity, which seems to rule the world. Indeed, much of this book shows just how the weight of omnipotent Christian society has paralyzed human vitality.

To free oneself from this earth-bound paralysis, the human being must first dance. Nietzsche eulogizes the transcendent liberation of dancing in frequent metaphors: "One must still have chaos within, in order to give birth to a dancing star"; "I would only believe in a god who knew how to dance"; "Now I am light, now I fly, now I feel myself under me, now a god dances within me." This last sentence may recall the end of the prologue, in which Zarathustra claims the flying eagle as his own symbol, "the proudest animal under the sun." But in the later passage, the one who flies becomes a dancing god. This combination of ideal conditions—flight, dance, and mastery—results from the self- overcoming that forms the most essential trait of the *Übermensch*. The specific image of looking down at oneself perhaps best expresses the idea of self-transcendence. Elsewhere Zarathustra preaches that people must dance above and beyond themselves.[6]

An essential component of the rope-dancer's transcendent skill is balance. Such an artful poise characterizes the superior person, who attains the ultimate human freedom as a metaphorical eagle, upon the heights. Gaston Bachelard, focusing on the symbolism of height, builds a whole

4. Marion Faber, *Angels of Daring*, 36.
5. Friedrich Nietzsche, *Werke: Die Fröhliche Wissenschaft*, ed. Alfred Baeumler, 272.
6. Nietzsche, *Zarathustra*, 13, 14, 43, 22, 328.

interpretation on his vision of Nietzsche as an "aerial mentality." In *L'Air et les Songes* (*The Air and Dreams*), Bachelard devotes one chapter to Nietzsche and the psychology of ascent.

In part we may justify this reading of Nietzsche as "montagnard," the poet of the summits, by biography. He spent long periods at Sils-Maria, six thousand feet above sea level. Here, surrounded by heroic Alpine views, he conceived and wrote much of *Zarathustra*. But of course vertical imagery pervades not only this book but most of what he wrote. The striving toward what lies beyond man, beyond even the mountains he can scale, emerges as a basic Nietzschean trait. The title *Jenseits von Gut und Böse* best characterizes this philosophy of spiritual liberation.[7]

Bachelard closes his chapter by quoting one of Nietzsche's most seemingly paradoxical lines, from the mystical poem "an Hafis": "You are the depth of all the heights." Here we find a parallel to the split identity of the rope-dancer/jester. The necessity of the acrobat's fall shows that he belongs to the depths as well as the heights. Only in his *Untergang* (descent) does he truly attain the summits of the *Übermensch*. One thinks of "Stirb und werde!" (Die and become!) in Goethe's "Selige Sehnsucht." But Zarathustra preaches that the *Superman* need not wait for actual death to be reborn. In "Der Wanderer" he tells himself "Peak and abyss—now they are one!"[8]

Yet there is a larger significance to the rope-dancer, beyond his symbolic function for Zarathustra and his book. First of all, only Zarathustra comes to see the dying man after his fall. "Then the crowd dispersed, for even curiosity and terror grow tired."[9] We note some of the same hostility to the public that marks "Le Vieux Saltimbanque." Only Zarathustra reassures the rope-dancer that he lived courageously, and promises to bury him. Zarathustra takes the corpse into a forest, where he lays it in a hollow tree. Although he explains this unconventional burial as protection against wolves, it has a deeper symbolic meaning. By enclosing the rope-dancer in a living organism, Zarathustra endows him with continuing life.

Moreover, the prophet absorbs the aerialist's spirit when he sleeps through the night by the corpse. On awakening, Zarathustra feels himself reborn. "Zarathustra slept for a long time, and not only the dawn passed over him, but also the morning. But finally he opened his eyes: with awe he saw the forest and the stillness, with awe he saw into himself. Then he got

---

7. For an interesting survey of "aviation and angelism," see Felix Ingold, *Literatur und Aviatik*. He treats "the ascension of the lyrical self (from Baudelaire to Mallarmé and Nietzsche) as an anticipation of aviatorial titanism." The bulk of this book traces the influence of classical angelology on the modern literature of flight from Kafka to Arp.

8. Gaston Bachelard, *L'Air et les Songes*, 185; Nietzsche, *Zarathustra*, 168.

9. Nietzsche, *Zarathustra*, 17.

up quickly, like a sailor who suddenly sees land, and rejoiced: for he saw a new truth."[10]

Again we recall Goethe, who gives Faust a similar rebirth at the beginning of *Faust II*.

> The pulse of life beats once again,
> in order to gently greet the ethereal dawn.
> You too slept through this night, earth,
> and now breathe anew at my feet.
> You begin to surround me with joy,
> you excite a mighty will
> to strive forever toward the highest life.[11]

We might well compare the role of Margarete to that of the rope-dancer. What both Faust and Zarathustra have experienced through these characters determines their later lives. Both men are closely involved in the deaths of the two victims, which bring spiritual rebirth. Both heroes assimilate their crucial perceptions of these figures into their new consciousness. Hence both Margarete and the aerialist serve as catalysts for renewed action. Here lies their vivid posterity, their immortality.

Faust relates generally to Zarathustra as a model of heroic striving. Indeed, the *Erdgeist* addresses Faust as an *Übermensch* in the first scene of *Faust I*, line 490. Critics have also noted the "ascensionist imagery" of the rope-dancer in Euphorion, the Icarian son of Faust. F. D. Luke even speaks of a "Euphorion complex" as a literary parallel for what psychologists call "the Icarus complex." Luke also pursues the psychology of ascension in saying that Zarathustra's prose expresses "an exhilarated euphoric state . . . evidently the manic phase of a manic- depressive temperament, both aspects of which are . . . fully expressed in Zarathustra."[12]

The links of *Zarathustra* to Goethe go beyond Faust and Wilhelm Meister. Indeed, in arguing that the *Übermensch* stands for the ultimate artist, R. J. Hollingdale finds the Superman actualized in Goethe. Despite the slim evidence for this claim, we may agree that Goethe's ideas pervade the book, specifically in relation to the rope-dancer. In the chapter cited above from the *Lehrjahre*, Wilhelm not only idealizes the aerial act as a spiritual, even political, force, but he also specifies the means of achievement as the creation of unity. "I admire the cleverness of these artistes, with which they make even meagre offerings effective, and the way they create a *whole* out

10. Ibid, 20.
11. Goethe, *Werke*, 3:148.
12. F. D. Luke, "Nietzsche and the Imagery of Height," in *Nietzsche: Imagery and Thought*, ed. Malcolm Pasley, 109, 112.

of the clumsiness of their children and the virtuosity of their stars. Thus they first gain our attention, and then most pleasantly entertain us."[13]

Although Wilhelm calls this show merely agreeable entertainment, we must note the crucial Goethean ideal he finds here: oneness. The artistic unity that Wilhelm admires translates readily into the larger realm of moral wholeness. The same goal of spiritual unity in *Zarathustra* links it to such Enlightenment ideals. Like Faust, who anticipates him, the Superman aims to transcend his fragmented life and become a unified being. Hence we may build an arch connecting Goethe to Nietzsche. The Revolution that Goethe hailed and Nietzsche hated brought an inevitable decadence that grew throughout the century. Goethe, the classical humanist, hoped to regain wholeness through the moral influence of art. Nietzsche, seeing only the fragments left by the political process, sought integration through a renewed heroism.

WEDEKIND

Like Nietzsche, Wedekind also wanted renewal. For both writers, this rebirth could come only by destroying the false moral values of bourgeois society. Nietzsche sought polemical means to this end, whereas Wedekind created human images for such change in his plays. Specific links lie in Karl Hetmann and King Nicolo as Nietzschean "madmen." And our rope-dancer relates closely to another character: Wedekind published a collection of aphorisms by the Marquis of Keith as "Also Sprach der Marquis von Keith."

Here I shall discuss the three figures most clearly linked to Nietzschean values, which Wedekind attaches to the popular player. Lulu, Nicolo, and Hetmann all perform for the public, and all become martyrs to their ideals. Moreover, they function as the three archetypes composing Wedekind's allegorical circus world: Lulu the animal, Nicolo the clown, and Hetmann the acrobat. The ultimate tragedy of Hetmann lies in his unwitting identity as a clown, but essentially he represents the doomed idealist, that mental acrobat portrayed by Wedekind in his essay "Zirkusgedanken" (1887). Let us start with Lulu, the tantalizing fruit of Wedekind's first decade of serious writing.

Lulu (1892–1905)

Lulu performs as both dancer and acrobat, first encouraged by Dr. Schön and then coached by her partner, Rodrigo Quast. But we quickly grasp her

13. Goethe, *Werke*, 7:98, italics mine.

true identity in the prologue to *Erdgeist (Earth-Spirit)* (1898), where the ringmaster introduces her as a serpent. Lulu belongs to the circus ring, the only home of natural morality for Wedekind. In her he creates his most positively Nietzschean figure, one who transcends the mere outsider status of the "mad" Hetmann and Nicolo. To be sure, Lulu lacks the *Übermensch* quality of self-transcendence. Yet she embodies for Wedekind the most ambitious image of Nietzschean animal morality. Only she represents a true beast: "the *true* animal, the wild, beautiful animal."[14]

To understand Lulu as a wild animal, we must examine her image in both *Erdgeist* and *Die Büchse der Pandora (Pandora's Box)* (1905). In the first play, we learn that she has no real parents; Schigolch simply found her in the street at the age of seven. Soon thereafter, Schön discovered and further "rescued" her for his own purposes. By marrying her off to Dr. Goll, Schön insured her availability while keeping himself free for his own advantageous union. In this early history of Lulu, we note right away a perversion of the Pygmalion theme. Lulu stresses this "nurturing" aspect of her relation to Schön. "If I belong to anyone in this world, it is to you. Without you I would be—I won't say where. You took me by the hand, fed me and clothed me when I tried to steal your watch. Do you think one forgets that? Anyone else would have called a policeman. You sent me to school and taught me manners. Who besides you cared at all about me? I danced and modelled and was happy to earn my living that way."[15]

With Goll Lulu has more exclusively the role of the trained animal, for he literally plays the tune. When he commissions her fateful portrait from Schwarz, her sexual exploitation takes an aesthetic turn. From the first scene of *Erdgeist* onward, we see that Schwarz uses Lulu to project his own naive artistic fantasies.

Hence the first trait we associate with this "wild beast" is her exploitation by men who represent several levels of capitalist society. Financier, artist, publisher, and gambler all attempt to profit sexually or socially from owning Lulu. In Schön, her chief antagonist, we see most clearly the essential links among sex, power, and money. Not accidentally, he displays an obsessive concern with both his sexual freedom and his prosperity. The ultimate exploitation of Lulu by her murderer, Jack the Ripper, implies the destruction of this wholly materialistic world from within. Indeed, we may see Jack as the ultimate symbol of Victorian corruption, expressed in its barbaric relations between the sexes. In this light, Jack becomes merely the executioner of the sentence already passed on Lulu by Schön. Lulu, symbol of all

14. Frank Wedekind, *Gesammelte Werke*, 3:8.
15. Ibid, 3:47.

the ills created by male domination, must die as she has lived: a martyr to patriarchal culture.

Much of the criticism on the Lulu figure depends on the concept of the *femme fatale*. The earliest such woman is the talmudic first wife of Adam, Lilith, who gives Lulu her name. In both Marlowe's and Goethe's *Faust*, Lilith practices magical powers that threaten men. Delilah offers another image of the biblical temptress; Helena exemplifies the type in pagan antiquity. More specifically, we may trace the *femme fatale* to the medieval figure of *frô welt*. We see her still in sculpted form on the portals of Gothic cathedrals: a beautiful noblewoman in front, yet devoured by demons in back. Medieval poetry also shows the danger of this woman who is both lovely and hideous. This dualistic image of seductive worldliness evokes the two aspects of woman in medieval culture: idealized beauty versus demonic power. Wagner's *Tannhäuser* offers both types of woman in the courtly Elisabeth and her opposite, the wanton Venus.

But Lulu belongs to a special tradition in the literature of the fatal woman: the half-animal. Hence she represents not only the lure of the flesh, but also female guilt. Indeed, the larger issue she invokes concerns an ultimate cultural problem, the concept of woman herself. Since Lulu is part animal, does her power stem from natural qualities or from her human will? In the first case, she acts helplessly, according to physical drives; in the second case, she intends to destroy men. Wedekind seems to incriminate Lulu, for he calls her Pandora, the woman sent to earth by Zeus as revenge on men for the theft of fire. And we may readily see Lulu as taking revenge on the many men who have stolen her own identity.

Yet if we place Lulu among her peers, women who are also half-animal, the question of guilt becomes more mysterious. To take a familiar example, the undine in Goethe's "Der Fischer" (1778) has no trouble luring the fisherman with her promise of a watery paradise. In thus reversing the relation of fisherman and fish, hunter and victim, this woman also seems to take her justified revenge. Yet one of the closing lines implies that the man himself wills his death: "She half-pulled him, he half-fell."[16] Like her cousins, Heine's Lorelei and Giraudoux' Undine, this mermaid probably stems from Homer's Circe. Romantic literature abounds in such beings: sprites, elves, sylphs, swans. We see them still in Romantic ballets—*Giselle, Swan Lake, La Sylphide*—where they usually draw men to their downfall. Yet in most cases, the man responds all too willingly to this magical attraction. So it would be simplistic to assign guilt to the *femme fatale* alone.[17]

16. Goethe, *Werke*, 1:153.
17. Nina Auerbach notes the Victorian fascination with the mermaid, a combination of

Ultimately such half-women convey a mythic message about the dangers man faces when attempting to return to nature. Here Rousseauism adds a romantic tinge to the ancient figure of the deadly woman. This same Rousseauist view of Lulu as half-snake emerges from Friedrich Rothe's interpretation. Lulu, he says, embodies "the essential problem of *Jugendstil,* the question of how the natural relates to the social." We see this conflict mounting in the latter half of the nineteenth century, which Mario Praz labels as the heyday of the fatal woman. The emerging liberation of women may have helped to form this widespread image, but so did the previous dominance of the "fatal man," "the Byronic hero." As the heroic ideals of Faustian, revolutionary figures faded, powerful women began to appear. The *femme fatale* dominates the imagery of the Symbolists and others of the *fin de siècle.* The complex of Judith, Herodias, and Salome alone recurs like a leitmotiv in the works of Moreau, Mallarmé, Wilde, Khnopff, Beardsley, Strauss, and Hofmannsthal.[18]

In exonerating Lulu, Hans Mayer contrasts her with the tradition of earlier women who willfully ruined men: Merteuil, Marwood, Judith, Delilah. But "the female demons in Lulu's retinue are existentially unconscious. . . . The great anticipation in this development was Carmen, the gypsy woman . . . without rights and morality who belongs nowhere." (Merimée's novella dates from 1846, the Bizet opera from 1875.) However, Mayer continues:

One can still follow the reasoning behind Carmen's actions. She always seeks out the stronger, more successful man: the better man, in a word. And the Delilah of the operatic world [Saint-Saëns, 1877] is a traditional seductress, a Philistine, a tool of the priests enjoying seduction and treachery. Lulu, however, evades any such explanation. She is neither foreign, Philistine, nor gypsy. *Her femaleness itself is the cause of her strangeness.* A writer in the Enlightenment tradition, . . . Wedekind came to create the new female phenotype for the counter-Enlightenment: the bourgeois Delilah.[19]

Wedekind himself likened Lulu to Salome. In an essay published posthumously, he looks back on the Berlin premiere of *Erdgeist,* contrasting his

---

Eve and the serpent. "In her mysterious hybrid nature, whose humanity is only an appearance, the mermaid becomes an emblem of Victorian womanhood generally" (*Woman and the Demon,* 96). In chapter 6, I discuss the lure of the demonic for the nineteenth century as a retreat from humanistic values.

18. Friedrich Rothe, *Frank Wedekinds Dramen,* 40; Mario Praz, *The Romantic Agony,* 216.

19. Hans Mayer, *Outsiders,* trans. Dennis Sweet, 109, italics mine.

own view of Lulu-Salome with that in later productions. The traits he associates with Lulu do not clearly belong to the tradition of deadly women: naturalness, honesty, childlikeness. Accordingly, Wedekind criticizes those
versions of the character that ignored "the refined Lulu."[20] Hence we see
some paradox in her image as savage beast. Yet Wedekind, portrayer of all
the irrationality he found in the human subconscious, would see no problem in this woman as both primitive and sophisticated. His two plays show
above all that Lulu exists as a projection of many male fantasies, which run
a wide gamut of psychology.

Wedekind gives us woman as product, designed to meet the needs of
male sexuality. Indeed, the very concept of the *femme fatale,* expressed in
literature written mainly by men, characterizes a male view of women.
Indicatively, the male counterpart for the fatal woman, Don Juan, appears
more heroic than dangerous. The male author/reader may project his wishful self-image of power onto the countless seductions of the Don. But Lulu,
the female Don Juan, bears a deadly warning, for women in patriarchal
culture must serve only the aim of procreation.[21]

The varied meanings of Lulu's many names show that she represents
more than a *femme fatale.* Schigolch first named her Lulu, but in the second act of *Erdgeist* she tells him that name sounds like something "before
the flood": a clear reference to Lilith. Another possible source is Zola's
Nana (1880). Men find this woman irresistible also, for she too embodies
natural sexuality. And here too a corrupt society finds her purity intolerable.
Actually, Wedekind took the name from a popular pantomime he saw at the
Nouveau Cirque in Paris, Félicien Champsaur's *Lulu* (1888). This piece,
later turned into the novel *Lulu: Clownesse Danseuse,* greatly benefited
from the appearance of the famous clown Footit as Harlequin. As for Lulu,
she assumes the role of a literally heartless Columbine. However, she
resembles Wedekind's Lulu only in her seductive dancing. Wedekind uses
Champsaur's cruel Lulu as a mere springboard.

Each husband gives Lulu a new name. Goll dubs her Nelli, an inversion
of Helen. Schön calls her Mignon, and Schwarz chooses Eva. This variety of
names reflects not changing identities but the particular need of each man
to possess her as his own. Nonetheless, as Schigolch remarks, the principle
remains always the same. In all her incarnations, Lulu represents the sexual

20. Wedekind, *Werke,* 9:440.
21. Ariane Thomalla, *Die "femme fragile": Ein literarischer Frauentypus der Jahrhundertwende,* gives a thorough account of the expectable complementary figure, the *femme
fragile.* This searching study of the repressed male sexuality in Aestheticism extends from
Poe and the Pre-Raphaelites to Beer-Hofmann.

attraction of woman. The specific names that Wedekind gives Lulu, like the titles of the two plays themselves, reveal his positive concept of this essential being. Consider first Eva, the ideal of innocence lured into evil. Apparently Schwarz ignores this latter aspect of Eve, for the news of her non-virginal past prompts his suicide. As Lulu says, he is too blind to see either her or himself. Hans-Jochen Irmer notes that if the name Eva refers to Lulu's past, the name Mignon refers to her fate.[22] Most obviously, Lulu resembles the enigmatic dancer-child: abducted, mistreated, lonely within a hectic society that cannot contain her. Like Mignon, she too becomes the martyred innocent.

We note other resemblances in the relation of Mignon to Meister and Lulu to Schön. Both women cannot exist alone in a menacing world; both find a protector, a savior, in the experienced man. Another link between the two women lies in their silence. When Schwarz bombards Lulu with questions, she responds, "I cannot answer, I don't know." We recall Mignon, who says, "Don't make me speak, let me be silent, for I must keep my secret." For both figures, silence does not conceal willfully, for they simply cannot speak of what they do not understand themselves. Finally, both characters long for a home. This home signifies not a known place already lost but a potential locus of identity.[23]

Like Mignon, Lulu strives to find a self. She pursues that quest through rebellion, which we see most clearly in her role as Faustian Erdgeist. In defying the world as given, Lulu gains an identity stronger than any of those around her. Despite her actual lack of power, she achieves a freedom unattainable to all the men who can never truly possess her.

The most pervasive and enigmatic symbol of this quest for identity appears in the portrait of Lulu as Pierrot. One can hardly exaggerate the importance of this picture for our understanding of her. We see it in all but two scenes in the two plays; it sets the plot in motion at the beginning of *Erdgeist;* it follows Lulu, similarly tattered, to her death. Tilly Wedekind calls the picture "almost mystical." Therefore we must investigate the relation of Lulu to Pierrot, her famous colleague in the theatrical arts.

Like her many costume changes in *Erdgeist,* act 3, the portrait reveals the essential aspect of Lulu. She appears primarily as a costumed image, a woman performing for male viewers. Indeed, Schwarz speaks of the Pierrot costume as part of her body. And the discussion of costume in act 3 shows again how clearly each different image expresses what each man perceives in Lulu.

22. Hans-Jochen Irmer, *Der Theaterdichter Frank Wedekind,* 136.
23. Wedekind, *Werke,* 3:33; Goethe, *Werke,* 7:356.

Escerny. I think she looks too ethereal in the white tulle.
Alwa.   I think she looks too animal in the pink tulle. The white tulle shows
         better the child in her nature!
Escerny. The pink tulle shows better the woman in her nature![24]

The specific character of Pierrot gives Lulu her most complex identity. First of all, although Goll commissioned her portrait, she chose the costume herself. Moreover, in one of the two scenes where the picture does not appear, she asks for it, as if she misses some part of herself. Hence we perceive an instinctual link to Pierrot—at least to what his image signified at the turn of the century. Critics have often tried to relate Lulu to the popular clown of the Parisian circuses that Wedekind frequented. By the 1880s, Pierrot had lost most of his melancholy insouciance and had gained a more raucous, even menacing, character (see chapter 6). Wilhelm Emrich tries to link him with Lulu in their eventual mastery over their supposed masters. But he gives no examples for this version of Pierrot. Such usurping of power characterizes not Pierrot but Harlequin, so Emrich may confuse the two figures. However, he does suggest something helpful in speaking of the sad mixture of the genuine and the false in both Pierrot and Lulu. "The figure of Pierrot always—already in Watteau's picture—shows a bewildering mixture of deceptive appearance and genuine nature, of concealment and openness."[25] The picture of Lulu also both reveals and disguises her true nature.

Like Pierrot, she is an innocent, yet she also uses her naiveté to gain an advantage. Indeed, she loves masquerade itself, so we cannot take any one aspect of the complex Pierrot as definitive for her. Noting the shepherd's crook that Lulu holds in the picture, we may compare her innocence to the rococo pretense of naturalness that courtly figures adopt in Watteau's paintings. Aptly enough, the figure of Pierrot furthers this connection, for Watteau often links his aristocrats with *Commedia dell'Arte* figures in an idyllic landscape (see chapter 7). In suggesting something similar for Lulu, Wedekind shows that she relates to her social world, symbolized by the men seeking to dominate her, as the *Commedia* actors relate to the artificial world of the rococo court. Of course, the theatrical world usually connotes illusion and artifice; yet here, ironically, Lulu as performer represents the natural, the authentic, enmeshed in the falseness of society.[26]

24. Wedekind, *Werke*, 3:70.
25. Wilhelm Emrich, *Protest und Verheissung*, 211.
26. Audrone Willeke disputes this view of Lulu. She takes issue with "the Nature-Society dichotomy," arguing that "Lulu as dancer, as acrobat, as Pierrot, . . . the entire circus world represented in this play is not Nature, but rather Art" (letter to author, 3 February 1985). Although I agree with this perceptive conclusion, I still cannot ignore the crucial

Wedekind confirms another likeness between Lulu and Pierrot in describing her and Schön as the opposing principles of instinct and rationality. "I wanted to show the destruction of the human consciousness, which . . . overestimates itself, in conflict with the subconscious of Lulu." Schön, in his utter self-awareness, represents the blind egotism of his society. Lulu, as the asocial person with no self-consciousness, relates well to Pierrot. Only in his decadent, Symbolist incarnations does the clown gain awareness of himself. Essentially he lives as much by instinct as Lulu does.[27]

Edward Harris suggests another, biographical meaning for the shepherd's staff in the portrait. Discussing the Pygmalion figure as part of Wedekind's adolescent sexual fantasies, he quotes from a letter of 1881, written in Aarau: "You can understand that, for the idyllic shepherd's life I am leading up here, I needed a shepherdess. So I created one in my mind, and called her Galathea." (Galathea appears in the eighteenth century as the name of Pygmalion's creation.) Harris finds this figure in Wedekind's later poetry and in the idyll "Felix und Galathea," where she represents a "sexually compliant idealized version of himself." The idea of Galathea, the female creation of the male artist as an externalized image of himself, stems from post-Ovidian versions of the fable. More specifically, Harris interprets this "Wunschbild" of Wedekind as a masturbation fantasy. Thus we may readily see Galathea-Lulu-Pierrot as androgynous images of their creator.[28]

Apart from helping to explain Lulu-as-Pierrot-shepherdess, the idyllic Galathea also relates to Lulu's androgyny. Already in the first act of *Erdgeist*, she tells Schwarz that Pierrot's trousers have allowed her to escape his advances. In a long skirt she could not have done so. Male clothing again protects Lulu when she escapes the police by changing clothes with Bob, the elevator boy. Other hints of androgyny occur in the identity of Mignon: the name Mignon enjoyed a vogue among Parisian lesbians at the turn of the century, and Goethe's figure is herself a sort of hermaphrodite. When she meets Meister, she is about the same age, twelve, as Lulu is when she meets Schön. Furthermore, Mignon's egg-dance, a kind of ritual tribute to

role of instinct in Lulu. Therefore I find Wedekind typically ambivalent in his treatment of this artiste. Elizabeth Boa might agree with me, for she too stresses "an ambiguous response to the patriarchal ideology." Unfortunately, my book was already in press when Boa's *The Sexual Circus* appeared (Basil Blackwell, 1987), so I was unable to work with it. However, her title alone suggests that the book develops a view of Lulu similar to mine. She also pursues some rich and original comparisons: *Manon Lescaut, La Dame aux Camélias, Minna von Barnhelm*.

27. Wedekind quoted in Emrich, *Protest*, 211. We recall Kleist's positive image of the puppet as more graceful than the human dancer. Although Lulu bears the negative puppet aspect of being manipulated by men, her dancing also shows an almost superhuman freedom. Willeke suggests a fruitful comparison of this freedom in Lulu with what Kleist sees in the puppet.

28. Edward Harris, "Liberation of Flesh from Stone: Pygmalion in *Erdgeist*," 46.

animal fertility, recalls Lulu's erotic dancing. Finally, in the lesbian Gesch-
witz, Wedekind gives a summary symbol for the tragic ambivalence of the
sexes in society.

In general, of course, we may see in Lulu's "wildness" her way of living
according to primal drives, a "masculine" trait. But Wedekind questions
the social habit that arbitrarily assigns such social behavior to a specific
gender. His daughter, Kadidja Wedekind, recalls such sexual ambivalence
as part of Wedekind's own androgyny. "His Franziska was a fantasized
female self—what he would have liked to be as a woman, and hence she
was both female twin and beloved. She was a boyish ideal—the wishful
image of an era when sameness and similarity are more attractive than
strangeness. She was self-sufficient, a free woman superior to convention
and bourgeois mores."[29]

This last sentence particularly fits Lulu also. Indeed, she shares with Franziska, the female Frank of 1911, the Faustian defiance that expresses the
attitudes of their creator.[30] We hardly need to state that Wedekind himself
stands, clearly outlined, behind most of his protagonists. But the critics
have not much noted his identification with Lulu. Perhaps because Wedekind often played both the ringmaster and Jack the Ripper, interpreters have
associated him with her antagonists. However, he links himself unmistaka-
bly to the martyrdom of Lulu in the foreword to *Pandora,* written in 1905 to
defy the censors. Here Wedekind compares his defense of the play to the
self-defense of Christ before the Sanhedrin. All three heroes—Lulu, Wedekind, Christ—had to martyr their own true morality to false bourgeois
norms.

The last reason why I mention this case, considered a norm, in relation to the
verdicts given on my play, is the difference between bourgeois morality, which
the judge must protect, and human morality, which transcends all earthly justice.
In all three judgments against my play, prostitution was labeled as immoral and its
practice as sin. . . . But honorable poets in all times have felt called upon to
defend the victims of prostitution against general condemnation. And Christ said
to the priests and the judges, "Truly I say unto you, the tax-collectors and the
whores will enter the realm of God before you."[31]

29. Quoted in ibid., 47.
30. Hans Mayer also sees a Faustian dimension in Lulu. "Lulu was to become a central
figure in the literature of warning, precisely like the popular tale of Doctor Faustus at the
end of the sixteenth century. The literature of warning, however, is always ambivalent.
One reads it filled with both fright and delight. It demonstrates where one ends up if one
does not have oneself under control (in which a more universal control is glimpsed).
Faustus is taken away by the devil; Lulu meets her end as the victim of someone who
murders for kicks" (*Outsiders,* 112).
31. Wedekind, *Werke,* 3: 106.

Rothe is the only critic who cites likely sources for the portrait motif: Wilde's *The Picture of Dorian Gray* (1891) and Giraud's "Pierrot Lunaire" (1884). As for the Wilde novel, which Wedekind probably knew, the portrait of the title plays just as "mystical" a role as Lulu's does. However, Lulu's portrait ages only expectably, as a parallel for her own aging; Dorian Gray stays magically young while his picture ages. The relation of image to subject in both works expresses a central problem for *fin-de-siècle* aesthetics. In both cases we see that the author cannot take nature as it is. Both artists pose haunting questions about the validity of our perceptions.

"Pierrot Lunaire" offers more concrete links to the idea of Lulu as Pierrot. Rothe describes a letter written by Wedekind to Karl Henckell, dated 11 September 1893, in which he notes both the recent German translation of Giraud and his work on the first act of *Erdgeist*. In this German translation of "Blancheurs Sacrées" as "Das Heilige Weiss" ("Holy Whiteness"), we readily see the link to Lulu. Here the images of purity transcend their merely physical whiteness.

> The white of swans and snow,
> of the lily and the moon,
> was a four-fold holy symbol
> in Pierrot's time.
> It meant scorn for all earthly contentment,
> scorn for the commands of all slave-souls in its noble, silent power.
> The white of the swan and the snow triumphs
> through its own purity![32]

We note here some Nietzschean features. The eulogy to whiteness as a symbol of natural purity may recall Nietzsche's praise for absolute values that transcend the impurity of ordinary life. Such contempt for the normal would readily appeal to Wedekind, as would the parallel longing of the decadent poet for "Pierrot's time." All three ideas pertain well to Lulu, the purely natural being in conflict with a decadent society of *Sklavenseelen*. Here again, we find evidence for the view of Lulu as Nietzschean *Übermensch*. This defiant-aggressive side of her nature may seem incongruent with the traditional image of the melancholy Pierrot. Yet by the end of the century, as Giraud's verse shows, he could represent just this superior figure.

32. Quoted in Rothe, *Wedekinds Dramen,* 43. Regarding whiteness, we often find it in Symbolist visions of women, in both literature and painting. Think of Maeterlinck, Wilde, Munch, Whistler. Wolfgang Pehnt finds the concept of white central to the *fin de siècle,* since it expressed the secret desires of the era (in Thomalla, *"femme fragile,"* 47).

We have already noted the "pierrotic" lack of self-consciousness in Lulu. This trait belongs to a larger element in her nature, her intuitive arationality. She shows remarkable intuition in her recurring prophetic dream of being murdered by a sex maniac. Her foreboding shows more than clairvoyance, however; it also reveals the death wish of the *femme fatale*. Like Carmen and Salome, Lulu knows that the conventional world cannot tolerate her honesty. For all these women, a life of candid sexuality brings inevitable death. In their seductiveness we see the increasingly conscious desire to die. Eventually, the masochism of the instinctual woman makes dying welcome, as we see in the last scene of *Pandora*. Lulu tells Jack, with pointed ambiguity: "I like you so! Don't let me beg any longer!" For her, death brings release from the intolerable life of the prostitute. As Lulu already told Schön, she cannot love "on command." She prefers death to that dishonesty.[33]

The importance of dance for Lulu confirms her instinctual nature. Only in dancing can she reveal her true self; only thus can she live as a free person. Critics have tended to neglect the courage of such honesty, which Lulu demonstrates admirably at her moment of greatest danger. When the cowardly Schön demands that she shoot herself, Lulu denies that she should feel guilty for her life. "I have never sought to appear as anything other than what people took me for, and they have never taken me for something other than what I am."[34] This openness forms part of the ultimate "animal" identity of Lulu. The creature—beast or dancer—who communicates by physical means alone cannot lie. Here lies the clue to our fascination with such mute beings. Like Mignon, Carmen, and Salome, Lulu dances out the enigma of that mysterious, haunting realm beyond words. Her language of movement has a power akin to sexual expression. Hence she inspires both adoration and fear.[35]

In sum, then, this "wild beast" embodies the vitalist morality of the primi-

---

33. Wedekind, *Werke,* 3:192.

34. Ibid., 3:95. Carmen reacts the same way when José threatens to kill her. Indeed, she taunts him, displaying her death wish. In this respect, both Carmen and Lulu recall Don Juan, who prefers death to the sacrifice of his free sexuality. All say no to the figures of convention, who finally kill them. I refer to Don José, Schön, and, in Mozart's opera, the Commendatore.

35. Again, in Hofmannsthal's *Elektra* (1903), we see the enigmatic power of the dancing woman whose honesty forces her self-destruction. This figure, just as symptomatic of the *fin de siècle* as Lulu, performs a true dance of death, climaxing in both the murder of Ägisth and her own death. Comparing Elektra with other *femmes fatales,* we see that artists find the figure fascinating because of the ambiguous freedom her dance represents. Like Carmen or Elektra, the Salome of Beardsley and Moreau displays a passion for movement that symbolizes ultimate freedom. But for all these dancers, the escape from human limits brings its exact opposite, death.

tive, just the antidote needed for corrupt capitalist society. Lest we fail to see Lulu as necessary, Wedekind gives this idea to Alwa. At the beginning of *Pandora*, the playwright says that effete modern art needs contact with earthier elements. What he says goes equally well for all of European culture, according to Wedekind: "The curse of our recent literature is that we are too literary. We know only those questions and problems that arise among writers and scholars. Our point of view does not extend beyond our own peer group. In order to get back on the track of a powerful art again, we must move as much as possible among those who have never read a book, whose simplest animal instincts guide their actions."[36]

As for Lulu's supposed immorality, her power to destroy men, it is clear that men bring such revenge on themselves. Like Epimetheus in the fable of Pandora, they invite their own downfall. Indeed, their need for Lulu seems too great to resist, as if their evil values sought the catharsis of death. That rather dramatic idea may remind us of several political and social philosophers at the turn of the century. Spengler, for instance, like Novalis a century earlier, saw a willing apocalypse as the necessary stage preceding a true revolution in culture. Later on, other voices—even that of Rilke—welcomed the war in 1914 as a similar sort of purging.

We may cite yet another reason for condemning Lulu: Wedekind's rejection of the contemporary women's movement. His bitterest caricature of the suffragette appears as Bertha Launhart in *Hidalla* (1904). And Wedekind specified in letters his distaste for female political activists, thereby revealing his own illogical prejudice. After all, we see their male counterparts as outspoken heroes in most of the plays. Dagmar Lorenz removes most of the seeming paradox in this situation, for she shows that the author rejected only the "conservative" wing of the women's movement that sought political rights. Like the German Socialists, he believed that the patriarchy had to die in the private realm before women could enjoy public equality.[37] These views may remind us of those American southerners who claim that legally desegregated schools can not change deeply conditioned race bias. Wedekind, the supposed socialist, also believed that the state could not legislate morals.

Perhaps the clearest vindication of Lulu comes from the contrast afforded by one of her famous progeny: her namesake Lola-Lola in Heinrich Mann's *Professor Unrat* (1905). In her, Mann shows his admiration for Wedekind, but his *femme fatale* has inherited only the external aspects of Lulu. Far

---

36. Wedekind, *Werke*, 3:125.
37. Dagmar Lorenz, "Wedekind und die emanzipierte Frau: Eine Studie über Frauen und Sozialismus im Werke Frank Wedekinds," 39.

from being beyond good and evil, Lola symbolizes the truly immoral seductress. Deceptive and grasping, she has none of the involved concern that Lulu shows for Schigolch and Schön. Lola willfully ruins the hapless professor who, unlike Schön, has given his lover only dogged devotion. The 1930 film version, with Lola played by Marlene Dietrich, offers a virtual caricature of the complex Lulu. Her hard-won freedom takes the distorted form of cruel selfishness.[38]

Finally, we must return to Nietzsche. In Lulu we see the peril and the exemplary daring of the *Übermensch.* "I love those who can live only as the condemned, for they are the ones who cross the abyss." Lulu knows that she must live as one condemned. Yet her inevitable death points the way for us. In that exemplary sense she too "goes across" to a better life. Since such courage still seems utopian, we must hail Wedekind's vision.

König Nicolo (1902)

Almost all the critics belabor the presence of Wedekind in Nicolo and Karl Hetmann. Indeed, some see in the plays little but fictionalized catharsis for the author's professional crises. Yet the characters do have autonomous value; we need not know of the parallels between them and Wedekind to perceive the significance of the plays. Moreover, the relation between the two characters goes beyond what several critics reiterate, namely that Wedekind intended Nicolo as a pathetic self-portrait and Hetmann as a vindication for the widely misunderstood Nicolo. Going beyond this obvious layer of meaning, I see the two men as opposing examples of "the world upside-down." Again, as in the Lulu plays, Wedekind demonstrates a Nietzschean reversal of values. The king as willing jester and the prophet as unwitting clown express this inversion in opposite ways.

Although Wedekind did not write the prologue to *König Nicolo* until 1909, it sums up the basic idea of the play with admirable economy. Nicolo and his daughter, Alma, present the two masks of the play, king and jester, as universal elements found in everyone.

Nicolo. Now no laughter! You too are fools,
      As blind as I. I'll prove it to you right away. . . .

---

38. Mayer sees a more complex daughter of Lulu in Ruth, the bourgeois wife revealed as a prostitute in Harold Pinter's *The Homecoming* (*Outsiders,* 117–20).

Alma. And who are you anyway, who have assembled here?
          You all seem so different in shape, like works of art
          selected by some great artist of life.
          And yet I'll name two beings,
          which necessarily rule in you all:
          A *small* king and a *great* fool. . . .
Nicolo. So take our play as a gay picture of human dignity,
          And if it overflows with madness
          Then you may consider in true earnest
          That it depicts *essential* human dignity.[39]

One clear implication here recalls Shakespeare: "All the world's a stage." Second, the image of humanity to emerge will contain both majesty and foolishness. True human dignity unites these opposite traits. Immediately the players set the stage for a drama of constant reversals. Indeed, each turn of the plot depends on just this swing from the noble to the earthy, from high to low.

This alternating pattern characterizes the modern tragicomedy. A bare account of the plot confirms such a definition. Nicolo has lost his throne because of his dissolute habits. Banished on pain of death from Umbria, he and Alma escape from their guards and continue to live there in disguise. While working as a tailor's apprentice, Nicolo commits the crime of *Majestätsbeleidigung* (insulting royalty), which he intended only as self-criticism. Here we find the first absurd irony of being king-as-serf; a complementary comedy ensues when he is tried, imprisoned, and banished again, all for insulting himself. On release from prison, Nicolo begins a new life as an actor. But the audience takes his own tragic story as comedy, and Nicolo becomes a buffoon. Such role reversal reaches its climax when the new king, Pietro, a former butcher, weeps at the moving performance of the supposed clown. Without further ado, Nicolo finds himself the official jester at his own court.

The denouement, continuing the interplay of tragicomic masks, involves the love of Pietro's son for Alma. When Nicolo refuses to ban the marriage, Pietro banishes him yet again. This ultimate irony proves too much for Nicolo, who dies while vainly trying to assert his true identity. The court believes him mad. Finally, however, the dead Nicolo finds vindication through Alma, who confirms his claims. A shocked Pietro orders him to be secretly buried in the royal crypt so that no one can accuse Pietro of making a king his jester.

The general term *tragicomedy* suits the genre of this story. But more spe-

39. Wedekind, *Werke*, 4:105–7.

cifically, the play explores on several levels the carnival theme of an inverted world. The ritual succession of festival, containing both death and rebirth, parallels Nicolo's own fall and rise. Hence both he and the play gain a mythical dimension.[40] Here may lie an explanation for the unusual time and place chosen by Wedekind. None of his other plays take place in medieval Italy; indeed, his polemical message seems tied to contemporary Germany. In fact, the censors of the Lulu plays might have proved less troublesome if the conditions depicted did not refer so clearly to German society.

But Wedekind's intention for the setting of *Nicolo* probably had nothing to do with censorship, which he always defied. It seems more likely that he simply found the most suitable frame for his king-as-fool in what Bakhtin calls "the carnival culture" of Italy in the waning Middle Ages. Bakhtin, like Huizinga, specifies this period as climactic for the carnival spirit of order upset. And Italy recalls the pagan underpinnings of classical comedy, where Bakhtin locates the origin of carnivalization.

This mythic aspect of the play also illumines Nicolo's moral side. The three levels of death and rebirth he undergoes not only echo the ritual resurrection of ancient festival, but also force him to assume successive new identities. As a king, Nicolo was vain, selfish, and corrupt, but each new mask he must wear progressively erodes his former character. In accepting the humiliation, even the ridicule, that accompanies each new role, Nicolo demonstrates his true nobility. He readily accepts banishment, imprisonment, and serfdom, for he knows that these conditions express necessary stages in his life. Indeed, only his behavior in these roles finally establishes his actual character. He had to sink to the lowest level of humanity to truly deserve his elevated status. Nicolo recognizes the necessity of his fall early in the play. In the second scene he tells Alma, "If I could laugh at my past, who knows, my child, whether we would regain our place at the full table!"[41]

This necessary process reminds us of many figures ennobled by a fall from grace. The gospels portray Christ as preaching that one must lose his life in order to save it. Aptly enough, we associate such paradox with fools (see chapter 6). Moreover, such foolish wisdom belongs to the mythic basis of the Nietzschean reversal. Hector MacLean links Nicolo to Sophocles' Oedipus. He too loses his kingdom, lives among the poor, and finally gains insight by discovering his true identity. For Nicolo, the moment of insight arrives when he becomes the jester-king. "This is the climax of his career, the power which has grown out of humiliation. The fool, replacing the king,

40. Hector MacLean, "The King and the Fool in Wedekind's *König Nicolo*," 29.
41. Wedekind, *Werke,* 4:118.

brought freedom; the license of the fool [brought] wisdom and truth."[42]
Nicolo as jester becomes a truly noble man, for only the fool has the power
of moral recognition.

Karl Hetmann, der Zwergriese (1903)

Hetmann offers many contrasts to Nicolo. Most obviously, he never becomes an actual clown; indeed, the offer of a position as "dummer August"
prompts his suicide. Unlike Nicolo, Hetmann never abandons his assumed
role as a leader of men. He doggedly plays the Messiah until his rigidity
ruins him. To the biographical critics, this figure represents Wedekind par-
odying himself. And to be sure, the League for the Training of Beautiful
People offers the perfect parody for Wedekind's utopian eugenics. Hetmann's self-inflicted martyrdom to an absurd beauty-cult confirms his
comic identity. This "giant dwarf"—himself an absurdity—embodies the
idealist as sacrificial clown.

Long before creating Hetmann, Wedekind supplied a key concept for
understanding this character. In "Zirkusgedanken" (1887), his essay claiming the moral primacy of the circus performance, Wedekind sees in the
aerial act a symbol of idealism. The trapeze artist reminds him of the
"abstract-sublime" idealist, who adores "the naked idea." Hetmann fits
well into the professional categories of such people: lonely prophets and
would-be saints, political rebels, poets and philosophers. These people
"project their self-generated ideal directly toward heaven, in order to
admire it there as an eternal, divine revelation. . . . They make their whole
lives dependent on this projection, without any deeper tie to the real world.
They express their individuality by all kinds of leaps, twists and athletic
feats, which young people and especially women find entrancing."[43]

This description satirizes the life of Hetmann, whose tireless lecturing on
the utopian ideals of his cult draws a rapt audience. Despite his physical
ugliness, women pursue him. Naturally, the capitalists he attracts seek to
commercialize his appeal, and here lies his undoing. The circus director
Cotrelly, seeing Hetmann's actual absurdity, wants to employ him as a
clown. Unlike Nicolo, Hetmann prefers death to ridicule; he hangs himself.
The account, in "Zirkusgedanken," of the "aerial" idealists who fall recalls
Hetmann's fate.

They are so utterly obsessed with their idea that, even in the direst misery, they
feel themselves far superior to humanity. However, if a catastrophe occurs, if the
rope supporting their great mental system breaks, then everything—their belief,

42. MacLean, "The King," 32.
43. Wedekind, Werke, 9:301.

their confidence—collapses from an unmistakable blow of fate. Then no doctor of body or mind can help them. They plunge downwards from their dizzying heights and break their necks. Often this fall comes in the form of suicide.[44]

Here we have the *Übermensch* parodied. Because Hetmann rigidly clings to a doctrine without value, he must fall. Like Nietzsche's aerialist, he too loses self-confidence because of a mocking observer. But the rope-dancer falls despite his skill, due to human frailty. Hetmann falls because pride dominates his skill. His idealism proves useless when challenged, for he cannot transform it into human shape. Hetmann's "abstract-sublime" character dooms him for life in a world that requires change.

Nicolo offers the best counterimage of flexibility. He too has ideal values; indeed, he exemplifies unselfish love, sacrifice, and humility, just what Hetmann lacks. Nicolo becomes both fool and wise man, but Hetmann stays merely a freak. Comparing Hetmann to Nicolo, we find the prophet more comic than the jester, and the jester wiser than the prophet.

CARL ZUCKMAYER: *KATHARINA KNIE* (1929)

Like Wedekind, Zuckmayer lived for a time among circus people. Both authors identified with these showmen as fellow artists. But, less expectably, they also admired, even envied them. Such feelings may recall Banville and other French poets, who found in the aerialist a model of artistic skill and daring (see chapter 2). But the envy of the German writers has less to do with aesthetics than with practical life. Like Nietzsche, they see moral values in the circus performance; their artistes appear more as human beings than as performers. The problems of these people have a mainly moral dimension, which gives their stories a didactic tinge.

How, then, do Wedekind and Zuckmayer perceive the popular player? In general, they tend to glorify the independence of the artiste as superior to the established order of the bourgeoisie. For Wedekind, the honesty of animal instincts forms the core of the circus milieu. Only here can one find a ready antidote to corrupt, capitalist society. Zuckmayer focuses on the wandering life itself as a symbol of freedom. But both writers address the same social problem that characterizes their era: the integration of "outsider" values into conventional culture.

Of course, one may argue that artists have always stood outside society. At least since Roman comedy, which used only slaves as actors, the performer has represented a lowly species of humanity. Homer and Plato

44. Ibid.

doubted the morality of all artists, who necessarily court corruption in their pursuit of beauty. Accordingly, then, artists have usually struggled to liberate from its confining norms the society that opposes them. The outsider figure furnishes the means for this liberation, since "literature forever deals with exceptional cases."[45] Hence my claim of particular importance for this feature in the Modernist period may seem based on a narrow view. However, when we consider the social and political conditions surrounding writers from Nietzsche to 1933, we must grant a heightened need for their unconventional values. Imperialism, nationalism, the gross inequities of the *Glanzwelt,* sexual repression, and anti-Semitism as ideology all characterize this time as especially ripe for the reforms introduced through art.

Characteristically, Zuckmayer focuses on the problematic nature of social integration for the outsider. Like most of his titles—*Barbara Blomberg, Der Hauptmann von Köpenick, Schinderhannes—Katharina Knie* seems to offer an individual portrait. Yet in all these dramas we find the painful but necessary process of a person becoming part of a group. In this play the classically simple plot describes the heroine's journey of self-awareness, her vain attempt to substitute a landed life for the circus wagon where she was born.

In the leitmotiv "You have to know where you belong," we find two related themes: the universal human search for a true home, plus the problem of survival itself for the wandering circus. Zuckmayer makes a metaphor for the personal quest from the dilemma of Katharina, the scion of a famous circus family who craves the stability of a peasant life. However, the double burden of acute inflation and cheaper amusements threatens her troupe. Not only does their life already verge on poverty, but a future in competition with film and radio looks even worse.

Like the Naturalists, Zuckmayer cannot avoid the problem of heredity, especially in a play patriotically centered in one region. Therefore, again like the Naturalists, he focuses on the nucleus of heredity, the family. Zuckmayer chooses a family name immediately linked with the European traveling circus: Knie. Hence the audience readily associates his characters with the revered tradition of an actual family. Vater Knie, still the star of his troupe in his late sixties, represents the proud bearer of an art practiced for generations by his forebears.[46]

45. Mayer, *Outsiders,* 5.
46. The story of a venerable circus family had already captured the popular imagination of the nineteenth century. Holtei's *Die Vagabunden* (1852) went into many printings. Edmond de Goncourt's *Les Frères Zemganno* (1879) also belongs partly to this genre, for it tells much about the actual and virtual family of a wandering troupe. A recent Czech favorite is *Cirkus Humberto* (1942) by Edward Bass. Andreyev gave the subject dramatic

Knie asserts the superiority of his people when the police suspect them of stealing oats from a local farmer. "These men suspect us of theft and take advantage of us because we are wanderers and live in regular wagons, instead of your stuffy old apartments. You may say we have no honest work, but we say to hell with your honesty, which is far too meagre for us, we have our own respectability, and you can't find a speck of dust on it!"[47] This incident with the police has both ironic and tragic overtones. Ironically, Katharina herself has stolen the oats for her starving donkey. Furthermore, she has stolen them from Martin Rothacker, the farmer who has attracted her for a long time. Later she becomes his apprentice and eventually his fiancée.

The deeper tragedy, however, the unwilling recognition by Knie that Katharina must leave him, relates more centrally to the idea of the play. Naturally, he can hardly accept his daughter as a thief. Behind that fact lies the unbearable truth that his family is declining. Katharina's mother died in childbirth; Knie has not remarried; and Katharina herself seems unsuited for the profession. "She is missing something of the real artist—she lacks something inside."[48] Hence Katharina, offering a dubious future, symbolizes the extinction of her line.

The decadence that Katharina embodies parallels the general decline of her generation. The play often reminds us of the human shrinkage demanded by the economic miseries of the twenties. It shows this loss concretely in terms of the family. Not only Knie and Katharina but also Rothacker and his mother compose only half a family. Rothacker opposes Knie in the traditional manner of the suitor, placing Katharina between their two poles of wandering and stability. Yet Rothacker's mother determines his fate just as surely as Knie does Katharina's.

Neither child can break free from a life conditioned by a single powerful parent. These two Freudian pairs cannot complete a family group, despite the instinctual efforts of the young couple. Similarly, the old woman Bibbo recounts to Katharina her life of successive broken marriages. As for children, her good dozen have mostly disappeared. The only full family offered

---

form in *He Who Gets Slapped* (1915). The protagonist, He, recalls Katharina Knie: while she wants to abandon the circus for the conventional world outside, He seeks refuge there from his worldly miseries. There too, the author stresses the warmth of family feeling among the vagrants.

47. Carl Zuckmayer, *Meisterdramen*, 152. Unfortunately, my English translation cannot capture the earthy authenticity of the Rhenish dialect. Zuckmayer meant to write a *Volksstück*, a *Heimatsstück*, evoking the character of a particular locale. Even for the non-native reader, this dialect creates a comic pathos that transcends the conventional stage language of high German.

48. Ibid., 171.

in the play appears briefly in the third act. And their future seems perilous too, as the troupe can hardly afford to feed them.

In sum, then, a principal theme of this play reminds us of the subtitle of Thomas Mann's *Buddenbrooks: Verfall einer Familie* (1901). We might even compare Knie to Thomas Buddenbrook, for both men perceive the end of their noble family in their own children. Speaking compulsively of decline, both characters suffer from helpless guilt. Since they know that the time goes against them, they can only try to uphold their standards while waiting for death. However, Zuckmayer presents a hopeful resolution to the problem of family decline, for Katharina returns to the circus when her father dies. Although she had planned to marry Rothacker, her experience of Knie's death convinces her that she belongs in his place. Accordingly, the play ends as she assumes his directorial role. The hectic movement of the closing scene shows that, despite its degeneration, the circus rolls on.

Katharina. (quickly, firmly) Are all the wagons greased? Let's go! To the horses! Onward!
Julius.   Let's go, kids! (Runs off, the others follow.)
Bibbo.   (to Katharina, as if drunk with joy) We're going! We're going!
Katharina. As long as we live! (She goes to her father's wagon, while the horses begin to stamp, chains are rattling, wheels are creaking—she sits down on the threshold of the open wagon door, motions to Mario) Play!
Mario.   (jumps up next to her, curls himself at her feet, plays the harmonica.
The wagons roll across the stage.[49]

The joyous release of frustrated energy in this ending expresses the rightness of Katharina's decision. Zuckmayer shows her as conditioned by her

49. Ibid., 217. In chapter 8 I compare this ending with that of the Bergman film *The Naked Night*. There too the tragic dilemma of poor performers finds resolution in their drive to keep moving. In both the play and the film, the survival of such people depends on their ability to overcome their losses by simply going on. A similar determination pervades the last scene of Brecht's *Mutter Courage* (1940), when the heroine again saddles up. Indeed, this play shows intriguing links to *Katharina Knie*. The rolling warehouse symbolizes the opportunism of Courage herself, just as the neat circus wagon shows the self-sufficiency of Vater Knie. Although Courage is no performer, she shares the lot of all wanderers; like them, she must literally attach her life to the wagon. In both plays, the authors pose troubling questions about the morality of the vagrant life. And both authors set their action against a backdrop of dire economic need. Moreover, Brecht may have acknowledged a source here by naming Courage's daughter Kattrin. And Kattrin may have received her poignant muteness from Zuckmayer's Mario. Although this Italian player can speak, his lack of German makes him virtually speechless. He communicates mainly through mime and music. Kattrin is an actual mute, who uses her silence heroically, to save others. Both figures bear a pathos that transcends the power of speech. Such similarities in the two plays offer evidence that the plight of Germany in the twentieth century had roots in the Thirty Years War.

upbringing, as determined for the circus life. In this regard she resembles the hero of the classical *Bildungsroman,* who also follows a seemingly self-willed path that turns out to be mysteriously directed by other forces. She, like Heinrich von Ofterdingen, has left her original home to return to it on another, more conscious level of awareness. Her journey, like his, answers the question "Where are we going?" with "Always homeward." Both characters struggle for individuality but find it only among those they have abandoned. In discovering their interdependence with others, they integrate their lives into a community. However, the result of this action differs in each case. Heinrich will participate in society, whereas Katharina must remain outside it. Her identity depends on the permanent wandering dictated by circus life. For her, the Rothacker farm represents isolation; only vagrant circus people can form her family.

The determinism of wandering belongs to the oldest imagery of circus folk. In the language of Vater Knie, "You can't get a cat away from the house, and you can't get a Knie away from the wagon." Indeed, the wagon symbolizes Knie. No less than its counterpart, the tightrope, it forms the center of his life. Both symbols bespeak the instability that distinguishes life on the move from bourgeois security. And they both represent transcendence. The immaculate Knie wagon represents not only a far cry from Thomas Mann's image of "gypsies in green wagons"; it also recalls the "wandering temple" of Gwynplaine, the blessed freak in Hugo's *L'Homme qui Rit.*

Wanderers have always fascinated artists, and not only because of their identification with them. In the visual arts, we see a veritable parade of Bohemians from Callot to Picasso (see chapter 7). Since Baudelaire at least, such vagrants have received a romantic tinge in literature. In several of his poems and prose poems—"Bohémiens en Voyage," "Les Vocations"—Baudelaire evokes not only the pathos of the homeless but a special sanctity as well. In Mallarmé, Verlaine, Apollinaire, and Bergman, the wanderers acquire the transcendental aura of the Holy Family (see chapters 5 and 8). Füglister discusses comparable examples in Cervantes, Grimmelshausen, Arnim, Mörike, Gautier, Mérimée, and Pushkin. Rilke reaches a peak of identification with the wanderers in his "Fifth Duino Elegy" (1922). In them he sees all of us, who share their life of evanescence.

Despite Zuckmayer's admiration for circus folk, he gives them none of this romantic pathos. He concentrates instead on their earthiness, their toughness as survivors. Yet in Knie's case, the author cannot escape the transcendental implications of the aerialist. In his deathbed monologue, Knie relates his life to his death through the apt image of the tightrope.

I wonder if I can walk the tightrope up there. If not, I'd rather not go up at all. But I think you can do anything up there. Nothing is forbidden if you really need it. And you don't need any rope ladder either, because you are already so high up there isn't any place higher! . . . and all around nothing but heaven!—and there are the scales, and the little bear, and the lion and the goat, and the water-bearer, they all belong to the circus and to the menagerie—I've often thought, when you look up at a performance, and see someone on the high wire: he is going from star to star (he laughs lightly)—and do you know what they used to call us, five or six hundred years ago? They called us the men of heaven! Maybe they believed that we get up there more easily than other people.[50]

The aerialist as man of heaven: no figure of Faustian striving or Banvillian artistic ideals, but a popular icon. In Knie's death we see more than the extinction of a family tradition, for he represents an essential link between man and his gods. Like his ultimate forebear, Baudelaire's old clown, Knie symbolizes the decline of art in a world without transcendence. Not accidentally, Knie is a pious Catholic, who attends mass regularly. Thus we may see in him a sort of priest, a mediator between heaven and earth. Such may be the nature of any idealist, but Zuckmayer stresses the superhuman in making Knie an aerialist. Like Wedekind, Zuckmayer links literal and metaphorical heights. But whereas Hetmann falls victim to his own aerial ideals, Knie successfully tempers his morality with an earthy realism. This image of the aerialist retains much of the optimistic vitalism of Nietzsche's ropedancer.

THOMAS MANN

Throughout his career, Mann struggled to reconcile art with morality. He consistently portrays the artist as amoral at best and dangerously immoral at worst. Thus his view of art sharply opposes that of Nietzsche, Wedekind, and Zuckmayer. For them, the popular player alone embodies truth in a corrupt society; for Mann, the player shows that art depends on the falseness of illusion. Within this Platonic idea of art, Mann displays a variety of attitudes. Accordingly, his artist figures appear in several popular guises. I shall discuss the most notable of these types, focusing on the most concentrated image of the circus artiste in *Die Bekenntnisse des Hochstaplers Felix Krull* (1954).

Early Stories (1897–1903)

Starting with "Der Bajazzo" (1897), we find a principal theme treated by Zuckmayer: the disrepute of the popular player. The narrator here calls him-

50. Ibid., 206.

self "Bajazzo," the German version of Italian "pagliaccio," meaning buffoon. Despite his manifold talents in art, music, and writing, this man lacks the drive and discipline to become a practicing artist. Hence the rather free English translation of the title as "The Dilettante." One may read the story as a tribute by the young Mann to one of his powerful influences, Schopenhauer. From him Mann eagerly took the idea that for culture to flourish, will must unite with intellect. At the turn of the century, Mann perceived that these two elements had separated, leaving disillusion and inertia. His *Bajazzo* is, like Goethe's Werther and Keller's Green Henry, a failed artist. But only he of these three receives the epithet of clown. What prompted suicide for Werther has now become a laughing matter, for the artist has become a decadent figure.

For both the narrator and the author of this story, the identity of clown connotes a ludicrous inadequacy. With the label *Bajazzo,* the narrator expresses his helpless self-hatred. More essentially, however, he also reveals the deprecating view of the artist that he has inherited from his bourgeois background. Here lies the nucleus of a principal theme that Mann develops throughout his work: the irreconcilable duality between the artist's eccentricity, his "otherness," and bourgeois respectability.

Another aspect of the negative image of the artist emerges from "Das Wunderkind" (1903). The eight-year-old prodigy who gives a virtuoso performance for an adoring audience has the false glamour of the charlatan. As a complement to his "hype," the audience readily succumbs to the domination of this child. The satire verges on caricature, but it also has a deeper serious meaning. Indeed, this story anticipates the portrait of the artist as swindler in *Felix Krull.* And both the *Wunderkind* and Krull point forward to the tragic fable of corrupt power in "Mario und der Zauberer" (1929).

"Tonio Kröger" (1903)

Tonio recalls the *Bajazzo* in several ways. Their childhoods both include a doting and musical mother and a stern father, an indifferent school career, and a devotion to artistic pursuits. When the father in "Der Bajazzo" scolds his unproductive son, he speaks of clowning and jokes. The young Tonio recalls Konsul Kröger's similar disapproval and his admonition that they are no gypsies in a green wagon, but respectable people. This negative image of the wagon expresses just the opposite of its meaning in *Katharina Knie.* There the wagon summarizes the self-sufficiency of the wandering artiste; here it connotes all the defects of the vagrant. In the Mann stories, both the stodgy fathers and, surprisingly, their talented sons themselves see artists as simply clowns and gypsies. As inept, unstable outsiders, artists represent the opposite of what a bourgeois son must become.

We see how deeply Tonio has internalized this idea in his later return to his native city. Here the police detain him, for he resembles a criminal they are pursuing. Characteristically, Tonio has no identification papers, which adds to the suspicions of the officials. Finally, to satisfy their craving for printed matter, he shows them a manuscript, which settles the issue. However, during the proceedings, Tonio considers the simpler solution of just identifying himself as the scion of the famous Kröger family. Then they would realize that he is no gypsy in a green wagon. He does not do so, partly because he shares the doubts of the police about his repute. "And weren't these men of bourgeois respectability in the right? To a certain extent he agreed with them fully."[51]

Hence the artist sees himself as not only a clown and a gypsy but also an outlaw. In short, he has lost every trace of morality. This prejudice determines Tonio's identity crisis, which he cannot reconcile until the end of the story. Only his many experiences, climaxed by a relived confrontation with his youth, can free him from the duality of his nature as both artist and bourgeois.

Christian Buddenbrook (1901)

In his first major work, *Buddenbrooks,* Mann adds two new elements to this complex that forms the image of the artist: acting and sickness. Christian, the younger son, has behaved as an adept clown from the first scene of the novel onward. Indeed, the pleasure he conveys in displaying himself identifies Christian as the first actor in Mann's gallery of artists. But characteristically, this man suffers from the same lack of will that ruined his forebear, the *Bajazzo.* He too develops no career; he acts only in private, burlesque performances. Hans Rudolf Vaget calls Christian a *Komödiant,* but not in any professional sense. Instead, drawing on a dialectic proposed by Nietzsche, Vaget contrasts the parodistic Christian, the comedian, to the ambitious Thomas, the *Asket.* In this fraternal struggle lies the core of the family's decline.

Both Christian and the *Bajazzo* cannot outgrow their infantile aestheticism. Their idea of life recalls the puppet theater they loved as children. Indeed, this small-scale theater of life, where the imaginative child alone controls the action, provides the best metaphor for the protected yet playfully free world of the infantile artist. This metaphor, inspired here by

51. Thomas Mann, *Gesammelte Werke,* 9:249.

Wilhelm Meister's puppet theater—based on Goethe's own toy—recurs in many works about artists. Bergman's film *Fanny and Alexander* (1981) introduces the title character Alexander and his surroundings with an extended scene of puppet play. Bergman often draws on the puppet stage, as both reality (*The Magic Flute*, 1975) and metaphor (*From the Life of the Marionettes*, 1980). Accordingly, Bergman defines himself specifically as a child-artist. Fellini goes yet further in this vein, claiming that all artists live mainly in their infantile fantasy (see chapter 8).[52]

Christian follows the predictable fate of the dilettante. Ridiculed at home, he becomes a vagabond; he cannot work at any steady occupation; and he readily mixes with such questionable types as dancers and actresses. His many maladies point to an early death, and his hypochondria and hallucinations express the mental decline of the family. Quite the opposite type of artist, whose illness, however, also bespeaks decadence, appears in *Der Tod in Venedig*.

Two Figures of Death (1912)

Aschenbach does not fit directly into our gallery of artists who suggest the popular player. In fact, he contrasts sharply with all the characters surveyed so far, for his work succeeds famously. No one could think of Aschenbach as a clown, gypsy, outlaw, or dilettante. However, his story concerns the transformation of what he appears to be into what he actually is. And that spiritual core revealed here, that essence beneath the mask, exposes just the dubious figure that Aschenbach loathes: the artist as fraud.

Aschenbach confronts this fateful alter ego in two different guises on his trip. The first man sells him a ticket for the steamer to Venice. This Charon-figure "sat behind a table, his hat on the back of his head, a cigarette butt in the corner of his mouth. This man with a goatee had the bearing of an old-fashioned circus-director."[53] In the paragraph devoted to this seemingly minor figure, Mann stresses two dominant aspects of the man: death and histrionics. As for the former, his bony yellow fingers and his grimaces suggest a skeleton. Like several other death figures in the story, he presages Aschenbach's impending fate.

Specifically, the goatee points to the artist's satyric adventures to come. Moreover, this cashier's falseness implies all the duplicity of the Venice that

52. Another meaning for the puppet theater relates to Kleist's essay "Über das Marionet-tentheater." As I argue in the previous chapter, Kleist anticipates the narcissism of the modern artist. In Christian's "disgusting self-absorption" we see just this narcissism of the Kleistian artist (Mann, *Werke*, 1:595).

53. Mann, *Werke*, 9:470.

Aschenbach will indeed experience. "Ah, Venice! A city of irresistible attraction for the cultured, due to its history as well as its present charms." This theatrical type exudes deceit, from his melodramatic "salesman's flourishes," his "croupier's deftness," to his final pretense that business is booming. "'A pleasant trip, dear sir!' he cried, raising his arm, as if others were waiting to be served, although there was nobody."[54]

The other "artistic" figure of death appears in a climactic scene at the hotel. Now the cholera has spread so far that even the unwilling Aschenbach begins to admit to himself what is happening. A band of scruffy street minstrels, visiting the hotel, evoke the bright patina with which Venice, like Aschenbach, attempts to hide an underlying ruin. The leader of these musicians, a guitarist who also sings "a sort of baritone buffo," summarizes both the deathly aura of these infected people and their histrionic effort to mask it. Again, as with the cashier, the false appearance of well-being disguises a core of decay. And again, this deception perfectly mirrors Aschenbach's condition. But the buffoon adds a new element to the encounter with Aschenbach. He transforms the merely amusing comedy of the cashier into grotesque mockery.

Like the cashier, this player looks emaciated; he implies more intensely Aschenbach's approaching end. Indeed, his image conveys a terrible intensity in its combined illness, fraudulence, and depravity. His face, "furrowed by grimacing and debauchery," the swollen veins of his forehead, his leering mien, and his lecherous movements all add to the impression of a menacing seduction. With the phallic details of a skinny neck "with a strikingly large and naked-looking Adam's apple," Mann stresses the sexual exhibition of this performer. Finally, he resembles a devilish death's-head, with unruly red hair and brows, between which lie deep lines. These furrows suggest demonic power: "defiant, domineering, almost wild." This Harlequin truly bespeaks the etymology of the character as *hellkin*.[55]

This repulsive jester—"half pimp, half comedian, brutal and daring, dangerous and entertaining"—links sexuality and death, a key theme in the work. He also introduces the mockery of the devil into the story. When the smell of disinfectant emitted by this man overwhelms Aschenbach, he asks him if the plague has indeed arrived. Of course, the charlatan denies this obvious fact, to which Aschenbach replies, "That is good." The scene closes with a song in bawdy dialect, whose refrain consists of nothing but rhythmic laughter. This "fake, scornful laughter" releases a paroxysm of manic laughing in the audience. At this moment of truly infernal comedy, we hear

54. Ibid.
55. Ibid., 9:518.

the deathly cackle of the devil himself. Here Mann realizes his idea of the artist as "a mixture of Lucifer and clown."[56]

The object of this deadly hilarity is none other than Aschenbach, who has just gratefully accepted the lie that abets his self-willed death. More generally, the devilish laughter of this scene refers to the god-like artist who becomes a parody, a mockery of himself—in short, a clown. When this happens, Aschenbach's identity has died. As Mann explained: "The problem I had in mind particularly was that of the artist's dignity. I wanted to show something like the tragedy of greatness."[57] In this tragedy, Mann achieves a catharsis for all the fears of his previous artist figures. The *Bajazzo*, Hanno Buddenbrook, and Tonio Kröger all find a resolution here, albeit pessimistic, for their dualism as bourgeois artists. In his metamorphosis and death, Aschenbach shows that art belongs to "the abyss." Any artist pretending to respectability must eventually perish, for his life represents a lie.

Cipolla (1929)

The deceptiveness of the two figures of death in *Der Tod in Venedig* turns to blatant evil in the sinister magician of "Mario und der Zauberer." The link that Mann makes between the performing artist and dangerous power emerges from the title itself. Hypnosis, one of the most popular of "the black arts," conveys a special, personal meaning for Mann, who bore the family name of "The Magician." Accordingly, he signed many of his letters to family members with a simple "Z." for "Zauberer." Reflecting this elementary identity between Mann and his work, Peter de Mendelssohn entitled his biography of Mann *Der Zauberer.*

This story presents the performer as no mere *Zauberkünstler,* one who enchants an audience; Cipolla depends on exploiting and degrading live subjects. Accordingly, critics have tended to interpret the story as a political fable. Mann himself stresses its moral overtones. "Leaving aside the artistic aspects of the story, I should prefer to see its significance in the realm of ethics rather than politics."[58] Indeed, Cipolla is no creator in any Apollonian sense. Yet he shares enough traits with Tonio Kröger, Aschenbach, and Krull that we must consider him at least a perverted artist. Krull, after all, is an artist only in a parodic sense, yet readers usually see him as still another

56. Ibid., 9:520; Mann quoted in Hans Wysling, *Narzissmus und Illusionäre Existenzform,* 325.
57. Thomas Mann, *Briefe,* ed. Erika Mann, 123.
58. Thomas Mann, *Letters, 1889–1955,* ed. Richard Winston and Clara Winston, 186.

metamorphosis of the artist type. Mann also considered Joseph an artist, though he creates no art.

To see Cipolla's resemblance to our other artists, we need only consider his appearance and behavior. Everything about him bespeaks the charlatan, from his flamboyant costume to his easy domination of the crowd. In this latter respect we may view him as the ultimate version of Mann's first charlatan, Bibi Saccellaphyllaccas in "Das Wunderkind." Similarly, Cipolla's hunchback recalls that of a very early "artistic" man, little Herr Friedemann (1897). Likening Cipolla's hairdo to that of an old-time circus impresario, Mann repeats himself: he makes the same comparison for the cashier in *Der Tod in Venedig.* In his bizarre biographical remarks, Cipolla also introduces the shadow of Aschenbach. "My profession is demanding, and my health not the best; I suffer from a slight deformity, which prevented me from taking part in the war for the greatness of the fatherland. But with the power of my soul and my spirit *I conquer life,* which only means that *I conquer myself.* And I flatter myself that I have, with my work, aroused the respectful attention of the cultured public."[59]

My italics stress the resemblance to Aschenbach in this Nietzschean will to overcome a physical frailty. In fact, several facets of "Mario" relate it to *Der Tod in Venedig;* as Henry Hatfield suggests, we might think of the later story as "Der Tod in Venere." In both works, Mann conveys a sense of foreboding through the setting. Not coincidentally, both narratives occur in the "African heat" of Italy at high season. Such intense heat, which rots Aschenbach's strawberries and melts his cosmetics, also helps to explain the insane "Byzantinismus" of Torre di Venere and Cipolla himself. Similarly, both stories involve the unwilling but fated move of the tourists. Aschenbach originally settled on the island of Pola but felt somehow driven on to Venice. "Something within disturbed him, urged him onward, though he didn't know where."[60] Similarly, the management at the Grand Hotel in "Mario" forces the narrator and his family to move to the modest Pensione Eleonore. This hint of the great Duse, explained during Cipolla's act, reiterates the "theatrical" character of this town.

The problem of will dominates "Mario" more centrally than it does the tale of Aschenbach. His demise does result from an initial collapse of will, symbolized throughout his life by a clenched fist. But the breakdown of the Apollonian artist only initiates his crisis; it forms the premise, not the substance, of his story. In "Mario," the magician's "art" depends on his suspending the will of his subjects. Cipolla explains that their resistance has no

59. Mann, *Werke,* 9:731.
60. Ibid., 9:469.

relevance for the outcome of his card trick. "Your resistance will not change the result. Freedom exists and will exist; but freedom of will does not exist, for a will that seeks freedom reaches only the unknown. You are free to draw or not to draw. But if you draw, you will draw correctly—all the more certainly if you try to act more willfully."[61] Cipolla represents the most dangerous, dehumanizing effect that a performer can produce. Naturally, his "enchantment" appears as immorality, for Mann, the Platonist, always evaluates the experience of art in moral terms.

Felix Krull (1954)

In Krull, the artist figure who occupied Mann intermittently for most of his career, we have another *Zauberkünstler*. But Krull inverts Cipolla's demonic hypnotism, for he practices not subversion of the will but true charm. His "victims" all desire their domination by Krull, indeed to a comic degree. Some critics even contest his identity as rogue, since his public readily complies with his deceptions. Here Mann expands on a theme introduced with Cipolla: the wish of the audience for self-abandon. Krull's consummate histrionic gifts induce in those around him states ranging from passive acquiescence to ecstasy.

The trickster relates three capsule experiences at focal points in his three books. In these scenes of operetta, circus, and bullfight, he illumines the essential facets of his identity. His superior awareness contrasts with the herd reactions of the audience; one side of his own showmanship emerges in each type of entertainment. Like these performers, Krull can range from erotic arousal to a symbolic triumph of man over nature. By comparing what Krull stresses in each of these mythic events, we find not only a variety of alter egos but also a guide to his aesthetics.

Krull begins all three accounts with an extended description of setting and audience. Because of his obsession with effect, he thinks first of the reception given the artistic performance. As a born enchanter, Krull immediately notes whatever provokes a response. Since his own arts of illusion depend on *Wirkungsästhetik* (the aesthetics of effect), he naturally identifies with the tangible success of the players he sees. The audience for his first spectacle, an operetta, displays the attitude of Roger Shattuck's "banquet years" toward theater as a social event. The scene offers flirtatious chatting, heady perfumes, women fanning bosoms, all framed by "voluptuous frescoes" with "cascades of rosy nymphs." Krull devotes a long paragraph to the sensuous delights of this public display. Since churchgoing has

61. Ibid., 9:742.

provided his only experience of comparable size and grandeur, he calls the theater "a temple of pleasure." Krull echoes the disarmingly innocent irony of this phrase with his later view of the star actor as a god-like gratifier of human desires.[62]

This actor's name, Müller-Rosé, suggests both the frothy escape of the Krull family product, a cheap champagne, and the similar nature of the operetta itself. The account of the show revolves exclusively around this star; we get no idea of plot, music, or other characters. In this man's appearance, Krull stresses blatant artifice, for not even a boy of fourteen can believe in the reality of what he sees here. "All that was somehow not of this world."[63] Krull repeats the verbs *blenden* (to blind) and *entzücken* (to enchant) as the essence of this performance, which forms his aesthetics. As his first crucial experience of the theater, this chapter-long event offers Krull meager content but much style.

However, the truly determining part of this event does not occur onstage. Instead, when father and son visit the actor backstage, the young artist has a visceral confrontation with the essence of all performance: illusion. Suddenly the dapper figure of unbelievable grace becomes simply a middle-aged actor in grimy underwear. To add to the paradox, his dressing room reeks of sweat, filth, and greasy cosmetics; his dresser is just another unattractive man; and, most unbearable of all, Müller-Rosé's back is covered with active pimples. In short, the encounter fills Felix with disgust. The bubble of the rapturous performance could not have burst more explosively, for the dressing room scene continues to haunt him throughout his life.

In evaluating his impressions, Felix dwells on the relation of the actor to his public. Noting the audience's facile expressions as "silly and joyful," he expresses his disdain for "stupid self-abandon."[64] Krull shows his ultimate contempt for such people by comparing them to insects, charmed helplessly by the flame emanating from the stage. Yet the audience must know they are falling under the spell of illusion; they pay for just that deception. He concludes that both performer and viewer fulfill mutual human needs. Just as the actor wants public acclaim, so do the viewers seek his mimetic fulfillment of their deepest longings. The artist, then, despite his massive vanity, gratifies, even edifies, the rapt public. "He was able to make the crowd see in him their heart's ideal, and thereby to uplift and animate them immeasureably! . . . [A]nd if he gave them the joy of life, for which they sated him with applause, is it not a reciprocal satisfaction, a marriage of his and their desires?"[65]

62. Ibid., 8:29.
63. Ibid., 8:30.
64. Ibid., 8:32.
65. Ibid., 8:37

This rhapsodic tone recalls Wilhelm Meister's idealization of the rope-dancers. But Mann does not seriously refer to Goethe here. On the contrary, the merciless treatment of the pimply actor reveals the essential narrative pose as parody. Like Meister, the dazzled Krull claims to see in the popular player a transcendent value for the public. Yet the vocabulary in this last sentence suggesting sexual gratification—"a marriage of his and their desires"—mocks the Goethean ideal of moral edification at the theater. With these words closing the operetta chapter, Krull characterizes his view of life as sexual adventure. Here lies one of his strongest links to the phallic Hermes.

Krull devotes most of another chapter, the first in Book 3, to his next histrionic event, the Stoudebecker Circus in Paris. Some elements of this show recall the operetta: illusion appears here as virtuosity, and the audience again abandons itself in passive, stupid pleasure. And again, Krull elevates himself above them in perceiving the deception behind the spectacle. Moreover, he derives a sense of superiority from identifying with the artistes, whom he now sees as partners in the art of "tricks, devices, effects." Like them, he knows how to "milk" an audience; he too creates illusion to gain his desired ends. Krull sees himself as part of the players' profession in general, "of the profession of effects, of gratifying and enchanting people."[66]

Here we note the identical vocabulary—"delight," "enchant"—used earlier to describe Müller-Rosé's relation to *his* public. Krull now clearly sees himself as an artist of illusion. In focusing on what the show does to its audience, he identifies with the aesthetics of effect that Mann considered the worst feature of art. Moreover, Mann believed that all actors resembled Krull. "Every true player tends toward the circus, toward clowning and the jests of parody. His talent (something close to the animal, to the ape) and all else is ambition and childish awe for the ideals of the mind."[67] Krull exemplifies the amoral artist, the center of Mann's Platonic view of art as false by nature. Here, of course, in contrast to *Der Tod in Venedig*, Mann adopts a gaily ironic tone toward his con-man artist, for the *Confessions* burlesque the whole genre of the *Bildungsroman*. Specifically, Krull inverts the idealism of the hero in Goethe's *Dichtung und Wahrheit*.

The circus offers a more complex spectacle than the operetta. Characteristically, Krull first notes the physical excitement of this show. Brilliant color, constant movement, animal smells, and naked human limbs all combine in a full-blown attack on the senses. The primary psychological state of this audience stems from "the bewitching, tantalizing sensuality of the ring." To this stimulation the circus numbers add the thrill of fear, for Krull

66. Ibid., 8:210.
67. Mann quoted in Wysling, *Narzissmus*, 46.

calls the *salto mortale* the basis of them all. In combining carnal grace with utmost daring, the circus satisfies two profound needs in the public: sensuous pleasure and fright. Krull recalls Wedekind here, for the ringmaster in the prologue to *Erdgeist* invites the audience to view the show "with heady pleasure and cold horror." Krull says that the circus gratifies "by bodily attraction, which assaults the bloodthirsty crowd through exciting physical acts."[68]

The star of this show, the aerialist Andromache, introduces another new and crucial element into Krull's image of the artist. First Krull apostrophizes her consummate skill and courage, for she performs her death-defying act without a safety net. Second, her personal coolness, her sober professional air, has an equally compelling effect. In short, Krull worships her. Indeed, his awe for this goddess approaches religious fervor. But he also explains rationally why this "angel of daring" actually transcends humanity. For him, the aerialist provides more than a celestial metaphor for human ambition à la Banville or Nietzsche. Because of her sexual identity, this artiste defies any human definition. To be sure, she is a woman, as Krull observes in detail; yet her body appears androgynous. Like her name, suggesting both grandiose heroism and ambivalent sex, this body combines muscularity with boyish features. Krull interprets the double message of this body as a function of its craft. "She would have slipped . . . if this angel of daring had lowered herself as a mere woman, and would have fallen to a shameful death."[69] Andromache is superhuman, reminding us of Nietzsche's rope-dancer, the would-be *Übermensch* who falls only because *he* surrenders to the all-too-human weakness of uncertainty. Krull further specifies the super-human aura of this "girl of the air" by placing her atop his circus hierarchy. Both literally and metaphorically, Andromache stands closer to the angels than to the beasts, those at the opposite end of the scale represented by this show.

Krull views not only the androgynous aerialist but also her colleagues as not human. "What people, these artistes! Are they human at all?" It seems sentimental to include the clowns, for instance, in ordinary life. He calls them "side-splitting monsters of comedy, glittering monks of absurdity excluded from life, somersaulting hybrids of man and crazy art."[70] The "insane" profession of such people precludes them from having families, says Krull. He means by that something very like what Tonio Kröger says of the artist: he can never live as an ordinary citizen. Krull, then, sees at the

68. Mann, *Werke*, 8:202.
69. Ibid., 8:209.
70. Ibid., 8:203–4.

circus, in concentrated and ironic form, what Mann has been saying throughout his career. He transforms into sublime comedy the same dilemma that bore tragedy for Aschenbach.

As for Andromache, her androgyny relates her to many similar figures in both this and other works by Mann. Indeed, the earnest tone Krull adopts when describing her, contrasting with his usual deadpan irony, shows that Andromache raises an essential concern for Mann. Considering her ambivalent sex in its broadest meaning as duality per se, we see that she reiterates Mann's pervasive theme: the artist's split identity. Take only one comparable example from Tonio Kröger. In decrying his uncertainties to Lisaveta, he says, "Is the artist a man anyway? Ask a woman about that! I think we artists share the fate of those castrated papal singers."[71]

Krull's ambiguity reaches from the many costumes of his childhood to his paradoxical emptiness, the void behind his many masks. What Erich Heller calls his "hermetic ambivalencies" recall the constant transformations of both Krull's patron-deity, Hermes-Aphrodite, and the element named for it, mercury. Felix finds the first earthly parallel for the divine pair in a brother-sister couple who mysteriously fascinate him from a balcony. Hence they appear elevated, god-like. We get hints of Krull's bisexuality from his relations to Count Venosta and Lord Kilmarnock. Other dual beings appear in the confusing pair of Spanish women Zaza and Zouzou. And a final sexual duplicity closes the book in the outrageous exchange of Senhora Kuckuck for her daughter.

Such dualities ultimately concern what Charles Neider calls "the artist's intermediary position." This critic interprets the artist's ambivalence less broadly than I did at the end of chapter 2. Namely, he sees here a psychoanalytic clue to identity. "All that Mann has written about the artist . . . disguises a basically sexual motif: the ambivalence between masculine and feminine traits in the artist . . . more expressly stated, the artist's ambivalence between his father and his mother."[72]

Other critics see the double image that fascinates Mann as a sign of his striving for integration. Herein lies perhaps the only theme seriously proposed in *Krull,* the theory of underlying universal oneness in nature that Professor Kuckuck espouses. "The artist . . . does many things, but univer-

---

71. Ibid., 9:229.
72. Charles Neider, "The Artist as Bourgeois," in *The Stature of Thomas Mann,* ed. Charles Neider, 353. Neider claims this basic conflict for all the major artist-figures. His analyses are mostly convincing; yet he may overstate the case in calling all Mann's artists Oedipal neurotics. For a discussion of actual androgynes in Apollinaire, Cocteau, and Picasso, see my "Art and Androgyny: The Aerialist," *Studies in Twentieth Century Literature* (Summer 1989).

sality is his need, and unity his obsession. Such is the oneness ironically concealed behind the narrative disunity of the picaresque, the acquisitive and the amatory episodes of the mobile rogue."[73] Of course, the urge toward wholeness goes back to Goethe. At the beginning of this chapter, I claimed a similar link between Nietzsche's rope-dancer and the aerialists in *Wilhelm Meisters Lehrjahre*. Again, we see unity as the ultimate goal of the transcendent artist.

The last theatrical event that Krull treats, the bullfight, transcends the realm of art in its fully mythic confrontation of man and beast, civilization and nature. Krull does not directly discuss the complexities of this spectacle, for he focuses mainly on the artful dynamics of the performance. Surprisingly, he does not identify with the masterful bullfighter; Krull admires the acts described, but he remains objective. His preoccupation with Senhora Kuckuck's heaving bosom distracts both him and the reader. In any case, Krull does not see the bullfighter as the kind of artist represented by either Müller-Rosé or Andromache.

The bullfight differs from the previous two shows in many respects. First, as usual, Krull observes the crowd. This one gathers from afar in the streets around the arena. They clearly differ from the theater or circus audience. These people, despite the dense traffic they must negotiate, behave with a sober dignity befitting their national rite. Krull contrasts their serious, even reverent, mood to "that nasty herd-like mood of the crowd at vulgar sporting events."[74] Naturally, the restraint of this quasi-religious drama evokes the elitist in Krull, not the illusionist who loved the pretense of the previous shows. Indeed, the ardent sobriety of the bullfight reveals some paradox in a logical comparison with that other arena spectacle, the circus. Although the bullring offers far bloodier sights, it does not stimulate the raucous self-abandon of the circus audience. On the contrary, the bullfight, despite its savagery, resembles a church ritual in all its grave ceremony.

Yet we might expect the folkloric expression of the Spanish festival to produce some hilarity. Consider, for instance, the wild crowds, unbearable to Goethe in his account of the comparable folk celebration, the Roman Carnival. As we saw in the previous chapter, that spectacle creates "a modern Saturnalia, ending in general delirium." The difference between the Carnival and the bullfight lies in their origins in different stages of one religious myth, the death and resurrection of the god. Whereas the Carnival celebrates the reawakening of spring that results from the sacrifice of the

---

73. Robert Heilman, "Variations on Picareque," in *Thomas Mann: A Collection of Critical Essays*, ed. Henry Hatfield, 151.
74. Mann, *Werke*, 8:402.

deity, the bullfight enshrines that ritual death itself. As Kuckuck explains, the slaughter of an animal created a fertility rite, meant to appease the gods and bring a bountiful harvest. Hence the sacrificial death of the beast ultimately preserved mankind. This sacred act survives only in the bullfight.

The linking of the three spectacles in *Krull* suggests a wealth of comparisons among them. On one level, they constitute a progression backward in time, from the most trivial, decadent amusement to the most primal, symbolic mimesis. The circus occupies a middle ground: it exhibits the human skill that elevates man above the animals while it also gives a mutual wish-fulfillment to actor and audience. In short, the circus has both primitive and decadent faces. Despite all its false glitter, it still contains an image of truly heroic achievement in Andromache. She embodies what Wedekind calls the "abstract- sublime" part of the show; for Krull she is simply superhuman. The operetta, on the other hand, is all lies, whereas the bullfight is all skill, grace, and daring. In contrast to these two pure forms, the circus displays a heady mixture, which may help to account for its universal and durable appeal. Of the three shows, only the bullfight has a moral dimension. Hence the sobriety of its mood and hence the inability of the amoral Krull to identify with it.

The bullfight and the animal act at the circus may offer the most fruitful comparison among these performances. Krull does not speculate on the fact that both shows juxtapose man and beast as performers. Both also render an essential drama of power. Man always tames the beast, so both spectacles confirm the widespread belief that civilization will survive. Does the bullfight simply dramatize more violently the same myth that the circus stages? I think not, for the bullfighter kills the bull within him, whereas the circus performer keeps alive the inner beast. The circus exploits animals to remind the public of its own animality; the bullfight destroys the bull to save mankind.[75]

Finally, all three spectacles dispense with speech. Even at the operetta, music accompanies the sung words, which stylize rather than reproduce natural discourse. Both the circus artiste and the matador perform without words. Such forms of theater that go beyond language appeal directly to

75. For a suggestive commentary on the bullfight as distinct from the circus, see Michel Leiris. "I am a fervent admirer of bullfights, for more than at the theater—and even more than at the circus, where everything is lessened by being identically repeated, anticipated and stereotyped each evening, whatever the danger—I have the impression of watching something real: a ritual death, a *sacrifice* more valid than any strictly religious sacrifice, because here the sacrificer is constantly threatened with death, and with a bodily catastrophe—being caught on the horns—instead of the magical, i.e. fictional disaster which threatens anyone entering into too abrupt a contact with the supernatural" (*Manhood,* 64).

Krull, whose own essential art also transcends the verbal. Already in the scene backstage with Müller-Rosé, Felix notes that sense impressions effect him far more potently than words do. He has hardly listened to the conversation between the actor and his father, since his disgust for the scene has overpowered his perceptions. "For what we apprehend through the senses is much stronger than what we perceive through words."[76]

Later on, Felix acknowledges that his own true medium lies beyond speech. "My element is not verbal communication; my deeper interest lies in those ultimate, silent regions of human contact; . . . where the most profound meeting, trust and union recreate the mute condition of original mankind to perfection."[77] Although Krull speaks in an erotic context, we may take his remarks as characteristic of his general need to go beyond the rational plane of life. Hence the legitimate stage holds no appeal for him. Only movement and gesture, the mysterious language of the body, make possible that ultimate communion he seeks.

In this will to transcendence, we note again the link to Hermes, who served as mediator between men and the gods. Krull too becomes a kind of god, although he never fully sheds his simultaneous identity as rogue. Interpreting the several levels of this character, Robert Heilman makes an analogy between "picaro-victim . . . artist-audience . . . and deity-mankind." Indeed, those responding to Krull need "to show faith, to yield belief," which bespeaks "a debased religious feeling." "One would expect con men to flourish in skeptical ages."[78] So Felix, the magnificent fraud, has a divine aspect too. In ending his career with this divine artist of deceit, Mann mitigates his persistent attack on the immorality of art. Here lies an ultimate tie to Nietzsche, whose rope-dancer symbolizes the moral uplifting of man through art. Mann could never find such truly ideal values in the artist; yet he approaches a positive Nietzschean aesthetics in the transcendent laughter of *Felix Krull*.

BÖLL: *ANSICHTEN EINES CLOWNS (THE CLOWN)* (1963)

Between the sublime wit of Krull and the decadent pathos of Hans Schnier lies a notable cleft. Indeed, one may see little to connect these two books: Böll treats *Vergangenheitsbewältigung* (overcoming the past) through the eyes of a failing but virtuous mime; Mann ignores actual politics to explore

76. Mann, *Werke*, 8:35.
77. Ibid., 8:92–93.
78. Heilman, "Variations," 53.

the artist as successful rogue.[79] But these two works do relate through that very morality that Krull eschews, for Schnier is the last moral man in a corrupt society. Mann gives us total irony, whereas Böll, despite his keen humor, has the deeply moral earnestness of Nietzsche himself. Schnier represents the only rope-dancer we have left—lame, to be sure, yet still performing inwardly.

Several traits link this clown with Oskar Matzerath: childlikeness, withdrawal, failure, an ironic laughter masking despair. Moreover, their stories emerge from an absurdly tragic world of Nietzschean reversals. Yet Schnier's insistent morality distinguishes him from the amoral Oskar. Indeed, since the clown appears only four years after the dwarf, he may represent an anti-Oskar: Böll's reply to Grass. Böll presents *Vergangenheitsbewältigung* through a traditional fool figure, the only good man in an evil world. Oskar has far more complexity. Accordingly, Böll creates pathos, which Grass rigorously eschews.

We cannot help liking Schnier, but Oskar eludes our sympathy. Schnier is above all an artist, Oskar above all a parodist. Schnier has a specific, credible clown character, based on the *Commedia* Pierrot, the loser in love. Oskar contains such a wealth of figures—historical, fictional, and mythic—that we cannot believe in his reality. Böll usually satirizes with gentle resignation, while Grass often pillories his victims. As for the history they document, Schnier makes a clear protest; Oskar mixes his defiance with other motives. Ultimately the two books treat their similar topic in sharply different ways. The epically expansive canvas of *Die Blechtrommel* contrasts with the modest "views" of the mime. In short, Grass inflates, Böll deflates.

In the first sentence of the book, Schnier appears as a problematic performer in the sense of Kleist. "It was dark already when I arrived in Bonn, I

79. Of course, Mann implies much about the inflated theatricality of the Wilhelminian era in *Krull*. Naturally, a creature like Krull could exist only in a climate decadent enough to stress the facade rather than the substance of life. Compare, for instance, the *Schauspielerei* of the virtuoso writer-narrator in "Ein Eisenbahnunglück" (1908). "One appears, one shows himself to the jubilant crowd; not for nothing is one a subject of Wilhelm II" (Mann, *Werke*, 9:426). See Walter Sokel, "Demaskierung und Untergang wilhelminischer Repräsentanz," in *Herkommen und Erneuerung,* ed. Gerald Gillespie. Like his actual forebear, the swindler Georges Manolescu (born 1871), Krull expresses the hollowness of his time. Yet Mann does not deal overtly with this historical situation; he considered the book "very pre-war and pre-political." In 1916, at least, he hoped that its "supra-political" tone would endear it to the public (Wysling, *Narzissmus,* 41). That he contradicted himself a month later, stressing the "socio-political meaning" of Krull, shows that he too saw the implicit layer beneath the surface. "At that time he was obviously somewhat confused about his work" (ibid.). In any case, Mann does not directly present the German past as a crucial problem, while Böll does just that.

forced myself not to yield to the *mechanical movements* that have developed in the course of traveling for five years."[80] Specifically, Schnier is talking about the resigned automatism that has overtaken him, especially since his lover, Marie, left him. But on a deeper level, he also shows the content as well as the style of his life as pantomime. Because of his endemic conflict with the hypocrisy of all the elements in the society around him, the mime can only "act out" his existence. Critics often call his plight existential, for he says "I am a clown, and I collect moments."[81] Not only on stage does Schnier fragment universal human images; but his own life also does not cohere.

In the detailed depiction of arrival that follows the first sentence, quoted above, Schnier recalls his own piece, "Arrival and Departure." There the audience consistently confuses the two subjects, whereas in this actual arrival the mime confuses hotel and train station. The first comedy in the book arises from his asking at the ticket window for his room number and trying to give his train ticket to the hotel porter. Here we think of Bergson, who defines the comic as "something mechanical encrusted on the living."

Hence the first paragraph relates Schnier to two statements, by Kleist and Bergson, of the paradox of human automatism. This first paragraph contains one further, biographical clue to Schnier's impossible ambivalence: his straddling of the Protestant and the Catholic. Though he was born Protestant, his confused parents have nonetheless sent him to a Catholic school. So his theological disputes with the Catholic Marie go back to a basic personal conflict.

Another allusion in this first chapter confirms our image of Schnier as a Kleistian artist. Having recently turned to drink as a consolation for the loss of Marie, he describes the perils of alcohol as disastrous for a clown. When drunk, he loses the very basis of his work—precision—and laughs at himself. In this moment of "desperate coldness", Schnier stiffens into a marionette. The crisis comes when the metaphorical thread breaks and he falls. Such a calamity has just occurred, for he fell last night during a Chaplin act and injured his knee. Characteristically, Schnier still tries to imitate Chaplin, the greatest mime in our era. He still strives for his highest ideal, though he knows he is falling.

This knee damage has deep import. The clown can not only no longer move onstage in the literal sense, but he has also lost grace in the Kleistian metaphor. Of course, he has already lost the grace of Marie's love, but now his art deserts him too. And now, just as Kleist's dancer is fully aware of his

---

80. Heinrich Böll, *Ansichten eines Clowns,* 11, italics mine.
81. Ibid., 294.

movements, so must Schnier fully recognize his fallen condition. He criticizes the "Catholic" need for total awareness of even the simplest pleasures, such as drinking wine. Hans tends to equate innocence with goodness. Hence his own new consciousness threatens his virtue.

Schnier shows his self-awareness by referring, in this first chapter, to the gutter where he eventually ends up. "I thought of the gutter where I would lie someday. For a clown nearing fifty, there are only two possibilities: the gutter or the castle. I didn't believe in the castle."[82] In this portentous fall, Böll links physical and theological grace, just as Kleist does. Thus the Kleistian aspect of this clown goes deeper than his personal pantomime of an inauthentic life.

The injured knee worsens overnight, and Schnier must cancel his tour. Here starts the plot: because of this injury, he returns to Bonn and experiences the four hours of conversations, memories, and introspection that compose the novel. However, the swollen knee has more essential, even "existential," meaning for Hans, since it ends his life as a puppet. What critics find in Kleist's puppet-like characters—the Marquise of O., Alkmene, Kohlhaas—we also see in Schnier. Like these characters, he also has

the unshakable self-assurance and inner certainty that is the mark of innocence. As in Kleist, the primary conflict in Böll's world is that between innocence and worldly crookedness, between the purity of the simple, natural soul and the envious arrogance of the twisted careerist. But, whereas in Kleist innocence and justice win the battle in the end and force the world to acknowledge them, the contemporary author makes a distinction between the obvious physical victory that goes to the wicked and false, and an intangible, ill-definable spiritual or moral victory that the just obtain for themselves.[83]

At this point we may relate Schnier beyond Kleist to Nietzsche. Böll has specified Kleist as a strong early influence, but not the more problematic Nietzsche. However, Schnier's primary moral demands, which have nothing to do with Kleist's puppet, hark back to Zarathustra. Therefore Nietzsche, although less visible in the text than Kleist, has equal importance for our understanding of the clown.[84]

82. Ibid., 17.

83. Walter Sokel, "Perspective and Dualism in the Novels of Böll," in *The Contemporary Novel in German*, ed. Robert Heitner, 34.

84. See Bernd Balzer, ed., *Heinrich Böll: Werke, Interviews I (1965–1978)*; Viktor Böll and Renate Matthei, eds., *Querschnitte*. Critics have already discussed the other clear references to Kleist in the novel; see especially Ralf Nicolai, "Die Marionette als Interpretationsansatz zu Bölls *Ansichten eines Clowns*," and Manfred Durzak, "Über das Marionettentheater von Heinrich von Kleist," *Jahrbuch des Freien Deutschen Hochstifts*. The

As the book develops, we see how closely the mime profession relates to the ethical stance of protest. Hans does not just happen to become a clown; his work arises naturally from his plight as outcast. Ever since his sister's needless death, provoked by his opportunistic parents, Hans has felt driven to closely observe and dramatize the myriad ills of his world. Thus caricature provides his sole means of dealing with the reality he perceives.

But Schnier does more than pillory the powers that be; his real forte lies in rendering everyday life. His "Representing of Daily Absurdities" shows his love for ordinary people, his respect for the human condition. Schnier puts into the best part of his mime all the compassion he misses in society. Like Böll's work, the clown's art has much warmth and humor.

More than most artists, the mime builds his art from observed reality. Naturally, his acute memory must preserve details, which his technique then renders for the public. Schnier tends to equate human sensitivity with this sense for detail, which he finds lacking in Catholics. One thinks of the famous remark, attributed to both Flaubert and Fontane, that God lives in the details. Schnier's attention to small things makes his mime an art of fragments. He excels at evoking moments, but he cannot capture the whole. "My pieces Dancing Couple and Going to School, Going Home were at least artistically passable. But when I tried The Life of Man, I fell into caricature again."[85] Hans cannot make connections in his art because he has found none in his life.

Characteristically, the details of Marie's body mean everything to Hans, yet he has never succeeded in making that deeper mental contact with her that might have created a lasting union. He thinks of her hands, her hair, her breasts; he poignantly recalls her natural way of screwing on the top to the toothpaste tube. Yet her thoughts that he remembers concern only their disputes. This attitude prompts a feminist reading of the book by Evelyn Beck, who oversimplifies Schnier's subjectivity. (She also needlessly attacks Böll.) In particular, Beck distorts Hans's loving attention to the moment with the toothpaste top into "seemingly obsessive voyeurism." On the contrary, I see him as haunted by that movement for two reasons that have nothing to do with the voyeur. First, the personalizing gesture fascinates the mime, and second, he simply loves the physical being of Marie.

Yet Schnier alone is not to blame for his fragmentary relations to others. Both his family and the larger social group it represents have cruelly re-

---

only hint of Kleist that commentators have ignored is the moment when Schnier plays blind to annoy his father. As Ilse Graham, *Heinrich von Kleist,* stresses, the symbolism of "their eyes being opened" in Genesis plays a major role for Kleist. As for the link of Kleist's essay to Nietzsche, see Hanna Hellman, "Über das Marionettentheater," in *Kleists Aufsatz über das Marionettentheater,* ed. Helmut Sembdner, 30.

85. Böll, *Ansichten,* 123.

jected his need for community. And Marie, victim of all the hypocrisies of the Church, has left him. Hans craves unity no less than Felix Krull does. Both types of modern artist bespeak that longing for wholeness that we have traced beyond Nietzsche to Goethe. As Peter Gay shows, "the hunger for wholeness" continues well into the twentieth century.

Schnier as an artist of fragments relates closely to the child. In his awareness of the small, the clown develops a gift for the childlike. "The lyrical side of childhood I do very well: for a child even banality has grandeur, it is strange, disordered, always tragic."[86] Hans feels an instinctual tie to the imagination of the child, for he too lives much of his life in fantasy. Here indeed, say Freud and others, lie the roots of all artistry, in the free psyche of the child who survives in the creative adult. Moreover, Hans understands the attitude of the child because he still feels like one himself. Essentially he functions as an innocent within a depraved adult world. His art grows from both these links to childhood: fantasy and isolation. He stands outside society in a double sense, as an infantile artist.

In this respect, some critics call Schnier adolescent. By this term they criticize his tendency to passively decry current conditions without acting to change them. This view usually depends on a perceived link to Holden Caulfield in J. D. Salinger's *The Catcher in the Rye*, which Böll himself translated in 1962. Indeed, Schnier shows the Holden-like infantile traits of compulsive complaint, subjectivity, and self-pity. Yet, as with many artists, such unpleasant habits complement the vivid imagination that engenders art. Holden, though displaying a brilliant verbal wit, is no practicing artist. And one doubts that he will ever attain the discipline that Hans has mastered in perfecting his art.

We perceive another childlike side of Hans through his narrative style. He recounts the events of his life through subjective first-person recollections, so that past and present often intermingle. Without clear causal links, this narrative bears the intensity and directness typical of children. Yet the supremely self-conscious tone of the satire counteracts any general impression of innocence. Naturally, Hans most resembles a child in talking with his father, the only person from his past to appear in the book. Their conversation, occupying the longest chapter, reveals most of the sources of Hans' condition as outsider. Father and son relate here as power does to purity. Schnier implies this relation in the first chapter, when he says he will end in either the gutter or the palace. Later on, he specifies his role as court jester. "In the thirteenth century I would have been a nice court jester, and not even the cardinals would have cared if I were married to Marie or not."[87]

86. Ibid., 124.
87. Ibid., 115.

Schnier plays the role of the naysayer, the figure of protest at the center of power. Accordingly, his father represents the king of that court built on the *Wirtschaftswunder*. Hans, the only one who perceives the rottenness of that society, strikes a Hamletic pose of despair masked by laughter. He has managed to function within that world he loathes because he has become the jester that Hamlet only identifies with in Yorick. Like Oskar Matzerath, Schnier as modern Hamlet rebels against the court by impersonating his alter ego, the Fool. Schnier fits particularly well into the tradition of the court jester discussed above in chapter 2.[88]

Blanche, Triboulet's daughter in *Le Roi S'Amuse*, initiates the jester's enmity for the duke; so does Marie provide a fulcrum in Hans' opposition to his father/society. We see a similar triangle of ruler-republican-woman in Lessing's *Emilia Galotti* (1772), in which the virtuous father confronts the tyrant through the same seduction motif that activates the plot in Hugo. The man of the people in Schiller's *Kabale und Liebe* (1784) is a musician, just one step away from a court entertainer. In John Osborne's play *The Entertainer* (1957), the decadent life of Archie Rice represents a protest against the patriarchal, Edwardian world of his father. Here the daughter again forms a fulcrum, for Jean tries in vain to rescue Archie from his inevitable decline, just as Marie tries to save Schnier.[89]

Osborne's play presents other parallels to Schnier. As with Hans, Archie's talent is declining, the public deserts him, and self-pity drives him to drink. Professionally, both men recall the classic decadent entertainer, Baudelaire's old clown, whose audience now ignores him. In Chaplin's *Limelight* (1952), Calvero also exemplifies the man in decline. But his plight, like that of the *saltimbanque,* stems from aging and the consequent disdain of the public. Archie compounds that inevitable problem with alcohol and cruelty to all those around him.

---

88. Nietzsche defines the court jester as extraordinary in his inability to compromise the truth to suit his hearer. In "Wem ein Hofnarr nötig ist" ("He who needs a court jester"), he says the very beautiful, the very good, and the very powerful can learn the truth only from their jester: "a being with the privilege of a madman, not being able to adapt himself" (*Werke: Morgenröte*, ed. Alfred Baeumler, 265). Elsewhere, Nietzsche deprecates the fool as a liar. "Mere fool! Mere poet! mouthing only pretty things / intoning behind your fool's mask / climbing around on liar's verbal bridges / on rainbows of lies / between false heavens / roaming around, creeping about— / you mere fool! mere poet! You—the suitor of truth?" (*Der Fall Wagner*, vol. 8 of *Nietzsches Werke*, 410.)

89. Theodore Ziolkowski discusses the other triangle involving Schnier as Pierrot, Marie as Columbine, and Züpfner, Marie's husband, as Harlequin. In "Vom Verrückten zum Clown," Ziolkowski plausibly identifies the other personnel in the novel with similar types in the *Commedia*. Sommerwild and Kinkel resemble the old doctor and Pulcinella; Schnier Senior plays the domineering Pantalone (Marcel Reich-Ranicki, ed., *In Sachen Böll*, 3d ed. [1970], 353).

Schnier, at twenty-seven, is not aging, and he treats others with compassion. Indeed, he differs basically from Archie, who displays all the vices commonly linked with show people. As a con man, Archie resembles Felix Krull, yet his consistent failure makes him less amusing than pathetic. However, despite such differences, both Archie and Schnier represent the protest of the lonely comedian against social decay. Here lies a major theme for Osborne: the isolated man, alienated from others by a crass consumer society. One could formulate the essential Böll similarly, with the addition of the German past as a determinant of present ills.

Moreover, both Osborne and Böll symbolize social degeneration in the clown's enmity for his father. Billy Rice opposes his son more clearly than the elder Schnier does Hans, for Billy is a professional rival. Archie eventually kills his father by trying to exploit his former stage fame for a comeback. When Billy dies in the wings, the jester has destroyed the symbol of that old world he hates. Schnier remains untainted by the corruption around him, but Archie cannot do so. He partakes of the same hypocrisy that has formed his society; he is both product and victim of imperial England. Osborne uses Billy's death, representing the Edwardian music-hall tradition, as a metaphor for the decay of Britain, reflected in the Suez crisis. So this work also deals with *Vergangenheitsbewältigung*.

Both Osborne and Böll point to family decline as the root of the clown's problem. Osborne renders the mutual alienation of three generations. The three Schnier children have either died or isolated themselves because of their parents' callousness. The other son, Leo, scorns parental expectations just as clearly as Hans does, for he becomes a monk. Indeed, he has sequestered himself completely; Hans at least stays close to people through his work.

Böll starts to compare the brothers when a child equates them. In search of Marie, Hans calls Kinkel, a friend of hers, and the son answering the telephone asks who is calling: Schnier the theologian or Schnier the clown? This charming question sums up a key idea in the book: the double character of Hans as both clown and Christian. Like Böll, Schnier mitigates his biting satire with compassion. Accordingly, he disdains the rich and favors the poor, for he practices a populist brand of Christianity. Theodore Ziolkowski speaks of Böll's "anarchic-Christian humanism," which suits Schnier also.[90] Wilfried van der Will coins a similar term for this clown: "the worldly saint."

The comparison to the officially virtuous brother culminates in a long-

90. Theodore Ziolkowski, "The Author as Advocatus Dei in Heinrich Böll's *Group Portrait with Lady*," 7.

awaited and disillusioning talk on the telephone. Leo says he will give Hans money, but his slavish obedience to monastic regulations prevents his coming now, when his brother desperately needs "the presence of a human being." The bitter failure of this conversation, the last in the book, signifies ultimate despair for Hans; even his own "Christian" brother will not help him.

The telephone that conveys this crucial message forms both the chief narrative vehicle and the primary symbol in the book. Hans communicates tellingly with a rich variety of people, but only through mechanical means. The telephone symbolizes his isolation, his interiority. Characteristically, he must rely on an instrument to make contact with others, just as he depends on his body to silently communicate his art. In this reliance on the telephone, we might compare Schnier to K. in Kafka's *The Castle,* who also thinks he may save himself by speaking with the sources of power. K. too seeks the grace that Schnier craves in the shape of Marie; K. knows only that his grace lies inside the castle of God. And both men have trouble making contact through their telephones. K. gets only faulty, garbled reception, so he cannot grasp the message. Schnier can hear perfectly well, but he finds meagre understanding on the other end of the line. Finally, Schnier stops trying to reach the castle, represented by the powerful church people he talks to. Indeed, he does not court their favor at all. K., by contrast, desperately seeks to ingratiate himself up above. Schnier simply rejects the impenetrable bastion as evil.

Böll often underlines the moral superiority of Hans, who sees himself as the most suffering martyr in an evil world. Right away, in fact, the epigraph from Romans 15:21 links the lowly clown with the highest blessing. "To whom he was not spoken of, they shall see: and they that have not heard shall understand." Characteristically, Böll later puts these same words into the mouth of a fool at the monastery. This man, who has fallen from grace into the job of receptionist, serves as surrogate brother and alter ego for the fallen Hans. Their hilarious talk ends with the citation from Romans, which we may now see as the most revered literary legitimizing of Nietzschean reversal.

Here lies an essential message of the novel: Böll's final reckoning with the moral absurdity of his country. Twenty years after committing the greatest evil in history, the Germans are prospering as never before. In both biblical and Nietzschean terms, we have the reversal of all values. What better way to "hold up the mirror to nature" than through the eyes of the only pure one, the Fool?

Wolf Lepenies finds in all literature the expression of the fool. "Whether we speak of the jester or the poet, it makes no difference: the fool-function ('Narrenfunktion') of literature stands beyond doubt." Judging by its context, this pregnant sentence refers to the diversion from boredom that the fool provides. However, I see that aim as only superficial; ultimately, the clown plays a political role. Think of Bakhtin, who finds in all carnival forms the essence of parody (see chapter 6). For what is parody, if not the mocking of the dominant order? Albert Bermel speaks of the "equalizing impulses" of comedy. As we have seen, most works featuring jesters have reformist tendencies. Thus such comedians belong to the literature of protest. Triboulet and Rigoletto, Fancioulle, Fantasio and Valerio, Ubu Roi, Schnier, Archie Rice, Oskar Matzerath: all present aspects of the histrionic attack on power. Grass specifies the futility of this attack in the present age, when writers no longer deign to exist as jesters. "Fools have a relation to power, writers seldom do."[91]

In the motif of holding the mirror up to nature, Schnier partakes of another Fool tradition, that of Till Eulenspiegel. This complex figure incorporates aspects of the blasphemous Harlequin that anticipate Faust and Don Juan. In medieval German chapbooks, Till maintains a steady rebellion against all sources of authority. His name indicates his habit of portraying, through mimicry, the follies of mankind. The war of comic pranks, practiced by Till on almost everyone inside respectable society, often brings him close to the gallows; yet his beloved Nell always saves him. Schnier relates to Till not only in his pose as protesting outsider but also in his populism. Like Till, Hans sides with the poor against the powerful. The hero of the *Volksbuch* provides another alter ego for the mime whose art reveres ordinary people.

We have another modern Till, not yet noted as relevant to Schnier, in the hero of Gerhart Hauptmann's verse epic *Till Eulenspiegel* (1927). Like Hans, this angry man protests against postwar conditions in Germany. He also tours the land with shows for the people, and he too subsists on meager reward. However, this Till practices a more direct satire than Hans does, for his entire "act" consists of holding a mirror before the faces of his astonished public. By contrast, Hans gleans only private meaning from his mirror. He uses it mainly for facial exercises, but confronting his face causes such anxiety that he must immediately run to Marie to see himself in her eyes.[92]

91. Wolf Lepenies, *Melancholie und Gesellschaft,* 95; Albert Bermel, *Farce,* 45; Günter Grass, "Vom mangelnden Selbstvertrauen schreibender Hofnarren unter Berücksichtigung nicht vorhandener Höfe, " 194. Stuart Evans claims that rulers are now their own fools. "Today's caesars / Spell out their own acrostic of doom, . . . / . . . and each tyrant is a temperer / Of public mood, each hierophant is a crowd-pleaser, / Each soothsayer monitors himself. Who needs the fool? / Take away the fool and let the senile sages drool / Over their moral porridge in the clinics of the emperor" (*The Function of the Fool,* 77).

92. Böll, *Ansichten,* 175.

Hans often refers to his monkish nature, which goes beyond monogamy. Among his many complaints he lists melancholy, which he associates with mysticism. Melancholy, defined by Jürgen Vogt as grieving memory, relates Schnier again, ironically, to the jester: this man combats melancholy. Lepenies claims that the capitalist age has foisted the ruler's sorrows onto the jester; lacking an audience, the Fool must now divert himself.

Hans adds the marionette to this melancholic self-image as both monk and clown. Indeed, recounting his drunken performance as mechanical, he immediately thinks of a mystical condition. "I made myself into a marionette; and it was bad when the string broke and I fell. Monks must go through a similar state in contemplation; Marie used to carry around a lot of mystical literature, and I remember that the words 'empty' and 'nothing' occurred often there."[93] This link of the mystic with the marionette suggests the silence of mime that gives Hans his identity. Moreover, the image of the mystical performer goes back to Villon. The medieval Tombeur de Notre Dame, perhaps the first sacred clown, is precisely the monk-jester that Schnier fancies himself.

Hans reiterates the blasphemous link of Christ and Fool in imagining the pope as Harlequin. "I decided to go to Rome too, and request an audience with the Pope. He had something of the wise old clown about him, and anyway Harlequin came from Bergamo."[94] The pope as Harlequin: that image may ironically express the guiding idea of this chapter. Not by accident did the *Commedia* figures spring from hallowed ground. The comedian, according to all the writers discussed here, belongs to the extraordinary realm of the spirit. Whether he symbolizes heroic aspiration or its opposite, the nihilist laughter of Mann's buffoons, the player evokes a heightened awareness of life. Nietzsche puts both of these possible poles into *Zarathustra,* which develops from the double idea of the rope-dancer combined with his jester. Idealism, it seems, cannot survive without the complementary pull of sobering reality. Accordingly, the performers viewed here range, as Böll might say, from the pope to Harlequin. Such antic personnel renders transcendent images of the human condition.

93. Ibid., 13.
94. Ibid., 218.

One can't confuse these street players with actors. Their spectator must be pious, for they celebrate silent rites with a difficult agility.

—Apollinaire, on *Les Saltimbanques*

The idea of the artiste as a transcendent figure belonging to another realm does not emerge from the German tradition only. Indeed, we may trace this image to ancient acrobatic fertility rites. In this synchronic chapter I shall explore the myth of the extraordinary player as three major modern artists distill it into one poignant symbol: the boy *saltimbanque*. Naturally, many of the themes treated in historical sequence above—isolation, commercialism, silence, the infantile—recur in these works. So the triptych I propose, two poems bridged by a painting, sums up a tradition (see figure 3).

Rilke absorbed not only Picasso's *Les Saltimbanques* (1905) in his fifth *Duino Elegy* (1922) but also the broader imagery of the European street show. So did Apollinaire, whose "Un Fantôme de Nuées" ("A Phantom of Clouds") (1911) refers clearly to Banville, Baudelaire, and Mallarmé. Less obviously, the other players of Gautier, Hugo, the Goncourts, and Laforgue also helped to shape these writers' images of the *saltimbanque*. As for the painting itself, it deeply touched both poets. Rilke lived with it in 1915, and Apollinaire reviewed it lovingly in 1905.[1] Picasso himself, whose images haunt our consciousness, reflects perhaps the broadest scope of forebears. He does not consciously point to Villon, nor to Kleist's marionettes, nor to Nietzsche's rope-dancer; yet they all nourish his painting.[2]

TWO POEMS: MYTHIC IMAGES

To my knowledge, no one has yet discussed the close resemblances between Rilke's elegy and Apollinaire's poem. Only three critics treat Apollinaire's work in detail: Ingrid Schleifenbaum, in her study of the *Ondes*

---

1. See L. C. Breunig, ed., *Apollinaire on Art,* trans. Susan Suleiman, 13–16. For more of Apollinaire's critical and lyrical response to Picasso, see the calligram "Pablo Picasso" in *Il y a* (1925).

2. In chapter 7 I show that Picasso consciously refers to Manet, Velasquez, the Le Nain brothers, and Watteau. These painters create an imagery of wanderers/players that parallels the literary tradition of the transcendent artiste.

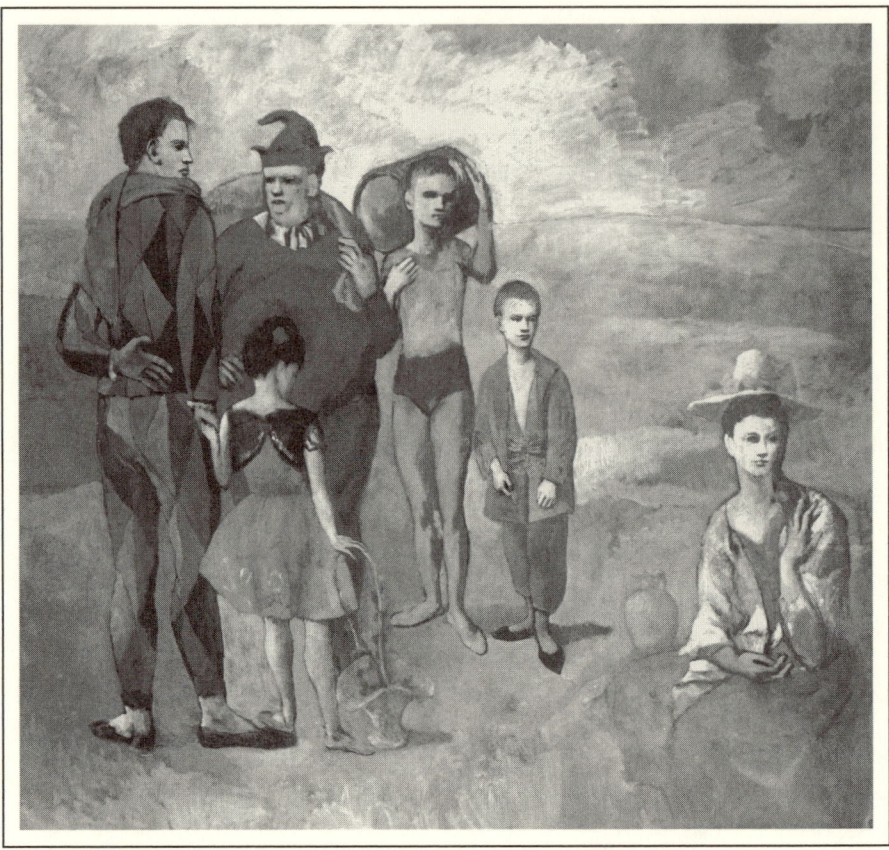

Figure 3. Pablo Picasso, *Les Saltimbanques* (1905). Courtesy of the National Gallery of Art, Washington.

(*Waves*), and S. I. Lockerbie and Anne Greet, in their commentary on the *Calligrammes*. Neither of these discussions mentions Rilke.[3] In comparing the works of Rilke and Apollinaire, I do not seek to "prove" Rilke's debt to Apollinaire. Instead of offering actual signs of influence, itself a difficult concept, I consider the more suggestive link of shared motifs.

I do not claim that "Un Fantôme de Nuées" anticipated Rilke's elegy or that Rilke consciously borrowed from Apollinaire. On the contrary, since

3. Jacob Steiner, *Rilkes Duineser Elegien,* still offers the most complete guide to the elegies. For studies of the *Fifth Elegy* especially, see Marion Faber, *Angels of Daring;* Hans Jaeger, "Die Entstehung der Fünften Duineser Elegie"; Ilsedore Jonas, "The Shattered Image: Rilke's Reaction to the Artists of Expressionism and to Some Works of Picasso"; Katharina Kippenberg, *Rainer Maria Rilkes Deutung des Daseins;* Dietgard Kramer-Lauff, *Tanz und Tänzerisches in Rilkes Lyrik;* Eudo Mason, *Lebenshaltung und Symbolik;* and J. R. Salis, *Rilkes Schweizer Jahre.* Kenneth Batterby, *Rilke and France,* surveys his subjects without mentioning Apollinaire.

Apollinaire's poem appeared only in Les Écrits français and Le Nouvel Imagier before its publication in Calligrammes in 1918, Rilke may not have seen the work before finishing his elegy. Besides, we have no evidence for considering this poem one of the several sources for Rilke. Nor do Rilke's letters show any familiarity with Apollinaire.[4] However, the question of whether Rilke knew of "Un Fantôme" has minor importance. The significance of the striking similarities between these two works rests in the common themes underlying modern artists' perception of the street performer. This shared material points to a circus mystique that has long attracted artists and writers.

Thus my textual comparison of these two poems may reveal a venerable mythic substructure. Accordingly, my focus does not simply rest on either work. Instead of embroidering further on previous criticism devoted to each poem, I shall discuss the two in their most significant mutual context, that is, as works inspired by a street circus. I shall concentrate on the motifs common to the artistes and their show in both texts. Related figures in Apollinaire's "Saltimbanques," "Crépuscule" ("Twilight"), and "Le Musicien de Saint-Merry" ("The Musician of Saint-Merry") will help to specify his image of the saltimbanque.

A brief narrative account of the Rilke and Apollinaire poems may orient the reader unfamiliar with them. In "Un Fantôme," the narrator views a small street circus at work in the Latin Quarter. First he describes a burly weight-lifter, an old organ-grinder, and three younger men. After the public has performed its ritual of coin throwing, the show begins with the ceremonious act of a boy saltimbanque. The "music of forms" of this "small transcendent spirit" occupies most of three long strophes. After the boy disappears, the others again lift weights and juggle; but the audience has seen a "miraculous child."

In his elegy, Rilke introduces the wanderers by a question that relates

---

4. Despite this seeming ignorance of Apollinaire, Rilke may well have known his art criticism. Since 1902, when Rilke first came to Paris, Apollinaire had been publishing his distinctive views of the current art scene in various journals. Indeed, he first became known as an art critic and only later as a poet. Of course, Rilke may not mention Apollinaire because he did not share his taste for the avant-garde. Rilke learned much from Cézanne, but he could not appreciate Gauguin. He seems indifferent to the great innovators then in Paris; nowhere does he mention the revolutionary shows of the Fauves— Matisse, Dérain, Rouault—or Kandinsky, Delaunay, Léger, Gris. His passion for Picasso does not surface in the letters until 1915, and even then he discusses only the "Harlequin" pictures up to 1905. Here he does see the emerging cubism, but he never notes its hint at abstraction (see note 8 below). An actual acquaintance of the two poets remains only an intriguing possibility. As secretary to Rodin in 1905–1906, Rilke did meet many writers and artists, but we do not know if Apollinaire was among them. In any case, it seems ironic that Rilke ignored a true peer in French poetry, while he revered the decidedly minor Francis Jammes.

them directly to all humanity. The first lines describe, albeit elliptically, a group of tumblers: an old weight-lifter, a muscular young man, and a young boy who smiles despite a life of physical and emotional pain. His "seldom tender mother" ignores the loving look he casts toward her. We also see a young girl, who further evokes the exploitation of players by the public. The poem closes with a complex image of artistes who produce only a technical virtuosity. In their inevitable death, however, they may attain the perfection of art.

Apollinaire begins his poem with a prosaic description of time and place. In fact, he originally wrote the first ten lines in prose. The next four lines state even more directly that such *saltimbanques* belong mainly to the past.

> These people who perform in the open
> Are beginning to be rare in Paris
> In my youth one saw much more of them than now
> Almost all have gone to the provinces[5]

Here Apollinaire sets the tone of witness for the poem, which characterizes his relation to the subject. He writes to record a decadent sight, the surviving creators of a vanishing urban event. Also, by associating this disappearance with a nostalgia for his own youth, the poet places himself in the world of the *saltimbanques*. Already we find identification between poet and performer.

Our first explicit parallel to Rilke's elegy appears here. The original prose forms of both poems, along with their subjects and settings, correspond closely. Rilke first documented the street circus of his elegy, seen also on Bastille Day in the Latin Quarter, in a letter of 1907. The nostalgia that Apollinaire evokes does not surface in the elegy, but it does appear in this letter, where Rilke speaks of the old weight-lifter. "But Father Rollin, who lifted the heavy weights, works no longer and says nothing. . . . He could still beat the drum; they should never think that he got tired. . . . The weights have been sold, they are not fashionable any more, and the children belong to a new era."[6]

In another of his own sources for the elegy, the prose poem "Saltimbanques" (1907), Rilke transforms the witnessed event into street theater. Here we have the same Rollin family and the same Luxembourg gardens as in the letter. But Rilke soon focuses on the three generations the show presents.

5. Guillaume Apollinaire, *Oeuvres Poétiques,* ed. Marcel Adéma and Michel Décaudin, 193.
6. Dieter Bassermann, *Der Späte Rilke,* 415.

First he notes the boy, then his grandfather, and finally the woman—both daughter and mother—who is the true bearer of the *saltimbanque* heritage. In the prose poem, Rilke evokes pathos for the boy and admiration for the old drummer, but he implies that only the woman displays the unique talent characteristic of the profession. Especially in contrast to her husband, who has no blood tie to the tradition, she embodies the inheritance of the troupe. "She has the thing inside. You have to be born with it."[7] This figure also recalls Zuckmayer's Katharina Knie, whose crisis develops from this very position as scion of a venerable circus family (see chapter 4).

In contrast to the quotidian reality of Apollinaire's "Un Fantôme," Rilke's elegy suggests the inscrutable. Rilke starts and ends with a question, and the initial query seems to emanate from Picasso's painting. "But who *are* they?" is an apt response to this esoteric picture. Both it and the poem depict "mysteries played in the street," a paradox that pervades the image of the *saltimbanque*. The Symbolist *Les Saltimbanques* recalls Mallarmé's notion of poetry as enigma; all these works point toward abstraction.[8]

Next Apollinaire locates his tumblers very specifically, in a small square near St. Germain des Prés. He further links these artistes with their own proletarian tradition by placing them near the statue of Danton. In Rilke's letter, the artistes also occupy a central Left Bank spot: in front of the Luxembourg Gardens, facing toward the Pantheon.[9] Both settings show us a familiar event in a popular milieu. In fact, as Apollinaire says several times, this kind of street entertainment belongs to the working class, even to the criminal underworld. "Belgian cities raised at arm's length by a Russian worker from Longwy . . . / Another resembled a tough thug . . . / Didn't he look like a spruced-up pimp."

7. Rainer Maria Rilke, *Werke in drei Bänden,* ed. Ernst Zinn, 3:459, 461.

8. Philippe Renaud, "Ondes, ou les Métamorphoses de la Musique," *Apollinaire et la Musique,* 25. Rilke himself seems to have noticed the urge toward Cubism in the four clearly delineated diamonds on the sleeve of the dead Harlequin in Picasso's gouache *La Mort d'Harlequin* (1905). "One could almost comprehend the later Picasso through this one four-toned surface, as if, after Pierrot's (*sic*) death, the shattered world could only reunite in such beautiful fragments" (quoted in Herman Meyer, "Die Verwandlung des Sichtbaren," *Zarte Empirie,* 313; see also Charles Dédéyan, *Rilke et la France,* 3:189).

9. Here lies a probably unwitting echo of Banville, who asks in his *Pauvres Saltimbanques* if these players are not indeed "legitimate" artists, except for lacking the hope of recognition by any academy. For surely the most prestigious *académie* is this very Pantheon. "Saltimbanques, and poor ones at that, these inspired poets, these comedians drunk with passion, these eloquent voices, these fiddlers, these genial marionettes who must first weep . . . and then make the crowd weep, then laugh! For, if you please, what is the saltimbanque if not a free, independent artist who works miracles to earn his daily bread, who sings under the sun and dances under the stars, without hope of ever entering the academy?" (p. 4).

Artists often associate the street showman with vice. Baudelaire, for instance, makes the strong-man lover in "A Une Jeune Saltimbanque" a target of the police. Wallace Fowlie cogently traces this link between the poor player and crime to Villon. Not accidentally, the melodrama favored by proletarian audiences dwells on violence and horror. Thus the street of the famous *Funambules* in nineteenth-century Paris became known as the *Boulevard du Crime*.

In the film *Les Enfants du Paradis,* Carné and Prévert build a narrative axis by juxtaposing popular entertainers and criminals. Hence the little pickpocket mime that introduces Baptiste to Garance has central symbolic value for the film (see chapter 2). The title of part 1, "The Street of Many Murders," specifies the extremes to which a low-life milieu can lead. Indeed, the "boulevard of crime" received its name as much from events outside the theaters as within. Prévert fulfills the promise of this title at the end of part 2, when a climactic carnival leads to the murder of the Count de Montray. These two crimes—the pickpocket's initial petty thievery and his enemy's final, perfectly staged ritual murder—enclose a principal theme of the film.

Apart from visualizing Bakhtin's carnivalization of life and death, this sequence of scenes recalls what Apollinaire said of Picasso's *saltimbanques* in 1905. "In Rome, at carnival time, there are some masques (Harlequin, Columbine or *cuoca francese*) who at dawn, after a night of orgy sometimes ended by murder, go to St. Peter's to kiss the worn toe of the statue of the prince of apostles. These are the beings who would enchant Picasso."[10] Camus makes the same link of carnival and murder in his film *Black Orpheus* (1959). Here the Mardi Gras revels of Rio aptly mask the pursuit of Eurydice by the figure of Death. Deftly merging the pagan and Christian myths, Camus ends this carnival with the death of the two lovers.

We have already seen the artiste involved in deadly sins. The prince in "Une Mort Héroique," himself an artist, virtually murders his alter ego, Fancioulle. Triboulet/Rigoletto abets the crimes of his master, the duke. Of their relation, the jester says, "I am the man who laughs, he is the man who kills." But his complicity makes Triboulet a killer too. Hugo's other buffoons—Habibrah, Gwynplaine—confirm the link to the diabolic. Like Baudelaire, Hugo sees in laughter "a sign of the satanic."[11]

Our other players also relate closely to the criminal. The demonic Oskar at least collaborates in his father's death. Krull's con games seem benign in

---

10. Breunig, *Apollinaire,* 13.
11. Quoted in Victor Brombert, *Victor Hugo and the Visionary Novel,* 180.

this context; yet he, like his respectable cousin Tonio Kröger, raises the problem of immorality in art. Cipolla embodies the most dangerous charlatan. Like the totalitarian state he evokes, the conjurer kills by dehumanizing. Bergman's magician has less disastrous results, but he implies a similar scurrility for art. By contrast, Fellini's players are simply harmless illusionists (see chapter 8).[12]

But back to our *saltimbanques*. Before they perform, we again read of the spectators' poverty. "The music stopped and there were negotiations with the public / Who threw down on the carpet, sou by sou, two francs and a half / Instead of the three francs that the old man had fixed as the price for the show." Here we see a characteristic difference between the two poems in the handling of similar material. Rilke also uses the motif of coins hurled down by the public, but not until his final lines.

> Wouldn't they then throw down their last,
> saved-up, always hidden and unknown, yet ever-
> valid coins of happiness before the finally
> truly smiling pair on the stilled
> carpet?[13]

These coins symbolize not poverty but salvation. Rilke's acrobats are dead, for only in death might they achieve perfection, both in their craft and in love. Such perfection would save all the participants in this posthumous scene, as the viewers' eternal coins of happiness have evoked a finally genuine smile in the tumblers. Apollinaire's last lines readily compare to this last strophe; he too specifies a startling reciprocity of spectator and performer in this "miraculous" scene. And here too this reciprocity connotes salvation. "But each spectator searched within for the miraculous child / Century oh century of clouds."

This last line recalls Rilke's strikingly similar "Squares, oh square in Paris, endless showplace." Both lines, at a crucial point in the poem, denote the transcendence of the quotidian event into infinite space. But Rilke diverges from Apollinaire in specifying death as the necessary prelude to the final scene. On his "infinite stage" we find Madame Lamort herself. Accordingly, Rilke's closing scene of epiphany occurs in the subjunctive. While Apollinaire continues with the narrative past, stating historical actuality, Rilke

12. The general view of the player as scurrilous goes back to the *Commedia* at least. It also thrives in our own time. Joseph McCarthy gave to actors the current epithet for sin: Communist. For a massive study of this bigotry, see Jonas Barish, *The Antitheatrical Prejudice.*

13. Rilke, *Werke in drei Bänden,* 1:461.

transports his show into a hypothetical future. From the dividing line in the poem and the words "there might be a place," we know that this scene has no reality. Thus Rilke's ultimate stage represents the site of death and resurrection. By contrast, Apollinaire only implies death, in the figure of the sickly boy.

Images of sickness, associated with rose colors, abound in "Un Fantôme." The first juggler wears a sweater of "rose vio / let that you see on the fresh cheeks of certain young girls close to death." "Thus that man wore on his back / The mean color of his lungs." Even the small boy wears "pulmonary pink." Apollinaire gives reddish colors this deadly aspect so persistently that we must note the combination as essential to his meaning. Indeed, the rose "full of treachery" reflects the basic paradox of this scene. Just as the rosy hue of health belies the destitution of these players, so does their sordid ambience surprise us by producing a miraculous child.

Rilke also couples the rose color with impending death. In his French prose fragment "Saltimbanques" (1924), the endangered artiste wears an intense red. "The wire was so high that it went above the lights. Suddenly she was among us again in her too-rosy suit. It was another rose which, up there, exposed to the immense night the absurdity of her constant peril."[14]

But in the elegy Rilke associates an actual rose with the street show. "The rose of observing" represents the scene of tumblers surrounded by spectators. Just as the petals of the rose unfold, so do the onlookers come and go; the spectacle itself resembles the pistil of a flower. This complex image dates from the time when Rilke saw the Parisian *saltimbanques* described in his letter of 1907. We know of their origin from the poem "Die Gruppe" ("The Group"), in *Der Neuen Gedichte, Anderer Teil* (*New Poems, Part II*) (1908).

Here we find the earliest lyric version of an event comparable to that in the letter. In the sonnet's central image, the dynamics of the public watching a street circus resembles the chance arrangement of a bouquet. That Rilke should later compress this detailed vision into a single rose does not surprise us, since roses pervade his imagery. He even willed that a rose, in both stone and verse, adorn his grave. Starobinski associates Rilke's rose with the celestial one of Dante's paradise. The overtones of mystic salvation implied in that vision fit well into the context of Rilke's elegy.

In Picasso's painting, rose colors highlight the composition repeatedly. Rose-colored flowers, if not actual roses, adorn both the woman's hat and the girl's hair and basket. And the general tonality of this painting shows why we place it in Picasso's Rose Period. Theodore Reff notes that several

14. Rainer Maria Rilke, *Sämtliche Werke*, 2:714.

nineteenth-century artists depicted circus scenes in reds because those colors dominated in actual circuses.[15] He and other critics further speculate on the role the circus milieu played in Picasso's turn from the somber mood of his Blue Period to the warmer hues of the Rose Period.

Round shapes also form a common feature of the painting and both poems. In the painting, the figures stand in a semicircle, the main definition of the work. Other round forms echo this composition: the edge of the basket, the woman's hat rim, the boy's drum, the Grecian urn. In the elegy, Rilke adds to his rose the roundness of a tin platter rolled by a strong man, the "cheap winter hats of fate," and the "lovely urn." Circular forms in "Un Fantôme" appear in the spectators' circle, the points of the compass that the boy salutes, the ball on which he balances, and his cartwheel. Beyond the symbolism of completeness, perfection, and cosmic space, we find both the Christian cross of the compass points and the image of a god balancing on a sphere. Thus the boy's act, referring to both Christian and pagan realms, bears truly universal meaning.

Furthermore, the many phonetically rounded sounds of Apollinaire's verse—*tours, entourait, roulant, tournant, boule, moulait*—suggest that both the idea and the form of the circle provide the basic symbolism of the poem. Here we note Apollinaire's general fondness for circles, which several critics have discussed. "From the earliest poems onward, the circle is a fundamental element of organisation."[16] Moreover, Greet and Lockerbie refer to the "circular aspects of time" that recur in the poetry. Willard Bohn gives many examples of round symbols—wheel, target, halo, moon, umbilicus—that we may compare with the cartwheel of the boy *saltimbanque*. This cartwheel, forming the climax of his act and embodying its cosmic significance, recalls Bohn's explication of the large wheel in "Lettre-Océan." "As a simultanistic *tranche de vie*, in which time and space are temporarily frozen, the large wheel begins to take on the appearance of a full cosmology."[17] The circle's simultanism suggests the nonlinear narrative in both art and literature of our time. Roger Shattuck links the rejection of "progress and development" to the basis of Modernist aesthetics in "The Art of Stillness."[18]

We may wonder if Apollinaire's circles were prompted by their profusion in contemporary painting. As an art critic, he knew well the work of Delaunay and Léger, who thoroughly explored roundness in both organic and abstract forms. Picasso too, as in *Les Saltimbanques*, used circular

15. Theodore Reff, "Harlequins, Saltimbanques, Clowns and Fools," 35.
16. Jean-Claude Chevalier, *Alcools d'Apollinaire*, 82.
17. Willard Bohn, "Circular Poem-Paintings by Apollinaire and Carrà," 264.
18. Roger Shattuck, *The Banquet Years*, 350.

shapes in his many other treatments of *saltimbanques* around 1905. And the bullring, another round form, fascinated him later on. Kandinsky evolved representational round shapes into abstract circles. Arp and Brancusi also concentrated on spherical forms. One reason why Modernists treat both the circle and the circus may lie in the primitive character of both images. Such basic shapes as the triangle, the arch, and the circle recur often in the work of van der Rohe, Gabo, and Calder; the latter loved the huge space of circuses. Critics often call childish the simple forms of Miró and Dubuffet. In their search for a new art based on ancient principles, these modernists may well have found archetypal significance in the circus ring.[19]

Since Apollinaire revered *Les Saltimbanques,* along with the other Rose Period works, we might conclude that much of what he saw there inspired his poem. First, his "deadly" rose colors may hark back to the rosy tones of these paintings. Second, Apollinaire's round forms recall those in *Les Saltimbanques.* Finally, the suffering of his players may also derive from Picasso. Thus it is tempting to read "Un Fantôme" as variations by Apollinaire on Picasso's main theme. However, some critics suggest that the canvas gained its Symbolist aura from Apollinaire's poetics. In any case, the elegy, though also inspired by *Les Saltimbanques,* shares less with it than with "Un Fantôme." Reddish colors do not predominate here. And the round shapes, though recurring as motifs, do not bear the essential symbolic weight that they do for Apollinaire.

Like the moribund *saltimbanque* in "Un Fantôme," Rilke's artistes also show suffering and pain. In one of the first striking images in the elegy, the carpet on which the tumblers perform is "Laid on like a bandage, as if the suburban / sky had injured itself." The notion of injury thus enters the poem early. Soon afterward, we see the effects of a harsh life in the "withered, wrinkled lifter," who recalls Apollinaire's old organ-grinder, also appearing first among the group. But Rilke's boy offers the most persistent and pathetic images of suffering. Inspired by the child at the center of *Les Saltimbanques,* this boy has always known pain, which he received "as a toy." His daily routine of difficult acrobatics suggests the constant peril of the tumblers' life. Such strenuous exertion contrasts sharply with the natural grace that emanates from Apollinaire's boy.

In Rilke's relentless evocation of pain, we find a major difference from

19. Sherry Buckberrough, *Robert Delaunay: The Discovery of Simultaneity,* confirms my suspicions at length, devoting about half her study to the "pan-European 'circular era' in 1913" (136). She never mentions the interest of the "circularists" in the circus, but her discussion of round forms in Kupka, Duchamp, Braque, Picasso, the Futurists, and Chagall makes that affinity inevitable.

Apollinaire. However, like the grace in the boy of the clouds, the paradoxical smile of this child transcends his cruel milieu. Both children represent the hope that redeems the poverty and sickness, the whole sordid life of the artiste. Here the smile, an often important symbol for Rilke, occurs at the center of the poem, connecting with the final triumphant smile of the dead lovers at the end. Thus implying divine love, the smile saves both the *saltimbanques* and the life of art that the elegy evokes. In "Un Fantôme," the perfectly graceful boy redeems not only the players and their wretched existence but also the audience. "Each spectator sought in himself the miraculous child." We recall the striking line from Apollinaire's 1905 review of Picasso: "These tormented ones awaited a savior."[20]

THE BLESSED BOY

We have already noted the connotations of divine blessing in Oskar Matzerath. Indeed, several of our childlike artists bear transcendent features. The clown Furlani has a purifying, innocent grace; Josefine the mouse appears to some as a redeemer of society; Schnier the mime enjoys a moral superiority over all his peers. All these figures recall first the claim of Schiller, Baudelaire, and Freud that the artist is a mature child. Second, they suggest that this child-artist points beyond our conventional order. Baudelaire explicitly links boy and creator as exceptional beings in "Les Vocations" (1864). Here the child identifies with just those traits of the Bohemian artistic life that we find in "Un Fantôme": the "music of savages," poverty, and homelessness. And, as in the poem, the fraternity of boy and narrator bespeaks the vulnerability of all these outsiders. "There was something in his eye and his bearing of a *fatal* precocity, which usually bars sympathy, but for some reason *excited mine*. So for a moment I had the bizarre idea that I had an unknown brother."[21]

In Mallarmé, the sanctity of the child-artist grows to mythic proportions. Two prose poems in particular, "Pauvre Enfant Pâle" (1866) and "Réminiscence" (1888), enshrine the enigmatic boy player, who suggests redemption through art. In the first piece, the narrator addresses, in eight ritualistic paragraphs, the miserable orphan singer of the street. This boy exhibits two traits that clearly survive in Apollinaire's child *saltimbanque*. First, although his utter isolation points to death, his undaunted spirit will live on; second, he emerges as a Christ figure, redeeming all who hear him. The crime this outsider will commit, like his inevitable hunger, results from pov-

20. Breunig, *Apollinaire*, 15.
21. Charles Baudelaire, *Oeuvres Complètes*, ed. Claude Pichois, 1:335, italics mine.

erty. We have already seen both these facets of the entertainer's life, fasting and crime, in Apollinaire's poem.

The transcendence that this boy accomplishes through music and dance is only implied by Mallarmé in the boy's sacrificial beheading. Hence the street singer appears more the innocent savior and less the redemptive artist. The motif of decapitation may remind us of the headless acrobat in "Un Fantôme de Nuées."

> The second saltimbanque
> Wore only his shadow
> I watched him a long time
> His face escapes me entirely
> He's a headless man

In this image, the sense of things lacking, of absence, recalls Mallarmé generally. Specifically, this man of shadow, suggesting death, seems related to the earlier moribund boy. For both figures, the player's intense spirituality may cut him off—literally—from physical existence. Mallarmé stresses this notion of bodily transcendence in his frequent suggestion of ascent. "And your lament is so high, so high, that your bare head, rising in the air as your voice does, seems to want to leave your little shoulders."[22]

As for the savior quality, consider the weighty line "Have you ever had a father?" We recall that not only the expectable Hamlet but also Christ had a father problem. "My father, my father, why hast thou abandoned me?" echoes throughout the piece. The title suggests the Christ child, that "little man" of the second paragraph. The final one completes a satisfying circle with its image of the urchin-poet-savior who came to pay for our sins. The formulation "You will pay for me" is suitably ironic, since no one has paid the boy at all.

We have already seen an extreme, even comic, version of the denial of physical life in Kafka's hunger-artist. There too, the player sublimates hunger to a purified spirit; at least that is the starver's ideal. The difference between him and the earlier figures lies in his fraudulence. In both boys, transcendence seems possible. But Kafka ruthlessly negates any fulfillment for his deceptive artiste. He cannot redeem the narrator-sinner, as in Mallarmé, or the spectators, as in Apollinaire, because his "art" contains only self-display.

In "Réminiscence," the orphan gains in Hamletic mystery what he loses in martyrdom. Like Shakespeare's prince, this fatherless boy identifies with wandering players. He confronts not the harsh counterworld of indifferent

---

22. Stéphane Mallarmé, *Oeuvres Complètes*, ed. Henri Mondor, 274.

society in "Pauvre Enfant Pâle," but instead a seductive fairground. Accordingly, he senses here the kindred spirit of the outcast, the homeless; the boy acrobat he meets becomes a brother.

Indeed, this urchin, like the boy in Baudelaire's "Les Vocations," gains a spiritual family among the performers. In the first sentence, the boy glimpses a future like theirs, for they draw him away from the conventional world of his peers. He, like the players, belongs to that other realm of fantasy created by the theater. And again, as in "Pauvre Enfant Pâle," Mallarmé associates all these figures with food. The white cheese the acrobat eats arouses the narrator's hunger, both physical and spiritual. The whiteness of this sacramental meal, likened to snow and lilies, suggests the same blessing for this boy that redeems the orphan of "Pauvre Enfant Pâle."

Both Mallarmé's boys stand outside society. The poor pale urchin can never enter the respectable world, nor can the orphan find true parents. Longing to join the fair, the orphan readily contrasts with the later *pitre châtié*, who escapes it. Indeed, we may see the *pitre* as the adult version of the boy orphan. The young tumblers of Rilke and Apollinaire, however, belong firmly within the performing sphere. Like Picasso's central figure, these boys function as adult players. Indeed, their professionalism arouses more wonder than pity, for they exhibit both the skill of the trouper and the toughness of the street child.

Rilke's tumbler owes more to Mallarmé than does Apollinaire's "child of the clouds." Intent on his adept routine, this boy only hints at destitution in his thinness. But Rilke's young acrobat suggests mostly the pain of daily practice. This ordeal, along with his longing for love, imparts a pathos that recalls the wretched condition of the *pauvre enfant pâle*.

THE *SALTIMBANQUE* FAMILY

Not only the boy savior but also his human setting, the family, links the two poems and the painting. In all three works, the troupe of artistes forms an actual or virtual family. In the painting, we find a possible family group, including grandfather, son and daughter, and three grandchildren. Rilke conceived the group this way; when he saw the painting in 1915 he probably associated the fat older man with the Père Rollin of his Paris days, and the young woman with his daughter. Several art critics view the painting as a "family portrait" of Picasso and friends. Certainly the dominating Harlequin is a self-portrait, and the ample acrobat is Apollinaire; critics take the two boys for Max Jacob and André Salmon.[23]

---

23. For contrast, see *The Soler Family* (1903), an actual family portrait. Again, Picasso

Indeed, this canvas appeared as a personal document in a 1981 exhibit at the National Gallery in Washington, D.C. E. A. Carmean, curator for this show, not only identifies these figures as Picasso's friends but also claims that the woman is Fernande Olivier, Picasso's mistress in 1905, and that the girl is an orphan whom Fernande briefly adopted. Carmean does not reject the traditional view of the picture as "a timeless frieze of symbolic and poetic images"; instead, he seeks to "ground one theme in the other."[24] By this phrase he seems to mean that an anecdote underlies what the uninformed viewer perceives as more universal meaning.

However controversial this argument may appear, it does lend an astonishing validity to both our poets' familial visions of the Picasso canvas. Rilke selects from the group what is called the Freudian family: two parent-lovers, a son, and a daughter. His poem essentially depends on his vision of the mother-son relation, which has marked Oedipal overtones. The son steals furtive, loving glances at his mother, who seldom shows tenderness. Carmean ignores this view of the painting, for he attributes the coldness of the supposed Fernande to the girl.

Rilke clearly follows Picasso in focusing on the boy. The painter highlights the boy with the blue of his tunic, the brightest tone on the canvas. This color, though far from brilliant, is still a vibrant contrast to the somber blues of the recent Blue Period. But Rilke goes further in featuring the boy, for his smile is the symbolic key to his whole poem. Indeed, the image of the child, often juxtaposed to lovers and to death, recurs in most of the elegies. In the first, fourth, and sixth elegies, the important idea of "the young dead" develops in different contexts. The child's death that closes the fourth elegy leads us toward the boy in the fifth elegy, whose smile transcends the death implied in his milieu. This smiling boy has further significance for the whole *Duino* cycle in that Rilke composed this elegy last. Thus we may find resolution in its hopeful image of the boy as redeemer.

Apollinaire presents five figures, but they form no true family. Instead, he gives us three generations of males: the old man, the boy, and three adults. Thus, although no woman graces this troupe, the three generations represent the continuity implicit in the family. Especially since the boy is "born" from under the old man's barrel organ, we sense the range of life between birth and death.

---

places the group in a semicircle, with no recognizable background. And he again highlights one central child in blue. But there ends the likeness between the two canvases. The Soler picture presents a family outing, complete with hunting gear and picnic; the *saltimbanques* tell no comparable story, despite their props. Indeed, the girl's flower basket and the Grecian urn complicate the setting more than they explain it. The varying gaze of each player adds complexity to a canvas full of problems. The Soler group, all staring outward to the painter, suggests little beyond the commissioned family portrait.

24. E. A. Carmean, *Picasso: Les Saltimbanques*, 50, 54.

Apollinaire may have had another Picasso work in mind when he put this pair of young and old at the center of his poem. *Le Joueur d'Orgue de Barbarie (The Organ Grinder)* (1906) offers a close visual parallel to the two complementing each other in the poem (see figure 4).[25] The old man here resembles the one in Apollinaire, for he also looks "thin and savage" with his graying beard. And he too may dream of the future, as Apollinaire says of his man. But the two works have a deeper resemblance in juxtaposing youth and old age. In the poem this link occurs at the climax of the boy's act, lines 63–71.

Indeed, this moment when the boy clearly transcends his milieu is the high point of the poem. The most potent symbol of this milieu is the old man himself, the boy's counterpart. If the boy represents a new, "miraculous" music, the old man stands for the venerable *saltimbanque* tradition. One thinks of the great forebear by Baudelaire, the old clown who compares similarly with the young girl—"dream of poets"—in "A Une Jeune Saltimbanque" (1845). This pair of poems gives an archetype for our theme of old and young players. The latter poem dates from Baudelaire's earliest efforts, and "Le Vieux Saltimbanque" characterizes his final view of the clown-poet.[26]

In *The Organ Grinder,* the two figures connote a different aspect of the street show. Sitting close together, the two do not touch, nor do they seem aware of each other. Like those of the larger group in *Les Saltimbanques,* these two look away from each other, yet both their physical closeness and their costumes inevitably unite them. Here, in fact, we sense a rapport, a tenderness in the way the boy leans against the man's seat. Sharing a moment of rest from their act, the two reflect the stillness that follows strenuous work. Such moments recur often in Picasso's images of circus folk. Accordingly Reff uses this motif of resting *saltimbanques* as one of his four categories for Picasso's "circus" works.

The Organ Grinder relates most essentially to "Un Fantôme" in its focus on the pair that evokes the range of the street show. In both painting and poem we see that these vagrant players have a life fully circumscribed by

25. In several of the *saltimbanque* paintings, Picasso unites similar contrasts between players. Two works of 1905 juxtapose a mature strong man with a fragile girl. In *The Acrobat,* the massive male lifts his small colleague with one burly arm. *The Girl Acrobat on the Ball* links round shapes, which Picasso associated with the female, and squares, which connoted for him the masculine.

26. I accept the tentative attribution to Baudelaire for "A Une Jeune Saltimbanque" (Baudelaire, *Oeuvres Complètes,* ed. Pichois, 1:1260). "Les Vocations" offers a related kind of polarity to "Le Vieux Saltimbanque." In the former, the narrator sees the Bohemians positively, through the eyes of the boy; in the latter, he sees the old clown negatively, through his own eyes. In the child's naive longing for the free, exotic life, Baudelaire shows just the opposite of his horror at its outcome.

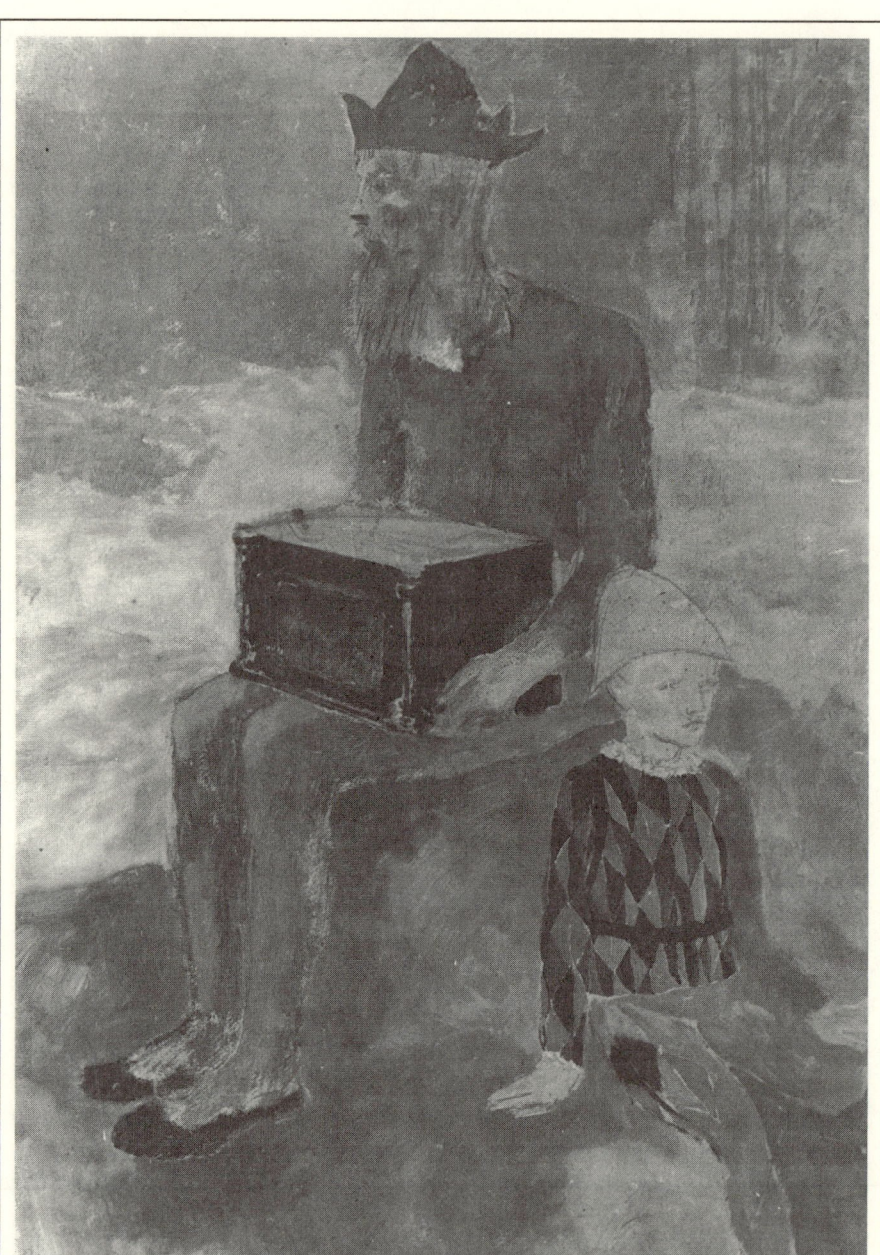

Figure 4. Pablo Picasso, *Le Joueur d'Orgue de Barbarie* (1906). Courtesy of Kunsthaus Zürich.

their profession. From childhood to old age, these people live bound together by their performance of skilled routines, inherited from ancient ritual. Constant interaction with the ordinary public heightens their cohesive identity as *saltimbanques*. Both the painter and the poet render them as remarkable, haunting, even magical in their suggestion of another life beyond our common human lot.

A similarly mythic quality emerges from a comparable photograph by Eugène Atget, *Joueur d'Orgue* (*The Organ Grinder*) (1899) (see figure 5). Again a young trouper works beside an old man; they too depend on each other to complete their act. Their union appears more subtly in their touching fingers than in Picasso's bodily juxtaposition of the pair. These united hands at the center of the picture bind its two halves, youth and old age, as framed by two shutters. The barrel organ supporting the hands provides the focus of the composition.

As in the Picasso painting, the instrument is the basis of the show. Without the music of this organ, the performers would be as incomplete as acrobats without props. The main difference between these two pictures lies in the beaming smile of the girl in Atget. Both old men bespeak passivity and fatigue, but this player radiates a joy that transcends all else in the picture. What a difference between this exuberance and the tentative smile of Rilke's boy![27] Atget's joyful young singer counteracts the sadness of the street life that the old man summarizes. By contrast, Picasso's figures convey a monotone sobriety.

Returning to the family theme, we may compare the related group in Apollinaire's "Saltimbanques." Here we find actual families. This troupe, wandering through the landscape, has an idyllic air of long-standing intimacy. Always together, these families constantly traverse the land. Hence they contrast with the players in "Un Fantôme," who orchestrate a specific event. This complex poem builds to a dramatic climax and closes with an epiphany, whereas "Saltimbanques" simply proceeds from image to image. Here especially, with his characteristic lack of punctuation, Apollinaire renders an art of juxtaposition. One thinks of the endless parade of gypsies in Callot's four etchings *Les Bohémiens* (1622) (see figure 6).

27. She recalls what Henry Miller says of circus clowns: "They are emancipated beings. For them the world is not what it seems to us. They see with other eyes. . . . They live in the moment, fully, and the radiance that emanates from them is a perpetual song of joy" (quoted in Dean Jensen, *Center Ring: The Artist*, 85). Similarly, Arthur Trottenberg sees in Atget's image the same rejuvenation of the hand organ that Proust evokes. "I had been apprised . . . by hearing a barrel-organ, playing beneath the window 'En Revenant de la Revue,' that the winter had received, until nightfall, an unexpected, radiant visit from a day of Spring" (quoted in Trottenberg, ed., *A Vision of Paris: The Photographs of Atget, the Words of Proust*, 117).

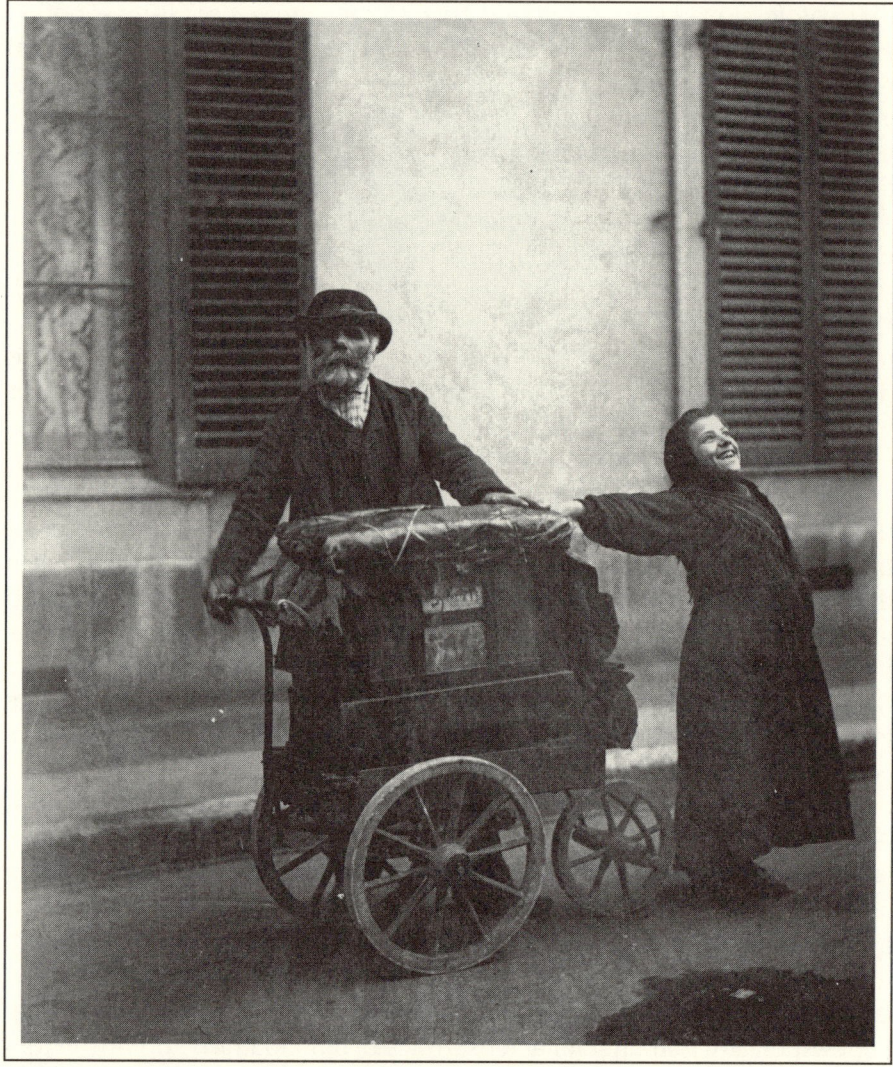

Figure 5. Eugène Atget, *Joueur d'Orgue* (1899). Gold-toned printing-out paper, 9⅜" x 7". Courtesy of The Museum of Modern Art, New York.

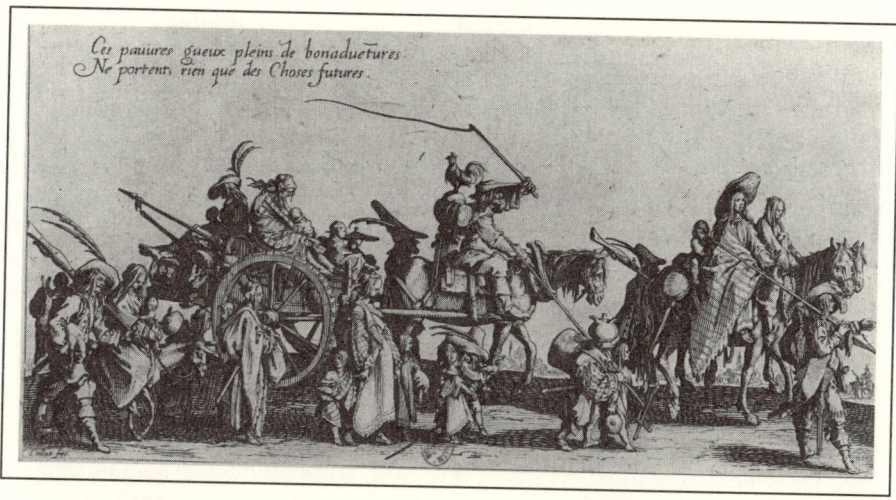

Ces pauures gueux pleins de bonadueñures
Ne portent rien qué des Choses futures.

Figure 6. Jacques Callot, *Les Bohémiens* (1622). Courtesy of the Bibliothèque Nationale.

Füglister finds in this series a source for both this poem and Baudelaire's "Bohémiens en Voyage" ("Bohemians Enroute").[28] The motto on the first etching clearly suggests two lines in Baudelaire and Apollinaire.

Callot: These poor wretches full of adventure
      Bring only news of the future
Baudelaire: . . . these wanderers, who glimpse
      The familiar realm of portentous shadows
Apollinaire: He seemed to dream of the future

All three artists associate their gypsies with the future. Perhaps they do so because of the link with prophecy of the arch-exile, the wandering Jew Ahasuerus. Callot implies this meaning in another of the four etchings, which bears the motto "Aren't these brave *messengers* / Who wander through foreign countries" (italics mine). Füglister ties this vision of the vagrants with what they meant for Baudelaire. "The nomads who, like the Israelites, traverse the desert, represent for Baudelaire the chosen people, to whom he wanted to belong, if not as a man, at least as a prophetic poet."

According with the endless, universal quality in Callot, "Saltimbanques" seems unreal. Like the old man in "Un Fantôme," these wanderers are dreaming. Hence they connect with that "other world" of the subconscious. At the middle of "Bohémiens," the men search the heavens, mourning their "absent chimeras." At the middle of "Saltimbanques," the adults

28. Robert Füglister, "Baudelaire et le Thème des Bohémiens," 104–28.

follow their children "while dreaming." However, Baudelaire's visionary tone contrasts with Apollinaire's quotidian detail.

Rilke's elegy, subtitled "Die Fahrenden," also stresses the eternal roving of the tumblers, but here it has the negative connotations of homelessness and vulnerability. His family lacks the remarkable cohesion of Apollinaire's wanderers. That paradox of homely affection among the homeless also pervades "Bohémiens en Voyage." We may readily compare this poem with "Saltimbanques," for both works render an idealized image of vagrant families. The final word of each poem, *futures* in Baudelaire and *passage* in Apollinaire, implies transcendence.

In sharp contrast to the wretched urban *saltimbanques*, these wanderers partake of the organic nature they inhabit. Indeed, such families have a special sanctity: in "Bohémiens," they inspire miracles wherever they pass. Their cohesion, despite the lack of any roots, represents the social integration, wholeness, and continuity of the ideal family. In spite of their actual evanescence, these gypsies suggest immortality.

Apollinaire even sees the Holy Family in the circus family. In the first version of "Saltimbanques," a mother suckles her son, specifically Jesus. Again, in his description of domestic circus scenes, the mother is "glorious and immaculate." Here Apollinaire probably refers to *The Harlequin's Family.* But in *The Acrobat's Family with a Monkey,* where the mother cradles an infant and the father lovingly looks on, Picasso more clearly evokes the blessed aura of the Holy Family.[29]

In all four poems, then, the vagrants relate to a realm beyond the ordinary human one. This transcendent view of the wanderers should not surprise us, for it recurs throughout the *saltimbanque* literature. Perhaps the ultimate forebear for the tradition of the blessed performer is the Jongleur de Notre-Dame. In this moral tale, the Virgin herself descends from heaven to bless his acrobatic worship. At his death, she transports him into paradise. Naturally, the monks of the monastery revere the Jongleur as a saint. Such sacred clowns persist: think of the grieving buffoons of Rouault, the resurrection of Petrushka, the holy fools of Bergman and Fellini. Fowlie makes this joining of sacred and profane a major subject of *Love in Literature.* Lescek Kolakowski sees the polarity of priest and jester as necessary for any healthy society.

French poets of the nineteenth century also saw the miraculous in their artistes, who resemble the Jongleur by being, suitably, aerialists. We have already noted the *sauteur* of Banville's "Le Saut du Tremplin" (1857), who soars from his springboard into the sky. Crashing through the stars, he tran-

---

29. Apollinaire, *Oeuvres,* 1056; Breunig, *Apollinaire,* 15; Carmean, *Picasso,* 34.

scends his violent death and attains a haunting immortality. In his *pitre châtié* of 1887, whose greasepaint is "his consecration," Mallarmé takes up the same metaphor of transcendence. This fool also seeks to escape his confinement through a window he tears in his tent.

This same motif of liberation from the stage appears again in the ballet *Petrushka* (1911). The wretched puppet bursts through the wall of his booth, which is really a prison cell. Like Banville's clown, he ascends from the stage; his soul appears above the crowd that has just seen his straw body die. As Fowlie suggests, Petrushka has a forebear in Mallarmé's *pitre*. The ballet develops the modern image of man as puppet, unable to break the bonds of his meager character. In chapter 6, I shall show that such "hollow men" pervade our art.

The boy *saltimbanques*, through their literally saving grace, relate to another realm more closely than do these forebears. In all three examples—Banville, Mallarmé, and the ballet—the clown strives to escape his condition through deliberate acts. These boys, however, show no conscious will to transcendence. They appear as innocent vehicles of some mysterious force that shapes the fate of the *saltimbanques*. Besides, the sickness of these boys predetermines them for that other world, which the earlier figures reach only through exertion. The boys are already "beings tied to death."[30]

The motif of the sick child suggests a decadent society. We think of Goethe's Mignon or of Munch's painting *The Sick Child*. In a flourishing culture, the child represents health, growth, freedom. But in the decaying world of the urban poor, the ailing child arouses our pity for his innocent suffering. Thus the figure acquires pathos. Furthermore, when such a frail being must labor for a living, he becomes heroic. Hugo gives us perhaps the first such child in the *gamin* Gavroche, whose paradoxical goodness belies the brutality of the streets where he lives. Gavroche's self-sufficiency, as well as his unlikely charisma, reappear in Apollinaire's boy.

Hugo shows us the paradox of a corrupt world producing a miraculous child; Apollinaire focuses on the suffering of that world. In Rilke, the brave, loving smile of the boy contradicts the tumblers' milieu of bitter hardship. Related texts confirm that the child symbolizes the transcendent purity of

30. Ross Chambers, "Frôler ceux qui rôdent: Le Paradoxe du Saltimbanque," 356. Circus figures often live close to death. Apart from the obvious fact that they constantly imperil their lives in dangerous feats, *artistes* often appear as decadent types, frail and sickly. Kafka's equestrienne in "Auf der Galerie," whose pink-and-white skin recalls the deadly rose of Apollinaire's players, has tuberculosis; his *Hungerkünstler* attains suicide through starvation; Daumier's buffoons seem to suffer from something more endemic than mere hunger. The common motif of Pierrot's death may ultimately refer to the archetypal function of the clown as a haunting figure (see chapters 6 and 8).

disreputable players. Max Jacob offers the baby genius of the zany girl in "La Saltimbanque en Wagon de Troisième Classe" ("The *Saltimbanque* in the Third-Class Car"). Or consider the many images of the circus infant as Christ child in Picasso, Chagall, and Bergman. All such works stress the poverty of outcasts living on the margin of society. In them all, as in Mallarmé and our two poems, the child player appears as a mitigator, a sign of redemption.

THE VISUAL SETTING

Apollinaire and Rilke share some lesser symbolism that further reveals the condition of their troupers. The carpet in the elegy, mentioned above, marks the stage for the acrobats. Critics have marveled at Rilke's carpet, "lost in the universe," as a verbal evocation of Picasso's enigmatic painting. Although the description of this worn carpet occupies only three lines, it renders a compressed image of the tumblers' eternal homelessness.

> as though from an oily
> smoother air, they come down on the threadbare
> carpet, thinned by their everlasting
> jumps, this carpet forlornly
> lost in the cosmos.

The word *carpet* also ends the elegy, thus reaffirming the emblematic value of the artistes' performance.

Apollinaire devotes a whole strophe to his carpets, the only description of the poem's setting.

> Many dirty carpets covered the ground
> Carpets whose wrinkles won't come out
> Carpets almost all the color of dust
> Where several flecks of yellow or green persist
> Like a tune that haunts you

These carpets, like the one in Rilke's elegy, have a clear basis in fact. In even the most modest street show, the artistes use some kind of decorative mat to lend ceremony to their act. Such special rugs appear in contemporary circuses, and they probably go back to the ancient ritual sacrifices that framed the first acrobatic acts. In Daumier's *Saltimbanques on the Move* (1840s), the clown carries such a mat under his arm. And in his *Les Saltimbanques* (1850s), a boy sits on a similar rug (see chapter 7).

Rilke's and Apollinaire's carpets have a close parallel in the ballet *Petrushka* (1911), in which two street dancers spread out their mats before competing. In our two poems, the carpets symbolize a very old civilization. They suggest both past splendor and its demise. Like the *saltimbanques*, these rugs embody a decadent condition, connoting the decay of European culture. Faded and marred, the rugs still show some haunting specks of history.

Here Apollinaire evokes on a grander, cultural scale that same persistence of memory that prompts the second strophe. "In my youth, one saw much more of them than now." Considering these lines along with the fifth strophe (lines 18–22), we see that these performers indeed belong to the past. Their dilapidated rugs, like their age-old routines, root them in the very beginnings of mimed performance. And, just as the stains on the carpets persist, like a phrase of music that "pursues" one, so does the ritual act of the artistes haunt the spectators.

Apollinaire introduces this enigma of music, another deeply cultural experience, before the show starts, so we can readily connect it with the later metaphorical music of the boy. Lockerbie and Greet refer to this image as a transference "from the real to the imagined."[31] They see the whole poem in this way, as a gradual progression from the prosaic to a mysterious, even magical, world. Rilke, on the contrary, shows little of daily routine, offering the reader his transcendent vision right away. So does Picasso, who immediately presents enigma.

Like the associative music of the show, the faded carpets closely link the performers with their audience. The rugs summon memory in the spectator, born of the same venerable culture as both the rugs and the artistes. This memory connects the audience to its own history as participants in a spectacle. Both Apollinaire and Rilke transmute, by means of their carpets, the ordinary props of performance into transcendent unifying symbols. Ultimately, these signs illumine both the ancient roots of the street show and its complex cultural tie to its audience.

THE POETRY OF THE *SALTIMBANQUE*

The main identification between Apollinaire and his boy performer lies in the metaphor of music and dance as poetry. Scott Bates shows that the poem's title implies this primary link of poetry between Apollinaire and his boy. Since the image of clouds connotes poetic vision for Apollinaire, the

31. Guillaume Apollinaire, *Calligrammes*, ed. and trans. Anne Hyde Greet and S. I. Lockerbie, 389.

boy of the clouds must also be a poet. We recall Baudelaire's albatross: "The poet resembles the prince of the clouds." Descriptions of the boy's act as "music so delicate," "with so much harmony," show that the child's redemption of the scene also constitutes a rebirth of music. Besides, as Philippe Renaud stresses, the boy emerges from under the barrel organ. His act arises out of the traditional, mechanical music; his art renews the old. "And that music of forms / Destroyed that of the barrel-organ." Thus he transcends his own heritage of the street performer, with its routine, even ritualized, style.[32]

However, referring to the boy's act solely as music belies the boy's import as a dancer. He creates his effects as much by body gesture as by acrobatics, and he makes no actual music. Indeed, the child's gestures may recall Mallarmé's evocation of dance as "a poem detached from all verbal means," as "bodily writing."[33] Many writers of the time—Symons, Rimbaud, Yeats, Hofmannsthal—perceived dance as an essentially mystic experience. As Frank Kermode shows, poets of the *fin de siècle* saw in all the silent arts a more fully expressive medium than language, which they found inadequate.

When we compare the "music" of this boy of the clouds with the flute playing of his kindred performer, the Musicien de Saint Merry, we see that both types of art have magical effects. As for the boy, his transcendent act recalls Apollinaire's reaction to Picasso's *Les Saltimbanques:* "One cannot confound these saltimbanques with actors. Their spectator must be pious, for they celebrate silent rites with a difficult agility." Likewise, the musician enchants his helpless lady listeners, just as the child's dance induces epiphany for his audience.

In "Crépuscule," we find another magical scene, indeed a sort of mystery play produced by the god Hermes as Harlequin. To Richard Stamelman, the many sides of Hermes appear as aspects of Harlequin himself. Here we confront perhaps the deepest level of magic, in the poet's identification with

32. For Mallarmé, the barrel organ gives not a mechanical sound but rather a magical suggestiveness. In the prose poem "Plainte d'Automne," this "instrument of the sad" makes him "dream desperately." Its "joyously vulgar tune," like a romantic ballad, makes him weep. And, as a sign of his emotional involvement in this sound, he does *not* do what the spectators of Rilke and Apollinaire do: toss coins. Contrasting with their ritual gesture, this poet insists on isolating, "savoring," the aural moment. Accordingly, he also cannot look at the artiste producing the sound. Typically, the transcendent Mallarméan event contains an absence. The barrel organ also plays a significant, albeit invisible, role in the creation of the ballet *Petrushka*. One of the popular songs Stravinsky used in his score was "Elle avait un' jambe en bois," which he heard from the organ-grinder under his window at Beaulieu (Charles Hamm, ed., *Petrushka: An Authoritative Score of the Original Version*, 178).

33. Mallarmé, *Oeuvres*, 304.

his artistes. The Musician of Saint-Merry serves as alter ego for the poet, for he leads the parade—a carnival sight—"playing the song that *I* sing and that *I* composed" (italics mine).[34] The boy's mysterious new poetry stands just as clearly for Apollinaire's own ideal of poetry reborn, "a new and humanist lyricism."

As for the elegy, Rilke also identifies with his artistes. At the purely biographical level, the boy *saltimbanque* resembles the boy Rilke in his frailty and his strained relation to his mother. But more significantly, the poet identifies with the metaphoric poetry of the tumblers' act. For him, this routine represents not only the painful demands of creation but also the questionable value of technique itself. "The pure too-little" that denotes the acrobats' act points further to the inadequacy of skill per se.[35] Like many of his peers—Mann, Kafka, Hofmannsthal—Rilke expressed haunting doubts about the justification of the artist's pursuit.

Not accidentally, these writers often render the conflict of art versus "Life" through the metaphor of the artist as wanderer and/or showman. We recall Tonio Kröger's ambivalence toward "gypsies in green wagons," or the declining Aschenbach as rouged buffoon, or Kafka's *Hungerkünstler,* that ultimate parody of the artist. Indeed, several critics characterize the fifth elegy as just such an attempt to justify the life of art. Ultimately, this common feeling of European writers of the war generation, this need to choose between art and "Life," reflects the end of *l'art pour l'art.*

THE SEARCH FOR SELF

What Stamelman calls "the search for self" lies at the root of the fascination for the *saltimbanque.* Ever since Banville first specified the artiste as also an artist, writers and painters have identified with these alter egos in performance. Two texts already discussed here, Banville's *Pauvres Saltimbanques* and Baudelaire's "Le Vieux Saltimbanque," evoke mainly the misery of the artistic life. Baudelaire finds kindred among all the poor, since, as he says in "Les Veuves," poets are "irresistibly attracted to all who are feeble, ruined, wretched, orphaned."[36] Hence the appeal of the *saltimbanque,* who is all of that and artiste also.

34. Apollinaire, *Oeuvres,* 189.

35. For an opposite, positive reaction to skill itself, again within the circus context, see Jean Cocteau and the Goncourt brothers. In the essay "Le Numéro Barbette," Cocteau glorifies the technique of the burlesque performer as exemplary for all artists. In similar terms, the Goncourts contrast the honest skill of the circus with the mere acting of the legitimate stage, which depends on illusion (*Journal,* ed. Robert Ricatte, 171).

36. Baudelaire, *Oeuvres,* 1:292.

The player's wandering life is a principal source of identification for Rilke, Picasso, and Apollinaire. All three creators lacked roots. Here lies a cogent reason for Picasso's closeness to circus folk during his Rose Period. Contemporary sources show that the artist, still feeling tied to Spain, could not truly settle in Paris. Artistically too, Picasso admired the resilience and virtuosity that these players inherited from the *Commedia dell'Arte*. And he saw in their art of improvisation a parallel to the resourcefulness that poverty forced on him. Picasso specifically identified with Harlequin, for he often painted himself as that daring, agile, and clever clown. Unlike artists of the nineteenth century, he never saw himself as the melancholy Pierrot.

Both poets also had no home. Rilke never even established a territory, moving from country to country, from castle to castle of aristocratic friends. His travels, like Apollinaire's, formed a basis for his art. We may see all the work of these poets, along with Picasso's, as a search for self. Thus the poems and the painting discussed here, proceeding from identification with the *saltimbanque,* are essential to the these three oeuvres.

To sum up: Both poems give us street circuses, with similar personnel. At the center of both shows and the painting, we find a "magical" boy, whose innocent grace redeems the suffering of his peers. Furthermore, the ritual-like act of Apollinaire's boy and the paradoxical smile of Rilke's child symbolize the salvation of the audience too. Both poems close with an epiphany of universal import. This artistic revelation suggests to Margaret Davies the beginnings of that "moral synthesis," uniting "the poetic, creative spirit in all men," that she finds dominant in Apollinaire's late works.[37] Rilke's last strophe, with its image of a triumphant posthumous spectacle, also connotes the salvation of humanity through art. Here we find the deepest common meaning in the two poems. Creation demands suffering, but it may unite and redeem mankind. Art requires the miracle of the uniquely blessed poet, yet, paradoxically, it belongs to us all.

37. Margaret Davies, "Poetry as the Reconciliation of Opposites," in *Order and Adventure in Post-Romantic Poetry,* ed. E. M. Beaumont et al., 182.

6 FROM PIERROT TO PETRUSHKA
The Anti-Hero of the *Commedia dell'Arte*

> Only a straw-stuffed puppet this modern hero!
> **—Wallace Fowlie, *Love in Literature***

Critics have long hailed the 1911 ballet *Petrushka* as a pivotal work in the development of modern music and dance. In his recent entry in *Groves Dictionary of Music*, Jeremy Noble notes Stravinsky's score as a turning point in his evolution toward bitonality. Boris Asaf'eyev claims that here Stravinsky "finally reaches a fulfillment, with it he steps out firmly in front of his generation."[1] Mikhail Baryshnikov calls the puppet *the* dramatic role of the century. And no one can ignore the influence that Michel Fokine's inventions have had on all "character" and crowd movement since *Petrushka*.

Accordingly, commentators find a wealth of deeper significance for this work. We may group most of their views into two categories, which sometimes overlap: the biographical and the political. The biographical side emerges most clearly from a contemporary review by Cyril Beaumont. In "Petrushka in London," he identifies Nijinsky with his role. "Did he, in one of his moods of dark introspection, feel conscious of a strange parallel between Petrushka and himself, and the Showman and Diaghilev?" Similarly, Vera Krasovskaya speaks of Nijinsky as "Diaghilev's captive." Baryshnikov, echoing Krasovskaya, goes still further in tying the ballet to Nijinsky's life. "The parallel between Petrushka's situation and that of Nijinsky in his relationship to Diaghilev and the Diaghilev regime is quite clear. . . . The role of Petrushka was not deliberately and literally based on Nijinsky, but . . . various aspects of his behavior and his real life must have contributed unconsciously to the creation of this great masterpiece."[2]

Some critics intensify the idea of Diaghilev dominating Nijinsky into a broader sociopolitical oppression. Harry Burke sees in the ballet "a symbol of the Russian people in the hands of its rulers." Baryshnikov also speaks of liberation as the theme of *Petrushka*. "It reflected the growing sensitivity of all artists to the freedom of the individual . . . ; it is about small people torn

---

1. Boris Asaf'eyev, *A Book about Stravinsky,* trans. Richard French, 20.
2. Beaumont quoted in Charles Hamm, ed., *Petrushka: An Authoritative Score of the Original Version,* 191; Vera Krasovskaya, *Nijinsky,* trans. John Bowlt, 351; Mikhail Baryshnikov, *Baryshnikov at Work,* ed., Charles Angell France, 219.

apart by fear and hate and humiliation, and their inevitable rebellion. Those feelings can emerge to control the destinies of the individual, no matter how primitive and deep the mask he hides behind may be." Theodor Adorno generalizes this idea into a more sweeping historical evaluation. In the ballet he finds "a premonition of the coming drama of the individual in an age of mass production and mechanisation, in which personality tends to be submerged.[3]

Finally, Edith Sitwell typifies the image of Petrukska as all-too-human. Others have echoed her view, but is has no rival for sheer sentimentality.

We know that we are watching our own tratgedy. Do we not all know that little room at the back of our poor clown's booth—that little room with the hopeful tinsel stars and the badly-painted ancestral portrait of God? Have we not all battered our heads through the flimsy paper walls—only to find blackness? In the dead Petrushka, we know that it is our poor wisp of soul that is weeping so pitifully to us from the top of the booth, outside life forever, with no one to warm him or comfort him, while the bright-colored rags that were the clown's body lie, stabbed to the heart, in the mire of the street—and, with Claudius, we cry out for "Lights, lights, more lights."[4]

Osbert Sitwell shares his sister's enthusiasm for the ballet, but his analysis goes far deeper. Indeed, I believe he was the first critic to probe its essential substance. Sitwell calls *Petrushka* "as symbolic a creation of its time as *Don Giovanni*." He even compares the influence of this ballet on its own era to that of myth on the Greeks. "*Petrushka* was, in its scope as a work of art, universal; it presented the European contemporary generation with a prophetic and dramatized version of the fate reserved for it, in the same way that the legend of the Minotaur summed up . . . the fate of several generations of Greek youths and maidens." Wallace Fowlie also finds mythic values in the puppet-hero, seeing in him a model for the "hollow men" of Eliot and Joyce.[5]

More recently, observers have tried to place the ballet within its own historical context. Since 1971, when the Béjart company revived *Le Sacre du Printemps,* the Diaghilev ballet that followed *Petrushka* in 1912, critics have noted that both works foreshadow the revolution. Asaf'eyev asks, "Did not this pre-revolutionary psychic excitation and nervous impetuosity bespeak both a demand for emotional release, and the absence of it?"

3. Burke quoted in Hamm, *Petrushka,* 18; Baryshnikov, *Work,* 221; Adorno quoted in Roman Vlad, *Igor Stravinsky,* 18.
4. Sitwell quoted in Hamm, *Petrushka,* 189.
5. Osbert Sitwell, *Great Morning,* 241; Wallace Fowlie, *Love in Literature,* 95, 117.

Arlene Croce may go too far in claiming that the idea of *Sacre,* namely "the individual destroyed in the name of the race, would become the apocalyptic message of the Russian revolution." She even interprets this ballet "as a sign that the end of civilisation was at hand." Croce makes no comparable claims for *Petrushka,* but she finds broad cultural relevance in the cult that has developed around Nijinsky in all his roles. "The notion that a ballet dancer could be part of the intellectual history of his time is starting to seem less absurd to us than it once did."[6]

Let us first question the validity of such claims. Can we accept these grandiose views of *Petrushka*? Does it indeed render a modern myth of primary cultural value? To answer these questions, I shall interpret this work in the broad context of origins, a matter not yet fully settled. Most accounts trace the work mainly to Russian folk puppet plays, themselves called *Petrushka* after their title character. In his study of the *skomorokhi,* Russell Zguta argues that these itinerant actors and musicians grew out of an indigenous East Slavic tradition. Their characteristic puppet shows seem to have developed from ancient seasonal fertility rites. The best known of these festivals, *Maslenitsa,* celebrated the killing of winter and the welcoming of spring. Here we may see some very close source material for our ballet, set amid the Shrovetide Carnival.

But I argue that the soulful character of Petrushka in the ballet, as well as his ironic resurrection, cannot stem directly from popular sources. Although the creators of the ballet intended to evoke the haunting, even grotesque, quality of the Russian Carnival, the result was much more than a fond look at folk art. Stravinsky himself implies other sources: "I was not attracted by any folklore element in *Petrushka,* always being prompted by something very different from that." By contrast, Stravinsky evoked the aura of the *skomorokhi* more directly in his later ballet *Le Renard* (1916). Here we find not only the animal characters typical of the pagan plays but also the typical anticlerical tone, with the fox disguised as a nun. It seems significant for my claim of mainly non-native sources for *Petrushka* that the librettist for *Le Renard,* Ramuz, had no ties to the avant-garde theatrical ideas of Blok and Meyerhold.[7]

Accordingly, I hope to show that *Petrushka* owes its essential debts to "something very different" from popular forms: namely, the theatricality of Blok and Schnitzler, mediated through Meyerhold's productions. I refer to

6. Asaf'eyev, *Stravinsky,* 24; Arlene Croce, "Inside the Ballets Russes," 158.

7. Vera Stravinsky and Robert Craft, eds., *Stravinsky in Pictures and Documents,* 66. I thank Simon Karlinsky for alerting me to *Le Renard.* In "Stravinsky and Pre-literate Russian Theater," he gives a compelling analysis of the four types of Slavic spectacle that the composer uses in his ballets (*Nineteenth Century Music* 6, 3 (1983): 232–40).

Blok's verse play *Balaganchik* (The Puppet Booth) (1906), directed by Meyerhold, and to Schnitzler's pantomime *Der Schleier der Pierrette* (The Veil of Pierrette) (1910). Meyerhold himself created an important bridge between these works and the ballet with his adaptation of the Schnitzler piece, *Sharf Kolombiny* (Columbine's Scarf) (1910), which he dedicated to Blok.

In sum, my argument concerns the three crucial innovations in the ballet. First, the puppet himself is a lyrical, pathetic Pierrot, rather than the traditional Punch-like buffoon of the Russian street fair. Second, he rises from death. Third, the ballet gives a finally ironic view of its own story. This last feature, stressed above all by Stravinsky, marks *Petrushka* as a mockery of stage conventions. Ultimately asking what *is* real, *Petrushka* joins the tradition of European Symbolists—Pirandello, Craig, Maeterlinck, Evreinov—in combatting Stanislavskian Realism.

Characteristically, such innovators often used puppets, which have belonged to the avant-garde since the Middle Ages. In tracing the ballet to the important but now forgotten plays of Blok and Schnitzler, I suggest that this work displayed all the leading tendencies in the drama of its day. Virginia Bennett even speaks of "the Petrushka era." Moreover, the ballet continues to have this representative value for us. No one now plays the Blok and Schnitzler pieces, while *Petrushka* survives as a popular staple in the ballet repertory.

BACKGROUND

My study starts with the known origins of the ballet, well documented in memoirs and letters of its creators. Stravinsky, Fokine, and Benois all left detailed, albeit conflicting, accounts of their collaboration. One fact emerges clearly from all their statements: the prime motive for the work lay in their shared nostalgia for the Shrovetide fair of their youth. As Benois has said, they wanted to offer "a kind of memorial" to the *balagani,* or fairground puppet shows. Since 1901 the regime's campaign against alcoholism effectively banned such shows.

The main character of these shows, Petrushka, played a significant role in the memories of all three collaborators. Stravinsky even speaks of the piano in his original score as a puppet quarreling, in harsh, percussive cries, with its antagonist, the orchestra. "I had conceived the idea of a puppet suddenly let loose, who, with cascades of diabolic arpeggios, exasperates the patience of the orchestra, which, in its turn, replies to him with menacing fanfares. There follows a terrible tumult which, after its paroxysm, ends with the sad and plaintive silencing of the poor puppet." So far, so good; I do not deny the immediate impetus for the ballet in the attempts of its creators to enshrine a primary folk icon.[8]

But let us look further back than the conscious aims of the three artists themselves. Ideally, of course, we should consider Pierrot's European lineage, which may go back to antiquity. Allardyce Nicoll highlights traits of the second slave in Attic comedy that recall the gluttony and stupidity of the earliest Pierrot figures in the *Commedia*.[9] However, it must suffice here to limit our tracing of origins for Petrushka to Romanticism. Since around 1850 the sad clown has thrived in the work of French painters and writers. Think only of the best-known ones: Gautier, Banville, Baudelaire, Daumier, Verlaine, Laforgue, Rouault, Picasso. In England, Dowson and Beardsley contributed to the modishness of the melancholy Pierrot of the *fin de siècle*. Later on, Klee, Beckmann, and Heckel used anxious clowns to express the growing malaise of prewar Europe. There is little danger of reaching too far in cataloguing subliminal influences on Benois, the chief librettist for the ballet. His awareness of all the arts, in both historical and current styles, surpassed that of any other collaborator.

In claiming Benois as mainly responsible for the libretto, I do not neglect the collaborative nature of the ballet. Not only did Benois, Stravinsky, and Fokine jointly achieve a *Gesamtkunstwerk;* but Diaghilev also gave an initial spur by suggesting that Stravinsky combine his first two compositions, *Petrushka's Cry* and the *Russian Dance,* into a ballet about the Russian Carnival. But even Stravinsky finally regarded Benois as the true author. As for Benois' knowledge of all the arts, he himself introduced the young, naive Diaghilev to the riches of European culture. Indeed, the later hostility between the two stemmed from Benois' sense that Diaghilev did not appreciate all he had learned from the older man.

MEYERHOLD IN CONTEXT

For my limited aim of tracing the specific sources for the ballet, I shall stay within the immediate sphere of Benois. When we look for Pierrot and puppets in this close context of art in Russia between 1905 and 1910, one creator stands out distinctly: Vsevolod Meyerhold, the most innovative and influential director of his time. After his break with Stanislavsky in 1904, Meyerhold staged the most daring productions of the international avant-

---

8. Alexandre Benois, *Reminiscences of the Russian Ballet,* trans. Mary Britnieva, 325; Eric Walter White, *Igor Stravinsky,* 194. Such nostalgia marks several modern works dealing with circus or street performers. Compare Rilke and Apollinaire in chapter 5 and Fellini in chapter 8.

9. Allardyce Nicoll, *Masks, Mimes and Miracles,* 72.

garde.[10] The plays of Strindberg, Wilde, Maeterlinck, Pirandello, Sologub, Mayakowsky, and Toller all took revolutionary form on Meyerhold's stage.

So Benois' susceptibility to the work of this director can hardly surprise us. We know from contemporary reviews that both men saw each other's productions, which usually elicited only negative responses. However, Benois specifically praised *Sharf Kolombiny* in his scathing review of Meyerhold's *Don Juan* (1910). And we also know of Meyerhold's own involvement with the Diaghilev ballets, for he himself appeared, as the sole non-dancer, in Fokine's *Carnival* (1910). Significantly, he played Pierrot, as he had already done twice before. In Schöntan's *The Acrobats* (1903), Meyerhold portrayed the clown as an aging man; in *Balaganchik* (1906), he created a lyrical, ironic Pierrot, in whom critics saw a poignant self-portrait. In Meyerhold's interpretation, Pierrot represented the sublime yet unhappy isolation of poetry, of art misunderstood.

In his essay "Balaganchik" (1913), Meyerhold suggests that the actor of the *Commedia dell'Arte* approximates a puppet in his stylized use of mask, gesture, and movement. Like Kleist, Meyerhold and many of his colleagues saw in the puppet an ideal actor. They glorified not the Kleistian mystical grace of the human image in wood but rather its lack of individuality. Many playwrights and directors of the late nineteenth century decried the cult of the actor that had developed by then. Craig found modern actors too egotistical to do justice to the play itself. He sought a return to the ideals of Greek drama, in which the intention of the poet reigned supreme. The actor, enlarged for the amphitheater audience, wore masks, padding, and huge buskins. He thus became depersonalized, indeed a virtual puppet.

Craig found other models in the Japanese Noh drama and medieval morality plays, which depend on masks, declaimed recitative, and stylized pantomime. He pleaded for an actor "plus fire and minus egotism." "The actor should copy the marionette, who, by dispensing with human personality, could concentrate the spectator's attention . . . on the essential conflict of the drama." Duse expressed this same urge toward purifying the stage when she exclaimed: "To save the theater, it must be destroyed. The actors and actresses must all die of the plague. . . . They make art impossible."[11]

In *A Theory of the Stage* (1897) Arthur Symons argued that puppets could correct the overly technical, analytic aspect of contemporary drama by giving the playwright a simple, direct means of expression. Accordingly,

10. For the stormy relations between Meyerhold and Stanislavsky, see Paul Schmidt, ed. and trans., *Meyerhold at Work,* and Marjorie Hoover, *Meyerhold: The Art of Conscious Theater.*
11. Edward Gordon Craig, "The Actor and the Über-Marionette," 7, 10.

he advocated movement and all kinds of nonverbal theater. "The foundation of drama is that part of the action that can be presented in dumb-show. . . . Puppets provide the vehicle for reducing that action to its simplest and purest terms."[12] George Bernard Shaw echoes this idea of the puppet as the essence of drama in his preface to the history of marionettes by Max von Boehn.

I always hold up the wooden actors as instructive object-lessons to our flesh-and-blood players. The wooden ones, though stiff and continually glaring at you with the same overcharged expression, yet move you as only the most experienced living actors can do. What really affects us in the theater is not the muscular activities of the performers, but the feelings they awaken in us by their aspect; for the imagination of the spectator plays a far greater part there than the exertions of the actors. *The puppet is the actor in his primitive form.* Its symbolic costume, from which all realistic and historically correct details are banished, its . . . grimace expressive to the highest degree attainable by the carver's art, the mimicry by which it suggests human gesture in unearthly caricature—these give to its performance an intensity to which few actors can pretend, an intensity which imposes on our imagination like those images in immovable hieratic attitudes on the stained glass of Chartres Cathedral, in which the gaping tourists seem like little lifeless dolls moving jerkily in the draughts from the doors, reduced to sawdusty insignificance by the contrast with the gigantic vitality in the windows overhead [italics mine].

In this remarkable inversion of the expected imagery, Shaw implies that people are mere dolls and puppets have a god-like monumentality. This notion harks back to what Craig said of the origins of the modern puppet in archaic stone images of the gods. According to his research in archaeology, the first marionettes of India represented a huge divinity. Our oldest relevant document, the account of a Greek traveler in 800 B.C., tells of the "noble artificiality" of the marionettes in a temple theater at Thebes. Tracing the origins of all drama to worship, Craig reflects the same urge for transcendence that moves Mallarmé to envision theater as sacred ritual. Indeed, several factors worked to foster transcendental values from the 1800s onward: Wagner, a Catholic renascence, anti-Darwinism.

Craig ends his essay on the *Übermarionette* by waxing messianic on what the puppet can do for the theater.

Weeds . . . grow quickly, and that wilderness of weeds, the modern theater, soon sprang up. The figure of the Divine Puppet . . . has made me love . . . what we now call the puppet, and to detest what we call life in art. I pray earnestly for the

12. Symons quoted in Peter Arnott, *Plays without People,* 75.

return of the Image . . . the *Übermarionette;* and when he comes again, . . . it will be possible for the people to return to its ancient joy in ceremonies . . . once more will Creation be celebrated . . . and divine and happy intercession made to Death.[13]

This Divine Puppet bears iconic value, again recalling Mallarmé and his religion of art. Moreover, Craig's purifying attitude reflects a typically Mallarméan trait of Symbolism. The ideal Symbolist art, like mysticism, must purge itself of all worldliness.

The puppet thus offers to a corrupted theater the purity of the silent human icon. What may seem like reduction has the actual advantage of abstraction. "The marionette . . . reduces the limitless complexity of the human being to the simplest of gestures, which are projected by a small amount of wood, paint and string. This acute simplicity of expression, however, affords the marionette an advantage over the human actor, for the marionette is the sum of a specific number of unvarying characteristics and is therefore an ideally perfect type. . . . It represents, it is an idea, and nothing more."[14]

By the end of the century, this ideal abstraction had endeared the marionette to the avant-garde. Rejecting crass realism, Symbolists fell in love with mime, shadow plays, and puppets. *Ubu Roi* (1896), that landmark of Modernist aesthetics, appeared first as a puppet show by the schoolboy Alfred Jarry. Schnitzler wrote a cycle of puppet pieces and pantomimes, of which *Der Schleier der Pierrette* is only one. In all these formative works, Schnitzler demonstrates that the nonverbal figure contains the essence of drama. Maeterlinck experimented with various unrealistic devices, striving for what we might call the soul of all soulless things.

Laforgue, Barrie, Craig, and Hofmannsthal also wrote for puppets and mimes, and even their conventional plays depend on nonverbal dramatic means: *Commedia* figures, dance, veils, mist. These writers not only create that "theater of silence" espoused by Maeterlinck but also realize the "purely visual spectacles" foretold by Gautier in 1842 (see chapter 2). Continuing this tradition, the theater of the absurd eschews psychology to focus on those external values conveyed by the silent actor. Beckett and Ionesco continue to treat their dehumanized characters like puppets. Indeed, Beckett's work exhibits a progressive silencing.[15]

---

13. Craig, "The Actor," 14–15.
14. Henry Schmidt, *Satire, Caricature, and Perspectivism in the Works of Georg Büchner,* 73.
15. Compare what Ionesco says about the roots of his work. "If the essence of theater lay in the enlargement of effects, it was necessary to enlarge them even more, to underline them, to emphasize them as much as possible. To push the theater beyond that intermedi-

All these seekers of a new theater—Meyerhold, Maeterlinck, Duse, Craig, Symons—want ultimately to get rid of words, of rationality itself. They express a need, characteristic of Modernism, for the primitive. In creating abstract styles, they contribute to the "barbaric" aspect of modern art. They find puppets and related nonverbal means fascinating, for they feel "the undying thirst for the non-rational and the mysterious."[16] At the root of this phenomenon lies that retreat from industrial society that also characterizes the mime discussed in chapter 2. We see the same impulse intensified in *l'art nouveau* and *Jugendstil,* with their proliferating vegetation. Think of Gustav Klimt, whose human figures often merge with aquatic forms. In Munch's work, a demonic nature even overpowers his frail, nervous people. In such artists we see a retreat from the human.

In *Petrushka,* the dualistic puppet-man shows this focus on the non-human already in progress. Below I shall trace this tendency to Hoffmann and the Romantic critique of mechanistic attitudes in the industrial era. As for Meyerhold, perhaps the single greatest influence on the ballet, we may now see why he found in marionettes the key to rejuvenating the thespian art. Rejecting the stale imitation of "real life" arduously cultivated by Stanislavsky, Meyerhold sought a return to the roots of all performance in mask and movement. A few quotations may briefly convey the larger aesthetic implications of his idea of mime.

Words in the theater are only embellishments on the design of movement. Cannot the body, with its lines and its harmonious movements, sing as clearly as the voice? . . . The puppet has created a world of enchantment with its incomparable movements, its expressive gestures achieved by some magic known to it alone, its angularity which reaches the heights of true plasticity. . . . The puppet does not want to become the exact replica of man, . . . it wishes not to copy but to create. . . . The mask enables the spectator to see not only the actual Arlecchino before him, but all the Arlecchinos who live in his memory. Through the mask the spectator sees every person who bears the slightest resemblance to the character.[17]

In this last quotation Meyerhold suggests that the mask, like the puppet, universalizes character. Hence it too creates abstraction. Here lies perhaps Meyerhold's strongest link to the *Commedia* tradition, which designed its

---

ary zone that is neither theater nor literature was to put it back into its proper framework. . . . What was needed was not to disguise the strings that moved the puppets but to make them even more visible, deliberately apparent, to go right down to the very basis of the grotesque, the realm of caricature, to transcend the pale irony of witty drawing-room comedies" (quoted in Martin Esslin, *The Theater of the Absurd,* 91).

16. Enid Welsford, *The Fool,* 272.

17. Edward Braun, ed., *Meyerhold on Theater,* 124, 142, 128, 129, 131.

comic characters according to local stereotypes. Indeed, he seems to have surpassed the Italian comedy, for he defines his actor as an *Übermario-nette*. This concept developed from his Biomechanics, a system based on photographic studies of movement.[18] Here again, we note the tendency to idealize through abstraction. In fact, we may see the supermarionette as a late manifestation of the urge for the abstract in *l'art pour l'art*.

With the concept of the *Übermarionette*, Meyerhold reaches the logical end of his antirealism, the attempt to get rid of "life" on the stage. Like other ultimate symptoms of the radical opposition of art and life, the superpuppet became an impossible ideal. Herbert Marshall shows the ironically "total-itarian" aspect of this attitude. "[The theory] was a weakness of his theater, for in the end every actor and every role was but a reflection of the puppet master. Meyerhold was the *regisseur par excellence*, the director, the dic-tator, which in itself was a reflection of the dictatorship of the Party he served. And he eventually starred himself as the 'author of the spectacle' because he was its director, actor and dramatist."[19]

Later on, Schnitzler gave his negative judgment of the Titanism ex-pressed in both the *Übermarionette* and its source. "You say: A Superman. Pardon me, I didn't notice him. What I saw on your hallowed stage—Although it had a human mask—Was only a Super-puppet."[20]

Now let us return to Benois' receptivity to Meyerhold's ideas. Since the director played Pierrot as a poet and also viewed the actor as marionette, one might combine these two related elements—Pierrot-puppet and poet—into one. That, I claim, is just what Benois did. He thus created a new iden-tity for Pierrot: the puppet as a desolated artist. Benois gave Petrushka a soul, for he transformed the brutish Punch into a lyrical Pierrot. This doll felt love, grief, humiliation; in short, his mind made him "a Hamlet among

18. On Biomechanics, see the detailed translation in Hoover, *Meyerhold,* 311–15. A similar system also appeared at this time in the Dalcroze mime school. As for the *Übermarionette*, Meyerhold insisted that he developed his idea independently from Craig, who had already coined the term in 1908. "Do away with the actor, and you do away with the means by which a debased stage realism is produced and flourishes. No longer would there be a living figure to confuse us into connecting actuality and art; no longer a living figure in which the weakness of the flesh were perceptible. . . . The actor must go, and in his place comes the inanimate figure—the super-marionette we may call him, until he has won for himself a better name" (Craig, "The Actor," 11). The super-puppet has deeply influenced subsequent acting styles. Think of Brecht's insistence that his actors "rigidify" themselves; Ionesco writes clipped, staccato sentences, forcing the actor to speak mechanically. Compare the opinion of Jean-Louis Barrault that "the good actor must have something of the robot in him" (quoted in Toby Cole, ed., *Actors on Acting,* 230).

19. Herbert Marshall, *A Pictorial History of Russian Theater,* 125.

20. Schnitzler quoted in Martin Swales, *Arthur Schnitzler, A Critical Study,* 260.

puppets." This identity forms the most novel invention for Pierrot in the twentieth century. Moreover, the new figure merged the popular art form of the puppet with the fine art form of the Romantic Pierrot. Here indeed may lie one chief reason for the survival of *Petrushka:* it combines, in one satisfying performance, the two poles of culture, both learned and popular. Few works of art have ever achieved this synthesis, and accordingly, they have become classics.[21]

FOUR PIERROT PIECES

Let us now look at our four basic texts. First, here is my description of the ballet adapted from the libretto *Petrouchka:*

Scene 1. In the midst of a Shrovetide fair, on a puppet stage labeled *The Theater of the Living,* an old Charlatan produces for an amazed crowd Petrushka, the Moor, and the Ballerina, who perform a wild dance. The Charlatan's magic has imbued them all with human passions, but Petrushka suffers more than the others. He feels more deeply the cruelty of the Charlatan, his own slavery, his exclusion from ordinary life, his ugliness.

Scene 2. After the show, Petrushka seeks consolation from the Ballerina. In his box behind the stage, he implores her affection, but the flighty creature only flees in horror.

Scene 3. The Moor, however, brutish and evil, readily seduces her with his splendid appearance. Just as their love scene begins, Petrushka intrudes, mad with jealousy, and the Moor throws him out.

Scene 4. Outside, the fair has reached its raucous height. Suddenly, cries burst from within the theater; the puppets rush out; the Moor kills Petrushka with one blow of his sabre. The wretched puppet dies in the snow, surrounded by the suddenly still crowd. The magician, whom a policeman has come to question, hastens to calm everyone, and in his hands Petrushka becomes a doll again. The puppeteer shows that the head is wooden and the body mere straw. The crowd disperses. The Charlatan, now alone, sees in terror that Petrushka's ghost appears above the roof of the puppet stage. The figure threatens the old man and leers mockingly at all, including the audience in the theater, whom the Charlatan has fooled.

---

21. Richard Buckle, *Nijinsky,* 159. Stravinsky created a truly popular dimension for his score in using five Russian folk melodies, along with some more popular music. "The palette on which Stravinsky mixes his colors for the Carnival scene is rich and varied: besides Austrian dances of the same period, we find a French music-hall ditty of the early 1900's ('Elle avait un jamb' en bois') and . . . traditional Russian folk songs of no particular period" (Hamm, *Petrushka,* 204).

Here is an eyewitness account of the immediate predecessor of the ballet, the pantomime *Sharf Kolombiny* (October 1910):

The frivolous Columbine, betrothed to Harlequin, spends a last evening with her devoted Pierrot. As usual, she deceives him, swearing that she loves only him. Pierrot proposes a suicide pact and himself drinks the poison. Columbine lacks the courage to follow him and flees in terror to the wedding-ball, where the guests await her impatiently. The ball begins; while a quadrille is playing, Pierrot's flapping white sleeve is seen first through the window, then through the doors. The dances, now fast, now slow, turn into an awful nightmare, with strange Hoffmannesque characters whirling to the time of a huge-headed Kappellmeister, who sits on a high stool and conducts four wierd musicians. Columbine's terror reaches such a pitch that she can hide it no longer, and she rushes back to Pierrot. Harlequin follows her, and when he sees Pierrot's corpse he is convinced of his bride's infidelity. He forces her to dine before the corpse of the love-stricken Pierrot. Then he leaves, bolting the door fast. In vain Columbine tries to escape from her prison, from the ghastly dead body. Gradually, she succumbs to madness; she whirls in a frenzied dance, then finally drains the deadly cup and falls lifeless beside Pierrot.[22]

Now for my account of *Der Schleier der Pierrette* (January 1910):

Scene 1. Pierrot's room. Pierrot despairs at the faithlessness of his beloved Pierrette. She suddenly appears in bridal array, but declares that she wants to stay with him. Both should drink the poison she has brought. Pierrot finally empties his glass, but she does not. Horrified at his death, Pierrette flees, forgetting her bridal veil on the floor.

Scene 2. Rejoining the anxious Arlecchino at her wedding party, Pierrette begins to dance. A vision of her dead lover repeatedly pursues her, holding the veil. When the specter vanishes with it, she runs after him. Arlecchino, now furious, follows her.

Scene 3. Pierrot's room. Arlecchino, seeing Pierrot's corpse with the veil nearby, begins to understand. First incredulous, then mocking, he finally leaves Pierrette, locking her inside. Going mad with horror, she begins a dance of death, which climaxes when she falls dead beside Pierrot.[23]

Lastly, here is an edited eyewitness account of *Balaganchik* (December 1906):

Scene 1. Some sophisticated talkers, the Mystics, discuss a strange maiden who appears. Pierrot sees in her Columbine, but they insist she is

22. Eduard Braun, *The Theater of Meyerhold*, 102–3. For a somewhat conflicting view, see Hoover, *Meyerhold*, 65.
23. Arthur Schnitzler, *Gesammelte Werke*, 2:321–36.

Death. The confusion grows when this woman, having sworn never to leave Pierrot, goes off with Harlequin. Suddenly the author appears, disclaiming what these actors have said; he wrote a simple tale of two lovers threatened by a third party but finally united.

Scene 2. A masquerade. Lovers dance with their mistresses, maskers laugh and flirt. Pierrot wonders if Columbine is made of flesh or cardboard. Harlequin claims that nobody knows how to love, life is like a sleep, and he will break the spell and get into the live world. But when he jumps through the window, he only bursts through the painted set and falls to the floor. Then Death comes to the ball and all the maskers flee; only Pierrot walks toward her with outstretched arms, and Death is transfigured into a lovely girl. The author again walks in, but when he is about to rejoice at such a happy ending, everything disappears. Harlequin dies, bleeding of cranberry juice; Pierrot is left alone, knowing that his beloved, Death or Lady Beautiful, is indeed a puppet. Is it Pierrot's diseased mind that turns all into cardboard? Or is Columbine the Eternal Feminine, the image of beauty and spirit? The audience was left with all these questions when the sets were pulled up and the end of the show announced on an empty stage.[24]

PIERROT

In juxtaposing these four works, let us first look at their comparable elements. Perhaps their lowest common denominator lies in the figure of Pierrot-Petrushka. Who, then, is this clown? He originates in the beginnings of the *Commedia,* in the latter half of the sixteenth century. Probably two peasant clowns, Pedrolino and Pulcinella, form a common source for the later Pierrot, who appears recognizably in name and dress a century later. From around 1680 to 1840, the character develops from the two poles of the clever, agile Harlequin and the cloddish side of Pedrolino.

But around the middle of the nineteenth century, which saw the most famous evocation of the clown by Jean-Gaspard Deburau, Pierrot exhibited other traits also. He still often resembled the zanni types in being stupid, gullible, and violent. Additionally, though, Pierrot became pensive, melancholy, even soulful. Gautier adds a political aspect to this blend of traits in a review of 1847. "Pierrot, wan, lanky, dressed in his pale costume, always beaten and always hungry, is the ancient slave, the modern proletariat, and the pariah, the passive and disinherited being."[25]

24. Marc Slonim, *Russian Theater,* 215–16.
25. Gautier quoted in Vivienne Rubin, *Clowns in Nineteenth-Century French Literature,* 168.

Actually, Jules Janin had already implied a proletarian identity for Pierrot in 1832. He called the figure Deburau created "by turns gay, sad, sickly, robust, cudgeling—a musician, a poet, a simpleton, always poor, like the common people."[26] Already Janin shows us how expandable the Pierrot character had become. Gautier was probably his broadest interpreter, but other artists also contributed a variety of images for this character. The white clowns created by Verlaine, Mallarmé, and Laforgue, as well as the popular Pierrots of Daumier and Willette, tended to obscure the original peasant character of the buffoon. By contrast, these figures embodied the complexities of the post-Romantic poet himself. In particular, Verlaine and Laforgue gave a lasting identity to the clown-as-poet.

Indeed, Edward Lockspeiser sees a source for our ballet puppet here, for he refers to "Laforgue's pathetic spirit in *Petrushka*."[27] In such a phrase, Lockspeiser seems to overlook the important difference in consciousness between Laforgue's elegant dandy, Lord Pierrot, and the unaware puppet of the ballet. Petrushka is indeed pathetic, but his passive suffering stems more from the Pierrot of Deburau than from the cooly rational Laforgue. Ultimately, as Robert Storey has shown, Laforgue's self-projection as Decadent Pierrot-poet led elsewhere, beyond the literary metaphors of nineteenth-century France, to Eliot and Stevens.

Whether or not Benois knew the landmarks of this venerable Pierrot tradition behind his Petrushka, we cannot ignore the Russian puppet's ties to his ancestors. Stravinsky calls him "a sort of guignol called Pierrot in France, Kasperle in Germany, and Petrushka in Russia, . . . the immortal and unhappy hero of every fair in all countries." Fowlie sees the same universality in Petrushka's forebear, the French Pierrot. "As all women were in the painted virgin of the Italian Renaissance, so all men are in the painted clown of modern France."[28]

Other commentators also point back to various aspects of the traditional Pierrot. Léonide Massine, an admired interpreter of Petrushka, stresses his exploitation by others. "Dupe and victim of both the impresario and the Moor," the clown is "a tragic figure symbolizing innocence caught up in a world of corruption." Benois himself stresses the puppet's artistic side and its fragility. He claims that Petrushka represents "the poetical principle," evoking "the vulnerability of the poetic spirit." Probably Benois recalled, consciously or not, the lyrical despair of Blok's Pierrot. Ultimately, of course, this type of soulful clown goes back to Deburau. But only in

26. Ibid., 181.
27. Edward Lockspeiser, *Music and Painting*, 108.
28. White, *Stravinsky*, 194; Fowlie, *Love*, 114.

Balaganchik could Benois find this poetic character as specifically a puppet.[29]

Perhaps the most sweeping assessment of Petrushka comes from Krasovskaya. She relates our clown to the familiar "little man" of Pushkin, Gogol, and Dostoevsky. "Invisible threads link this character with [the older figures]. . . . Their forced affectations disguised their souls stifled by fear and grief. With Nijinsky the role of Petruska embodied . . . the tragedy of his epoch."[30]

Krasovskaya's view of Petrushka reminds us of what Gautier implied in 1847. Both critics see the outcast clown as characteristic of his time—be it the prelude to 1848 or 1917. Storey shows that the roots of the link that Gautier makes between the clown and his proletarian public lie in the identification of the observing Romantic artist with both parties. "The Romantics, suffering from Byronic *mal du siècle,* saw themselves as disinherited as Pierrot or *le peuple.* . . . Deburau the *saltimbanque* entered a Romantic mythology in which clown, artist and common man all found common cause. Paillasse, proletariat, poet: they were facile but inevitable identifications."[31] This trio of clown, artist, and public helps to explain Pierrot's remarkable power. As alter ego for the poet, he expresses the malaise of the declassed artist as mere entertainer. But more noticeably, we see his reflection in a broad variety of modern non-heroes.

In referring to "souls stifled by fear and grief," Krasovskaya touches on a type in European literature pervasive since the latter nineteenth century. Fear, doubt, indecision, and despair all infect the anti-heroes of an era still marked by post-Romantic disillusion. Flaubert's Frédéric Moreau, Grillparzer's Jakob, Keller's Strapinski, Joyce's Daedalus, Kafka's K.: such diverse figures show us the breadth of literary counterparts for the unheroic Petrushka.[32] The pantomime *La Peur* by Paul Margueritte presents a Pierrot whose paranoid isolation recalls Kafka's protagonists. We think especially of the terrified animal in his last story, "Der Bau" ("The Burrow").

Margueritte's piece, though not a major landmark in the Pierrot landscape, does provide another forebear for Petrushka, since fear forms one of

29. Léonide Massine, *My Life in Ballet,* 52; Benois, *Reminiscences,* 326.

30. Krasovskaya, *Nijinsky,* 177.

31. Robert Storey, *Pierrot: A Critical History of a Mask,* 109; idem, "The Pantomime of Jean-Gaspard Deburau at the Théâtre des Funambule," 3.

32. Several critics argue that a bourgeois culture precludes any heroism in the traditional sense: Edith Kern, "The Modern Hero: Phoenix or Ashes?" in *The Hero in Literature,* ed. Victor Brombert; Raymond Giraud, *The Unheroic Hero in the Novels of Stendhal, Balzac and Flaubert;* Wallace Fowlie, "Swann and Hamlet: A Note on the Contemporary Hero." For them, Petrushka would represent a popular embodiment of the same unheroic traits in the literary figures they discuss.

his primary traits. According to Margueritte, no one had yet seen in Pierrot this dramatic element. "The gay Pierrot has had his time. I don't want any more of the amorous, the servile, the comic figure. . . . My Pierrot is tragic. Tragic because he is afraid: he is fright itself, crime, anguish."[33]

Margueritte's contribution to the Pierrot figure lies in his deepening of psychological traits already implied by other poets. He intensifies what Gautier suggested, namely some complex passions lying beneath the mask of innocence. The neurotic self-consciousness of this clown in *La Peur* parallels similar anxieties in Pierrots created by other poets of the 1880s. In *Pierrot Narcisse* (1887), Giraud describes a race of unhappy people, the sons of Pierrot, who are beset by fear, longing, and inadequacy. Giraud's famous *Pierrot Lunaire* cycle (1884), immortalized by Schoenberg, reveals an almost surreal world behind the mask. In Verlaine's "Pierrot" (1882), the clown has lost all living identity, becoming a specter who haunts us.

> This is no longer the lunar dreamer of the old song
> Who laughed at his ancestors at the top of the door;
> His gaiety, like his candle, alas! is dead,
> And his spectre haunts us today, thin and luminous.
>
> And so it is, that amidst the terror of a long flash of
>   lightning,
> His pale blouse has the aspect, in the cold wind that carries
>   it away
> Of a windingsheet, and his mouth is gaping, so
> That he seems to scream under the gnawings of the worm.
>
> With the sound of a passing flight of night birds,
> His white sleeves make vaguely through space
> Mad signs to which no one responds.
>
> His eyes are two great holes where phosphorous creeps,
> And his flour renders more frightful still
> His bloodless face with its pinched nose of one near death.[34]

Surely our clown now approaches the end of his winding Romantic road of innocence, wit, longing, and subjectivity. I suggest that Verlaine's haunting Pierrot represents the spiritual death of the Romantic artist. No longer "the dreamer of the old song," he has lost his gaiety; his extinguished candle symbolizes the death of his soul. The third strophe of the sonnet evokes

33. Margueritte quoted in Rubin, *Clowns*, 181.
34. Translation in Robert Storey, *Pierrot*, 134.

the utter aloneness of the decadent artist, whose "mad signs" are meaningless. The line dividing genius from madness has become dangerously thin indeed.

Although this Pierrot is only moribund, he signals the demise of the heart that marks one end of Romanticism. We sense here a climactic moment in Pierrot's development throughout the nineteenth century, a point beyond which he can signify only decadence. Dying alone in the snow of the carnival, that grotesquely ironic herald of reborn spring, Petrushka puts an end to the Symbolist maze of inwardness. Utter subjectivity, we see, leads only to death.

This problem of the inner life, of spirituality, emerges from Stravinksy's earliest formulations: "I began to meditate an entire poem in the form of choreographic scenes . . . of the mysterious life of Petrushka, his birth, his death, his *double existence*—which is the key to the enigma, a key not possessed by the one who believes that he has given him life, the Magician."[35] Stravinsky wanted his clown to evoke the Hoffmannesque theme of the puppet called to life by a demonic master.

This idea had already enjoyed much success in the ballet *Coppelia* and the opera *The Tales of Hoffmann*. The new twist that *Petrushka* gives to this familiar material lies in its final, shocking irony for both the Charlatan and the audience. Here the clown's "double existence" acquires an additional dimension in the ridiculing of all mimetic representation. We see Petrushka as a puppet who suffers as a man; but the ending of the ballet shows that he was only a mock-puppet.[36]

With Petrushka's final appearance as the human ghost of the doll, we see that he has fooled both us and the Charlatan. His double life as puppet and man dissolves finally into the unresolved dualistic conflict between appearance and reality. Hence the ballet transcends the Hoffmannesque ambiguity of roles that remains well within the conventions of the stage. *Petrushka,* in mocking such mimesis, leaves open the question of ultimate reality, which the music evokes with memorably teasing laughter. Surprisingly, Diaghilev disliked the "note of interrogation" in its brilliant ending. He

35. Quoted in Vera Stravinsky, *Stravinsky,* 67, italics mine.
36. Petrushka's dual existence relates him to characters besides Coppelia. Indeed, many ballet libretti draw on mythic material that concerns the problem of separating human from animal beings. Consider Odette, the Swan Queen in *Swan Lake,* a woman trapped in the body of a swan by another demonic magician, Rotbart. Or think of Giselle, who appears as two different characters. In act 1, she lives and dies as a peasant girl in love; in act 2, she has become a sylph. Like Petrushka, the puppet-man, Giselle is a sylph-girl and Odette is a swan-woman. Fowlie hints at such a comparison in noting a reciprocal relation between Petrushka and Giselle. "The tragedy of *Giselle* is a fairy-story, and the fairy-story of *Petrushka* is a tragedy" (*Love,* 118).

asked Stravinsky to create a tonal finish to replace the last four pizzicato notes.[37]

Now for our three other Pierrots. Blok's figure, himself a puppet, most clearly resembles Petrushka. He too loves blindly, and his Columbine also rejects him for the virile Harlequin. Moreover, his character, like his fate, recalls Petrushka; this Pierrot again suffers and dreams, complaining finally of his lonely disillusion. As for sources, this type reminds us of Laforgue's Pierrot, with his *Complaintes* addressed to the cruel beloved. Indeed, Blok seems to have created even more of a cathartic alter ego than Laforgue did in his lyrical clown. Several biographers of Blok find an exact parallel for the triangle of Pierrot-Columbine-Harlequin in Blok's marriage. They see in *Balaganchik* a resolution in art of the conflicts among Blok, his wife, and Bely, his sexual and professional rival.

In any case, *Balaganchik* also originated as a dramatization of Blok's poem of the same title; thus the link to Laforgue's Pierrot is one of genre as well as character. Furthermore, the play contains much self-parody, a logical extension of the pervasive irony in Laforgue. The Maeterlinckian mystics show Blok's rejection, even ridiculing, of his own mystical poetry. And Pierrot's pathetic quest for the ideal of Woman, embodied in the paradoxically earthy Columbine, mocks the elevated concepts of divine Sophia in Blok's own Symbolist love poems. Such persistent self-parody leads Harold Segel to stress above all the anti-Symbolist character of this play. Hence Pierrot, again like Petrushka, satirizes his own story. Ultimately, he also mocks current theatrical convention. In the ballet, Petrushka laughs at the credibility of stage mimesis; in the play, Blok ridicules the macabre mysteries of Symbolist drama.

In both *Sharf Kolombiny* and *Der Schleier der Pierrette,* Pierrot has none of Petrushka's soulful suffering, nor does his character bespeak the artist. Indeed, he has hardly any character at all, so closely does the action focus on Columbine. Since Pierrot dies in the first scene, his only active function is to reappear as a specter to haunt the faithless Columbine. At the wedding party, Pierrette's vision of her dead lover repeatedly accosts her, with the symbolic veil in hand. In *Sharf Kolombiny,* Meyerhold echoes Schnitzler's vision-motif by showing only Pierrot's flapping white sleeve outside a window in the ball scene.

The figure glimpsed symbolically through a window is a stage technique conveying both mystery and romantic longing. Indeed, the use of windows in *Balaganchik* and the ballet may remind us that the framed view beyond an enclosed space forms a potent Romantic symbol. We shall see below

---

37. Benois, *Reminiscences,* 330; Igor Stravinsky and Robert Craft, *Expositions and Developments,* 156.

how other clowns attempt release through a window. But here, in *Sharf Kolombiny,* the window has only the symbolic function of recalling Pierrot. This piece of staging probably comes from Fokine, who used it in his *Carnaval* a few months earlier in 1910. However, the essential source for all these specters is Hoffmann. The aura of the grotesque in his tales had long enjoyed popularity among Russian artists. Besides, the ultimate significance of Hoffmann's ghosts—a Romantic probing of conventional reality— closely relates to what all our Pierrot pieces accomplish. Again, we see that the roots of the ballet reach far beyond its own time.

Furthermore, the visions of the dead Pierrot in Schnitzler and Meyerhold form a source for Petrushka's resurrection at the end of the ballet. Since no Pierrot before him had risen from actual death, the ghost in *Schleier* seems to be the sole origin for this crucial aspect of the puppet's story. Schnitzler again used Pierrot's return in his comparable pantomime *Die Verwandlungen des Pierrot* (1908). Here the clown, an actor, keeps reappearing to his lover Katharina, in different guises.

As Martin Swales has noted, Schnitzler often depicts the actor as a woman's sexual wish-figure, offering the endless variation of his delusive roles. Hence the Pierrot figures in both these pantomimes ultimately refer to the haunted perceptions of a faithless lover. These sexual specters relate to the final image of the risen Petrushka in that they all symbolize the questionable shape of reality itself. The dead clown's ghost asks the audience, just as Schnitzler's Pierrots ask their Columbines, "Did you think I was gone?" In other words, the ballet transfers the woman's shock to the audience.

LOVE AND BETRAYAL

In each of our four works, the plot depends on the classic triangle of Pierrot, Columbine and Harlequin. This basic structure, directly inherited from the *Commedia,* produces a standard action. Columbine, rejecting Pierrot's love, yields to Harlequin. In most of our examples Pierrot actually dies; in *Balaganchik* he suffers despair, a spiritual death. So we could summarize these plots thus: love, betrayal, death.

The beginning of this structure, Pierrot's love for Columbine, proceeds from his character and determines his fate. Indeed, this one trait, his luckless wooing of Columbine, persists from the earliest appearances of Pierrot onward. We may even see his secondary traits—fear, gullibility, suffering, despair—as results of this one determining role. Pierrot is the quintessential hapless lover, the born loser.

In the ballet, the Moor slays Petrushka as his rival for the Ballerina. Her rejection of the clown's awkward advances ultimately causes his death. This Columbine appears as a *femme fatale,* since Petrushka's attraction becomes truly fatal. When we look back to the immediate predecessors of the ballet, *Sharf* and *Schleier,* we find a Columbine even more clearly responsible for Pierrot's death. In both versions, her betrayal determines the action from the start. And here she also suffers the terrible punishment of madness, climaxing in a dance of death.[38] In *Balaganchik,* the earliest of our four pieces, Columbine appears as Death itself. Accordingly, Blok's play on the Russian word *kosa,* meaning both a hair braid and a scythe, shows that Columbine symbolizes both Woman and the Grim Reaper.

As we see in the account quoted above, this deadly woman merges confusingly with the figure of Love: "The Eternal Feminine, the image of beauty and spirit."[39] Blok gives us a parodied Symbolist evocation of Love-as-Death, a far cry from the Schnitzler-Meyerhold woman of clear psychological drives. The Ballerina in *Petrushka* closely resembles the cardboard Columbine in *Balaganchik,* who shows no human consciousness. She has only one line in the whole play, addressed to Pierrot: "I won't leave you." Whereupon she promptly goes off with Harlequin. Since both this Columbine and the Ballerina act automatically, the suffering and death they cause seem especially horrifying.

In her perfect flatness, the Ballerina contrasts fully with the soulful Petrushka. In conceiving this heartless automaton, Benois probably thought of the doll Coppelia, or Olympia in act 1 of *The Tales of Hoffmann.* Perhaps unwittingly, the real ballerina Natalia Makarova recalls the unconsciousness of the doll dancer in her response to a question about interpretation. The interviewer asked, "What is a ballerina to do if she has only technique, if she is as empty as a mannequin inside?" Makarova answered, "Either develop the habits of the inner life, or do not go into classical ballet, for it is not a circus!"[40] Makarova underlines the irony endemic to a profession that demands the transforming of intellectual understanding into purely physical language.

Among our four Columbine figures, only the Ballerina does not betray her lover. This doll merely rejects the clumsy puppet for his physically superior rival, the Moor. Thus her guilt has mainly symbolic value, for both the Moor and the Charlatan inflict the actual and spiritual death of the clown. In the three other pieces, Columbine actually loved Pierrot and now turns

38. Madness often precedes a woman's dance of death in works of this period. Compare Hofmannsthal's *Elektra* (1903) and the viceroy's wife in his last pantomime, *Gott Allein Kennt die Herzen* (1928). The coupling of these two motifs may stem from fairy-tale material, such as Andersen's *The Red Shoes.* There a girl must dance herself to death by the magic shoes of a demonic cobbler. Compare the modern ballet version of the story in the film *The Red Shoes.* We may readily see in all these examples the punishment of death inflicted on the woman who expresses her repressed sexuality in a wild dance.

39. Slonim, *Theater,* 216.

40. Natalia Makarova, *A Dance Autobiography,* 36.

faithless. This theme of woman's betrayal recurs consistently as a plot-axis in most of Schnitzler's *Commedia* pieces. I refer to four plays, two pantomimes, and a short story that he wrote between 1897 and 1910, all of which depend on the triangle of Pierrot-Columbine-Harlequin.

Der Schleier der Beatrice (The Veil of Beatrice) (1901) is a five-act verse-play; *Der Puppenspieler* (*The Puppeteer*) (1903) is a prose study in one act; *Der Tapfere Kassian* (Brave Kassian) exists as both a *Singspiel* (1903) and a prose burlesque (1904); and *Zum Grossen Wurstel* (*At the Big Puppet Show*) is a verse burlesque in one act (1905). The other pantomime, besides *Der Schleier der Pierrette*, is *Die Verwandlungen des Pierrot* (*The Transformations of Pierrot*) (1908). The short story *Die Toten Schweigen* (The Dead are Silent) (1897) gives Schnitzler's earliest version of the triangle, clearly focusing on the betrayal of the woman. Considering the number of settings that Schnitzler devoted to the theme of the *femme fatale*, we see that his Columbine figures symbolize one of his essential themes.

The fatal woman, whom Mario Praz opposes to the Byronic fatal man of the first half of the nineteenth century, becomes a major figure for artists of the *fin de siècle*. One need only think of the Lulu of Champsaur and Wedekind or of the many versions of Salomé—by Beardsley, Wilde, Strauss, Moreau, Klimt, Munch—to note how often this deadly seductress appeared. The death-dealing temptress, opposite to the life-giving mother, has biblical origins. Champsaur may even have had Lilith in mind when creating Lulu (see chapter 4).

The most novel variant on the classic *femme fatale* appears in Kuzmin's *Venetsianskie bezumtsy* (*Venetian Madcaps*) (1912). Here the treacherous Finette steals Narcisetto from his male lover, Count Stello, just to arouse the jealousy of her own lover, Harlequin. Madly infatuated with Finette, Narcisetto kills Stello. In a final scene whose arbitrary reversals recall Blok's puppets, Narcisetto first claims to love Finette, then to hate her.

Finette. Did you [kill him] for love of me, Narcisetto?
Narcisetto. Yes.
Finette. You love me then?
Narcisetto. I love nobody but the Count. I never loved
  anyone but him.
Finette. I see. So that's your great love for me, Narcisetto.
Narcisetto. I hate you, Finette—get away from me! Stello!
  Stello![41]

The homosexual pair seems unique in the *Commedia* literature. But

41. Michael Green, ed., *Mikhail Kuzmin: Selected Prose and Poetry,* 413.

Finette owes much to the evocations of Columbine that Kuzmin saw in *Balaganchik,* and to *Sharf Kolombiny.* Kuzmin certainly knew Blok's play, since he wrote the music for it. And since Meyerhold directed *Balaganchik,* it seems likely that Kuzmin also knew his later work.

THE DEATH AND RESURRECTION OF PETRUSHKA

Like Pierrot himself, his death has a considerable history. However, the clown does not actually die in many *Commedia* plays or pantomimes before the Symbolist period. A typical early example is Gautier's *Pierrot Posthume* (1847), in which Pierrot seems to have died but returns to life just in time to stop his wife, Columbine, from marrying Harlequin. In the most famous of these midcentury pantomimes, *Le Marrrchand d'Habits!* (1842), Pierrot does die, killed by the specter of the clothes peddler whom the clown had robbed and killed. Pierrot does not rise from death, but the rebirth motif appears again in the peddler's ghost.

We may regard *Marrrchand!* as a watershed in the development of the motif of Pierrot's death. Although this piece enjoyed no success in its own time, it has attained a curious fame through two depictions of it. The film *Les Enfants du Paradis* gives a romanticized version of the work. But Gautier had already eulogized the pantomime in his "Shakspeare aux Funambules," which appeared in the *Revue de Paris* in 1842. This essay is a landmark in the history of Pierrot's death: for the first time, a Romantic artist states the deeper, metaphorical meaning of the clown. Instead of the previous sentimentalized or foolish figure in the standard *Funambules* fare, Gautier portrays his darker side, the brooding "internal landscape" that clearly prefigures Petrushka.[42]

In particular, the treatment of death here departs from its earlier use as a vehicle for a comic surprise ending. Indeed, critics speculate that the public rejected this piece just because of its macabre visions. In any case, the many earlier pantomimes have none of the haunting, grotesque quality of *Marrrchand!* with its final "deadly waltz" of Pierrot with the ghost. Gautier claims for the work not only a dramatic effectiveness worthy of Shakespeare but mythic and moral value also. "This show contains a myth that is very profound, very complete, and highly moral, which need only be formulated in Sanscrit to produce a swarm of commentaries. Pierrot, who walks down the street in his white trousers, his floured face, preoccupied

---

42. Storey, *Pierrot,* 133. According to this meticulous scholar, Gautier himself wrote *Marrrchand!* For complex reasons, Cot d'Ordan claimed authorship, and Gautier merely explicated and promoted the work in his essay.

with vague desires: is he not the symbol of the still-innocent human soul, tormented by infinite aspirations toward the higher spheres?"[43]

Presumably the high morality Gautier finds here pertains to Pierrot's mortal punishment for his murder of the peddler. This moral tale seems hardly relevant to Petrushka, yet Gautier's last sentence contains the seeds of that tragic character. Pierrot's innocence, symbolized threefold by his white blouse, white trousers, and floured face, remains a determining trait in our puppet. And so does his "infinite aspiration," his tormenting spirituality. Of course, this last phrase has a more literal meaning for Gautier, since those "higher regions" of Pierrot's striving were social. He killed the old man to get the fine clothes he could not afford for the wooing of a duchess. Yet Gautier is also interpreting here; he goes beyond the facts of the story to find symbols of the human heart. What he saw in Pierrot became a dominant feature of the clown in the latter part of the century. As I noted above regarding Verlaine and Laforgue, the Pierrot from the 1880s onward became increasingly a symbol of inwardness.

However, this soulful quality, which seeks to transcend quotidian reality, has roots in the midcentury. Probably the earliest transcendent clown appears in Banville's "Le Saut du Tremplin." This *sauteur*, hoping to escape the confining bourgeois world of his audience, springs free from his scaffold into the sky, bursting his canvas tent to cavort among the stars. The artist becomes, if not a star himself, at least a member of the galaxy. What image could better portray immortality? This acrobat, along with Gautier's Pierrot, foreshadows the ballet clown. Later on, we will see their vaulting progeny in Mallarmé, Dowson, and Blok.[44]

Petrushka himself connotes transcendence, for he alone among the puppets has a human soul. But he rises above the carnival stage in a more literal way through his resurrection. No aspect of the ballet has received more varying interpretations than its last moments containing the clown's ascent. To evaluate such comment, let us study the sources.

Since the ballet began with Stravinsky's piano concerto, we must regard his concepts as determining. Also, I especially heed his remarks because Stravinsky overshadows all the other collaborators. In his significance for the century, we can compare him only to Picasso. According to the composer's first idea of the puppet, his return from death characterized the ballet. "The resurrection of Petrushka's ghost was my idea, not Benois'. . . . Petrushka's ghost is the real Petrushka, and his appearance at the end makes

43. Théophile Gautier, *Souvenirs de Théâtre, de l'Art et de Critique,* 65.
44. The clown's death continues to furnish Romantic pathos in Zuckmayer's *Katharine Knie,* discussed in chapter 4. Picasso paints the theme in *La Mort d'Arlequin* (1905). And Fellini uses the supreme parody of that elegiac moment to end *The Clowns*.

the Petrushka of the preceding play a mere doll." As for the ghost's final gestures, Stravinsky meant them to carry the crucial meaning of the ballet itself. "I had conceived of the music in two keys in the second tableau as Petrushka's insult to the public, and I wanted the dialogue for two trumpets at the end to show that his ghost is still insulting the public. I am more proud of these last pages than of anything else in the score."[45]

Judging by the variety of other interpretations for this ending, we must accept Stravinsky's claim that the choreography did not achieve his intent. Fokine himself expressed no desire that the ghost should mock the audience. "Here is what I staged for the concluding part of Petrushka's role: He hangs over the top edge of the Charlatan's tent and, with puppet-like gestures of his arms, curses and mocks his owner, to hysterical outcries in the orchestra."[46]

Accordingly, the critics have not agreed on the meaning of these last moments in the ballet. Richard Buckle thinks the specter "threatens to live forever." In this view, Petrushka would appear as the triumphant figure that Stravinsky disclaims. Herbert Fleischer finds a much broader significance here. "In the final music of Petrushka, human existence is ridiculed through the shadow of a puppet." Since the critics have so misunderstood Stravinsky's intention, we must bracket his remarks. That is, although his ironic vision of the clown surely shaped the score, it has not clearly emerged from the ballet as a whole. Hence we may accept as legitimate quite a variety of differing critical evaluations. Indeed, this breadth of suggested meaning may contribute to the enduring popularity of the work.[47]

Most commentators state or imply a final triumph for the artistic spirit that has deeply suffered from the brutal ridicule of others. Starting from this common point of interpretation, let us explore its implications. We must

45. Stravinsky and Craft, Expositions, 156. Critics confirm the effectiveness of this ending. "[Petrushka's] gesture is not one of triumph or protest, as is so often said, but a nose-thumbing addressed to the audience. The significance of this gesture is not and never was clear in Fokine's staging" (White, Stravinsky, 198). Moreover, musicologists confirm Stravinsky's pride in this ending of the score. Asaf'eyev sums up in particular the uniqueness of these passages. "The grotesqueness and incisiveness of this music is perceptible just because one is aware . . . of the deep seriousness of Petrushka's plight. The surface . . . is all mask, all color and design of high festivity. But never in the literature of Russian pantomime and ballet have the basic misery, wretchedness and humiliation of the world of 'masks'—of the universal Petrushka—been conveyed in music so terrible, so excruciatingly realistic. Never have the howlings of impotent despair been so drowned in the hubbub of an indifferent public. . . . Petrushka falls with a broken skull; in the orchestra, against a background of cymbals tremolo, the piccolo 'expires'; and a tambourine falls jangling to the floor. . . . The death of Petrushka—one single line of music—is as eloquent as many tens of pages of symphonic poems" (Stravinsky, 21).

46. Mikhail Fokine, Memoirs of a Russian Ballet Master, trans. Vitale Fokine, 193.

47. Richard Buckle, Diaghilev, 201; Fleischer quoted in Vera Stravinsky, Stravinsky, 66.

consider first the general meaning of resurrection and then its particular relation to Petrushka. The major, even definitive, example of rebirth is Christ. We may interpret this miraculous return in many ways, but perhaps its most basic character lies in paradox. The impossibility of life that transcends death gives a fitting climax to the life of Christ, which contained the deepest contradictions. The Jews scorned the King of the Jews; the saintliest man died as a common criminal; a crown of thorns symbolizes the oxymoron of his life. His gospel also depends on paradox. "The meek shall inherit the earth"; "One must lose his life in order to save it."

While most interpreters stress pathos in the life of Christ, a few see the comic aspect of its ironic reversals. "Strange to think, the death and rebirth of the god belong more fittingly to the comic than the tragic theater. . . . The figure of Christ as god-man is surely the archtetypal hero-victim. He is reviled, mocked—a comic scapegoat King."[48] Christ serves the same ritual function of martyrdom for mankind that the ancient sacrifice victim did earlier. Then, scapegoat rites merged with celebrations of seasonal change, so that the fool, focus of the ritual, was killed and later resurrected. One can hardly imagine a closer parallel to the action of our ballet, which even has the properly mythic setting of the Russian Shrovetide carnival. So we may see here not only Christian overtones but also their ultimate roots in pagan ritual.

Can we then call Petrushka Christ-like? He does show a decided resemblance to the Savior. First of all, his innocence distinguishes him from criminal forebears in the French pantomimes. Moreover, the mockery he suffers from both his audience and his peers connotes Christ's martyrdom. Like the Savior, the clown exists for the sake of all men; yet this very humanity ridicules and humiliates him. In this respect, the puppet represents a variant of the holy fool, the Fool of God, whose incarnations range from Parsifal to the tragic Christ- clowns of Rouault, Henry Miller, and Bergman.

Miller's Auguste in *The Smile at the Foot of the Ladder* (1948) and the literally martyred Frost in Bergman's *The Naked Night* (1953) are tragicomic images of the secular Christ. Chaplin, our contemporary Pierrot, makes his final statement about the clown's transcendence in his *Limelight* (1952), where Calvero (the man of Calvary) dies but lives on in the spirit of Teresa, his Columbine, and her art.

As for the tradition of the Holy Fool in Russia, we cannot directly relate Petrushka and these other transcendent clowns to that figure. The *salia* in Slavic countries were radical religious ascetics who manifested madness, either real or feigned. Emmanuel Quint, Gerhart Hauptmann's "fool in

48. Wylie Sypher, ed., *Comedy,* 220.

Christ" (1910), also belongs in this category. All these Holy Fools represent something different from our clowns, who are clearly sane.

Finally, Petrushka's resurrection bespeaks a Christ-like vindication of his life. This clown is the most wretched of the puppets; yet he alone transcends in death the misery of his life on earth. But what of the reborn puppet's problematic final gesture? His mockery of the audience, so dear to Stravinsky, goes beyond the tragedy implied in Benois' idea of the ballet as showing "the death of the poetic principle." In ridiculing the gullibility of the audience that has always mocked *him,* the clown transports the work into the ultimate irony of destroying all illusion. Does not this mordant closing contradict the benignly redemptive aura of the Christ figure? After all, Petrushka mocks humanity, he does not save it.

We can accept both aspects of this crucial ending without violating either Stravinsky's intent or our own perceptions. Viewing the character of Petrushka as only ironically Christ-like suggests a resolution for this seeming conflict. He resembles the Son of God in some respects only. Hence we may recognize the traditional Christ-like parts of the clown while also seeing him as something quite different: a vehicle for revolutionary ideas in the theater. The final human incarnation of Petrushka, laughing at us all, transcends the suffering Christ of his puppet role. Ultimately, he shows the superiority of the artistic spirit.

CARNIVAL AND THE GROTESQUE

The setting for the ballet, the Shrovetide Fair, gives an apt frame for the clown's death and resurrection. In the pagan roots of this Christian celebration lies the myth of nature itself reborn. As a parallel for the death of winter and the rebirth of spring, the sacrifice and later regeneration of the fool formed the climax for ancient seasonal rites. Moreover, the idea of carnival relates not only to the reborn Petrushka but to his whole ballet as well.

Carnivalisation, the term coined by Mikhail Bakhtin, may help us to understand the function of the ballet fair. The social leveling of the carnival creates an equality of unequals, a reversal of conventional relations. In short, the world is turned upside down. Festival thus releases the populace from the imposed order of its daily life; carnival brings catharsis. In his book on Rabelais, Bakhtin specifies antiquity, the Middle Ages, and the Renaissance as high points for the carnival spirit. The art of these eras accordingly reflects their underlying "reversal of all values." Not accidentally, Meyerhold also claims these three periods as exemplary for the art of acting. Many of his early productions embodied two of Bakhtin's basic ideas: carnivalesque laughter and the Romantic grotesque.

In the ballet, both the first and the last scenes evoke the carnivalesque cross-section of society. The puppets introduce yet another element into the hectic crowd scene, presenting the sudden contrast of wooden lifelessness, the opposite of the previously animated scene. Benois specifies the dramatic necessity of this difference: the contrast of live people at the fair with automatons would intensify the theatrical effect.[49]

In the final scene, again set in the framing carnival, the mixing of opposites reaches the deeper level of life and death. The sudden revelation of the dying puppet, felled amid the raucous crowd, has enough dramatic effect to create the climax of the ballet. Benois thus "carnivalized" Petrushka's death. Instead of setting the finale inside the tent, he revealed it amid the carnival crowd, its most potent dramatic contrast. Moreover, this outdoor dying suggests irony: here, just a while ago, the Charlatan had brought the puppets to life.

Benois includes in the first scene another feature typical of the Russian carnival, masked revelers. Various hellish creatures, even the Devil himself, belong to the standard personnel of such masqueraders. This demonic version of carnival differs sharply from the charming Biedermeier flavor of the comparable ballet *Carnaval* (1910). Here Fokine wove a gay pattern of intertwining amorous adventures, all spiced by the mystery of several *Commedia* masks.

A year later, Fokine's choreography in *Petrushka* embodied the opposite spirit of the grotesque carnival. One need only see the curtain for the last act of the ballet, with its flying demons that illumine the night sky, to sense the macabre revelry to come (see figure 7). The huge goat and crane heads appearing in this final scene are traditional devil figures of the Russian carnival. They belong to the realm of death, into which this climactic, carnivalesque scene transports the living. Such hellish beings dispel death through ritual. Their demonic laughter expresses a grotesque mockery of death.

The devil figures in the ballet relate it to *Balaganchik*, although Blok uses no actual carnival. In that play we find a counterpart to the masked revelry in the interlude of three masked couples. These couples serve only as vehicles for parody of the main triangle in the play, not as carnivalesque figures. However, the source for *Balaganchik*, Blok's poem of the same name, does contain demons, who terrorize the children both on the stage and in the audience. At this puppet show, a boy and a girl burst out crying when they see, instead of the expected queen, devils dancing amid flames to "infernal music." This surprise ending may remind us of the final reversal in the play,

49. Benois, *Reminiscences*, 326.

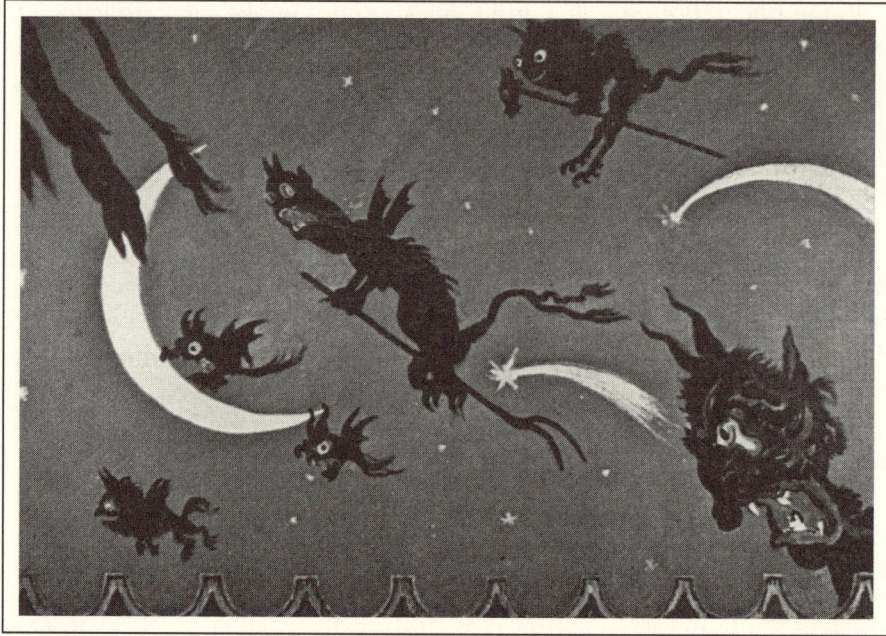

Figure 7. Alexandre Benois, *Petrushka,* drop curtain (1911). Courtesy of Nikita Lobanov.

when Harlequin dies and Pierrot survives. But even closer to the children's shock in the poem is the jolt felt by all at the end of the ballet.[50]

50. Blok, "The Puppet Show":

> Look, they've opened a puppet show
> For happy, good children,
> A little girl and boy watch
> The ladies, kings and devils.
> And that infernal music resounds,
> And a doleful violin bow whines.
> A terrifying devil has grabbed a chubby little child,
> And cranberry juice trickles down.
> Little Boy: "He escapes black wrath
> With a sleight of his white hand.
> Look: flames are approaching from the left . . .
> Do you see the torches? Do you see the puffs of smoke?
> That is the queen herself no doubt . . ."
> Little Girl: "Ah no! Why are you teasing me?
> That is the retinue of hell . . .
> A queen would walk in broad daylight,
> All garlanded with roses,
> And enamoured knights would carry her train,
> Clanking their swords."
> Suddenly a clown bends over the footlights

Schnitzler's pantomime also lacks the carnival, but he does supply a carnivalesque note by inserting the wedding-party scene between the two frame-scenes of Pierrot as corpse. This juxtaposing of a celebration of love, the thriving of life, with stark death creates the same grotesque contrast of opposite moods that we find in the ballet. And of course the specter of Pierrot, discussed above, furnishes a grotesque model for the resurrected Petrushka.

Meyerhold intensifies the carnivalesque aura of the wedding party in *Sharf Kolombiny*, for here the scene becomes demonic. The dances, first fast and then slow, become nightmarish: a conductor with a monstrous head sits high above his four grotesque musicians, who play for a whirling group of Hoffmannesque dancers. Along with his productions of *Don Juan* (1910) and *Balaganchik*, Meyerhold considered this pantomime crucial in his development. For my purpose—identifying *Sharf Kolombiny* as a source for *Petrushka*—the main significance of this piece lies in its grotesque style. For Meyerhold the grotesque conveyed "the horribly funny," which underlies not only the tragicomic effect of the clown but also the whole dark comedy of the ballet itself.

In analyzing *Sharf*, Konstantin Rudnitzki might almost be referring to *Petrushka*. "It modernized Italian masked comedy by placing it in the key of Hoffmann-like grotesque, a terrible dance on the boundaries of the amusing and the frightful."[51] Such ambiguity of mood, always playing between two extremes, characterizes all four of our pieces. In this respect, they all hark back to the kind of Romantic irony expressed in Hoffmann.

Moreover, the link to Romanticism has a cause more endemic than the popularity of the German poet. Essentially, the Pierrot figure common to all these pieces stems from the Romantic myth of the tragic clown. The ballet transforms this inherited image of Pierrot, developed from Gautier to Laforgue and filtered through both the Hoffmannesque and the native Russian grotesque modes. Accordingly, Richard Buckle stresses the broad European scope of the ballet. "Petrushka . . . had been designed in St. Petersburg; it had been composed mostly by the Lake of Geneva and on the Côte d'Azur;

And yells: "Help me!
I'm bleeding cranberry juice!
I'm bandaged up with rags!
On my head is a cardboard helmet!
In my hand a wooden sword!"
The little girl and boy begin to cry,
And the happy puppet show closes down.

(Translation in Virginia Bennett, "Russian *pagliacci*: Symbols of Profaned Love in Blok's *The Puppet Booth*," in *Drama and Symbolism*, ed. James Redmond, 144.)
    51. Konstantin Rudnitzki, *Meyerhold the Director*, trans. George Petrov, 166.

and it was finished and choreographed in Rome before being presented in Paris."[52]

Out of this wealth of accumulated imagery, the ballet creates not only a new figure but also a style perfectly suited to him: the grotesque farce. Indeed, the ballet merges two kinds of grotesque humor discussed by Bakhtin. He clearly distinguishes the Romantic grotesque, with its dark foreboding, from the ancient and medieval folk grotesque, characterized by brightness and renewal. This description of one thematic difference between the two styles recalls Petrushka. "The theme of the marionette plays an important part in Romanticism. This theme is of course also found in folk culture, but in Romanticism the accent is placed on the puppet as a victim of alien inhuman force, which rules over men by turning them into marionettes. This image is completely unknown in folk culture. Moreover, only in Romanticism do we find the peculiar grotesque theme of the tragic doll."[53]

What Bakhtin says about folk grotesque shows that the ballet also includes this earlier style in its treatment of carnival. We might even see a merging of the two types of grotesque within the clown himself, who represents both the Hoffmannesque victim and the regenerated spirit of carnivalesque laughter. In fact, the characteristic parody in Bakhtin's concept of carnival specifically reminds us of Stravinsky's intentions for Petrushka's final and essential ironic gesture. "In spite of their variety, folk festivities of the carnival type, the comic rites and cults, the clowns and fools, giants, dwarfs and jugglers, the vast and manifold literature of *parody*—all these forms have one style in common: they belong to one culture of folk carnival humor."[54]

The pantomimes of Schnitzler and Meyerhold also realize the theatrical mixture of grotesque farce, but in them the horrible outweighs the farcical. Expectably, Meyerhold's grotesqueries hark back to earlier writers. Beyond Hoffmann, he also revered Rabelais and Callot. In *Balaganchik,* we find a mixed style much closer to that of the ballet. Sudden mood shifts, dance-like rhythms, the constant surprise of arbitrary action: all these traits of puppet farce characterize the play. But Blok's original achievement lies in his merging of the farcical style with the grotesque. For instance, he ironically confuses the earthy Columbine with the transcendent Lady Beautiful, who is also Death. That Symbolist "quiet redeemer" appeared with utmost irony, for Blok transmutes her into a destructive force.

52. Buckle, *Diaghilev,* 195.
53. Mikhail Bakhtin, *Rabelais and his World,* trans. Helene Iswolsky, 40.
54. Ibid., 4, italics mine.

The grotesque irony of the love figure as Death also pervades the ballet, which depends on several such haunting paradoxes. The ludicrous clown, who also represents the sufferings of the spirit, and the manipulative Master whose puppet fools him typify the special kind of comedy that merges with foreboding. Just as a different, tragic show occurs behind the funny puppet theater, so do tragic themes lurk under the surface of the ballet. This work juxtaposes the farce of the traditional *Commedia* triangle with the horrors of imprisonment, brutality, and exploitation. Such a mixture leads far into the future, for we see its black comedy in several contemporary styles. Hoover points to Kafka, Beckett, Pinter, and Bond, but the list could continue, including Surrealists and Absurdists.

OTHER CHARACTERS

The Moor in the ballet corresponds to Harlequin in Meyerhold and Arlecchino in Schnitzler. Naturally, we may wonder why Benois changed this traditional figure from a mere rival to a gaudy savage. But Harlequin's origins help to explain this change. The character started as a haunting devil, masked in black. First the messenger of death, he later became its mocking mitigator. Laughing at death, the *hellkin* came to symbolize the force of life—specifically, fertility. Hence Harlequin became the eternal seducer. Like Don Juan, his noted progeny, Harlequin menaces the social order by his rampant virility.[55]

And so it is in the little puppet theater of the ballet: the Moor steals the Ballerina and slays Petrushka, ruining both the show and the Charlatan. Tamara Karsavina suggests this destructive role of the Moor by contrasting his "brutal, sensual hedonism" with Petrushka's "spiritual, suffering humanity." Benois calls the Moor the embodiment of "everything senselessly attractive, powerfully masculine and undeservedly triumphant."[56]

We know of several sources for the Moor. The most obvious one, noted by Benois, appears in the traditional intermezzo for the Russian puppet show. Here two Blackamoors, dressed in velvet and gold, furnish relief from

55. Jean Starobinski, *Portrait de l'Artiste en Saltimbanque,* 128; Jackson Cope, *Dramaturgy of the Demonic,* 106. Harlequin as thrilling seducer appears in the contemporary Harlequin romance. See Julia Bettinoti et al., *La Corrida de l'Amour: Le Roman Harlequin* (Montreal: University of Quebec, 1986).

56. Tamara Karsavina, "Benois the Magician," 76; Benois, *Reminiscences,* 326. Psychologists refer to "the Harlequin complex": women obsessed by the vision of a fatal lover. Hence we associate both love and death with Harlequin. "Death represents the demon lover—the symbol of a woman's own life urge, which is expressed paradoxically in the thought of yielding or dying" (D. C. McClelland, "The Harlequin Complex," in *The Study of Lives,* ed. R. W. White, 98).

the main action of Petrushka and his lady by hitting each other with sticks. This slapstick interlude stems from the comic intermezzo for the medieval morality play, itself based on antique models of Roman comedy staged between the acts of uplifting epic dramas.[57] For the Russian audience, the stupid violence of the Moor, who first caresses and then destroys a coconut, must have recalled just such antics in the familiar *balagan*.

Two other sources for the Moor lie in Meyerhold's work. In *Sharf Kolombiny,* a Blackamoor "proscenium servant" addresses asides to the audience and announces intermission. In the celebrated production of *Don Juan,* some liveried black boys have a good deal of stage business.[58] Meyerhold probably used these black figures for their suggestion of fantasy. They may recall the exoticism in Watteau that Hofmannsthal hinted at with his Blackamoor page in *Der Rosenkavalier* (1911).

In the ballet, however, the Moor adds more than a note of intriguing foreignness. Indeed, this black man contributes to the avant-garde aura here as essentially as do those invigorating Negro masks in Picasso's *Les Demoiselles d'Avignon* (1907). Both the Moor and those African heads express "a belligerent primitivism."[59] Like his close cousin, the Favorite Slave in *Scheherazade* (1908), this man projects the charisma of untamed sensuality. His wildness contrasts dramatically with Petrushka's repression, that symbol of sterile Western culture.

The Moor offers an early example of the primal quality in Modernism. Think of the Egyptian frontal profiles in Picasso, the childlike stick figures in Miró and Dubuffet, the hieroglyphic designs in Klee. William Rubin and other art critics discuss close parallels between tribal art and that of these creators of Modernism. As for his choreography, the Moor exemplifies the contact with the floor that characterizes modern dance. His role is the least "balletic" of all the figures in *Petrushka*. Nijinsky may well have had the Moor's stamping movements in mind when he choreographed the truly barbaric *Le Sacre* in 1912.

Here lies one reason why the London audience gave special acclaim to *Petrushka*. The Sitwells, born balletomanes, testified to the influence of the Ballets Russes on London. "The influence of these productions on English intellectuals is incalculable. The Ballets Russes certainly played a big role in shaping . . . the Bloomsbury movement, which supported it from the start."[60]

What reason can we find for this enthusiasm? An over-refined culture

57. Nicoll, *Masks;* Francis Cornford, *The Origin of Attic Comedy.*
58. Rudnitzki, *Meyerhold,* 153.
59. Roger Shattuck, *The Innocent Eye,* 240.
60. Sitwells quoted in Arnold Haskell, *Ballet Russe,* 72.

needed that whiff of barbarism. Diaghilev offered to Britain just what Wedekind hoped to give Germany with his savage plays. Think of what Alwa Schön says, in *Pandora's Box,* of the need for "animal instincts" in his effete culture (see chapter 4). Something similar occurred when the Britons "discovered" Brecht in the 1950s. His unvarnished hostility to the bourgeoisie helped their "angry young men" to revolutionize their own theater.

Our last figure, the Charlatan, plays a role determining enough to make him the fourth major character. Indeed, Harold Segel calls him, like the three *Commedia* figures, a mythical character. "[*Petrushka* is] an original story based on the archetypal figures of Petrushka, the universal clown and loser; the exotic, brutish Blackamoor; the fatally feminine Ballerina; and their despotic but not quite omnipotent master, the Charlatan."[61] Looking for sources for this figure in Meyerhold and Schnitzler, we find his parallel in the demonic Kappellmeister of *Sharf,* who himself grew out of the *Gigolo,* or Master of Ceremonies, in *Schleier.*

This conductor seems unimportant; yet he leads the hideous music that the musicians play after the enraged Arlecchino has smashed their instruments. In *Sharf,* Meyerhold omits this cause for the distorted, nightmarish music, which is simply the suitably grotesque sound of the weird orchestra. Dohnanyi's score, used by both Schnitzler and Meyerhold, may have offered some inspiration for Stravinsky, whose music for the ballet sounded comparably crazy to its first hearers. Even Pierre Monteux's orchestra players burst out laughing at their first rehearsal. And later, in Vienna, the orchestra was so hostile to what they called "dirty music" that they sabotaged the performance.

Meyerhold made his director the primary figure in directing not only the music but also the action. The grotesque Kappellmeister with his hideous band set the rhythm for the whole production. Moreover, he clearly expressed his guilt as manipulator of the tragedy by fleeing from the stage when the corpses of the two lovers appeared. Although the first production of *Petrushka* lacked this ending, subsequent versions used it. So we see that Meyerhold implied something that Benois emphasized in his Charlatan: the guilt of the malevolent puppeteer. This aspect of the character comes from the image of the mad creator-conjurer in several of Hoffmann's tales. Doktor Mirakel in *Die Abenteuer der Sylvesternacht* (New Year's Eve Adventures) (1814), Doctor Coppelius in *Der Sandmann* (*The Sand-Man*) (1817), and the title character in *Rat Krespel* (*Councillor Krespel*) (1818) all contributed demonic traits to this Faustian figure, who dared to compete with God in fabricating a human being.

---

61. Harold Segel, *Twentieth-Century Russian Drama,* 57.

We find the closest forebear for the evil master in *Petrushka* in Doctor Coppelius, from both the ballet *Coppelia* and the opera *The Tales of Hoffmann*. In the ballet, Coppelius tries to inject his doll with the life force of her lover, Franz. But Franz' fiancée, Swanhilda, foils Coppelius by destroying all the dolls in his workshop. Here we also have a hint of the Pygmalion theme, for the old man himself loves his "daughter," Coppelia. But in the opera, the creator has purely malevolent motives; he sells his doll, supposedly a real girl, to the highest bidder. And when he discovers that his best offer depends on fraud, he furiously breaks Olympia into pieces.

The destruction of both Coppelia and Olympia bespeaks a rejection of the mechanistic attitude to life begun by the industrial age. In both stories, real people conquer the robot that threatens their supremacy. Hence society punishes the doll maker for his defiance of human limits, and the conventional moral order triumphs. As for our Charlatan, his evil manipulations also find punishment in his final guilty terror.

Thus, although the main idea of the ballet does not lie in this Faustian theme of hubris punished, the figure from Hoffmann plays an essential role in the drama of Petrushka. Indeed, some commentators stress the enduring supremacy of the Charlatan over Petrushka. They note that as the magician exits, the ghost falls forward and finally hangs lifeless over the parapet of the theater roof. Hence, in this view, even the triumphant spirit of the clown cannot exist in freedom without its master.[62]

But I believe this final fall signifies not the puppet's dependence on the Charlatan but merely the end of the show. Petrushka falls over just as a puppet does when the puppeteer lets go of his strings. Now the story of the clown has ended, but we know from the previous moments of resurrection that his spirit lives on.

Besides, the last bars of the music have nothing to do with the Charlatan's power; they express instead Petrushka's defiance. First a row of ascending leaps in the trumpet duet articulate the specter's mocking question, namely, "Did you think the show was real? Did you think I was just a puppet?" Then the final four notes in the strings evoke the other, pathetic half of the clown's being, the trapped puppet. The lurking pathos of these last pizzicato sounds bespeaks the ineffable "double existence" of the puppet-man. Considering this music, it seems perfectly fitting for the ghost suddenly to become just a puppet again, reverting to his deceptive mask. So despite Stravinsky's stated dissatisfaction with the last moments, the choreography does give a haunting finish to this enigmatic story.

There is no demonic puppeteer in Schnitzler's pantomime, but one does

---

62. Baryshnikov, *Work*, 221.

appear in his comparable play *Der Puppenspieler*. Here we see the manipulator's eventual helplessness when truly powerful human emotions take over. We recall the Charlatan when one of the "puppets" tells the "puppeteer": "We danced on your strings. But your puppets slowly became quite human, didn't they?"[63]

Another comparable figure from Schnitzler, the director of a puppet theater, plays a key role in *Zum Grossen Wurstel* (1905). Throughout the play, this character carries on a farcical dialogue with the Author. We see immediately that these figures do not serve as demonic masters à la Hoffmann but as vehicles of satire. Like the puppet-play-within-a-play here, these two men parody the themes, characters, and ideas of Schnitzler himself. In this regard we think of Blok, whose *Balaganchik* had a similarly parodistic intent.

Besides, the titles of the two plays are almost identical, and *Wurstel* precedes the Blok play by only a year. Furthermore, the director/author figure gives ironic distance to both plays, serving as a mediator between the audience and the stage. Hence both Schnitzler and Blok surpass even Pirandello's later anti-realism in *Six Characters in Search of an Author* (1921). Here the author never appears; only the characters feel his effects.

Segel lists the author's appearance as one of the anti-illusionist devices used by the "Theatricalists." Some of these techniques clearly stem from the *Commedia dell'Arte*, but the author appearance does not. Bennett cites as precedent Rossini's *The Turk in Italy* (1814), in which the poet-librettist joins the action onstage. But such appearances seem rare before the end of the nineteenth century, when they began to form part of a complex of anti-realist devices.

We may distinguish two different functions among the various authorial figures in our four pieces. The Hoffmannesque evil masters in *Sharf* and *Petrushka* connote the grotesque, while the parodistic authors in *Wurstel* and *Balaganchik* suggest farce. The former two figures, like Hoffmann's madmen, simply create the play-within-the-play, so they do not challenge the Aristotelian framework of the drama. But the latter two authors represent the intrusion of Reality onto the stage. They negate the most basic assumption of mimetic drama: namely, that the author speaks only through his characters. Hence these men unmask theatrical art as pure illusion. Their mockery of ruling convention belongs to the dramatic avant-garde of the time.[64]

---

63. Schnitzler, *Werke*, 1:846.

64. However, such techniques were not new at this time. Tieck had already tapped the rich farcical vein of Romantic drama in his *Puss in Boots* (1797). This play used many means to destroy illusion, ending in a debacle similar to that in Schnitzler's *Wurstel*.

THEATRICALISM

The anti-illusionist appearance of the author in *Balaganchik* forms a major facet of its author's aesthetics. Segel's term *theatricalist,* embracing both *anti-realist* and *anti-Symbolist,* suits Blok and Meyerhold very well. Besides, the term denotes a positive dramaturgy, which also characterizes these artists.

Although the author does not appear in *Petrushka,* the clown's last moments create the same kind of disillusion that we find in Blok and Schnitzler. But Petrushka's implied question comes only at the end; hence it gives a greater shock than the author does in *Balaganchik.* In this question—"Did you think I had died, I was only a puppet?"—lies the closest link to Blok. In Blok's play, Pierrot says finally: "I'm very sad. Do you think it funny?" Both questions, addressing the audience directly, give a startling ironic end to the story. Pierrot's melancholy becomes Petrushka's mockery. The tragicomic tone of the play is gone, replaced in the ballet with burlesque. Specifically, Stravinsky insists that this last cry of the puppet's soul mocks the gullibility of the audience. Since we find none of this clear disillusioning of the spectators in *Sharf* and *Schleier,* we must consider *Balaganchik* the source for this crucial aspect of the ballet.[65]

Petrushka's parody of stage convention recalls his native origins. I refer to the *skomorokhi,* whose implied subversion of Christianity caused both church and state to summarily ban them in the tenth century. Like these scurrilous entertainers, the ballet clown also undermines the reigning system. Just as they kept alive the pagan culture that threatened Christian Russia, so does Petrushka represent the "theatricalist" avant-garde that threatens Realism. The public has long perceived the puppet—like his human counterpart, the mime—as a subversive figure.

As for other contemporary examples of such theatricalism, we find some devices similar to the appearance of the author. In fact, these examples may also have contributed to the ballet, since they too involve *Commedia* figures. Between *Balaganchik* and *Petrushka* came Evreinov's *Vesyolaya smert (A Merry Death)* (1908). Both Benois and Meyerhold saw Evreinov's plays at the cabaret theater he directed from 1910 to 1917, the Crooked

---

65. Asides to the audience have become common in our theater of anti-illusion since Brecht. However, when the author saves his address to the public for the end of the play, it has the effect of the last word. Compare the poignant line that Archie Rice throws directly to the audience at the end of John Osborne's *The Entertainer:* "You've been a good audience. Very good. A very *good* audience. Let me know where you're working tomorrow night—and I'll come see you" (quoted in Arnold Hinchliffe, *John Osborne,* 35). With this last bit of characteristic self-mockery, Archie captures both his own downfall and that of the music hall.

Mirror. So it does not surprise us to find similar techniques and attitudes in the work of all three directors. In the farce *A Merry Death,* Pierrot starts and ends the action with two long and hilarious monologues on behalf of the author. Adding to the blatant theatricalism of addressing the audience directly, Pierrot describes the characters in the play as actors playing their roles. Perhaps the ultimate mockery of stage pretense occurs when Pierrot insults the author.

You're going to be really surprised when you hear what the culprit guilty of per-petrating this strange . . . mockery has commissioned me to say by way of conclu-sion. . . . Neither your applause nor your hisses will be taken seriously. And I might add that if he's right, then I fail to see why anyone should take that author's play seriously, especially since Harlequin has no doubt already risen from his death bed and is now preening himself for the curtain call. Because, say what you will, actors aren't responsible for the playwright's wild ideas.[66]

Evreinov again defies mimetic convention in *Samoye glavnoye* (*The Main Thing*) (1921), when Harlequin tells the audience to end the play however they like. Furthermore, both the director and the manager then appear to give their variant ideas of the Main Thing. The director wants a prompt ending so that the audience can catch the last trolley home; the manager prefers the "smash ending" of fireworks. In Kuzmin's earlier play *Venetian Madcaps,* Harlequin and Finette end the piece by reminding us of their identities as actors.

Harlequin: Time is short, and we have to leave for Verona at once. It had com-pletely slipped our minds that we were due to appear there so soon that we'll hardly have time to get there. . . .
Finette (sings): Let not our deeds discomfort you or daunt, You honest burghers, pups and popinjays. What is our life if not a merry jaunt? Actors all of us in plays. . . .[67]

We find a famous forebear for all such mediation of the actor between author and audience, again within the clown literature, in Ernest Dowson's *The Pierrot of the Minute* (1893). Here Pierrot speaks the whole epilogue, itself a jab at realism:

The sun is up, yet ere a body stirs,
A word with you, sweet ladies and dear sirs,

66. Christopher Collins, trans., *Evreinov: Plays,* 18.
67. Green, *Kuzmin,* 415.

Although on no account let any say
That Pierrot finished Mr. Dowson's play.[68]

These lines ring particularly ironic when we consider that the actor who portrayed Pierrot indeed wrote them. William Peters, having commissioned the work from Dowson, granted the playwright's request that Peters end the play himself. Incidentally, the fireworks closing this play may have inspired Evreinov to use them in *The Main Thing*. The Dowson piece soon became famous all over Europe, probably due to the illustrations for its text by Beardsley.

In the same year, 1892, Leoncavallo's opera *Pagliacci* used a similar device, in the prologue sung by Tonio. This player explains that the author intends to show real passions on the stage, for his work is based on actual events. Indeed, Tonio claims, remembering these things still brings the author to tears. This motif of the author's tears may recall Baudelaire's "Le Vieux Saltimbanque" and "Une Mort Héroique."

A close link between *Pagliacci* and *Petrushka* lies in the play-within-a-play. Like the other anti-realist techniques noted above, the inner action reminds the audience of its distance, both literal and symbolic, from the stage. We see first the main play, which then frames the story within. This inner drama subtly demonstrates what the outer action cannot show. In the classic example of *Hamlet,* a dumb show "is just the thing / Wherein [to] catch the conscience of a king." The reduced and mute form of the inner play illumines the king's guilt more clearly than could a direct assertion. Not only guilty adulterers but all audiences may best understand the meaning of a play by grasping it indirectly, in an enclosed, even metaphorical way. Hence the use by revolutionary authors of the veiled message offered by both the puppet stage and the playlet framed inside the main play.

In both *Petrushka* and *Pagliacci,* inner scenes lead to the denouement of death resulting from the archetypal triangle of Pierrot, Columbine, and Harlequin. In the opera, the "played" scene exactly mirrors the actual relations of the actors. The jealous Canio, playing Pierrot, murders Nedda and Silvio, playing Columbine and Harlequin. Art has fully merged with life when Canio sings "The comedy is finished." In *Petrushka,* scenes two and three show us the inner life of the clown, who is really a passionate man. Like Canio, Petrushka discovers only in death the impossibility of his dual existence.

In *Balaganchik,* Blok suggests the inner play in several ways. In the first scene, Pierrot sits at the side of the stage, observing the Mystics. When this

---

68. *The Poetry of Ernest Dowson,* ed. Desmond Flower, 227.

scene ends as the Mystics collapse, puppet-like, over their chairs, we see the separate play of the masqueraders. These three couples parody the triangular relationship of Pierrot, Columbine, and Harlequin in the main play, thus creating a true play-within-a-play. Moreover, their action arbitrarily interrupts the narrative preceding their appearance. Only the broken thread linking the three main characters gives *Balaganchik* any unity. By thus stressing the jerky, puppet-like actions of his cardboard characters, Blok again demonstrates the artificiality of performance. Using one stage within another, he creates layers of unreality.

Similarly, the ballet's setting implies boxes within boxes. The main set— the ironic Theater of the Living—is a puppet stage within the larger area of the city fairground. Beyond this "theater" we see the embracing frame of St. Petersburg, clearly identified by its Admiralty Square. These three settings are framed by a second proscenium echoing the frame of the stage in the theater itself. And in this painted proscenium we see painted windows: yet another layer of boxes (see figure 8).

Is it by accident that this outer theater is blue like our sky, and that the reveal of a narrow strip of ceiling, painted in false perspective just above the gold-fringed helmet of its proscenium, is decorated with a yellow sun? Box within box: world within world. The artist is teasing us, suggesting that the "real" people in the crowded fair are as much puppets as the painted sawdust figures behind the curtain of the booth, or even that we, so safe beyond the footlights, are really puppets too.[69]

Finally, the crowd choreography in the first and last scenes of *Petrushka* creates yet another frame for the stage action. A mass of people groups and parts to reveal, then hide, the puppets. The crowd itself acts as a theater curtain.

Although Schnitzler's *Der Schleier* does not offer comparable examples of theatricalism, we find many of them in *Zum Grossen Wurstel*. Indeed, this 1905 farce offers a surprising number of links to *Petrushka*. Starting with the title, *Burleske in einem Akt,* we recall the designation of the ballet as *Scènes burlesques*. The main setting of *Wurstel,* the Prater in Vienna, also parallels the set for the ballet, Admiralty Square in St. Petersburg. Each place denotes the site of traditional popular festivities in the nation's capitol.

As for specifically anti-illusionist devices, *Wurstel* again bears comparison with *Petrushka*. Both works frame the *Commedia* triangle in a play-within-a-play. Indeed, Schnitzler manipulates two triangles simultaneously

69. Buckle, *Nijinsky,* 193.

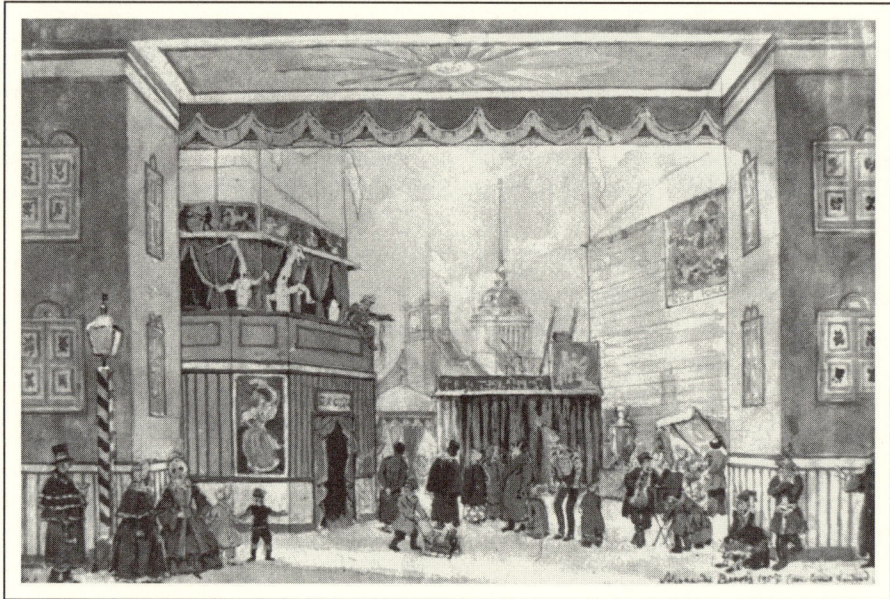

Figure 8. Alexandre Benois, *Petrushka,* drawing for first tableau (1911). Courtesy of
Nikita Lobanov.

in the self-parody of his puppet-play at the center of *Wurstel*. And some of
the people on his stage function as spectators, just as some of the members
of the audience turn out to be actors. Hence we have the same confusion of
spectacle with spectators that is implied by the many frames in the ballet.

Furthermore, just as the ballet puppets take over their own lives, so do
Schnitzler's figures burst out of their roles. Finally, a new character appears
and addresses the audience directly, just as Blok's Pierrot and Petrushka do.
Like many familiar anti-illusionist devices, the actor's direct address to the
audience has very old sources. Nicoll notes that *Commedia* players often
stepped out of character to speak with their spectators in the street. And the
skomorokhi often invited their audience to participate in the show. We may
even trace such techniques linking the actor with the spectator to ancient
drama. The prologue and the epilogue, like the Greek chorus, break the
mimetic artificiality of the stage action.

This new character in *Wurstel, der Unbekannte*, serves as an anti–deus
ex machina. Instead of untangling the inextricable net of the senseless
action, he abruptly cuts the strings of all the players. Thus the farce simply
ends unresolved, only to start again from the beginning. As in the ballet, the
question of reality versus appearance remains unanswered.

LIBERATION

Blok and Schnitzler use the conventional theater as a metaphor for illusion. Hence the titles of their plays denote the clearly illusionistic puppet stage, consisting of a box set on a platform. We assume that all the characters, like the puppets in the ballet, exist within this box, which delimits their world. This stage is traditionally small, since children form the audience for most puppet shows. However, the confined puppet space signifies more than mere realistic scale; essentially it stands for the imprisonment of the puppets themselves. The play symbolically shows us that these conventional characters are trying to escape from the limits of their given roles. Hence they subvert the author's pathetic wish to write a typical puppet play. The imagery of failed liberation climaxes when Harlequin, bursting through the paper set, falls to the floor.

We find parallels in the ballet. Again the setting reminds us of the puppets' confinement. In the first scene, the Charlatan unveils the puppets in boxes just big enough to hold them on stands. In the last scene, they burst from their stage to act out, like Blok's puppets, their own life. But especially in the second scene, Petrushka's cell, we see his essential imprisonment. He is a man not only trapped inside a puppet, but also imprisoned by his hopeless love for the unworthy, stupid ballerina.

This scene begins when the magician hurls the clown into his cell; it ends when he tears a hole through his wall to pursue the ballerina. This violent escape recalls Harlequin in *Balaganchik*, who bursts through the painted window. "Greetings, world! You're with me again! / Your soul has long been close to mine! I go to breathe the spring / Through your golden window frame!"[70] Harlequin's act represents a bursting out of mystical self-enclosure, which does not pertain to Petrushka. However, both clowns share the immediate impetus for their escape: the quest for love.

This common theme reminds us of a whole tradition of liberation imagery associated with circus figures. In Dowson's *The Pierrot of the Minute*, the clown also seeks to fulfill love by fleeing his present limits. Here the desired goal lies not in the springtime world but in heaven, where his beloved lives.

> Then, sweet Moon-Maiden, in some magic car, . . .
> Mount me beside thee, bear me far away
> From the low regions of the solar day;

70. Alexander Blok, "The Puppet Show," in *An Anthology of Russian Plays,* ed. F. D. Reeve, 174.

Over the rainbow, up into the moon,
Where is thy palace and thine opal throne;
There on thy Bosom—[71]

We find the closest precedent for the clown's attempted escape into love in Mallarmé's "Le Pitre Châtié." This fool also tears a hole in his tent to flee from his art into love. Like Petrushka and Harlequin, the *pitre* fails at liberation, for he cannot escape his vocation without losing his identity. Having burst through his confining tent, he tries to swim free in the waters of his beloved's eyes. But in these icy lakes the fool suffers the punishment of losing his greasepaint, his only consecration.

The sacral connotations of this vocabulary also recall Petrushka's Christ-like traits. Walter Strauss has suggested that Mallarmé intended an obvious pun on the words *pitre* and *prêtre*. Characteristically, he here played on linguistic similarity to convey the artist's priestly function. Strauss' claim pertains to all of Mallarmé's prose poems in the *Divagations* (1897), in which the poet grows from mountebank to poet-priest.

Fowlie, in relating all poets to the clown per se, deepens the tie between the *pitre* and Petrushka. He calls both the poet and the clown *chétif,* meaning pitiful.[72] The Russian suffix -*ka* in the name *Petrushka* contains only a familiar diminutive, but the -*ot* suffix in Pierrot has derogatory overtones. The very name of the French clown thus connotes a meager character. One might call any fool *chétif,* but the word's etymology makes it a particularly apt epithet for this fool. Derived from Latin *captivus* (prisoner), *chétif* pertains not only to the puniness of the clown but also to his condition and fate. For art truly imprisons the *pitre,* despite his attempt to escape its demands in romantic self-abandon. Like Petrushka, he cannot flee from the prison of art into "life," symbolized by love. Finally, both fools are punished for their attempt at freedom: the *pitre* suffers spiritual death, and Petrushka actually dies.[73]

The opposite of the pessimistic view of the artist in Mallarmé appears in the earliest forebear for all these figures, the aerialist in Banville's "Le Saut du Tremplin." This man also bursts through his canvas tent, not for the liberation of love but for freedom from his petty-bourgeois audience. Again, the clown rebels against the imprisoning conditions of his art. But, unlike the *pitre,* this *artiste* succeeds in his flight, soaring into the heavens and rolling

71. *Ernest Dowson,* 205.
72. Wallace Fowlie, *Love,* 115.
73. As for the name *Petrushka,* a Russian theater historian believes that the carnival puppet was named after a famous *Commedia* trouper of the eighteenth century, Pietro Miro, called Petrillo (Bennett, "Profaned Love," 150).

among the stars. Such euphoria characterizes Banville's circus types, but after him the escape of the artist figure acquires increasing pathos.

When we compare Petrushka to these two earlier clowns, we see his close kinship with the *pitre*. In Stravinsky's description of his original character, we sense the importance of that same rebellion against a role that characterizes the *pitre*'s downfall. "The real subject of [my work] was the droll, ugly, sentimental, shifting personage who was always in an explosion of revolt."[74] We may see in these words an unwitting description of the composer's own score as a rebellion against traditional tonality. In assessing this composition, we must remember that Stravinsky's style before 1911 still owed much to his teacher, Rimsky-Korsakov. And, although we find hints of Moussorgsky, Strauss, and even Debussy in *Petrushka*, the work as a whole portends the new styles to come.[75]

Banville's clown also revolts, but successfully. We may see his apotheosis in death as a climactic symbol of the supreme Romantic artist. The glory of his transcending the bourgeois world is reversed in the martyrdom of Petrushka's ignoble death. Even Petrushka's resurrection bears only ironic triumph; he rises *after* death, not *in* it, as the *sauteur* does. When we consider the period between Banville's poem and the ballet, 1857 to 1911, we see that the two clowns mark opposite poles of an era. The ballet shows us an ultimate reaction against Romanticism.

All our clown figures attempt release through some kind of window. Both Banville's acrobat and the *pitre* tear holes in their canvas tents; Harlequin in *Balaganchik* leaps through a painted window; and Petrushka hurls himself through his wall. Bennett offers an autobiographical explanation for the use of the window in *Balaganchik*.

When Blok has poor Harlequin leap out of a window into an abyss, he rather wickedly parodies Bely's symbolic jargon in an article originally entitled "Okno v vechnost" (A Window to Eternity), . . . in which Bely discourses on Nietzschean interpretations of music and drama. . . . Although Blok does not repeat the ardent outpourings of Bely . . . , he reifies them in Harlequin's actions, and he eerily mimics Bely's impassioned style in Harlequin's speech just prior to his undignified exit.[76]

74. Quoted in Vera Stravinsky, *Stravinsky*, 67.

75. "In *Petrushka*, Stravinsky finally acquired the mastery of concise, concrete, intensive musical speech, toward which he had been moving in his earlier works. . . . He had first to pull out by the roots the choking weeds of academic dogma that had flourished in a culture of security and prosperity and self-satisfied Philistinism. That Stravinsky did, and he thereby opened the way directly to *Sacre*" (Asaf'eyev, *Stravinsky*, 21, 23).

76. Bennett, "Profaned Love," 161.

I see here more than a reference to Bely, namely the Romantic tradition of window symbolism. Writers and artists of the nineteenth century often depicted a figure at a window as a symbol of enclosed, civilized mankind longing for the freedom outside. The notion of conflict between society and nature forms a basis for this symbolism. Indeed, the window seems inevitable in any image of rebellion against confinement. As we have seen above, the puppet figures of Blok, Schnitzler, and the ballet defy their limits in order to live independently of their masters. Thus we may understand their escape through a window as a metaphor for the freeing of the actor from stage mimesis, from the bonds of illusion itself.[77]

After Banville, the attempted liberation of all our clown figures fails. We may see in their failure the dead end of the Romantic idea of a spiritual, suffering artist, crushed by the brutal forces surrounding him. *Petrushka* does not signify "the end of civilisation," but it does represent the death of a major Romantic myth. The grotesque puppet parodies Benois' "poetic principle," beloved in literature and art since Gautier. Hence the whole ballet—music, choreography, and libretto—points forward to an ironic view of art. In the final figure of the clown mocking his own audience, we have a poignant image of modern art as burlesque.

77. See O. F. Bollnow, *Mensch und Raum;* Lorenz Eitner, "The Open Window and the Storm-Tossed Boat"; and my own *House and Individual.* For specific visual examples of the clown's imprisonment and escape, see Klee's *Pierrot Prisonnier* (1923) and Lipschitz's *Pierrot Escapes* (1927). Storey reproduces both these works in *Pierrot.*

7 A HISTRIONIC CANVAS
The Visual Arts

At the circus, most people see the surface that's funny, but a lot goes on.
—**Alexander Calder**

To fully understand modern images of the artiste, we must go back beyond Romanticism. An exhaustive study of the subject would start with antiquity, where we find the earliest pictures of acrobats and clowns. But within the limited space here, my argument must pertain to only the nearest and most familiar sources. So I shall start with Callot, who depicts both the origins of modern theater setting and the *Commedia dell'Arte* at work. Straddling the French Renaissance and Rabelaisian humanism, Callot portrays the players in his own theater of arabesque.

A century later, Watteau uses the same subject, the *Commedia* roles, but he evokes with them a different sort of drama: the private rococo masquerade. His famous *Gilles,* however, continues Callot's tendency to create portraits of individual actors. Domenico Tiepolo introduces social satire, even caricature, into his *Divertimenti* of Punchinello in daily life. With Daumier, the full-blown caricaturist, we enter the post-Romantic era of disillusion. Like his close colleague Baudelaire, Daumier uses the *saltimbanque* as a mirror of both political decline and artistic self-assertion.

Manet, that axis linking the nineteenth century with Modernism, returns to the image of Watteau's *Gilles* in *The Old Musician* (1862). His rendering of the boy in white, though less problematic than its famous forebear, raises similar questions about the player and mimetic art itself. Picasso, in his many images of *saltimbanques* in the Rose Period, extends Manet's musings into an existential statement. Finally, Beckmann allegorizes his contorted, demonic players. Evoking all the horrors of the totalitarian era, these figures give a tragic complement to the comic grotesque in Callot. The witty spectacle that began this study ends it as a painful pageant of imprisoning and death.

This chronology of the histrionic landscape since Callot gives only a selective sketch of highlights. Lack of space forces my neglect of such important artists as Gillot, Goya, Degas, Lautrec, Seurat, Matisse, Nolde, Rouault, Kandinsky, Calder, and Klee. Indeed, the reader may extend this list at will, for few modern artists have not treated some aspect of the popular stage. My criteria for choice are thematic: Which works best exemplify the principal ideas that emerge from the relevant images? Which works speak most eloquently to each other? And where do we find the keys to unlock the doors to the artist's perception of his theatrical alter ego? Naturally, we must probe beyond the surface of these images as deeply as we have searched behind the texts of the literature.

My selections focus on two main themes that emerge not only from the many pictures I have studied but also from the literature. So this chapter deals with some of the essential themes we have already observed: isolation, decadence, the child-artist, mimesis, transcendence, the commercializing of art. But here, thanks to the synoptic vision of the graphic artist, we may study these matters through two broad categories: the individual versus the group, and the death of the clown. Simplistic though these rubrics may seem, I believe they offer a means of telescoping—without reducing its potency—a huge body of images into a manageable sample.

All the artists considered here visualize the individual artiste within the performing group, evoking relations of great subtlety. And many of them also treat the second subject, the death of the clown, as an essential Western myth. In the most striking examples, the artist combines both themes. For instance Tiepolo, in *The Hanging,* shows the ritual death of a Punchinello, both mourned by other Punchinellos and executed by a hangman-Punchinello. In his *Les Saltimbanques,* Daumier evokes the end of life for the players when the audience does not come. Picasso actually paints the *Death of Harlequin,* attended by a tiny group of two mourning boys and a dog. Beckmann concretes the metaphor of the clown's death in the destruction of his own diseased society.

CALLOT (ca. 1592–1635): THE *COMMEDIA* AT WORK

Our earliest familiar images of the *Commedia* come from about 1622. In his twenty-four etchings *I Balli di Sfessania,* Callot pairs the leading personalities of a show that he probably saw at Italian fairs (see figure 9). For a long time critics tried to identify these scenes with specific troupes or places. Pierre Duchartre even illustrates the portable *Commedia* stage with the *Balli* frontispiece. However, Donald Posner disputes such close links between actual comedians and these etchings. He reads the title of the series as referring to the popular Neapolitan dance, the wild *moresca,* which Callot uses to evoke the fairground spectacle. No one has explicated the complex frontispiece as persuasively as Posner does, interpolating the phrases of a *moresca* song it contains. He doubts that Callot ever saw what he

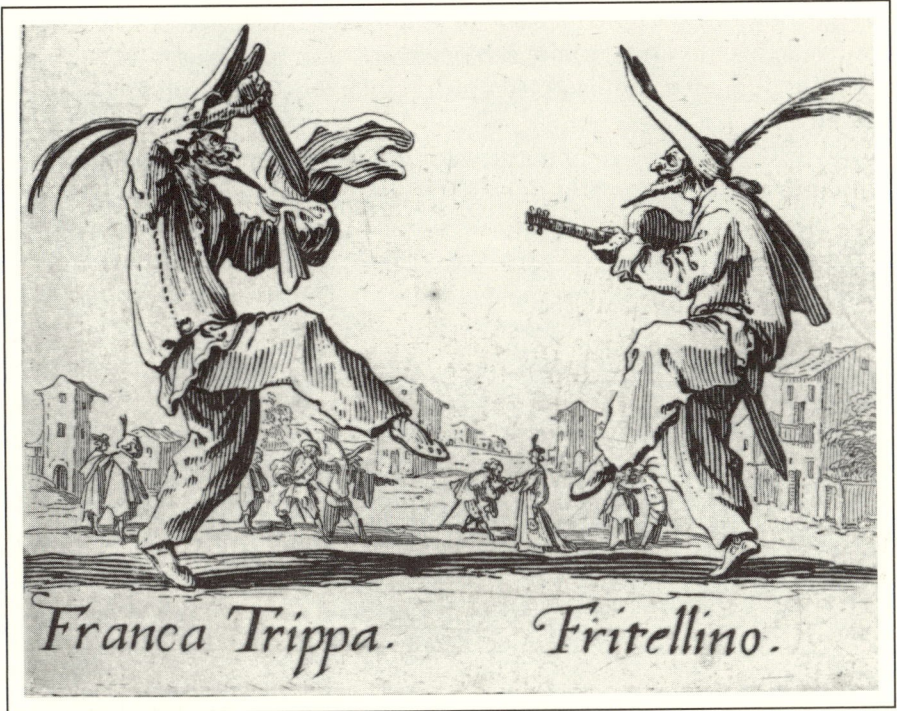

Franca Trippa. *Fritellino.*

Figure 9. Jacques Callot, *Franca Trippa and Fritellino,* from *I Balli di Sfessania* (ca. 1622). Courtesy of the National Gallery of Art, Washington.

depicted; instead, Posner thinks these pictures evolved from Callot's copying of a related series, the *Gobbi*.

Plausible though Posner's argument seems, I cannot accept the *Balli* as images of mere carnival dancers. First of all, the poses of these figures bear more narrative meaning than the mainly aggressive *moresca* does. Not all the figures dance, and several engage in mimed dialogue. Second, the attached *Commedia* names suggest some level of professional identity. So the series may represent the famous dance integrated into *Commedia* routines. Callot could well have invented this combination from the two forms he had seen separately.

Perhaps the contrast of scale gives these pictures their most striking effect. The foreground actors appear about three times the size of the background figures. Hence the players seem monumental, which suits perfectly their stereotypical nature. However, since the tiny distant scenes may depict some routines typical of *Commedia* shows, they also command our attention. Indeed, we can hardly envision these pictures without their background counterpoint. Callot never isolates his star actors, fascinating though they may be, from their social setting. This trait expresses something particular, even unique, to the subject: the *Commedia* exists only in relation to its audience. Here we see truly popular theater, played in the street, for and among the people.

The *Balli* shows no clear progression from one plate to the next, so we cannot discern a story. Nor does Callot individualize the actors, whose faces usually appear masked. However, the names of the roles played bulk large enough below the figures to form part of the composition. Instead of telling a story, then, Callot makes paired portraits of *Commedia* characters. Moreover, these figures considered together form a continuing parade. In fact, the *Commedia* troupes often used the Renaissance form of the festival parade to advertise their show. This idea of a continuous procession also dominates another of Callot's series of etchings, the *Bohemians*.

As noted above in chapter 5, these images of wanderers express the artist's fascination with the homeless. This trait, expanded into clear identification, appears again in the exiles whom Daumier portrays obsessively. For Callot, we may more modestly trace the link between his Bohemians and his actors: both groups live by improvising. For both wanderers and professional players, life has no predictable story. The parade gives an expectable form for the fugitives, who play no roles. Actors, however, seem bound by the mimetic conventions of beginning, middle, and end. And the typical *Commedia scenari* do follow Aristotelian rules. Yet Callot chooses to take these players out of all narrative context, for their plots do not interest him. He focuses instead on the appearance of these characters, which he makes into emblems of the fairground theater.

The means by which Callot creates these striking images recall several stylistic aspects of the baroque stage. First of all, we note the marked, often histrionic, gestures of these figures. Naturally, to be seen by distant viewers, the actors had to mime in a clearly "legible" style. Callot captures the climactic moments in these pantomimes in a telling way. Like a photographer, he sums up a dynamic action in one characteristic pose. Daumier and Seurat learned much from this kind of hyperbolic gesture.

Second, masks are an essential element in the portraits. Huge noses, fantastic wigs, and grimacing mouths all contribute to the impression of the grotesque. The term *grotesque,* often applied to Callot, has several senses here. The masks in particular create a vision of contorted, leering humanity. Another aspect of the grotesque appears in the bold, deeply shaded outlines of the figures. The restless rhythms generated by these arabesques exemplify the eccentricity that typifies the grotesque. Here lies an etymological link between grotesque style and Callot's vision: his forms have the shaded irregularity of the grotto. His dark contours, more than any other stylistic feature, may well account for his influence on the graphic media. Daumier even extends the thick outlines of his caricatures to painting (see figure 23). Like Hoffmann, who "could not get the figures of Callot out of his head," many artists saw the *Balli,* in particular, as Callot's legacy.[1]

Georges Sadoul's phrase "grotesque lyricism" suits these etchings well. Like other critics, he also stresses the animation of these players. Naturally, since their art consists in motion, Callot makes them appear dynamic. Even when standing still, the actors gain movement through the jagged, assertive outlines of their swords or wildly feathered hats. Moreover, they are animated in another, literal sense. Hoffmann, noting their beak-like noses and wild gestures, sees the combination of both human and animal traits. In this union of opposites, thought the Romantic poet, lies the pervasive irony of Callot. "Irony, setting man in conflict with the animal, mocks the pathetic activity of mankind. Irony lives only in a profound mind; hence the grotesque creatures of Callot, uniting beast and man, reveal to the sensitive observer all the secret allusions that lie hidden beneath the mask of buffoonery."[2]

A smaller group of etchings, the *Three Comedians* (1618), gives related yet significantly different views of *Commedia* characters. Again, Callot provides a dramatic contrast in scale: the actors tower, larger than life, over miniature scenes from the repertory. In the middle distance, Callot adds a pit of spectators, who watch both the player and the distant spectacle. The street framing that scene resembles a wing-and-border stage set in perfect Albertian perspective, yet the actor appears on the frontal plane on another stage. To add to the confusion, the source of light is inconsistent. One can hardly explain this arrangement as other than an imaginary hybrid of street and theater. In creating such a fantasy, Callot may again express his notion of the *Commedia* as mediating between life and art. However, the monumentality of these men, as well as their more formal setting, clearly frames them in a theater stage.

Some other contrasts to the *Balli* show Callot's tendency to portray an individual actor. Consider, for instance, *The Captain* (see figure 10). In contrast to the hectic activity of the *Balli* figures, this man stands utterly still, posed with the perfect self-assurance typical of his role. Moreover, he does nothing *but* pose, while the *Balli* figures appear at work. This static, statu-

1. E.T.A. Hoffmann, *Werke,* 7. Victor Hugo, for instance, whose literary theory depends on the grotesque, often refers to Callot. See Jean-Bertrand Barrère, "Victor Hugo's Interest in the Grotesque in his Poetry and Drawings," in *French Nineteenth Century Painting and Literature,* ed. Ulrich Finke; Victor Brombert, *Victor Hugo and the Visionary Novel.*

2. Hoffmann, *Werke,* 7.

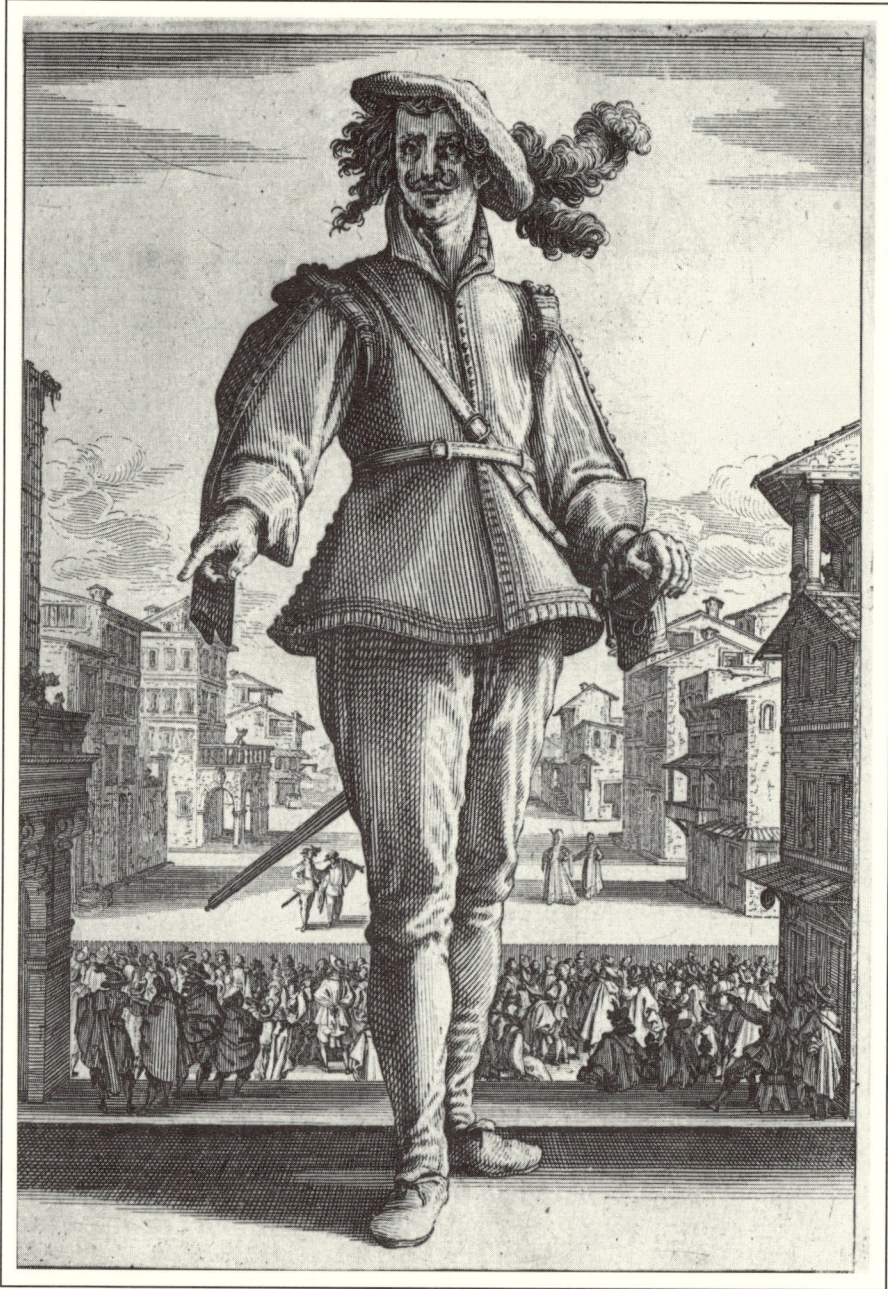

Figure 10. Jacques Callot, *The Captain* (1618). Courtesy of the National Gallery of Art, Washington.

esque person imbues the whole plate with a sobriety wholly lacking in the other series. Alone and unmasked, he relates to no one but the viewer. Hence he appears less as his assumed role and more as himself. Several critics have tried to identify these three players, but no one knows who they are. I see them as examples of that ambiguity between actor and character that has always fascinated artists. Think of Yeats: "How can we know the dancer from the dance?"

Art historians speculate on what attracted Callot to these scenes of comedy, dance, acrobatics, and earthy farce. One cannot readily infer the kind of personal identification that artists of the nineteenth century made with such burlesque performers; we know too little about Callot for such claims. Probably the universal appeal of dramatic, dynamic conflict best accounts for the attraction of these figures. All Callot's art, from *The Miseries of War* to the military catalogues, depends on drama. Not only his themes but also his composition, settings, and mood suggest the staged presentation.

But what does this dramatic style produce? How does it render Callot's vision of the players? Primarily, of course, it works through formal traits. The artificial scale, the contrast of huge versus tiny, the rhythmic interplay of group and individual: such features belong to the stage. Because Callot imposes such theatrical means on his material, we consider him the founder of the histrionic genre in the visual arts. Yet he goes beyond the formal by creating the sense of drama itself. Hoffmann has immortalized this ineffable quality in the phrase "das fremdartig Bekannte" (the strangely familiar).

For Hoffmann, Callot's appeal lies in just this evocation of the universally human that is also exotic. Meyerhold, another admirer of Callot, quotes from the same passage in Hoffmann's *Phantasiestücke in Callots Manier* (*Fantasies in Callot's Manner*) (1814) in his essay on the aesthetics of theater, *Doctor Dappertutto* (1908). "The element of deception is important in the dramatic grotesque, just as it is in Hoffmann. The same is true of Callot. Hoffman writes of this astonishing graphic artist: . . . there is something in the appearance of the life-like figures that makes them at once *familiar yet strange*."[3]

This paradoxical merging of the known and the unknown characterizes the mimetic art. Callot depicts the *Commedia* array of human types in all their earthiness; yet he also implies their transcendence. Does not all drama both display the ordinary and go beyond it? Ross Chambers echoes this idea of theater in Callot, Hoffmann, and Meyerhold. "The primary paradox

3. Edward Braun, ed., *Meyerhold on Theater,* 141, italics of Meyerhold.

of the saltimbanque is to live an oxymoron, that of the strange and the familiar."[4]

WATTEAU (1684–1721): ROCOCO-COURTLY MASQUERADE

Probably the most popular images of *Commedia* figures from the eighteenth century belong to the various *fêtes galantes* by Watteau, 1712–1718. Let us first consider *Pierrot Content* (1712) (see figure 11).[5] Like its parent image *The Jealous Ones*, now lost, this picture treats one variation of Watteau's constant theme, the dilemmas of love. The subtle, even inscrutable, expressions of these people take us a long way from the vulgar histrionics in Callot. Yet some features persist. Like the *Three Comedians*, Pierrot occupies center stage, framed by lesser types. His pose reveals nothing stereotypical, but his shimmering white centrality highlights him as clearly as monumental scale and climactic pose do the Callot figures. We find the same link to Callot's portraits in *The Italian Comedians* and *Gilles*.

Here we see Watteau's typical mannered juxtaposing of people from the theater and from daily life. No longer separated, as in Callot, by their own picture plane, the *Commedia* masks intimately mingle with their audience. Or else all these figures are nobles, some costumed and some not: no one knows their identity. Posner takes them all for actors at leisure.[6] In any case, disguise itself appears as a primary subject. And beyond this level of pretense, Watteau conceals the very meaning of the scene. What exactly is happening here? How do the costumed figures relate to the others? Does this masquerade depict a sort of courtly theater, or is it just a game of love? As in Callot, art and life intermingle; yet Watteau intensifies the ambiguity of role playing into questions about far more than the dramatic event.

One can readily see these pictures as musings on a social order threatened by impending decline. Put most simply, romantic emotion may soon overwhelm the rational control of traditional mores. Norman Bryson even speaks of "high passion" here: a surprising view of pictures that characteristically depict restraint. As for their overtones of social decadence, Bryson sees in the *Commedia* players offstage "the sadness of depleted

4. Ross Chambers, "Frôler ceux qui rôdent: Le Paradoxe du Saltimbanque," 348.
5. Only lack of space prevents my discussing three other such pictures, which exemplify the mysteries implicit in *Pierrot Content:* (1) *The Italian Serenade,* a portrait of a musical Pierrot, (2) *The Foursome,* featuring a provocatively off-center back view of Pierrot, and (3) *Do You Want to Conquer the Beauties?,* the image of a truly haunting, black-masked Harlequin. (See Donald Posner, *Antoine Watteau,* 87–89.)
6. Ibid., 57.

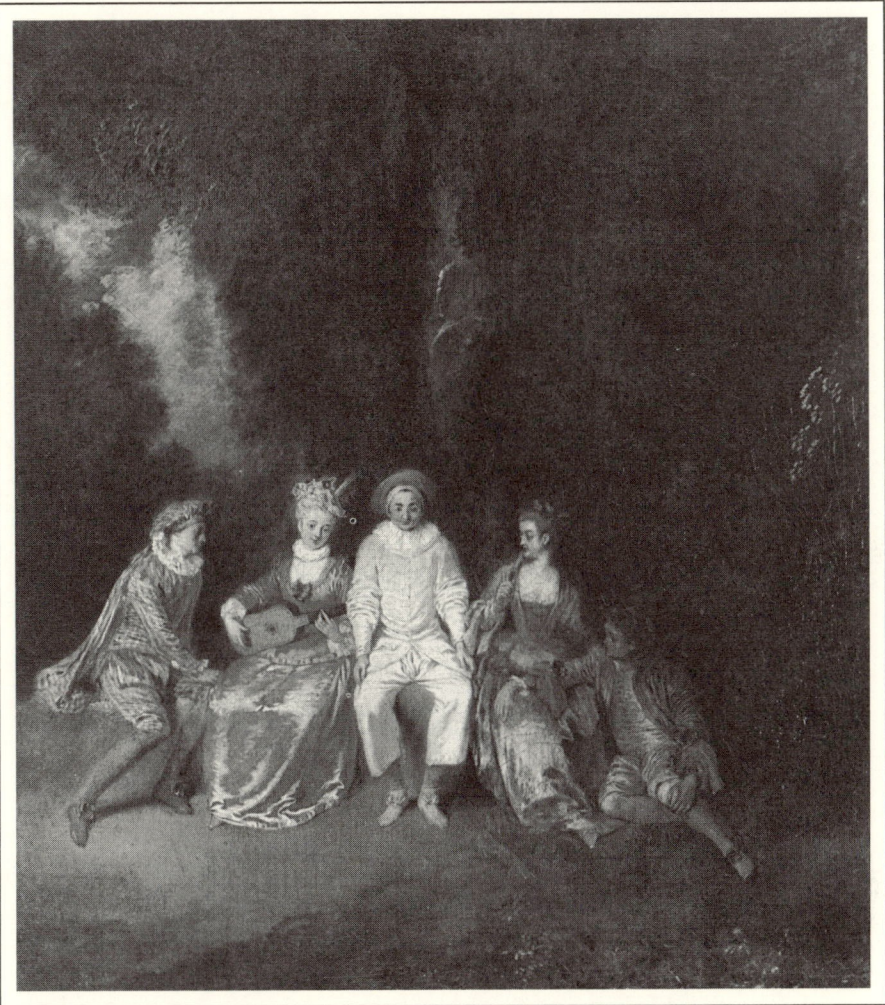

Figure 11. Antoine Watteau, *Pierrot Content* (1712). Courtesy of Foundation Thyssen-Bornemisza, Lugano, Switzerland.

signs."[7] However, despite such charming insights, no one has adequately explained the famous mystery of these images. Most critics finally admit that the *fêtes* reveal the ultimate riddle of love itself.

For my discussion, two pictures of *Commedia* players show more of Wat-

7. Norman Bryson, *Word and Image*, 82, 71.

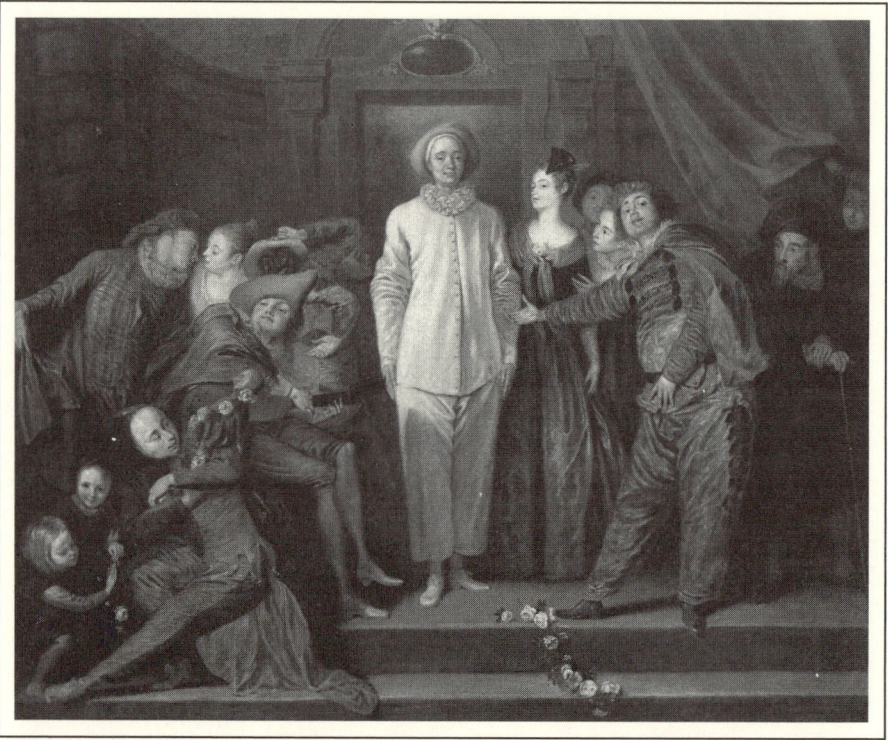

Figure 12. Antoine Watteau, *The Italian Comedians* (1720). Courtesy of the National Gallery of Art, Washington.

teau's view of the artiste than do the *fêtes*. *The Italian Comedians* (1720), unique though it is, also continues Callot (see figure 12). Here again we have a formal, frontal portrait of a star actor, highlighted by the surrounding company. Watteau omits the public, which looms large for Callot, and adds enough detail to the other figures to make a true group portrait. Instead of an artificially grandiose scale, he creates a credible scene in human size. No fantasy of the popular stage, this theater clearly addresses the quotidian life of the viewer. Our eye moves from left to right, from childhood through young love to self-assertion. The gleaming Pierrot gives an elegant center for this trip that finally declines into old age. According to this popular view, the picture belongs to the emblematic tradition of the symbolic *Steps of Life*. Merging the iconography of that theme with a play allows the painter to display simultaneously the whole span of human life and to miniaturize it.

This interpretation helps us to define the kind of theater enshrined here. These comedians play specifically the story of Man; the *Commedia* presents universal drama. But to that simple content we must add complex ambiguity. First of all, what is happening? Most critics assume that Watteau makes a portrait out of a curtain call. Posner settles for the epithet "a vaudeville farewell," but Bryson sees deeper significance in the choice of this particular aspect of the performance. "Watteau breaks with the Gillot precedent of illustrating scenes from plays, and selects instead . . . the moment when discourse ends: the curtain call."[8]

However, only three of the figures behave accordingly. The other players ignore the audience, assuming their typical poses in the play. Thus we cannot take this picture as a faithful depiction of actors standing for applause. Instead it seems to incorporate both the curtain call portrait and the capsule drama. We may compare this combining of function with Callot's *Balli,* in which foreground figures perform and the background miniaturizes actual scenes.

Another ambiguity surrounds the curtain partly raised at the right. As in some of the *fêtes champêtres,* Watteau poses teasing questions with this usual signifier of the stage. "In performance, the curtain divides the theater into two distinct zones: in front of the curtain audience, life, the absence of coded meaning; behind it stage, art, the area of meaningfulness. But when the performance ends, the division between the two zones breaks down; and during the curtain call it is impossible to tell whether we are still seeing the bodies of characters from the drama, or the asemantic bodies of actors out of role."[9]

In *The Italian Comedians,* the curtain call gains mystery through the idiosyncratic placing of the actors. Usually in a curtain call the drapes open fully, permitting the actors to step out in front and approach the audience, or the actors remain in tableau, well behind the opened curtain. But Watteau uses neither of these schemes, setting his figures in a flowing composition divided by the curtain itself. Clearly he uses its slanting drape to highlight Pierrot; the curtain not only echoes his line from head to elbow but also hangs just behind where he stands. Yet the clumsy lifting of the curtain by one figure disturbs its function as a clear divider of stage from audience. In any case, we cannot take the picture as a credible curtain call. This hybrid image begs rather than answers questions. Like the ambivalent curtain itself, the scene upsets our assumptions. Hence it negates the function of a curtain call, which we expect to leave us satisfied.[10]

In a famous article of 1952, Dora Panofsky attempts to reconcile two

8. Ibid., 79.
9. Ibid.
10. For suggestive Freudian musings on the curtain in film, see Daniel Dervin, *Through a Freudian Lens Deeply: A Psychoanalysis of Cinema.*

conflicting definitions of this painting: the group versus the individual portrait. Following a classic study of the Dutch group portrait, she concludes that Watteau combines in Pierrot both the "internal" unity of common purpose among the players and the "external" unity of his own stardom. "In being equally impervious to both the audience and his companions, in being almost unconscious of either the one or the other, he balances the two [unities] within himself. Watteau conformed to yet outgrew the conventions of the Dutch portrait. He utilized them for his own individual purpose: the isolation and glorification of Pierrot."[11]

By far the greatest confusion produced by this picture is its problematic Pierrot. He immediately draws our attention, not only by his gleaming costumes but also by his stillness amid motion. The rest of the company are all gesturing, while Pierrot simply poses, with utmost self-awareness. Moreover, he stands detached from the event. He clearly dominates the scene, yet he is also detached from it. With good iconographic evidence, Panofsky argues a resemblance to the Christ of the ecce homo tradition. Rembrandt in particular provides the model for three primary traits in the Watteau work: (1) the central figure isolated by a framing doorway; (2) two or three figures wedged behind the two protagonists; and above all (3) the presentation itself. "As Rembrandt's resplendant Pilate 'brings forth the Lord' and points Him out to the crowd, saying 'Behold the man,' so does Watteau's elegant rascal . . . present the impassive Pierrot to the audience. His mocking gesture, with hand outstretched, hand open, and thumb raised, may be described as a bitter parody of Pilate's."[12]

The martyred Christ relates well to Pierrot, who often played the scapegoat in *Commedia* pieces. Moreover, this picture displays several other links between the two men. Not one but two halos frame Pierrot's sublime face: his brimmed hat and the oval crowning the door behind him. To add to this obvious symbolism, white roses suggesting Christ point from the spectator to Pierrot. Finally, this clown seems to glow from within. Like a resurrected Christ, the figure itself radiates light.

Although we must grant some Christ-like traits to this ecce homo image of Pierrot, Watteau did not necessarily equate the clown with the Savior. Instead, we may see here the Pierrot who commonly stepped forward at the end of the play to pronounce the moral. Historical grounds further support such objections to the view of Pierrot as Christ. In Watteau's time, the fairground buffoon acted with all possible vulgarity; only the Romantic poets

11. Dora Panofsky, "Gilles or Pierrot?" 337.
12. Ibid., 339.

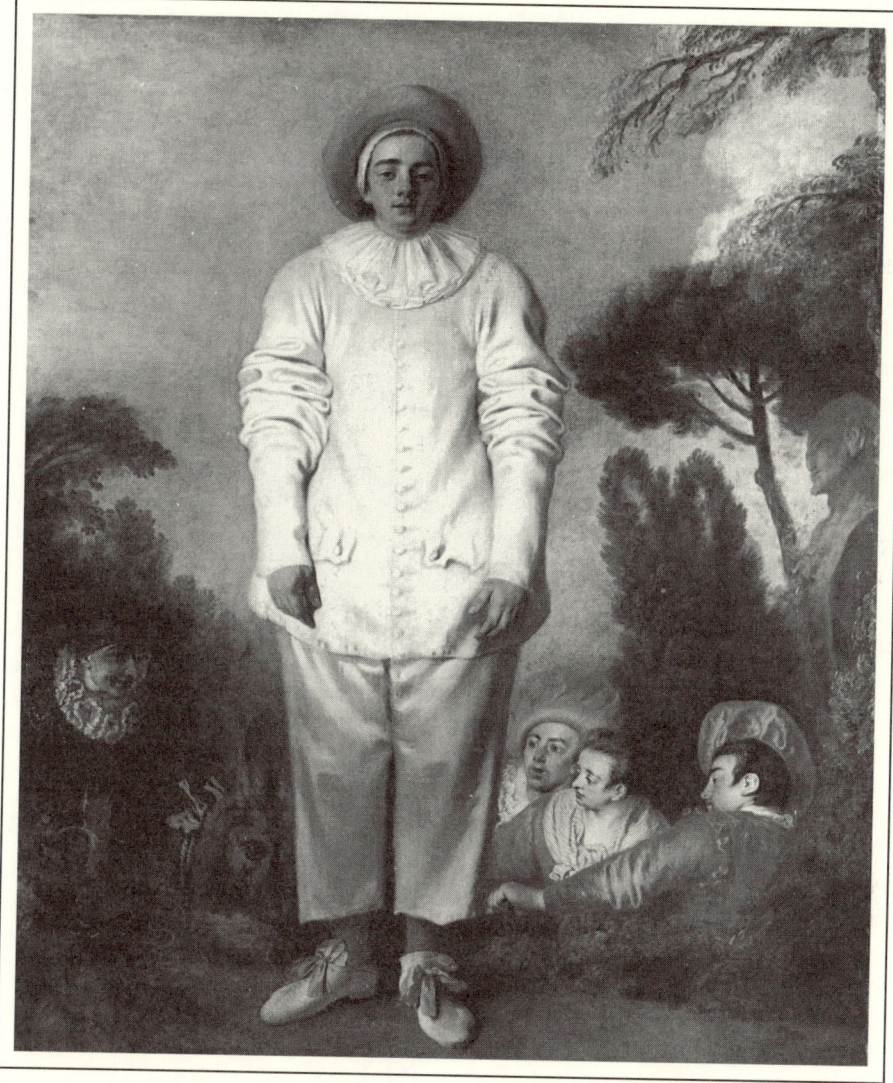

Figure 13. Antoine Watteau, *Gilles* (1721). Courtesy of Musées Nationaux de France, Orsay and Louvre.

and their followers invented the myth of the melancholy clown. Indeed, contemporary sources say nothing of sadness.

To evaluate this problem fully, we must turn to the climactic image of Pierrot: the *Gilles* of 1721 (see figure 13). No other picture has caused as much controversy, or had as much influence, as this one.[13] Even Posner,

13. The latest tribute to this *Gilles,* and certainly the most literal, is Joseph Cornell's box

resolute debunker of "the Watteau myth," would not doubt that *Gilles*, more than anything else, helped to promote the late Romantic idea of the sad clown-artist. However, we must remember that the work did not enter the Louvre until 1869. Hence it probably did not contribute to our "classic" images of the player in Hugo, Gautier, Banville, and Baudelaire.[14]

Right away the picture confounds our expectations of Watteau. It diverges so far from his usual pictures of *Commedia* types that historians have disputed the attribution. Here we have no *fête galante* or *fête champêtre*, no curtain call, no depicted stage scene, and—above all—no suave, proud Pierrot. True, Watteau may treat the Pierrot of *The Italian Comedians* as mock-heroic, but that man still appears dignified. The cloddish *Gilles* presents the exact opposite of the self-assurance expressed in both *The Italian Comedians* and its forebear, Callot's *Captain*. *Gilles* perfectly contrasts with the latter, who seem to say, "Look at me! Aren't I wonderful?" Watteau's clown appears instead as a true fool, drawing not admiration but mockery.

Watteau may well have found inspiration in Callot. Gilles' size and frontality recall the Captain, as does his placement in an elevated foreground space. We might view the clown's clumsy feet as a parody of the Captain's careful, balletic position. Moreover, the odd, undefined background space in Watteau, presenting mysterious half-figures, seems just as unnatural as the irrational depiction of space in Callot.

Watteau isolates this Gilles from his colleagues, even more so than he does the Pierrot of *The Italian Comedians*. There at least one figure relates directly to him, the man presenting the clown. And some of the others do focus on him. But in *Gilles*, no one seems aware of the central figure. Furthermore, his elevated position, with no framing architecture, monumentalizes him. Thus *Gilles* resembles an individual portrait much more than that of a group.

Accordingly, critics have tried to identify the subject as a specific actor. However, they can only guess at the origin and purpose of this painting, for it has an unusually obscure history. This huge canvas served as a shop sign for the café owned by the actor Belloni, a friend of Watteau. Both the actor and the painter fell ill and died in 1721, the same year when Watteau

---

construction *A Dressing Room for Gille* (1939). The artist cuts an identical copy of the Watteau figure in thirds, which he connects with ribbons. When one slightly moves the box, the puppet dances in his close-fitting, decorated room, his "poetic theater" (Sandra Starr, *Joseph Cornell and the Ballet*, 11).

14. Francis Haskell ("The Sad Clown: Some Notes on a Nineteenth Century Myth," in *French Nineteenth Century Painting and Literature*, ed. Ulrich Finke) raises important points in considering this phenomenon. However, as Robert Storey perceptively remarks, Haskell errs in not distinguishing between the sad clown, who himself feels sorrow, and the tragic clown, who arouses pity in the audience (letter to the author, 21 July 1981).

painted *Gilles*. Few critics resist the urge to see this picture as the final, aptly "difficult" self-portrait of a problematic artist.

Panofsky brings Watteau into the clown-Christ equation in two ways. Tracing the history of Pierrot as a distinctly French creation, she relates *Gilles* to two traditions, the theatrical *parade* and the artist's self-parody. As for the former, the painting illustrates a maxim taught by the educational *parade*: "In Washing a Donkey's Head One Loses the Soap," or "Love's Labors Lost."[15] Hence Watteau links Gilles, here as elsewhere, with the ass. This buffoon serves to rescue mankind from its foolishness, just as Christ saved it from sin. Iconographically speaking, Gilles belongs with the donkey, which also bore Christ to his Calvary. Perhaps the strongest statement of this linkage comes from Pierre Schneider. He speaks not only of Gilles-Christ and the ass but also of Watteau as suffering scapegoats. "Watteau, the painter of other people's passions, here represents his own life and career as a re-enactment of the Passion."[16]

The second definition that Panofsky makes for this canvas, the parodied self-portrait, depends on three engravings after Watteau that show an artist-monkey as both the artist himself and Pierrot. In the most arresting image, *Poorly Guarded Love*, Pierrot is an actual ape. To paraphrase Panofsky: If Watteau equals ape and ape equals Pierrot, then Watteau equals Pierrot. The parody here seems to involve less the suffering artist than art itself, which critics have long called "the ape of nature."

Linda Nochlin contradicts the deconstructive Posner by reiterating, even expanding, the classic view of Gilles as both the quintessential sad clown and the enigmatic artist himself.

Half-sacred in . . . silky whiteness, . . . Gilles [is] Christlike in his innocent exposure to the gibes of the crowd, the very prototype of the tragic clown, the clown with the broken heart, avatar of Pierrot Lunaire, He Who Gets Slapped, and Prince Myshkin—that whole galaxy of more or less holy fools whose existence has marked the art, literature and film of the modern period. Not the least of Gilles' roles is the double of the artist himself: here then we have the Clown Prince of Melancholy standing in for the Painter Prince of Evocation.[17]

15. Panofsky, "Gilles," 327.

16. Pierre Schneider, *The World of Watteau*, 103. The linking of both Pierrot and Harlequin with an ass probably comes from the *Commedia* repertory. Posner, *Watteau*, shows several pictures that pair either of them with a donkey (figs. 43, 48). One of Callot's *Balli* also features an obscene background action with two clowns and an ass (Gerald Kahan, *Jacques Callot, Artist of the Theater*, pl. 16). Tiepolo often puts donkeys into his Punchinello drawings, but he uses so many other animals—dogs, pigs, horses, even a giant crab—that the ass loses its iconographic meaning. Picasso offers a possible pendant to the ass motif with the white horse that often accompanies his *saltimbanques*.

17. Linda Nochlin, "Watteau: Some Questions of Interpretation," 71.

This last word, *evocation,* sums up Watteau's general legacy: an ineffable realm of reverie. Bequeathing to clown imagery the spirituality of Gilles, Watteau captures the evocative function of theater itself. In this use of the *Commedia* as a means, not an end, Watteau differs from Callot. While he too depends on pose and gesture, Callot focuses more on the total scene than on the subtle mime of individual glance, attitude, and bearing. Watteau communicates the essence of physical appearance.

As for Posner's objections to the Panofsky-Nochlin view of Pierrot, I find them unconvincing. Since Watteau never depicts scenes from actual *Commedia* repertory, we have no reason to expect that his Pierrot should conform to historical type. Indeed, looking at only the few images discussed here, we must conclude that all his Pierrots defy the bawdy style of the time. All wear that immaculate satin, "half-sacred" suit that separates them from their less transcendent colleagues.

In the *Commedia* plays, Pierrot had no such nobility. The ungainliness of the *Gilles* costume, with trousers too short and sleeves too long, merely exaggerates the same traits seen in other pictures. All these Pierrots wear the trouser leg well above the ankle, and the sleeve always bunches at the elbow. Not the costume but the oafish manner of this buffoon distinguishes him from these other images. Here, in fact, Watteau comes closer than anywhere else to the peasant buffoon of the fairs. Yet Posner and Nochlin object that this Gilles lacks all the bawdiness of the actual character. But why *should* a Watteau figure appear so earthy? To expect that is to demand realism, which hardly concerns Watteau.

To my mind, Bryson comes closest to stating Watteau's import for this subject. Stressing the improvisation of the Italian players on stock situations, he implies an affinity between their art and that of the painter. Like these virtuosi of theme and variations, Watteau also presents versions of the one comedy of love. We might call Watteau's repertoire an aristocratic *Commedia dell'Arte.* Just as the actors represent stereotypes who enact types of plot, so does Watteau evoke categories of love. Flirtation, pursuit, hesitation, withdrawal, faux pas: his keen modulation of these motifs, transcending the anecdotal, creates a catalogue of amorous mores.

DOMENICO TIEPOLO (1727–1804): THEME AND VARIATIONS

If Gilles exemplifies "the myth of Watteau," so does Punchinello symbolize the legacy of Venetian fantasy in Tiepolo. *Divertimenti per li Ragazzi* (*Entertainments for Children*) (ca. 1800) was his final work, a fitting testament to his prevailing spirit. These 104 drawings bespeak the end of the prerevolutionary era, when all of northern Italy capitulated to Napoleon.

The Venetian Republic fell in 1797. Thus these pieces contain a deep nostalgia, both personal and social, for the past, a sort of double decadence.

As for my two themes, the individual versus the group and the death of the clown, Punchinello exemplifies both. Indeed, he suggests an especially problematic relation between the single player and the company in his infinite duplication. Who is the original clown, who are the clones? Have the fools taken over the world? I shall venture some possible reasons for this striking situation, but no one seems able to explain it fully.

Punchinello also introduces a clear affinity with death that remains essential to all subsequent clown imagery. No one sees the players of Callot as close to death; nor do most critics see Gilles in this light. True, Michelet thought that the clown was saying "Farewell, people, I am going to die."[18] And we may view the whole genre of the *fête galante* as a symptom of decadence. But nowhere does Watteau clearly associate the *Commedia* figures with death. One might perceive subliminal morbidity here, but only by arguing that these figures oppose the inevitable end of their society with a melancholy game of love. Like the libertines in Schnitzler's doomed Viennese *Glanzwelt*, these nobles would be denying death by indulging in its opposite, erotic play. Whatever the merits of this idea, we must separate Watteau from Tiepolo when it comes to pictorially linking the fool with death. A quarter of the 104 *Divertimenti* deal with sickness, collapse, executions, last rites, burial, and mourning. Thus death plays a primary role in this visual biography.

The title page starts the series with the provocative image of a lone Punchinello contemplating his own tomb (see figure 14). Right away we confront irony: Domenico gives birth to this work with an image of death. To discover why he does so, we must look to political motives. After the fall of Italy in 1797, the image of Punchinello and all he suggested of popular life bore overtones of nationalism. Indeed, some historians of the time used such *Commedia* masks to prove the continuity they claimed for all classical culture.

Such nationalistic nostalgia often spurs memorials to the artiste who expresses the values of a vanishing society. Consider "Un Fantôme de Nuées," which Apollinaire sets near a famous revolutionary symbol, the statue of Danton. Furthering the patriotic aura, the *saltimbanques* perform on the eve of Bastille Day. Adding transience to this evocation of French street culture, Apollinaire notes the rarity of these troupers; most of them have deserted Paris for the provinces. *Petrushka* also developed as a fond farewell to the Russian puppet show, and so did *Les Enfants du Paradis*

18. Haskell, "The Sad Clown," 5.

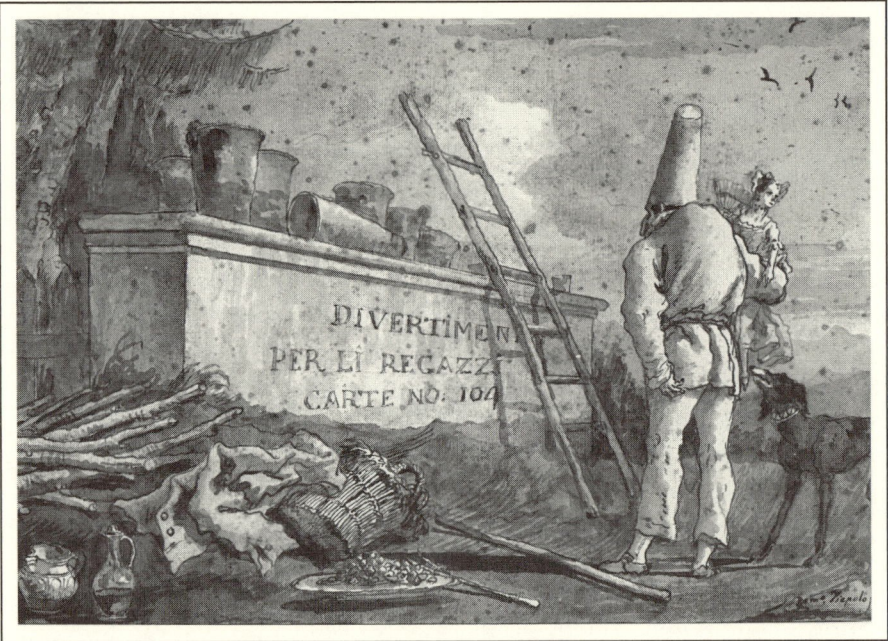

Figure 14. Domenico Tiepolo, *Divertimento per li Ragazzi,* title page (ca. 1800). Courtesy of the Nelson-Atkins Museum of Art, Kansas City, Missouri.

celebrate the French stage. This film made a particularly subversive protest against the enemies of its culture, for it miraculously escaped the Nazi censor. Like the *Divertimenti,* both the ballet and the film explode with carnival life, yet they all also show death lurking beneath its bright surface.

The *Divertimenti* form no continuous narrative. Like Callot, Domenico gives us a parade of images rather than a developing story. And like *Balli di Sfessania,* this series offers scenes of the masked popular player among ordinary people. However, Domenico radically departs from tradition by divorcing his Punchinellos from all theatrical context. Here lies their first mystery: their costumes link them to the *Commedia* stage, which appears nowhere. Even in the two scenes of performance, *Punchinello on the Tightrope* and *Punchinello on the Trapeze,* we see only a circus-like aerial act, no *Commedia* play (Vetrocq, pl. 31, S56). Whatever this character and his clones represent, their identity remains enigmatic.

Of course, Domenico gives his Punchinello the character well-established by *Commedia* troupes. Lazy, gluttonous, bawdy, quarrelsome, stubborn: such traits figure clearly in most of the drawings. But Domenico also evokes much more with this ubiquitous fool, who dominates every scene. Even as a dying or dead man, Punchinello attracts the full attention of all

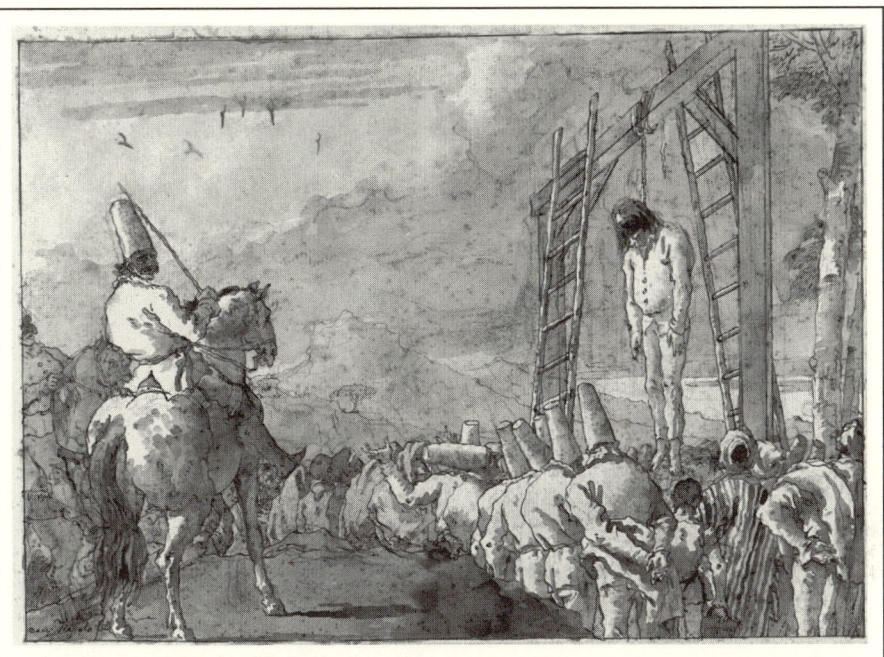

Figure 15. Domenico Tiepolo, *The Hanging,* from *Divertimento per li Ragazzi* (ca. 1800). Courtesy of the Stanford University Museum of Art.

around him. At the very least, this clown immortalizes the dying tradition of Italian folk humor. At the most, he symbolizes the independent, often defiant, imagination. The many images of Punchinello led away by police, imprisoned, even hanged, display his protest against authority. As we noted in chapter 5, artists often show the clown as criminal. Faced with the encroachment of the rational Napoleonic order, Domenico champions the immortal spirit of play. Hence Punchinello offers *Divertimenti* in a specially literal sense. His adventures not only divert us from the dull everyday world, but also evoke the principle of fun—folly, even madness—that all sane society needs.

Nonetheless, in the midst of his buffoonery Punchinello hints at tragedy. Certainly the title plate, with our hero studying his own death, introduces the series on a morbid note. And several plates allude to the martyrdom of Christ: *Punchinello Taken into Custody, The Hanging, Punchinello Collapses by a Wall* (Vetrocq, pl. 32; see figures 15–16). In the latter picture, a mock-Magdalen even rests at the foot of the fallen clown. Such iconography suggests the popular imagery of the gluttonous Punchinello as Carnival and the skeletal hag as Lent. Another plate, *Punchinellos in a Carnival Procession,* shows one figure on a donkey, surrounded by a merry crowd on

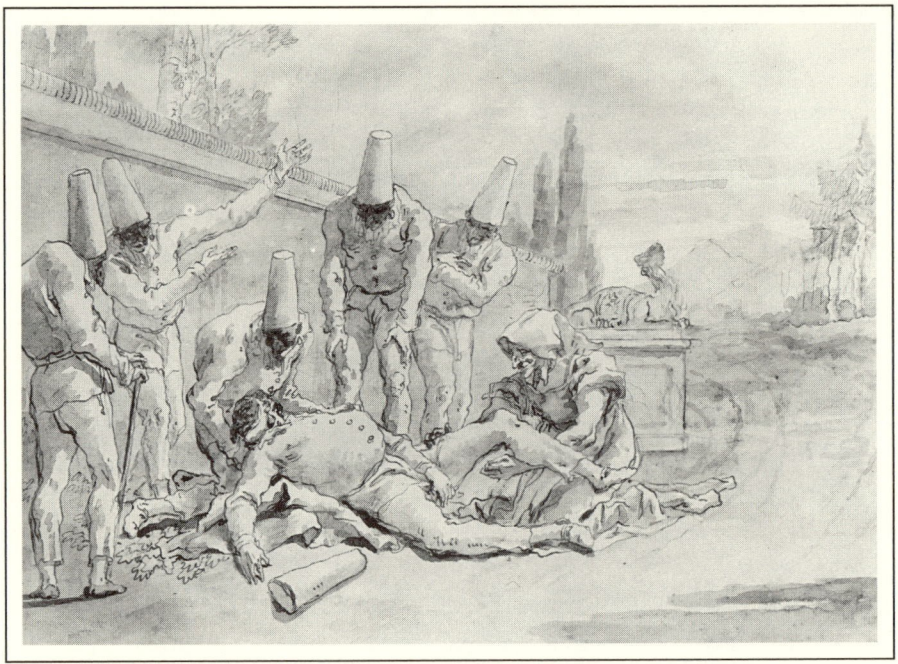

Figure 16. Domenico Tiepolo, *Punchinello Collapses by a Villa Wall,* from *Divertimento per li Ragazzi* (ca. 1800). Courtesy of the Stanford University Museum of Art.

foot. This scheme recalls both the pagan and the Christian pageant of the mockery, death, and resurrection of the scapegoat.

So the buffoon has transcendent aspects. His broad range of experience may suggest Everyman, yet his fate transmits no clear moral message. Since this multiple figure represents nothing historical, we must accept him as the artist's fantasy. In particular, his infinite duplication has no parallel before Domenico. Only a few plates present a family of identical clowns. Otherwise, we see interchangeable adults with no clear family ties. We seem to have a theme and variations. Marcia Vetrocq defines Punchinello as a symbol of role playing itself, "an infinitely recreatable work of art."[19] But perhaps we may find more specific interpretations by looking ahead, to our own time.

I find parallels for these many Punchinellos in the work of Prévert-Carné, Ionesco, and Handke. The film *Les Enfants du Paradis* closes with an unforgettable scene: Baptiste vainly pursues Garance through a wildly cavorting carnival. First a few celebrants in his own Pierrot costume call, "Baptiste! Have you seen Baptiste?" Soon they surround the mime, repeating this line in echoing mockery. As the story ends, the screen fills with hundreds of

19. Marcia Vetrocq and Adelheid Gealt, *Domenico Tiepolo's Punchinello Drawings,* 28.

Pierrots shouting, laughing, singing. Among the several layers of symbolic meaning here, the proliferation of Baptiste's chief role best relates to Tiepolo. Surely the authors knew Tiepolo's figures, but a closer historical precedent probably inspired this image: Deburau initiated a vogue for the Pierrot mask in society. The film pays tribute to just this link between the vulgar stage and the Parisian populace.

In *The Bald Soprano* (1950), Ionesco achieves hilarious confusion in an extended dialogue about a large family, all named Bobby Watson.[20] For Ionesco, not only identities but also objects proliferate like Punchinellos. In *The Chairs* (1952), he produces a mounting comic effect by filling the stage and overwhelming the characters with—what else?—chairs. "Objects themselves become a language."[21] Ionesco probably learned this technique less from Tiepolo than from silent comic films, which also pile up things. Indeed, he has stated his desire to create a pure comic form, as the Marx Brothers did. And as David Madden and Anthony Caputi show, much in the Marx Brothers film farces comes from *Commedia* tradition. Both Ionesco and Tiepolo owe their technique of comic repetition to their common theatrical forebear.[22]

Handke's play *Kaspar* (1967) exactly echoes Tiepolo, for it surrounds the original Kasperle, the German white-clown puppet, with many clones. The play also depends on theme and variations; repetition forms its essential style. We may see in this reproducible clown the mechanical repetition essential to a technological society, the narcissism of the contemporary mind, or the impossibility of being an individual in a world of clones. These interpretations, whatever their merits for *Kaspar*, shed little light on Punchinello. However, we may also take Kaspar's duplication in a broader sense, as a comic confusion of identity, which Handke uses for menacing effect.

The *Divertimenti* share some of these grotesque overtones, as do the Prévert film and Ionesco's plays. Just as Kaspar's teachers threaten his life, so do Ionesco's objects menace his characters. Humanity, it seems, may lose control of its fate. Do we not find a comparable meaning in Tiepolo? Threatened by political domination, the free Venetian spirit must run rampant to survive. In this light, the *Divertimenti* represent a last gasp for the classic

20. As I write, Garrison Keillor, on *The Prairie Home Companion* radio show, gets a similar laugh from telling of Edwin Shroder, who named all his five sons Edwin Shroder. The world of comedy is small indeed. However, I by no means belittle the importance of repetition for the human condition. More space here would allow a discussion of Kierkegaard's imposing essay. The reader may find some consolation for this lack in the various sources on comedy already cited: Sypher, Bergson, Bermel, Caputi, and Charney all skirt Kierkegaard, consciously or not.

21. Ionesco quoted in Walter Wager, ed., *The Playwrights Speak*, 124.

22. After thus linking Tiepolo with Ionesco, I found the revered Jan Kott confirming my claims. He also sees Everyman in Punchinello, and even suggests that Ionesco's characters should dress as the ubiquitous *Commedia* clown (*The Theater of Essence*, 104).

Commedia. Domenico correctly perceived that he was witnessing the end of an era, for subsequent images of these players assume a wholly different character. As the post-revolutionary world changed, so did its artistes, those barometers of the social climate.

DAUMIER (1808–1879): THE *SALTIMBANQUE* AS POLITICAL SYMBOL

A primary link between Tiepolo and Daumier lies in caricature. Although we cannot call the *Divertimenti* political satire, they do suggest social comment. In the development from Hogarth to Goya, the true forebears for Daumier, Domenico occupies a minor place, for his message remains obscure. Yet he points the way by firmly setting his player among the people. Daumier's *saltimbanques* suggest the suffering of human outcasts, not any Watteauesque ambivalence in their professional roles. Domenico provides a model for such figures, for he took the buffoon off the stage and into the street.

Like Watteau and Tiepolo, Daumier sees in the clown a symbol of social conditions. Since his images of *saltimbanques* reach from the 1830s to 1870, they offer a haunting profile of the decades, fraught with crucial change, from the July Revolution to the Commune of Paris. The following account of his developing imagery can give only a brief sketch of its significance in our context. Like Paula Harper, the most recent and thorough critic of these clowns, I take examples from the three decades in which the artist created his most telling *saltimbanques:* the 1840s, the 1850s, and the 1860s.

To begin with, we must examine one assumption shared by all writers on Daumier: his identification with the clown. As we saw in chapter 2, T. J. Clark sees this equation in terms of craft. Howard Vincent and Oliver Larkin stress the kinship of work; Judith Wechsler points to a shared hostility toward the bourgeois. Harper, refining these definitions of the obvious ties between Daumier and his buffoons, resists any blanket link with every type of player. Instead, in Harper's view, the artist relates variously to *paillasse, pitre, queue rouge, bonimenteur, aboyeur,* and *escamoteur* (rough equivalents: tumbler-juggler, fool, red-wigged musician, charlatan, barker, and prestidigitator). Analyzing the depiction of these species chronologically, Harper shows that one type dominates each decade. Her discussion thus profiles not only the development of a major mode in Daumier, but also its parallel, sociopolitical history.

To assess what Daumier added to the common image of clowns in the 1840s, we must review the traits that writers had assigned to them. Earlier poets—Banville, Musset, Champfleury—stressed a dichotomy that made the buffoon a positive figure for the bourgeois viewer. On the one hand, their *saltimbanques* endured wandering, neglect, even abuse; on the other hand, they displayed the heroism of the free imagination. Banville eulogizes both these aspects in *Pauvre Saltimbanques*.

The clown was such a rich symbol for the vanguard writers because he could embody these romantic antitheses: he could represent both the real condition of man, bound by contingency, and the dream of escape from it. And, in the minds of Banville and Champfleury, it was the artist and poet who understood and empathized with both experiences, who could make a bridge from the depths to the heights, show a path from imprisonment to freedom. This was one of the romantic hopes for an art which would be useful to all humanity.[23]

Another common view of the clown is sharply negative: the charlatan. Several contemporary sources describe the mountebank as a con man at best, an outright swindler at worst: *Physiologie des saltimbanques et du peuple* (anon., Paris, 1845) and *Paris-Saltimbanques* (anon., Paris, 1854). We readily recall Flaubert's definition, in his *Dictionnaire des idées reçues* (1850): "Artistes. All buffoons." Hugo creates perhaps the darkest such character in Triboulet (1832). True, the hunchback jester has some heroic traits; as an outsider, a rebel by definition, he must live literally by his wits. Yet the subtlety of this portrait lies in its merging of such virtues with evil motives. Like Jean Valjean, that saintly convict, Triboulet embodies the ambivalence of man, both angel and devil.[24]

Daumier assimilates much of this mosaic of the artiste, but he intensifies the pathos of destitution. His clowns completely lack that vaulting Banvillian idealism that life in the streets destroys. In the 1840s, Daumier distinguishes his *saltimbanques* from both this Romantic image and that of the popular print. *Saltimbanques on the Move*, a wash drawing in the Hartford Atheneum, strikingly contrasts with two contemporary lithographs of 1840 by Victor Adam: *Proverbes en actions* (*Proverbs in Action*) and *La Parade* (see figures 17–19). Daumier's work shares several features with these prints.

23. Paula Harper, *Daumier's Clowns*, 79.
24. Brombert sees all Hugo's clowns as demonic. Their laughter never expresses joy but instead animosity and hatred. Some, like Gwynplaine, transform their infernal laughter into revolution and redemption, but all are basically diabolic. Moreover, these malevolent jesters share a kinship with both the divine Creator and the artist—the *noir génie*. Hugo thus "points to the bond between the creative artist and the forces of darkness. Increasingly, Hugo seemed haunted by the belief that poetic vision depends on the dangerous intimacy with evil, that God and the artist join in a theology of shadows" (*Victor Hugo*, 168).

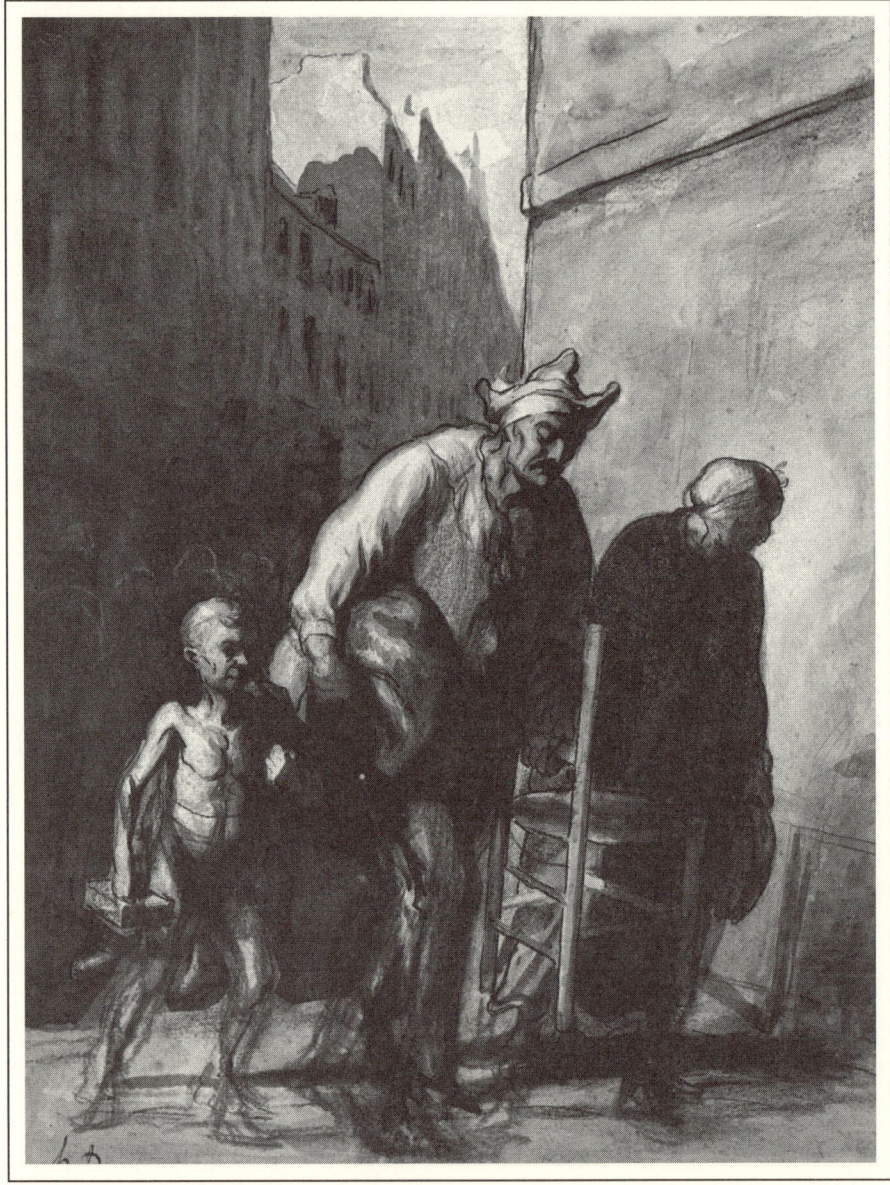

Figure 17. Honoré Daumier, *Saltimbanques on the Move,* (1840s). Courtesy of the Wadsworth Atheneum, Hartford, Connecticut.

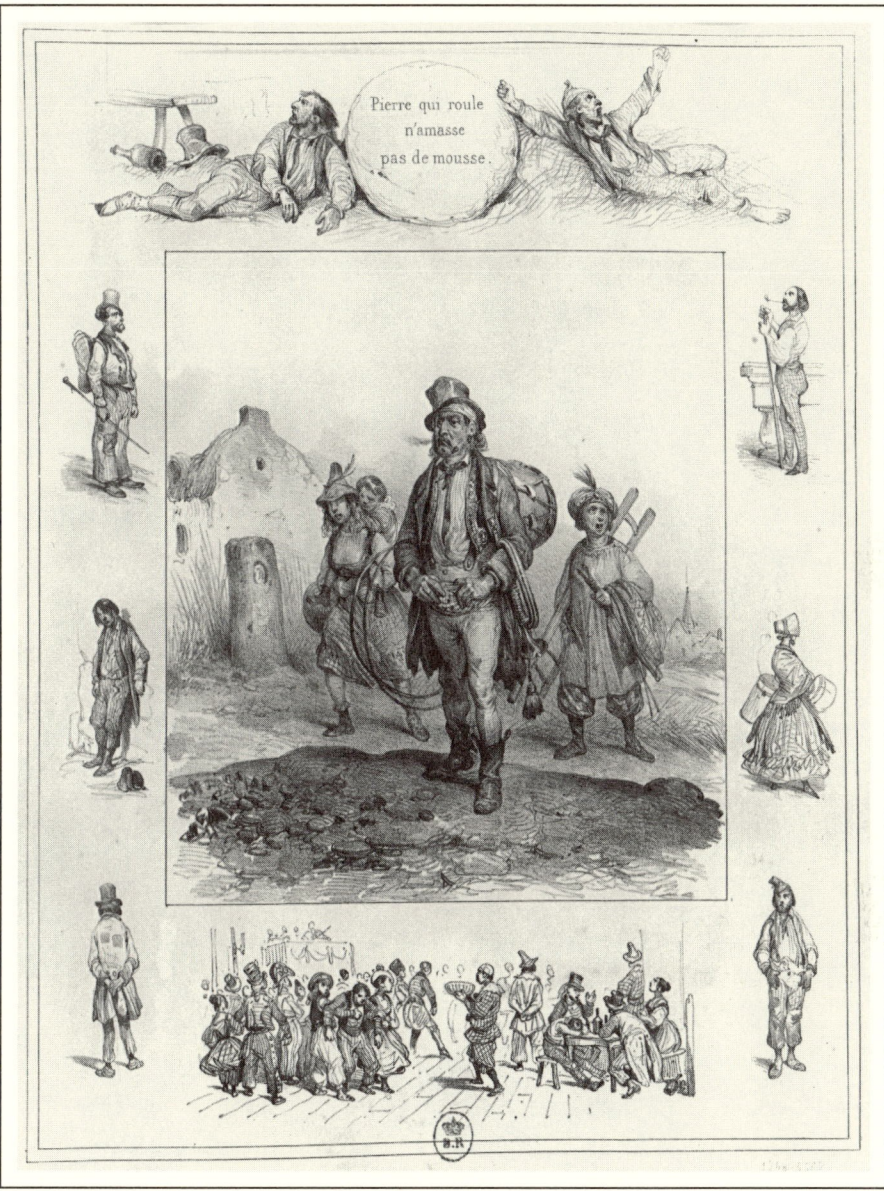

Figure 18. Victor Adam, *Proverbes en actions* (1840). Courtesy of the Bibliothèque Nationale.

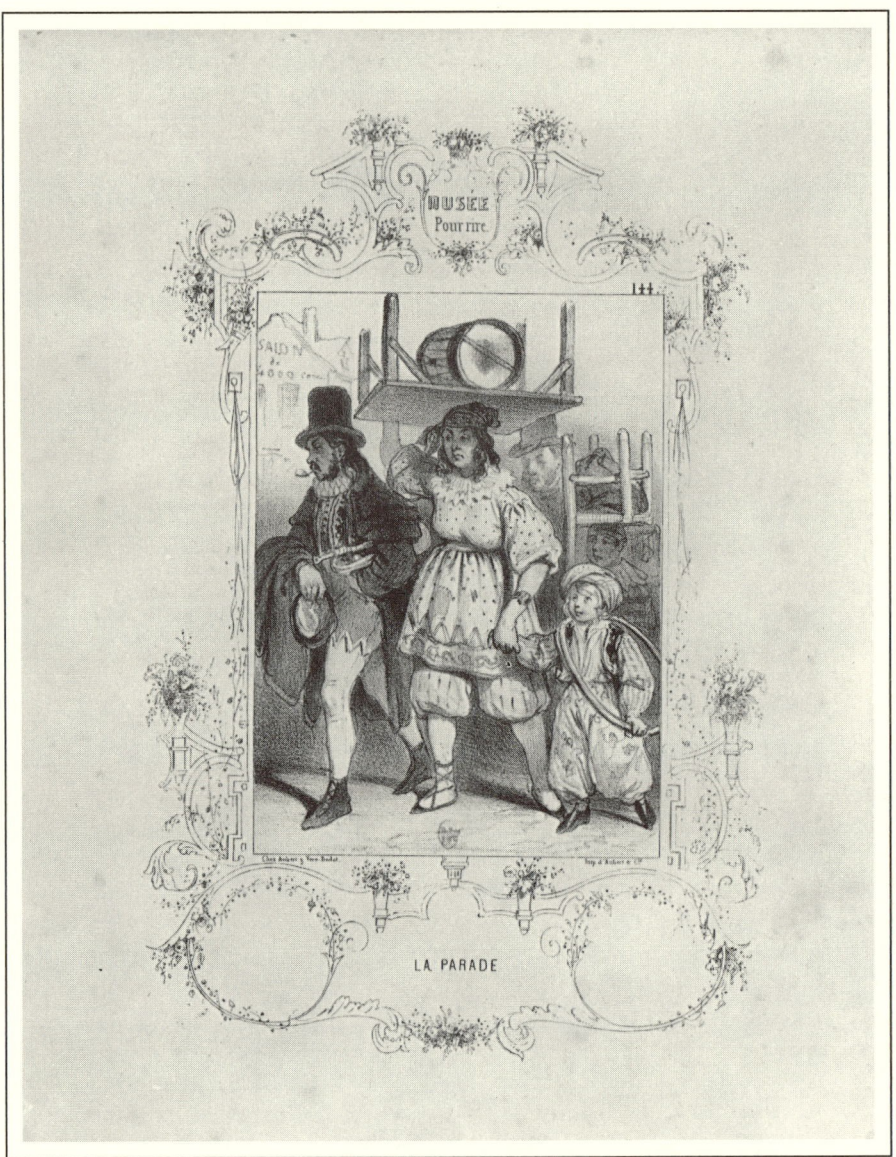

Figure 19. Victor Adam, *La Parade* (1840). Courtesy of the Bibliothèque Nationale.

He repeats the triangular composition of man, wife, and child moving forward diagonally; an outdoor setting; and the expectable props: chair—their "etymological bench"—mat, drum, and cashbox.[25] But Adam renders merely picturesque images of a quotidian event, while Daumier transmutes the ordinary subject into a concentrated vision of grim homelessness.

In contrast to Adam, who fills his prints with descriptive detail, Daumier strips away all but the essential from his image of a weary trio sharply outlined against an anonymous cityscape. Although Adam's figures also plod glumly onward, they lack that summary expression of the downtrodden that Daumier renders so poignantly. Accordingly, the prints bear oddly misfitting anecdotal titles, while Daumier's title *Saltimbanques on the Move* captures the mythic substance of his subject. The pragmatic homily attached to one print, "A rolling stone gathers no moss," has little to do with the aura of the *saltimbanques;* the title *The Parade* for the other one does not even fit the picture. The *parade,* as we shall see below, is the brief preview given to attract customers before an actual performance.

The Adam prints, a historian's delight, amplify their subject, while Daumier's work transcends his subject. Like his many versions of fugitives, Daumier's vagrants bespeak the very condition of wandering. Here Daumier transfers to the *saltimbanque* that heroic, even Homeric, treatment of exile that Callot implies. The woman, barely more than a faceless female specter, evokes the depths of physical and spiritual suffering. Her husband, as resigned as Baudelaire's old clown, embodies their life of mere subsistence. The bravely marching son looks young enough to show that his parents are old before their time.

Several aspects of this picture suggest the same Christ-like transcendence that critics have seen in Watteau's Pierrots. The cross composition, centering the clown in white, and his slumping, defeated posture connote the Martyr. We may compare this vision with that of the later watercolor *A Strongman and a Pierrot in the Wings* (1850s) (see figure 20). Here we must focus on the utter collapse of the buffoon, who may anticipate the misery of Van Gogh's *Seated Old Man,* his hands covering his face. Lending a transcendent aura to the image, a strong stage light bathes the Pierrot. Despite this clear source of light, something seems to illumine the man from within. Like Watteau's Pierrot in *The Italian Comedians,* this clown has the inward glow of the Savior.

Another related picture exemplifies this midcentury Christian treatment of Pierrot: Gérôme's *The Duel after the Masked Ball* (1857) (see figure 21). As Haskell notes, the popularity of this canvas may come more from its

25. E. A. Carmean, *Picasso: Les Saltimbanques,* 21.

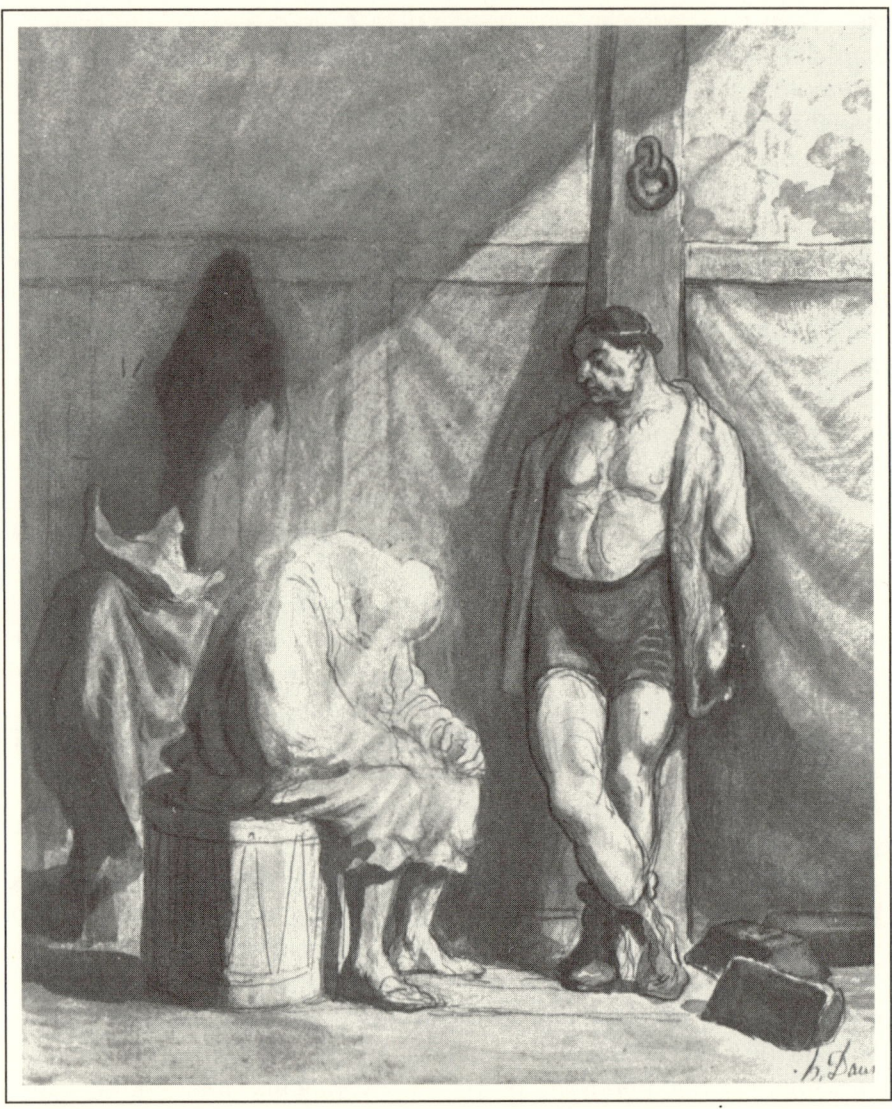

Figure 20. Honoré Daumier, *A Strongman and a Pierrot in the Wings* (1850s). Private collection, location unknown. Photograph courtesy of K. E. Maison.

mysterious story than from its Deposition scene. But for our pantheon of artistes, it ranks as the most blatant image, up to the midcentury, of the sacrificial clown. Indeed, I know of only one surpassing example: the martyred fool Frost, who is visually crucified in Bergman's *The Naked Night* (1953) (see chapter 8).

We have already noted the intimations of Christ by various writers.

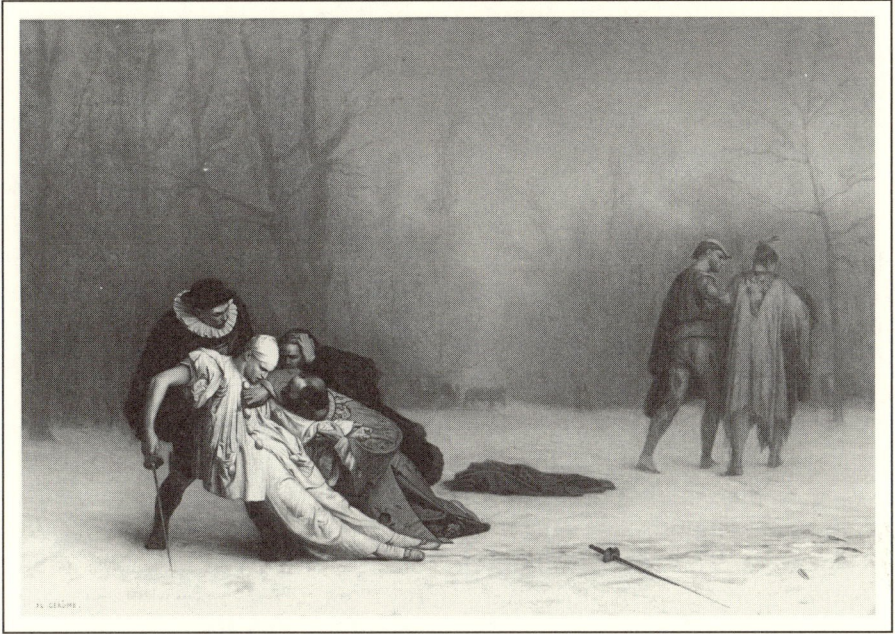

Figure 21. Jean-Léon Gérôme, *The Duel after the Masked Ball* (1857). Courtesy of Walters Art Gallery, Baltimore.

Gautier and Banville create transcendent players, but not until the 1860s does Baudelaire clearly link them with the Savior. His victimized old clown, like the haloed Fancioulle, delineates the modern sacrificial fool. Moreover, Baudelaire also makes the crucial counterpoint of the artist himself as alter ego. Variants of the equation clown = Christ = artist persist in literature, as we have seen in Grillparzer, Wedekind, Zuckmayer, Böll, and Grass. *Petrushka* offers a poignant example of this constellation, as do the films of both Fellini and Bergman.

In the graphic arts, the Christian imagery that also implies the artist starts with Daumier. Like Posner and Panofsky, I reject the "romantic" view of Gilles as Christ and/or Watteau. Of course, no one can ignore the ecce homo aspect of *The Italian Comedians;* yet we have no reason to see that Christ-like Pierrot as Watteau. And Tiepolo's Punchinellos allude to the Savior only by parody. *The Punchinello Infant in Bed with His Parents* exemplifies such burlesque treatment, for this blasphemous nativity scene includes the father in bed with the Virgin and child (Vetrocq, S2). As for Tiepolo's two pictures of the buffoon as a painter, they imply nothing transcendent in this pursuit (Vetrocq, S52, 28). Only *Punchinello Paints a Tiepolo* contains the specific self-mockery that marks the blatant artist-as-jester in Daumier's last caricatures.[26] So he is the first to seriously associate clown, creator, and martyr.

My explanation for the linkage depends on the historical situation. A loss of status forced the artist to identify with the *saltimbanque;* seeing the player and himself as martyrs to their public, the creator portrayed both as Christ-like (see chapter 2). This elevation of the artist exemplifies the secularization that had been happening since the eighteenth century. Put another way, artists of the nineteenth century tried to resacralize an art that had already lost its elevated character. "They tried to recreate the sense of the sacred which is missing from their *theatrum mundi* from now on: art alone, making man divine, can save the poet from this futile and profane comedy to which, in their eyes, bourgeois life reduces itself."[27]

Harper sees in the martyred *saltimbanques* of the 1840s a veiled portrait of Daumier's father. To me, this reading depends too much on biography. Why must these figures have any specific sources? Harper echoes the many attempts to identify Gilles with Watteau. Similarly, one often reads that Callot portrayed a particular *Commedia* troupe or that Watteau's *The Italian Comedians* displays the Riccoboni actors. E. A. Carmean offers an extensive example of this kind of interpretation for Picasso's *Les Saltimbanques.* Here the argument concerns a complex story involving Picasso, Fernande Olivier, and an orphan girl she briefly adopted. But such links, however fascinating, should not color our assessment of the works themselves.

This attitude works particularly well for Daumier, as both the man and his works retain their mystery. We know too little about his habits to simply infer that he makes portraits. "The problem with Daumier, as with the clown petitioner, is that he shares his public's anonymity—part by choice, part by necessity. He paints in secret, puts no dates on his canvases, exhibits little. He leaves us no clues to intentions, except the pictures themselves; the series repeat a message, extend it, qualify it, but for the most part we do not know whether they describe in particular or in general."[28]

However, we cannot help seeing the clown as an alter ego for the artist *in general.* Post-Romantic artists showed a growing need to exhibit themselves; Baudelaire summarized a trend in "laying bare his heart." And, as I note above, the tendency has spawned outright narcissism in our time. But the problem of identification raises some thorny issues in both art criticism and literary theory. How specific is any work of art? Even detailed titles do not remove the universality implied by the act of creation itself. As Ballanche said, "The story of a man is the story of man."[29]

26. See Judith Wechsler, *A Human Comedy,* pl. 161, and Harper, *Clowns,* pl. 77.
27. Ross Chambers, "L'Art Sublime du Comédien," 196.
28. T. J. Clark, *The Absolute Bourgeois,* 122.
29. Brombert, *Victor Hugo,* 172.

In the case of so socially relevant an artist as Daumier, perhaps we should take both points of view. Hence the *saltimbanques* belong concretely to their Paris sidewalk, yet they stand for all suffering players. We may better understand both perspectives if we explore the links between Daumier and his subject. First of all, the clown appears as his heroic image of the outcast-artist. This level of identification goes far back in history: think of Villon and his Jongleur, or of Walther von der Vogelweide, often complaining of his lot as begging troubadour. But the second level of identification in Daumier belongs strictly to his own time: the clown-artist as worker. "After the barrel-organ came the lithograph; the clown and the lithographer were not so very different; the son of a proletarian . . . is not so far from the son of a glass-maker."[30]

Perhaps Daumier's closest kinship with the mountebanks lies in just this professional link. The lithograph, Daumier's first achievement, represents the first truly public form of art. Only when it made possible cheap, mass reproduction could artists' images reach the people. Daumier's career as lithographer hence served the same function of publicizing a popular message that the street clown had performed for centuries. Half the Parisian populace was still illiterate in the 1830s, when *Le Charivari* and *La Caricature*, the main organs for Daumier, began to appear. Hence his work, seen by that large public lacking print media, found immediate acclaim. Like the *saltimbanque*, the caricaturist appealed to a class that had little other choice of entertainment.

Moreover, Clark suggests that Daumier, "working the stone," became less an artist than an artisan. Here lies the kinship of work. Both the lithographer and the buffoon now belong to the new proletarian class. Legally, of course, the Edict of 1853 deprived the street singer of most citizen rights. So he soon lost any recognized proletarian status that the Revolution might have conferred. But Daumier still saw enough likeness in his alter ego to continue showing their fraternity. For him, both artist and clown worked as bravely as any day laborer, since they all earned a meager living by performing their daily tasks.

The artisan in particular now stood on equal footing with the worker, whom the Industrial Age had also deprived of status. *Déclassé*, having lost all prestige attached to craft, Daumier saw himself as kin to the *saltimbanque*, whose artistry did nothing to mitigate his social and political stigma. As the Edict made clear, the law now saw the wanderers as dangerous, for their songs often denigrated the regime. What could better describe Daumier's plight? Think of his imprisonment for his infamous cartoon of Louis Philippe as Gargantua. The street player was regularly locked up for

---

30. Clark, *Bourgeois*, 122.

purveying similarly scurrilous fare in his medium of song, dance, and mime.

Wechsler states the equation of clown and caricaturist even more clearly. "He turned away from his society and to himself as caricaturist in his portrayal of the jester. . . . Daumier had earlier presented types with whom he might have identified, but never with such explicit self-reference. . . . The jester . . . is explicitly the caricaturist."[31] Of course, this claim refers only to Daumier's last phase, to the caricatures produced after 1867. Perhaps only then, with the detachment of age, could he mock himself as court jester. Besides, these late figures have a healthy wit that separates them from the earlier, wretched *saltimbanques*.

Moving into the 1850s, we find a pathos similar to that of *Saltimbanques on the Move* in the watercolor *Les Saltimbanques* (see figure 22). Here again, a family struggles to survive, but this picture stresses their performance, not their wandering. And by adding another child Daumier accents the familial troupe. Such a plea for the ordinary humanity of the players makes them less transcendent than the group in the earlier picture. Although a triangular composition again dominates the picture plane, an air of anxious occupation with the show precludes the sense of Christian martyrdom. Here Daumier underlines the hopelessness of those struggling to attract an indifferent crowd: a message clear to any performing artist.

In the 1860s, another type of *saltimbanque* picture emerges in *The Parade*.[32] Sharply contrasting with the grieving mood of *Saltimbanques on the Move*, Daumier's *Parade* portrays the hyperbolic barker at work. In 1839 Daumier had already used the *parade* stage to depict the staff of *Charivari* grimly selling their journal like any carnival item (Harper, pl. 16). In this lithograph, a determined hawker points to the goods while a drummer and a horn player draw attention to the scene. But in the 1860s a new tone emerges in such pictures: the player becomes raucous to the point of mania, even malevolence. A historical cause for this change may lie in the destruction of the Boulevard du Temple in 1862. This site of the *Funambules* furnished a natural center for street theater. When Haussmann razed

---

31. Wechsler, *Comedy,* 170.

32. In another study I shall compare several versions of the *parade,* which has attracted artists from many fields. Beyond Daumier, Seurat treats it repeatedly; a prose poem by Rimbaud ends with the haunting line, "I alone have the key to this savage parade!" (*Illuminations,* 1886). At the start of their film *Les Enfants du Paradis* (1944), Carné and Prévert immortalize the show before the *Funambules.* A cognate image of Venus on display appears in Mallarmé's "Le Phénomène Futur" (1864) (see chapter 2). Perhaps the best and most famous example is the ballet *Parade,* by Satie, Cocteau, Picasso, and Massine (1917). I suspect that this carnival event fueled the imagination of this variety of major artists because, as Daumier implies, it shows the ambivalent power of advertising.

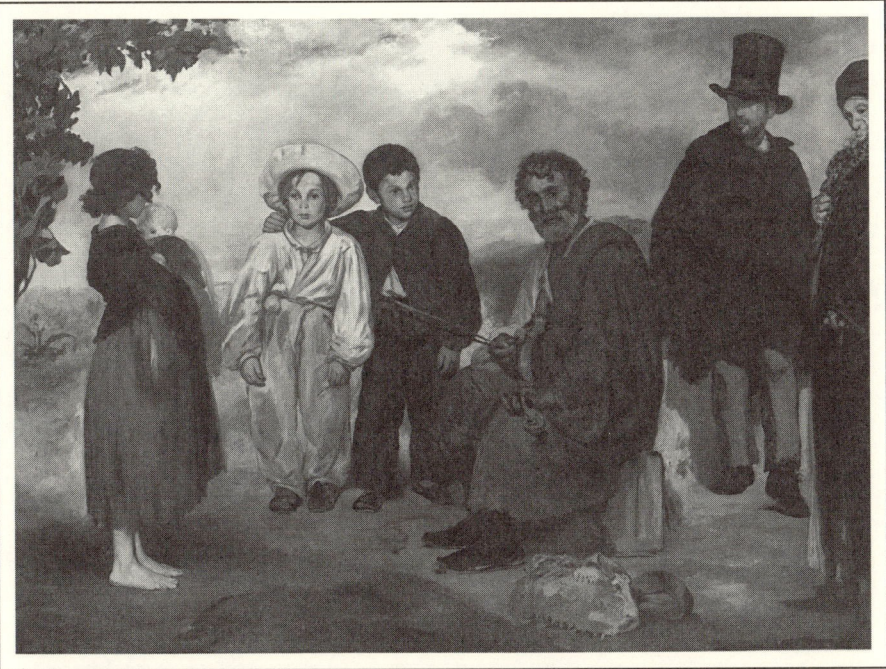

Figure 22. Honoré Daumier, *Les Saltimbanques* (1850s). Courtesy of Victoria and Albert Museum, London.

the street, the homeless players had to seek an audience more desperately than ever.

We may compare the earlier *parade* lithograph satirizing *Charivari* to the oil painting *The Strong Man* (ca. 1865) (see figure 23). The metaphor "The Age of Commerce" now evokes "The Age of the Empire," with its crass manipulation of the public.[33] The work may well express Daumier's fears about the threatening climate of propaganda in the 1860s. *The Strong Man* exemplifies the manic gesturing that typifies the style of the charlatan barker. (Seurat expands this motif in the histrionic flourishes of his *Le Cirque:* figure 1.) Such wildness belongs to the traditional popular view of the player as con man.

Indeed, Daumier intensifies this idea into a grotesque image of the sales pitch. We infer the importance of this theme for him, since he never renders the actual show inside but only the *parade* before it. In other words, selling subordinates performing. Appearance dominates essence. This situation already comments on the times. Yet the picture may evince a more specific,

33. Harper, *Clowns,* 164.

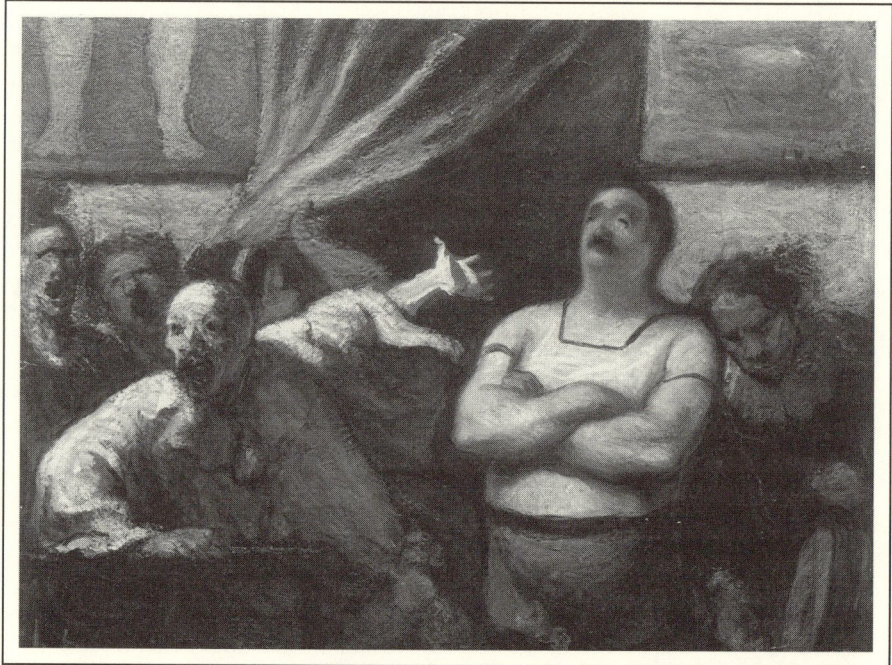

Figure 23. Honoré Daumier, *The Strong Man* (ca. 1865). Courtesy of the Phillips Collection, Washington, D.C.

more pointed attack on the Second Empire. Beyond the mania of advertising, Daumier shows the desperation of the regime to sell itself. If this picture gives his view of Louis Napoléon, it perfectly expresses what Hugo said: "The carnival is part of politics." In this light, the proud *Hercule* portrays the strongman of the Empire, "pink, plump, smug and imbecilic."[34]

This reading may gain credence if we compare the picture to the earlier *A Strongman and a Pierrot in the Wings* (see figure 20). Although we have the same pair, here they render a different theme: the contrast of weak and strong, the suffering of the hunched, Christ-like clown illumined—quite literally—by the matter-of-fact, vertical power of the athlete. Taking a political view of this picture, we might see the Pierrot-artist as tragically defeated by the herculean state. But the hyperbolic gesture of the later demonic Pierrot gives his message the political punch of caricature. *The Strongman and Pierrot in the Wings,* rendered with the delicacy of pencil, pen, and watercolor, lacks the stridency of the oil painting.

Not until the 1860s does Daumier incorporate the passion of his car-

34. Brombert, *Victor Hugo,* 176; Harper, *Clowns,* 166.

icatures into his painting. During the 1850s, his first decade of serious painting, he clearly divided his time between obligatory lithographs for *Charivari* and his private art of watercolor and oil. Naturally, the chiaroscuro of the prints increasingly pervaded the canvases. But only in his last active decade did Daumier create a unique fusion of the two styles. If his poignant caricatures left any doubt as to the "high art" of this maligned genre, the last paintings prove its emotional power.

Perhaps an old definition of caricature may best explain its lowly status in the hierarchy of Art: "Caricature is in painting what burlesque is in literature."[35] Indeed, the frenzied gesture of the Pierrot-barker in *The Strong Man* recalls the *Funambules*, the home of the stage burlesque. Most of the critics treat the mime that Daumier saw from the 1830s onward as a significant influence. Champfleury made a natural comparison between Daumier and Balzac: in them the bourgeoisie has "two severe historians."[36]

We may expand this relation to include Deburau. All three artists create a human comedy, though in different media. Both the mime and the caricaturist must perform daily for their public. Both depict their society through visual codes; both must invent a vivid language of gesture. In urban life they find inspiration. Indeed, they both build an art based on their own public and addressed to it. Perhaps the chief difference between the two media lies in just this relation between artist and audience. Both the mime and the caricaturist take "the people" as a subject, but only Daumier makes them his adversary. Only he invokes that ambivalent love-hate for the bourgeois that Baudelaire and Hugo express.

The link between Daumier and mime emerges most clearly in his economy. Like Deburau, Daumier sums up character and action with the bare essentials of appearance. Using gestural signs, he too articulates the most basic symbols of human experience. In *The Strong Man*, the frenetic splayed fingers of the barker's hand summarize the idea of the whole work. Starkly outlined at the very center of the canvas, this hand almost explodes the line bringing the triangular composition to its apex. It also points not only to the strongman but also to the void within. This screaming entreaty into darkness attracts our desire for fright. The Pierrot's grotesque head, capped in deathly white, recalls a skull. Harper likens the image to Goya's Black Paintings; we might think of Rembrandt also. Moreover, the free brushstrokes of the background heads prefigure Expressionism. The weary drummer at the right may suggest Rouault's sacrificial clowns.

35. Henry Fielding, quoted in Roger Shattuck, *The Innocent Eye*, 68.
36. Howard Vincent, *Daumier and his World*, 91.

Finally, I differ from all the other critics in my view of this picture. Namely, I see it as a parody of Watteau's *The Italian Comedians*. Probably Daumier did not make this link consciously, as he seldom refers to other artists. His debts to Callot and Goya are general and well assimilated. Yet I find the comparison of the two works inevitable in our context. On the one hand, an elegant theater of patronage offers an ecce homo; on the other hand, a raucous street show travesties the presentation of Christ as a smug brute. The differences of gesture and attitude in the two paintings summarize the poles of 1720 and 1860.

In conclusion, let us put Daumier in our thematic context. Unlike the players of Watteau and Tiepolo, Daumier's *saltimbanques* do not suggest the ambiguity of the group versus the individual portrait. Indeed, Daumier transcends the specifics of one image by creating poignant symbols of post-revolutionary disillusion. His buffoons bespeak an inevitable decadence. Both they and their society, he sees, must fall. The death of the clown implies the end of his culture. As one critic said of *The Parade*, "it has the smell of death."[37]

Many other artists have taken this elegiac view of the player; this study starts with Baudelaire's old clown and ends with Fellini's nostalgic *The Clowns*. In between we see variations on this theme in Grillparzer, Hofmannsthal, Wedekind, Kafka, Zuckmayer, Mann, Böll, Grass, and Tiepolo. So Daumier did not invent the idea. His innovation consists in merging the pathos of the dying clown with biting social comment. His buffoons marry art to politics.[38] No one before or after Daumier has left such a unique tribute to the popular player.

MANET (1832–1883): AMBIGUOUS PLAYERS

Moving from the passionate clarity of Daumier to the subtle suggestions of Manet may mean a long leap. But we find common ground in the 1860s, which saw major turns in the styles of both artists. Their seemingly dissimilar works show complementary reactions to the Second Empire. Except for some late and atypical works, such as the *Pierrot Singing* that anticipates

37. Jules Carétie, quoted in Oliver Larkin, *Daumier, Man of his Time*, 146.
38. Unfortunately, I have no room to discuss perhaps the most pointed example of this union, *The Parade*, owned by the city of Glasgow (Harper, *Clowns*, pl. 68). But Harper has argued the essential point: the work incorporates several ideas handled separately elsewhere. It gives a bitter summary of the old player's vain attempt to "tell the truth" to a country about to confront mighty Prussia in 1870 (ibid., 190). We need not necessarily see in this old but determined drummer the aging Daumier as court jester, but his timely message seems clear.

Modernist loose brushstrokes and abstraction, Daumier is very much "of his own time." This phrase, attributed to the artist himself, does not apply well to Manet.

Despite raging dispute over his significance, most critics agree that Manet hints at several traits developed fully in the twentieth century. Here I shall discuss only one painting, for it summarizes a new imagery for our familiar figures. Specifically, the boy in white in *The Old Musician* (1862) goes back to Watteau's *Gilles* (see figures 13 and 24). Moreover, the other gypsy types here refer to a tradition—Velasquez, Le Nain—that itself draws on Callot's *The Bohemians*. Hence Manet takes a pivotal place in my chronology, tying the past to Picasso, who brings this line of Bohemians to a climax in his Rose Period.

The Old Musician may first strike us as a patchwork of separate images. Beside the boy in white stands his opposite type in black, recalling Velasquez and Murillo; a barefoot gypsy girl with baby suggests the peasants of the Le Nain brothers; the top-hatted urban man refers, beyond Manet's own *Absinthe Drinker* (1859), to both Watteau's *The Indifferent One* and Velasquez's *The Drinkers*. The old violinist resembles figures by the Le Nain and an antique statue by the Stoic philosopher Chrysippus.[39] Naturally, this wealth of sources overwhelms us, blocking the immediate emotional response evoked by Picasso's similar *Les Saltimbanques*. Besides, the art critics' quarrels over sources have little to do with our context: namely the developing image of the entertainer. At best these critics may illumine the complexity of vision in Manet, which reflects the amalgam that the artiste had become in his time.

Comparing these figures to their contemporaries in Daumier, we do not see the pathos of homelessness, nor despair at the lack of an audience, nor any overt political message. True, Manet shared with Daumier, as with other creative artists around Champfleury, a general interest in "democratic," even "low," subjects. Naturally, as "painters of modern life," these artists included in their urban landscape the showman of the street. And many such artists displayed an affinity, depending on some degree of identification, with the patronless player. But Manet, at least, does not use his figures as metaphors for social conditions. Any message about his culture lies well beyond the surface, for Manet—rather like Mallarmé—cultivates concealment. He may have felt like Duranty: "Since a man must always expect his intentions to be misunderstood, it is preferable not to reveal them at all."[40]

What, then, does Manet show us with his company of assorted outsiders?

39. George Mauner, *Manet, Peintre-Philosophe,* 50, 78.
40. Duranty in ibid., 184.

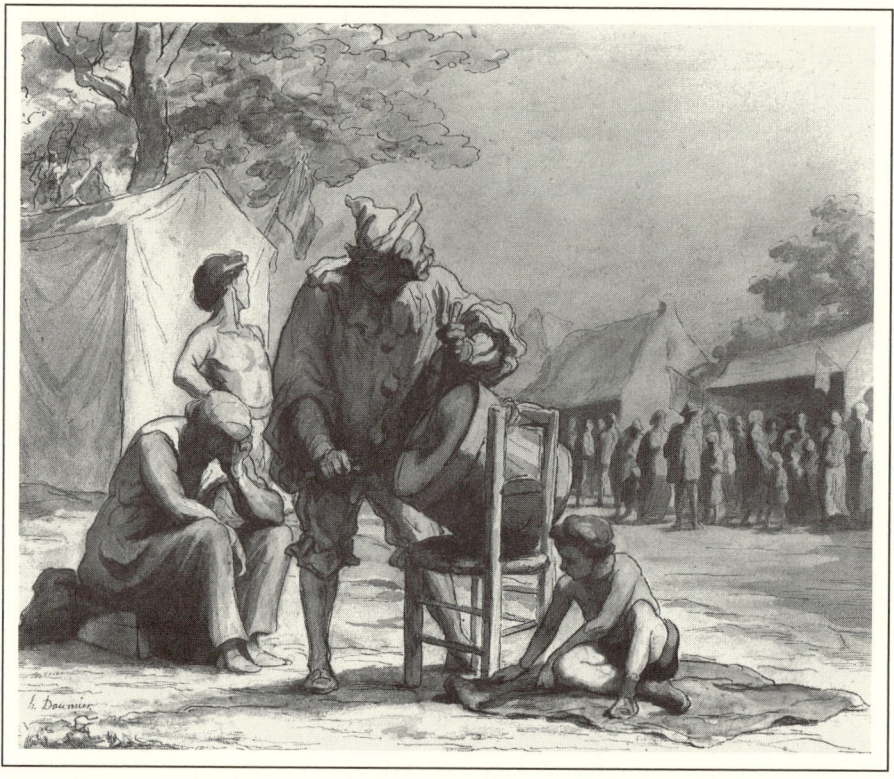

Figure 24. Edouard Manet, *The Old Musician* (1862). Courtesy of the National Gallery of Art, Washington.

A look through our thematic lens of the group versus the individual reveals a constant tension between the two elements. Indeed, this "group" has no clear unity of identity or purpose but seems merely assembled, motif-like, by the artist. And if he stresses one person, who is it? Only the title indicates the old man as subject; in fact, the light focuses on the boy in white. Moreover, both the pair of boys and the girl bear as much mysterious import as the old man. Picasso answers this question of focus by not making anyone the star of *Les Saltimbanques* (see figure 3).

In all his family groups, Daumier makes the husband-father the focal point. Manet still centers and titles his patriarch; but Picasso paints a decentered family arabesque. Both he and Manet look back to Daumier's *Les Saltimbanques,* with its two boys and its sympathy for the outcast (see figure 22). But by 1905 the group has become less a union of outsiders, as in Daumier, and less a cross-section of "picturesque" wanderers, as in Manet, and more a band of single professionals.

Instead of Daumier's family group, Manet focuses on the relation of youth to old age. Neither Daumier nor Picasso do this in their *Les Saltimbanques,* though Picasso does pick this subject in *The Organ Grinder* (see figure 4). The most obvious link between the old man and the boy appears in the violin bow that points directly to the two boys. George Mauner interprets this gesture not as an obvious ecce homo but as a pictorial tribute to *homo duplex,* that dualism that we have already seen pervading the nineteenth century. Hence the old man here, considered a "beggar-philosopher," points out the double nature of life from childhood onward.

The idea of the beggar-philosopher comes from contemporary sources. "The itinerant musician is a philosopher. He knows intimately the vanity of worldly glories."[41] Probably the Romantics first popularized this notion of naive wisdom among the poor; Manet found it too in Velasquez. However, we may also view this street player as a self-portrait of Manet. Considering his sophistication, we may find such a link absurd. Yet this identification of the artist with a "lowly" subject parallels the tie between Baudelaire and his old clown. The closeness of titles and dates for the two pieces seems hardly accidental: *Le Vieux Saltimbanque* (1861), *Le Vieux Musicien* (1862).

Of course, Manet cannot equate himself with the old man as literally as the poet does, but Mauner gives visual evidence for this claim. Namely, the centrality of the "artist" repeats the placing in Courbet's comparable painting *The Artist's Studio* (1855). This comparison lets us see *The Old Musician* as a sort of outdoor artist's studio. Here too we see an array of models surrounding the one who gives them posterity. Both works may thus serve as tributes to the profession of painting.

Courbet treats this venerable theme monumentally, with many large figures in complex relations. By contrast, Manet scales down the personnel, both in size and in scope. Yet he suggests a timeless universality with only six figures, for they all bear mythic meaning. Courbet puts himself at the center of his story of man; Manet masks his presence as one among the outcasts. To my mind, his picture better compares in this respect with Watteau's *The Italian Comedians.* In both these works, the image of life ranges from infancy to old age. In Manet too our eye finally rests on an enigmatic Pierrot. We may even see in the pointed bow a hint of the ecce homo gesture that dominates the Watteau work.

Of course, the boy as Gilles pays the clearest homage to Watteau. No other figure here evokes so well that staged, artifical aura that haunts us in the earlier piece. The critics discuss several reasons for this blatant reference to Watteau; for our context, a nostalgia for the tradition of Gilles seems

41. V. Fournel, quoted in Theodore Reff, "Manet's Sources," 43.

primary. Manet's boy may imply the survival of the *Commedia* in a world lacking imagination. Or the whole canvas may capture Manet's nostalgia for the innocence of the lower classes. This notion of the Romantics, already weakened in the 1860s by Darwinian anthropology and technology, still flourished among artists as primitivism. Manet recalls the Le Nain and Velasquez in this respect, but his juxtaposing of their primitivist imagery with the mannered Watteau makes this picture problematic. Indeed, our confusion may arise from just this disjuncture of sources.[42]

As for the boy, he adds still more mystery to the image in Watteau. Although his physical manner recalls the oafishness of Gilles, his face expresses something new. No longer gazing blankly outward, this boy looks soberly to the right. His face strikes us as too mature, too serious for a child; he shows the matter-of-factness of life in the street. This image of grim childhood may relate to Baudelaire's prose poem *La Corde* (1864), dedicated to Manet. The poet uses the actual story of the urchin Alexandre. Lovingly housed by Manet as his model, the boy abruptly hung himself. Baudelaire says as much about the attachment of the painter to the child as about his ostensible subject, the enigma of human nature. Similarly, *The Old Musician* captures the mysterious yet crucial connection between the artist and his wretched model.

Considering the primacy of primitivism in our century, we do well to note its importance in Manet. Apart from the problems raised by linking the Le Nain and Watteau, Manet heralds the paradoxical presence of the "naive" in modern art. Indeed, as William Rubin and others show, the Modernist generation created new styles out of their complex affinity with the arts of Africa, Oceania, and South America. Heeding the difficulty in calling all such diverse styles primitive, let us first note what Manet adopted from the Le Nains' rendering of peasants: separate figures lacking direct communication, awkward poses, a restrained bodily pantomime, and unbalanced compositions in a mysteriously empty landscape. This mere list recalls the "alienating" quality of Symbolism. A forebear for this psychological distance between figures appears in Tiepolo's *The Spring Shower* (see figure 25). This Mannerist image of several Punchinellos seen from behind antici-

---

42. Accordingly, I do not discuss the two figures at the right of this painting, for they only raise further problems with sources. Hanson, Mauner, Reff, and Fried all delve deeply into the iconography of the caped man, alias the rag-picker, and the so-called Turk, quack doctor, or Wandering Jew. Only in his latter incarnation does this odd, cut-off figure relate to the popular player. In chapter 5, I explore the links between all gypsies—as in Baudelaire, Callot, and Apollinaire—and Ahasuerus, the Jew condemned to wander the earth since witnessing the Crucifixion. This background is only marginal to our understanding of the performer in Manet.

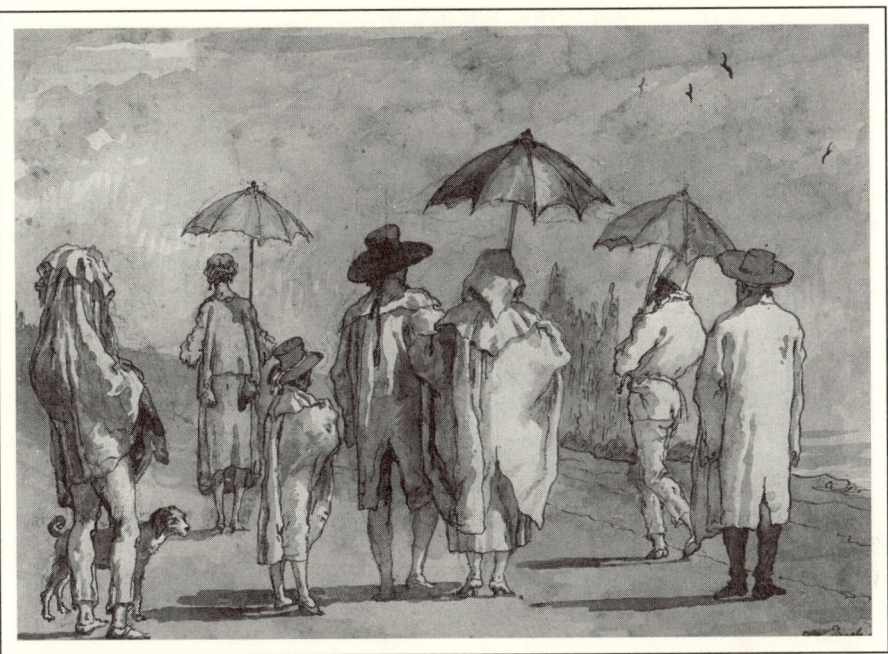

Figure 25. Domenico Tiepolo, *The Spring Shower* (ca. 1790). Courtesy of the Cleveland Museum of Art.

pates the composition of both Manet's *The Old Musician* and Picasso's *Les Saltimbanques*.

In the Le Nain, Manet, and such later artists as Moreau, Puvis de Chavannes, and Khnopff—not to mention Picasso—these problematic traits become central. In *The Old Musician,* despite the bodily contact of the two boys and the girl-infant pair, the disparate gaze of each figure creates a psychological distance. Picasso underlines this aloneness in *Les Saltimbanques* by the desolation of the landscape. He also exaggerates the blank gaze of Manet's figures. In *Les Saltimbanques,* the faces, turned in several directions, resemble masks. Both Manet and Picasso evoke enigmatic states of being. Whether we must call *Symbolist* such "mysteries in broad daylight" (to use Philippe Renaud's phrase) begs the question of much earlier art: in this context, Watteau's *Gilles*.

The violinist's direct outward gaze ties this picture to both the past and the future. His confrontation with the viewer gives urgency to the idea communicated, the player as *homo duplex*. We may compare this device to the *Commedia* habit of stepping up to the front of the stage to recite the moral of the story. Callot's Captain, the Pierrot in the *Italian Comedians,* and

Gilles all exemplify such a direct link to the audience. Champfleury compared the frontal pose of several figures in Louis Le Nain to just this conscious theatricality.[43] Hence he makes a novel tie between peasant and theatrical modes. Watteau does the same thing with Gilles, who is both clod and clown. Considering his origins in this very connection, the peasant player may not surprise us. Yet for the nineteenth century, one figure belonged clearly to nature, the other just as clearly to culture. Combining the man of the fields with the man of the stage means creating—yes, *homo duplex*.

The openly staged, theatrical image in *The Old Musician* shows Manet taking leave of representational art. As we saw in chapter 6, Blok and Schnitzler attack mimesis itself, for their actors drop their roles and address the audience. This shattering of illusion negates the Aristotelian fiction of the autonomous work of art. Manet's modernity lies in his parallel rejection of Realism. No longer the teller of a tale, however enigmatic (Watteau) or political (Daumier), his artiste simply stands before us. Bereft of the narrative ballast of three centuries, he prepares the way for those transcendent symbols of the human condition that emerge in our own time.

PICASSO (1881–1973): THE CUBIST *COMMEDIA* OF JAZZ

We have already noted some ties between *The Old Musician* and *Les Saltimbanques*. Again we see a semicircular composition, another arabesque flattened on the picture plane. Picasso also uses six figures. Other features of this work intensify what Manet only implies. His indefinite landscape, for instance, becomes a Waste Land here. And Picasso makes Manet's suggestive symbolism into a prominent trait. As Rilke saw, these people loom larger than mere players; their mystery transcends the evanescence of performing art.[44]

By the end of 1905, Picasso had painted the last of those many melancholy players who typify the concerns of the Rose Period. Of course, pensive Harlequins and Pierrots reappear, more or less recognizably, in later work; but gone is their world of wandering *saltimbanques*. Among the major subsequent works, only the stage curtain for the ballet *Parade* (1917) pays tribute to such player groups.

43. Michael Fried, "Manet's Sources," 48.
44. I discuss, more thoroughly than in chapter 5, the relations among *Les Saltimbanques*, Rilke, and other writers in my essays of 1981 and 1982.

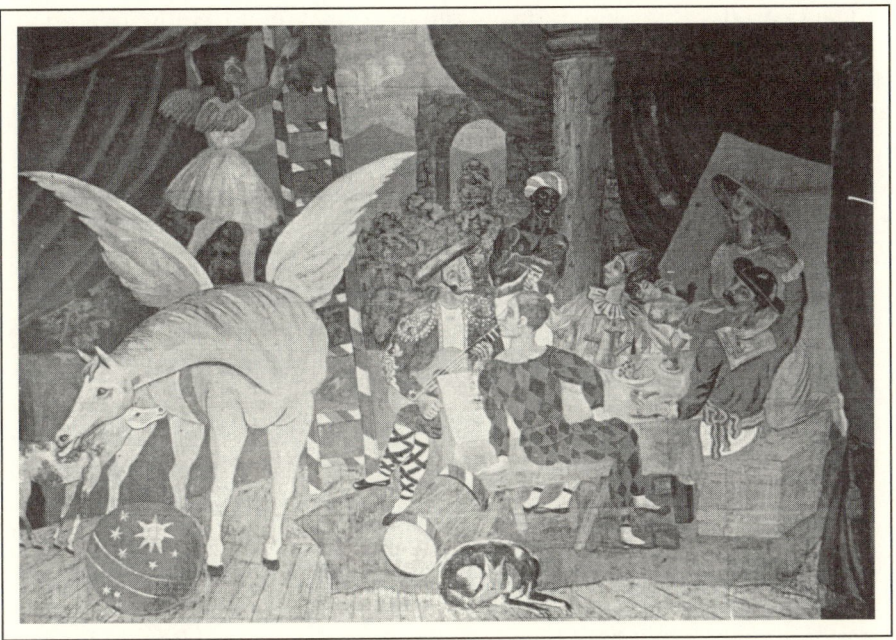

Figure 26. Pablo Picasso, *Parade*, The Overture Curtain (1917). Courtesy of Artists Rights Society, New York/Spadem.

In this complex image, Picasso combines an eclectic troupe —two Harlequins, Columbine, a Spanish guitarist, a black servant, a sailor, and a peasant girl—with several familiar props of his circus family: white horse, dog, drum, and ladder (see figure 26). An angel perched atop an artificially winged Pegasus, plus an acrobatic monkey, adds yet more novelty to this expanded repertory of images. Moreover, new types at the table diverge from the prevailing sobriety of the Rose Period. Several critics identify all these figures as members of still another group portrait of "Picasso's gang." Transcending the mere group portrait, the curtain integrates several complex strands of meaning into an ironic "artist's apotheosis." Here Picasso skeptically comments on "the artist's inspiration, [his] celebration of his activity, and [his] self-criticism."[45]

By 1921, the date of the two canvases called *The Three Musicians*, Picasso had already worked the Cubist vein for more than a decade. Accordingly, his manner had become synthetic, for he was progressively expanding his Cubist vocabulary. Like his other recurring motifs, Harlequin

45. Richard Axsom, *"Parade": Cubism as Theater*, 145.

had appeared in several forms, both closely and distantly related to Cubism. An example of the former, *Harlequin* (1915) flattens all pictorial elements onto broad surface patterns. We "read" these areas correctly only after perceiving the central Harlequin figure as a whimsical image of the artist himself.

Here Picasso resumes his identification with the agile player, who seems to dance like a puppet while clutching both painting and easel. The vague menace of this angular movement, like the black background and toothy smile, may link this picture with the death of Picasso's mistress, Eva Gouel, in 1915. Hence the personal background of the work leads directly to the *The Three Musicians,* which Reff considers a nostalgic portrait of the painter, Apollinaire, and Jacob.

Here Harlequin appears with both Pierrot and a non-*Commedia* companion, the musical monk. In the Philadelphia canvas, the monk plays a sort of accordion; in the New York version he sings. (I shall discuss only the New York work—figure 27—because it gives a more climactic statement of Picasso's last significant venture with the *Commedia* group. The Philadelphia picture, though provocatively decorative, lacks the classic rigor of the monumental New York piece.) As for this unusual trio, Reff traces it to earlier combinations of religious and theatrical figures, such as the studies of 1909 for *Carnival at the Bistro.* Picasso had already placed collages of the familiar players on a flat Cubist picture plane. Indeed, so summary is the stylistic effect in *The Three Musicians* that Pierre Daix calls the two versions an anthology, not of earlier artists such as Velasquez and Delacroix, but of "the Cubist Picasso himself." So far, so good, but what gives these visions their startling newness? How do they do more than merely rework the Cubist vision?[46]

First, the New York piece exemplifies one of our two general themes, the group versus the individual portrait. Here we see three imposing players equalized by the flat picture plane; no one has a starring role. Yet the painting does not inter-relate the figures psychologically. Instead, it simply juxtaposes them. This lack of narrative takes us far indeed from the anecdotal naturalism of the *Parade* curtain of only four years earlier. As for the story told by this trio, we see only that they perform vigorously.

Both the group in the *Parade* curtain and the artist family in *Les Saltimbanques* appear at rest. But these three robust players make us almost hear their staccato music. Their syncopated jazz rhythms, suggested by inter-

46. See plates 238, 240, and 283 in Douglas Cooper, *Picasso Theatre;* Theodore Reff, "Picasso's *The Three Musicians:* Maskers, Artists and Friends," 130–31; Pierre Daix, *Picasso,* 115.

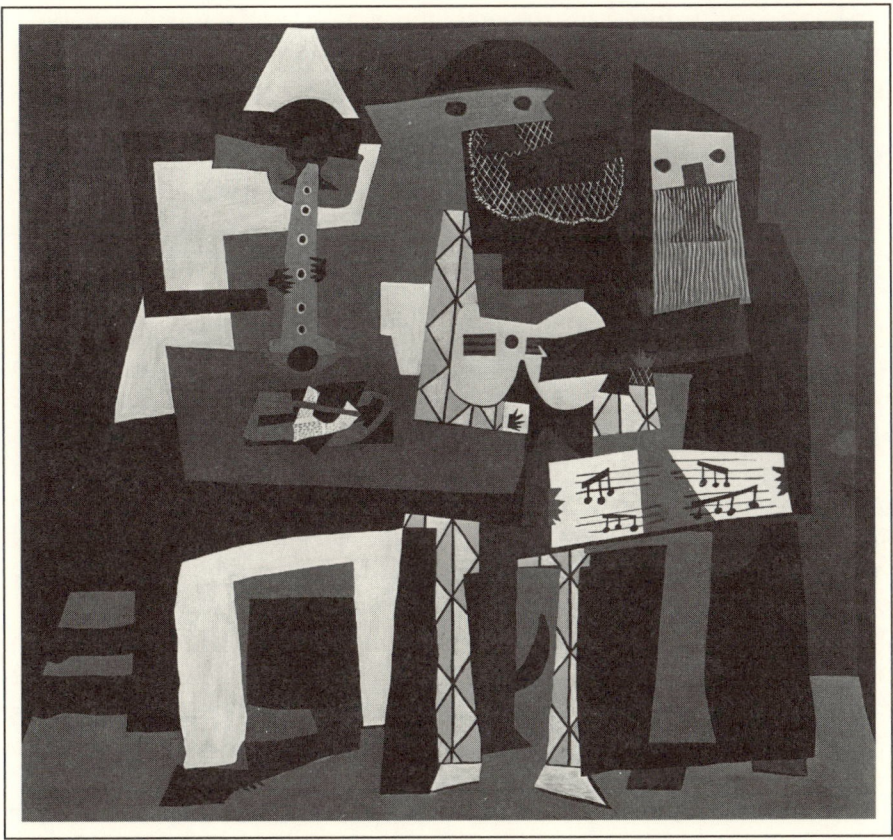

Figure 27. Pablo Picasso, *The Three Musicians* (1921). Oil on canvas, 6'7" x 7' 3¾".
Courtesy of The Museum of Modern Art, New York.

secting angular shapes, play the principal role here. Personalities and their relations recede in favor of performance. Moreover, the brown tabletop, recalling earlier Cubist works, suggests a hybrid image: the figural still life. Such depersonalizing goes along with the analytic quality of Cubism, which points ahead to full abstraction.

Several critics note the mysterious solemnity of this work. Reff and others refer to Seurat's *Parade* (1887–1888) as a source for this frontally iconic, hieratic image. The frozen poses of these players exemplify "the art of stillness" that Roger Shattuck notes as a summary trait of Modernism. Like Joyce's *Ulysses*, like Eisenstein's montage or Satie's disjunct harmonies, this painting juxtaposes separate units without clear transitions. Moreover, its densely overlapping planes impart the simultaneity of collage. Like earlier compositions of diverse material, *The Three Musicians* assembles a variety of shapes and textures: instruments, music paper, a lacy veil, a copious beard, and separate dog hairs. In sum, vibrant tensions among these areas articulate the essential conflict of the image.

To grasp the newness of this vision, we might again compare our two forebears, the *Parade* curtain and *Les Saltimbanques*. Their various complexities contrast tellingly with the monumental economy of *The Three Musicians*. In the *Parade* work, space recedes in several layers, the whole made ambiguous by the framing red drapes painted on the actual curtain. Similarly, the implied mental space is complicated by opposing right and left halves of the composition. On the right, we readily grasp the collegial gathering of artistes at rest backstage; on the left, we ponder a scene of mock mythology, complete with a falsely winged female Pegasus, who sports an angel bestowing the laurel wreath on an artist-monkey.

Here we have, to put it mildly, "reality versus myth."[47] *Les Saltimbanques* lacks such density, as it conveys virtually no space at all. And its story eludes all but the most informed viewer. Its visual intricacy lies in a subtle interweaving of tonal and figural relations. However, both *Les Saltimbanques* and the *Parade* curtain evoke rich visions of performers. *The Three Musicians*, on the other hand, evokes nothing beyond itself; it blatantly presents the sight and sound of a jazz band. As Richard Axsom notes, the *Parade* curtain recalls a Watteauesque conceit. *The Three Musicians*, by contrast, resembles an advertising billboard. In short, Picasso has replaced his earlier art of suggestion with that of bold statement.

These players evoke a specific kind of jazz. One look at their masks, or rather at their menacing dark eyeholes, tells us that they do the blues. Indeed, Picasso probably heard this somber music, which enjoyed a vogue in Paris after the war. The masks, however, connote more than a dark mood. On one level, we may see them as intensifying the dark eye areas in *Les Saltimbanques*. Already we sense a vague menace beneath the surface. But on another level these masks relate centrally to the very concept of Cubism that Picasso himself stated in 1914. As Gertrude Stein noted: "I very well remember at the beginning of the war being with Picasso on the Boulevard Raspail when the first camouflaged truck passed. It was at night, we had heard of camouflage but we had not yet seen it and Picasso amazed looked at it and then cried out, yes, it is we who made it, that is cubism." The mask, then, may serve Picasso as metaphor, a sign of form hidden, fragmented, and seen anew. Here indeed we have "concealment that is also . . . revelation, the familiar aspect of things disappearing while their normally hidden ones emerge."[48]

47. Axsom, *"Parade"*, p. 110.
48. Gertrude Stein, *Picasso*, 11; Theodore Reff, "Harlequins, Saltimbanques, Clowns

Synthetic cubism defines the style of *The Three Musicians,* but so does jazz itself: its zigzag, nervous rhythms and witty progressions, its brash, daring sound. We see the visual counterpart of that assertive sound in the bright primary colors that immediately assault the eye. Embracing both the comic and the solemn, both Blues jazz and this picture depend on surprise. Not only the famous command of Diaghilev, "Astonish me!" characterizes such avant-garde art; so also does the aesthetics of surprise in Apollinaire, who appears here as Pierrot-clarinettist. Part of Picasso's strong tie to his dead friend lies in his habit of constantly shifting styles. Accordingly, the blatant distortions of *The Three Musicians* seems to mock the surface naturalism of the recent *Parade* curtain.

However, several factors stabilize these "jittery Cubist puppets" into a grand classic image. First, the palette: highlighting whites and framing browns or blacks unify the brilliant color composition. Second, this imposing trio bears incisive symmetry. We sense the same classicizing balance in *Three Women at the Spring* of the same year. And in 1925 Picasso repeats the lively yet stable trio in *Three Dancers.* John Russell compares the classic triad in *The Three Musicians* to the three puppets in *Petrushka.* "Motionless in their upright pens, the Ballerina, Petrushka and the Moor have just a moment of stillness before the Russian Dance begins. . . . Mozart . . . had the same sure intimation when [he] decided to bring on the three maskers at the end of Act I in *Don Giovanni.*"[49]

In the context of both this chapter and Picasso's work, *The Three Musicians* has another kind of classic status. Namely, it exemplifies our second category, the death of the player, which constantly preoccupied Picasso. Reff claims that this canvas immortalizes the lost youth of the artist and his closest friends. Hence it continues his lengthy visual meditation on his own death. The young Casagémas' suicide provided only one of many sources for this pervasive imagery of dying from the Blue Period onward. *Les Saltimbanques,* that "landscape of death," *The Death of Harlequin* (1905), *Harlequin* (1915), and our *The Three Musicians* all seek to "overcome

and Fools," 31. Stein expands on this idea of Cubism in another context. "When I was in America I for the first time traveled . . . in an airplane and when I looked at the earth I saw all the lines of cubism made at a time when not any painter had ever gone up in an airplane, I saw there on the earth the mingling lines of Picasso, coming and going, developing and destroying themselves . . . and once more I knew that a creator is contemporary, he understands what is contemporary when the contemporaries do not know it yet" (50). Compare what Cocteau said in 1922: "It is tempting to photograph Greece from an airplane. You discover a completely new view of it. That is why I wanted to translate *Antigone.* From a bird's eye view, aspects of great beauty disappear, others come surging up. Unexpected juxtapositions, blocks, shadows, angles, reliefs are formed" (quoted in Christopher Robinson, *French Literature in the Nineteenth Century* [New York: Barnes and Noble, l978], 7).

49. John Russell, "In Detail: Picasso's Three Musicians," 18.

death through the magical power of . . . art."[50] Picasso painted this last picture near his crucial fortieth birthday, when he looked back on a brilliant youth with mournful nostalgia. These bold *Commedia* figures symbolize the best of what the *Bateau Lavoir* days had meant for the struggling but buoyant artist: avant-garde irreverence, boundless creative invention. In one Apollinairean word: adventure.

None of these traits had deserted Picasso in 1921, but his later images of performers bear less synoptic weight. Never again would he devote a major work to these players. The Pierrots and Harlequins of the twenties do not significantly depart from the conventions of portraiture. The portrayal of Jaime Salvado as Harlequin (1923) belongs mainly to the "Ingresque" sculptural figures.[51] And Picasso paints his son Paulo as both Harlequin and Pierrot (1924, 1925) using only the costume in striking but predictable ways.

Significantly, Picasso never again paints himself as Harlequin, his preferred alter ego until now. Soon the small circus setting that frames his artist-players yields to the grander bullring, where another drama plays between artist-matador and bull. Not only the personal metaphor of this one artist has changed; so also has the world around him. In Beckmann's work we see that the benign aura of the *saltimbanques,* like the prewar Europe that created them, had vanished.

BECKMANN (1884–1950): THE MENACE OF THE SHOW

Beckmann shows an aspect of circus players that we have not yet seen among painters: the modern grotesque. In contrast to Callot's merely stylistic exaggerations, the imagery of these gruesome performers reveals actual maiming, terror, and ultimate chaos. The earlier Nolde (1867–1956) and Ensor (1860–1949) saw the human condition in distorted ways that anticipate the horrors in Beckmann. Like them, he explores the dark side of the masked clown.

For Nolde, the mask offers rich challenges in both the form and the meaning of ritual. With the masked face both he and Beckmann evoke those primitive values dear to artists oppressed by their decadent society (see Nolde's *Still Life of Masks* [1911]). Nolde also paints savage dancers in the same kind of brutal color composition that Beckmann uses. For Ensor, the lurid mask expresses the constant struggle between good and evil, a primary theme for Beckmann. Furthermore, Ensor's mask often suggests an

50. Reff, "*Musicians,*" 138.
51. John Elderfield, *European Master Paintings from Swiss Collections,* 86.

allegory of death: see *Intrigue* (1890) or *Scandalized Masks* (1887). Beckmann also masks his figures as part of their immobilizing—a prelude to death. Ensor's *The Entry of Christ into Brussels* (1888) displays just what Beckmann's triptychs show: a modern vision of a primary myth. Not accidentally, both Nolde and Ensor insert in these social commentaries a self-portrait as mocking clown. Generally, all three artists evoke a sense of doom in the perceived world. Hence they create histrionic escapes into mythology, the macabre erotic, apocalypse. The animal masks and skeletons of Ensor's hallucinatory images foretell, a generation before Beckmann, the actual dehumanizing to come.

We have already met physical and spiritual cripples in *Ein Hungerkünstler* and *Die Blechtrommel*. Bergman, we shall see below, uses dwarves from Velasquez to measure a similarly deformed society in *The Silence*. Moreover, in much of what we have already considered, death lurks beneath a bright surface: think of Baudelaire's moribund clown, Daumier's gaunt buffoons, the hungry urchins in Mallarmé and Apollinaire. But only Beckmann makes destruction a driving force in his people. If we refer to Picasso's *Les Saltimbanques* as a landscape of death, we indulge in metaphor. But calling Beckmann's *The Dream* (1921) a scene of lethal violence gives a literal description.

The Dream portrays a war cripple in mordant clown dress, a blind organ grinder, and a Punch doll held by a peasant girl. Beckmann uses such familiar players in a new way, as symbols in the subconscious. The picture seems to visualize what Wagner said: "Art makes the unconscious conscious." In *The Acrobats* (1939), we again sense subliminal messages, for here the player appears on the stage of allegory (see figure 28). One critic refers to this drama as the chaos of human life; we must specify what she means.[52]

This imposing triptych first impresses us as chaotic. Especially the two flanking panels flaunt any spatial order but the strictly vertical. As in his works of the twenties, Beckmann develops here a Gothic flatness that uncomfortably crowds the picture plane. Furthermore, the figural scale varies in all three panels. The central figures stand about twice as large as those at left and right, and the tiny musicians—drummer boy and horn player—suggest dwarves.

Some scenes here offer relations that we can decipher. The central pair backstage enact a typical Beckmannesque erotic conflict, bespeaking temptation, threat, and violence. The left panel features another pair of acrobat-lovers, who consummate their act in midair. Above them hangs another familiar Beckmann figure: the aerialist who cannot move. Such a

52. Carla Schulz-Hoffmann and Judith Weiss, ed., *Max Beckmann Retrospective*, 277.

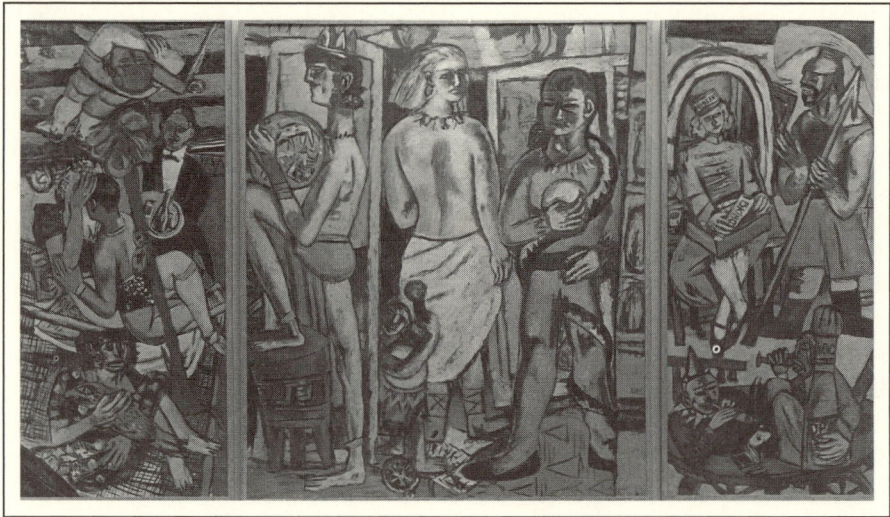

Figure 28. Max Beckmann, *The Acrobats* (1939). Courtesy of the Saint Louis Art Museum.

trapped player recalls the claustrophobic *The Trapeze* (1923). Beyond the Banvillian metaphor of acrobat as artist, we might see in this image Beckmann's own wartime immobility. But although the artist often paints himself as clown or acrobat, we may take the paralyzed player as a broader symbol of an imprisoning society. At the right we see an expectable clown with horn and a girl selling ice cream in the theater.

All the other figures defy clear definition, but critics have made brave attempts. The third large center person, a crowned seer-acrobat, may divine something from the globe he holds. Hence he would relate to the girl vendor, for she wears the uniform of a bellhop, a somewhat mythic figure in several other Beckmann works. In the triptych *Actors* (1942), Peter Selz sees a messenger of fate in the bellboy. The triptych *Carnival* (1943) presents a bellhop whose cap, from Berlin's Hotel Eden, specifies a particular fate: the expulsion from Paradise. Gert Schiff calls the dark drummer a cupid, but this boy lends a mainly demonic note to the perverted love scene he accompanies. No one explains the waiter bearing drinks at the left. Nor do the critics agree on the significance of the giant bird held by the grotesque woman at the left. (Indeed, some see this animal as a fish.) The Mars figure at the right portends the coming war, but a spear like his punctuates several earlier Beckmann pictures. In our context, the triptych *Carnival* contains three similar daggers, which point to the violence inherent in any Beckmann show.

We may best deal with this array of confusing images by first accepting their mystery. Even more persistently than the problematic Picasso, Beckmann defies our firm grasp. Although his pictures constantly challenge us to ask "Why?" they rarely yield more than fragmentary answers. The artist himself explained: "With furious tension one waits for the explanation of the secret. I *believe* in the unknown."[53] One tends to think of such mystery as typical of modern art, yet we have already seen comparable enigma in Tiepolo, Watteau, and Manet. Apollinaire, both the most modern and the most ancient of artists, saw in his *saltimbanques* "mysteries in broad daylight."

Perhaps our subject, the popular player, conduces to such indeterminacy, which I note at the end of chapter 2. Indicatively, three of Beckmann's most difficult works, the nine triptychs, deal with players: *Acrobats, Actors,* and *Carnival.* So we may see in these pieces a close kinship of idea and style. The histrionic life offers Beckmann spectacular metaphors for the "world theater" he inhabits. (Compare Stefan Lackner's title "Max Beckmann's Mystical Pageant of the World.") Beckmann said, "We all represent individual but endlessly changeable actors, who must play our own fated piece of life."[54] In short, we all participate in the carnival. Beckmann himself, as "The Barker," introduces *Circus Beckmann,* the 1921 set of drawings on contemporary life.

Once we settle for uncertain meanings in this carnival, some help emerges from a close study of the oeuvre. First we must note the significance of the triptych form itself. Few modern artists have painted such huge canvases with moral overtones. Gauguin's questioning allegories and Picasso's *Guernica* come to mind; so do the lesser works of Hans von Marées, Nolde, Munch, and Valloton. All such epic painting probes mythic material in posing the great moral questions. Lackner suggests Beethoven's nine massive symphonies, with their frequent tripartite forms, as a forebear for Beckmann's nine triptychs.

However, we find a closer model for his allegories in the medieval altarpiece. The intensely "spiritual" verticality of its side panels parallels the extreme subjectivity in Beckmann's flattened, crowded picture plane. Despite his tendency to parody, Beckmann takes up the transcendental aura of the Middle Ages. As for the conventions of the actual Gothic altarpiece, Beckmann ignores them. In particular, no clear story unites the three

53. Beckmann quoted in Peter Selz, *Max Beckmann,* 79.
54. Beckmann quoted in Friedhelm Fischer, *Max Beckmann, Symbol und Weltbild,* 159.

panels, nor do we see portraits of actual people, such as the noble donor of the altarpiece itself. Including the supposed self-portraits, Beckmann paints mostly hieratic figures who reveal the hidden, mythic sources of human behavior. The three panels together form a composite image: in *Acrobats*, of the performing life. Two references to the Parisian Médrano Circus further specify the setting. In the left panel, the letters *CIRCUS ME* appear, as does the name *Médrano* on the girl vendor's cap. During the winter that he painted this triptych, Beckmann spent several months in Paris. However, this location does not help us to interpret the work.

Acrobats renders the contemporary circus as a complex stage for the human drama of erotic tension, imprisonment, and impending destruction: in short, demonic love and death. The central man, whose snake may signify both the temptation and the constriction of sex, defies the imposing woman of comparable daring. Their shaded faces have a starkly ominous effect. This menacing pair may suggest caged wild animals circling each other before coupling. Such hints of the animal in human nature may recall Wedekind's circus; critics often link Beckmann's garish *Columbine* (1950) with Lulu.

A more positive image of love appears in the left panel. The entwined lovers here may relate, as those of Rilke's *Fifth Elegy* do, acrobatic and erotic skills. However, their cramped entanglement lacks the soaring freedom of the Rilke pair. Furthermore, they exist between two figures of anxiety, the immobile, self-enclosed aerialist and the hideous woman with her bird of prey. In fact, we might call this creature a bird of war, as its shape and color exactly echo the crest of the helmet worn by Mars, god of war, in the right panel. I find no accident in this symmetrical opposition, the clearest formal parallel in the work.

This horribly ugly pair, the woman at bottom left and the warrior at top right, imply most clearly the death that lurks just below the surface of every *Circus Beckmann*. Lesser anxieties emerge from the shadowy, deformed drummer boy and his dwarfish clown colleague at the right. The discomfort they all evoke recalls Oskar Matzerath and the Bebra troupe in *Die Blechtrommel*. Both Grass and Beckmann use dwarves to question our definition of the human.[55] Kafka achieves something similar with his animals who force us to ponder the line between beasts and people. Fools, cripples, freaks, apes, insects: all such personnel of the grotesque make us measure ourselves against prevailing norms. The vague fears they inspire thus bespeak our insecurity in the "normal" world.

The isolation of Beckmann's figures, ironically heightened by their close

55. Compare Leslie Fiedler, *Freaks*.

confinement, expresses the grim aloneness in his vision of humanity. Only the tangled lovers touch; all the rest seem absorbed by their own emotions. Hence they separate themselves as much as their cramped world imprisons them. However, such alienation is nothing new; we have noted it from Watteau onward. In particular, Picasso's *Les Saltimbanques* shows a similar self-enclosure among players. But how Picasso differs from Beckmann in the relation of people to space! Emptiness characterizes the settings of the Rose Period *saltimbanques,* whereas Beckmann always jams his canvases to the bursting point. In Picasso, we sense the lonely abandonment of wanderers; in Beckmann, players feel just as alone because they are trapped in their chaotic, cruel world. Thus the uniqueness of Beckmann's anxious dislocation lies in his torturing spatial constraint.

In *Acrobats* this constriction does much to create its grotesque foreboding. Not only can people not move, but they simply bulk too large for their space. Mirrors and screens further enclose them claustrophobically. And they have no access to a broader world outside, for total blackness lies beyond their windowless walls. The central panel shows the same kind of void behind the flat picture plane that menaces us in Daumier's *The Strong Man* (see figure 23).

One of the most striking interpretations of Beckmann's problematic space comes fromn Claude Gandelman. His essay on the simultaneous stage shows Beckmann's debt to the innovations of Erwin Piscator. Gandelman compares Beckmann's juxtaposing of loosely related scenes to the nonlinear stage presentations of events occurring concurrently. Of course, the frieze-like altarpiece often presents its material without clear narrative; but there the juxtaposed scenes appear as stages of the Passion, not as simultaneous actions.

Both the crowding of space and the enigmatic "freezing" of discrete events relate Beckmann, beyond Piscator and Max Reinhardt, to a general tendency of the time. He creates one type of what Shattuck calls "the art of stillness"—that psychic oneness of disparate things that we have noted above in Picasso and Apollinaire. These and other Modernists use a flat surface not to tell a story but instead to suggest hidden connections beyond the perceived world.

Such simultaneity depends on two features crucial for Beckmann: the free play of the unconscious, and a pervasive dualism. As for the former, we know from such pictures as *The Dream* and *Night* that Beckmann conceived his painting as a kind of prophecy, a playing out of his subliminal visions. Thus we may view the simultaneous panels of *Acrobats* as a painted stream of consciousness. This undramatic art juxtaposes opposites. Beauty and madness, good and evil, black and white coexist in this world.

Schiff recalls that Beckmann found examples of Greek mythology in the New York dives he visited.

Another key stylistic feature typifies Beckmann: the hectic color composition. We already saw how Picasso, in *The Three Musicians,* unifies the canvas with repeated color areas. For Beckmann, this technique is even more important, for it gives his only structure. Without their brilliant pigments balanced against thick black outlines, these paintings would lack any sense of order. The dark outlines recall Rouault, who also creates the effect of stained glass for subjects with religious overtones. In Beckmann's late works, the immobile look of stained glass becomes obsessive, as seen in *Columbine.* The tendency to iconic figures, another link to Rouault, also grows in his later work.

Indeed, Rouault's Christ-clowns form a pendant to Beckmann's players. Both artists see the suffering of vulnerable mankind in the circus, yet only Rouault dwells on its pathos. Although some critics call Beckmann Expressionist, I find his sources too broad—Fauve color, Cézannesque sculptural forms, Cubist flat fractured planes—and his "expression" too problematic for the epithet. Beckmann does not manipulate the viewer's feelings; indeed, his works have an anti-mimetic, anti-illusionist quality. Like *Petrushka* and kindred works, *Acrobats* simply presents the grotesque player for us to ponder. And again like the ballet, the triptych tends to burlesque mimetic conventions.

In surveying Beckmann's many symbolic images of players, we wonder why he chose the circus setting so often. I believe he found there both a metaphysical and a political vision of modern man. Masks, stereotyped roles, and the vulgar show reveal the essential nature of his reality. The variations on the circus theme delineate his view of human life as a mysterious, lonely, grotesque, and fearful performance. For Beckmann, such a condition characterized Europe in 1939. The political metaphor embedded in the circus may recall Balzac's *Human Comedy,* where nineteenth-century Paris frames another epic rendering of corrupt and brutal human relations.[56]

Taking the next step back to Dante, we observe that both the modern circus and the metropolis enshrine a particular kind of inferno. For Balzac, the city of greed determines everyone; for Beckmann, the gay surface of the popular show masks the amoral destructive forces ruling its world. We find a literary parallel for this duplicity in Christopher Isherwood's *Goodbye to Berlin* (1939). He describes the decadent cabaret as Beckmann paints the

---

56. Gert Schiff, "Die Ikonographie der Triptychen," in *Munuscula Disciplinorum,* ed. Tilman Buddensieg, p. 267.

circus. Beckmann was probably referring to such glittering sham when he wrote of "the little madness of the world" contained in *Acrobats*.[57]

The madness of this triptych has none of the positive, liberating attributes of folly that artists have long associated with fools. Going back to the beginning of this chapter, we might also call Callot's Baroque stage mad, but in a purely fantastic, harmless way. Beckmann, by contrast, shows us the demonic, "Northern" side of lunacy. In the next chapter, we will see how Bergman develops a similar haunting view of the unbalanced player.

However, we have already discussed comparable attitudes to art in Kafka. Beyond the grotesque hunger-artist, he offers us close comparisons to Beckmann in "Ein Bericht für eine Akademie" and "Auf der Galerie." In the former piece, the ape laughs at the alleged "autonomous movement" of human aerialists, who know nothing of true animal freedom. Such use of the circus scene recalls Beckmann's many paralyzed acrobats, who also mock human freedom. In "Auf der Galerie" we have perhaps the clearest verbal example of the literally fatal show, an allegory of life destroyed by the depraved society that drives it onward. Kafka saw the terror of the circus as latent in 1917; by 1939 it had become explicit.

57. Beckmann quoted in Schulz-Hoffmann, 277.

8 THE POPULAR SHOW IN FILM
Bergman and Fellini

The cinema is very much like the circus.
—Fellini

Bergman, born in 1918, and Fellini, born in 1920, share not only a similar age and similar fame as masters of their own vision. They have also absorbed the circus aura in remarkably parallel ways. Specifically, clowns and traveling troupes play a key role in the drama of their childhood, as demonstrated in *Fanny and Alexander* and *Clowns*. As directors, they show us many of the same aspects of the European circus. Their differing attitudes to the show characterize both their polar cultural backgrounds—Nordic Lutheran vs. Mediterranean Catholic—and their personal beliefs.

To my knowledge, no one has yet compared the works of Bergman and Fellini in detail, certainly not regarding this common theme. One of several casual links comes from Paisley Livingston, who merely states that both artists take the "curious spectacles" of the circus ring seriously, as "the correct point of departure."[1] However, the two men themselves sense a kinship that logically prompts comparison. Bergman calls Fellini "my little fratello." Fellini speaks of "Bergman's way of telling a story, the richness of his temperament and above all his way of expressing himself exactly as I feel a *showman* ought to—that is, as a mixture of *magician* and *conjuror,* prophet and *clown,* travelling salesman and preacher. . . . It is for this reason that my liveliest, warmest, most fervent admiration goes to . . . Bergman."[2] Not surprisingly, the two directors tried to collaborate on a two-part film, *Love Duet.* Despite its announcement in January 1969, the work never materialized.

Here I shall explore the deep affinities between these two directors as suggested by their shared focus on the vulgar spectacle. I shall show how insistently both men project their characteristic images of the player into their stories. Broadly different in outlook, the films discussed here still produce comparable conclusions. Both directors present their typical artistes in ways exemplified throughout this book. That is, both men identify with the primitive player, whom they see as transcendent in various ways. Their juggling of these elements—identification, the primitive, and transcen-

1. Paisley Livingston, *Ingmar Bergman and the Rituals of Art,* 67.
2. Anna Keel and Christian Strich, *Fellini on Fellini,* 99, italics mine.

dence—produces a similar evolution in each film, moving from seeming despair at the wretched life of the artiste to a celebration of the fantasy embodied in puppets and clowns. Both the wooden marionette and the human clown give signs of art as magic, one of the crucial aesthetic premises for both directors.

Comparing the two "circus" oeuvres, we see that *The Naked Night* is to *La Strada* what *Fanny and Alexander* is to *Clowns*. Bergman revises the miseries of *The Naked Night* with the joyous salvation of the players in *The Seventh Seal* and the manifold blessings of Alexander. Similarly, Fellini replaces the tragedy of Gelsomina in *La Strada* with the apotheosis of all buffoons in *Clowns*. Moreover, the child within the mature artist plays a crucial role for both directors. Put more pointedly, the circus lives at the core of the film.

BERGMAN

The Naked Night (1953)

Here Bergman presents his typically tortured artistes in a strongly negative light. The very first frames set the mood of chiaroscuro: shabby circus wagons cross an ominous dawn skyline. (We see the same striking movement in silhouette against the sky in the famous Dance of Death closing *The Seventh Seal*.) Cold wind and rain add to the dark tone of these first images, highlighting the players' vulnerability to nature. A ruined windmill also appears. John Simon and Robin Wood see in the broken-down mill a symbol of human collapse; Bergman has implied that he simply used what he found in the landscape.[3] Going beyond both these claims, we may take the windmill as a sign of the players' dashed quixotic illusions, which play a significant part in the players' downfall. Indeed, the film proceeds as an unmasking, a shedding of illusion. We may salvage at least that positive note from the prevailing gloom of its resigned ending.

A caged, pacing bear provides another key initial image: we soon learn that the destitute troupe had to sell all but this sickly animal, who thus represents the players' steady decline. Furthermore, by immediately associating the players with the beast, Bergman suggests their less-than-human status. Most important, the bear plays a symbolic role in the human dramas around him. As alter ego for Albert, the wretched director, and surrogate child for Alma, the clown's wife, he provides a focus for the agony of the two main couples. At the center of both their and the bear's experience lies

3. Bergman in John Simon, *Ingmar Bergman Directs*, 40.

humiliation, perhaps the prime feature of the artist's life for Bergman. When the suicidal Albert finally shoots the bear instead of himself, he achieves catharsis.

The film begins by retelling a crucially symbolic experience of the clown Frost. This flashback forms a play-within-a-play, which Bergman often uses to reveal layers of meaning. The event, an Expressionist Crucifixion, plays a genetic chord for the whole film, as it encapsulates the main action of the protagonists. The rest of the film, as Bergman says, forms a set of variations.[4] Moreover, this sequence has special import for our context, as it telescopes several themes we have already met in literature, ballet, and painting: the enmity of the middle class for wanderers, the clown as fool of love and sacrificial victim of society.

As the wagon nears the town, the coachman tells Albert what happened here seven years ago. Alma had left the circus tents to watch some soldiers on maneuvers nearby. They dare her to bathe naked in the lake, which she does; a boy fetches Frost to see the soldiers' raucous delight in the scene. With a silent scream, the clown sheds his costume and, though fearing the water, wades in to rescue his shamed wife (see figure 29). Since the boy has hidden their clothes, Frost pathetically tries to cover her naked body with his own. While the soldiers jeer hysterically, the clown carries his wife out of the water across sharp stones. Wincing in pain, he bears her on his back, just as Christ bore his cross. Finally, after falling twice, he collapses under this impossible burden. Alma, overcome with remorse, clings to him as the circus people bear him back to the camp. A final shot of the clown's costume, spread out like a cross, confirms that we have witnessed the martyrdom of Christ.

This flashback occurs wholly in pantomime, which gains further intensity by its technique. What looks like blinding Expressionist overexposure gives a surreal, nightmare quality to this primal scene. Glaring sun connotes anxiety for Bergman: "My nightmares are always saturated in sunshine. I hate the south, where I'm exposed to incessant sunlight." "When I see a cloudless sky I feel the world is coming to an end."[5] The silence of this white nightmare adds to its terror. Apart from bits of narrative by the coachman, only cannon shots and a crescendo of drumbeats accompany the clown's Calvary.

Like the silent film that partly inspired it, this sequence exploits both silence and symbolism. Shots of huge cannon barrels, for instance, crosscut with faces of leering soldiers, visualize the phallic impulse of the whole

4. Stig Björkman et al., eds., *Bergman on Bergman,* trans. Paul Austin, 86.
5. Bergman quoted in Peter Cowie, *Ingmar Bergman,* 115.

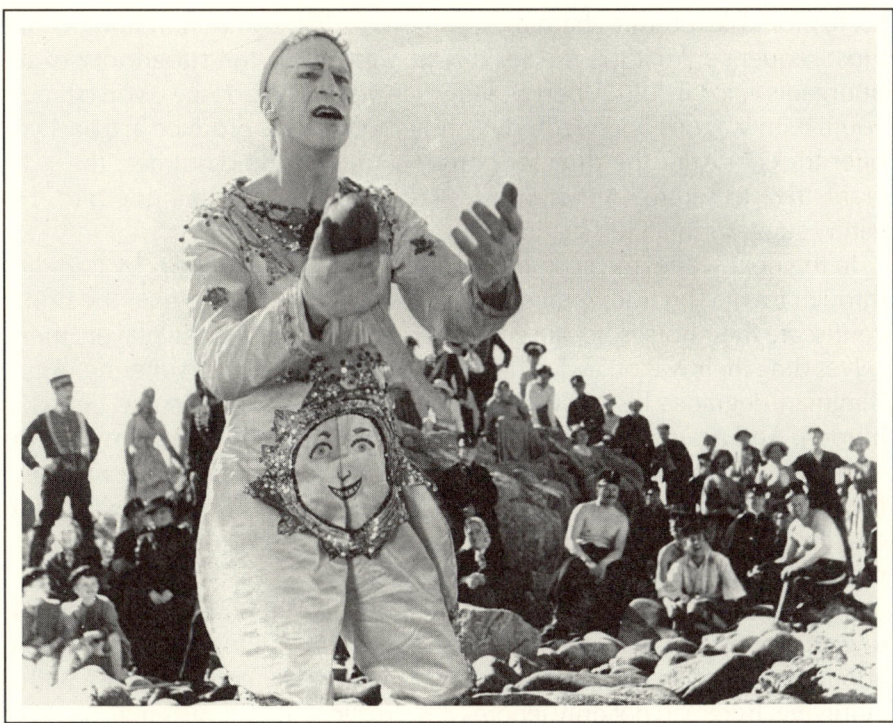

Figure 29. Ingmar Bergman, *The Naked Night,* Frost and Villagers (1953). Courtesy of Janus Films.

event. Similarly, Alma's nakedness connotes the unmasking that Bergman shows as one stage of humiliation. At first the vain woman takes the men's jeers as sincere applause; only the ensuing agony disillusions her. The water also has symbolic value, suggesting a baptism in human cruelty.

Turning literary, we might recall the sunny lake of Mallarmé's fool. Like that naked swimmer, Frost must immerse himself to pursue his love. And both clowns suffer punishment for that pursuit. Mallarmé also speaks of rebirth in water, and also implies the clown's transcendence. His grease-paint was "tout son sacre" (his anointing). In sum, both Mallarmé and Bergman reflect the tradition that we have traced of the fool as mocked Christ. See especially "Une Mort Héroique," "Ein Hungerkünstler," *Ansichten eines Clowns, Petrushka, The Italian Comedians,* and *Gilles.*

The next scene, contrasting with the grotesque enlargement of the flashback, returns us to the muted chiaroscuro of the circus wagon. Albert convinces Anne, his bareback-rider mistress, to accompany him to the town theater, where he hopes to beg some needed costumes for the evening show. Another scene of deep humiliation ensues. Overtly pertaining to the professional level, this shaming also implies the sexual humbling of the Frost sequence. First the theater director, assuming the superiority of the bourgeois actor, insults Albert as a lowly buffoon. "We despise you because you live in wagons and we in dirty hotel rooms; we produce art, and you offer tricks."[6] After the director consents to lend the costumes, the actor Frans tries to seduce Anne. She resists, but only after taunting him. His vanity suggests that their game of domination will continue.

In the next scene, the costumed troupe advertises the show by parading through town. The troupe members expect acclaim, but instead the police confiscate their horses because they have no license. As the players themselves drag their wagon away the townspeople jeer at their suffering. Again Bergman degrades his circus to the animal level; they become beasts of burden. And again we witness the enmity of the stable citizens toward the wanderers. This mob equals the soldiers in the flashback. We may also recall the same dualism in Banville's *Pauvres Saltimbanques,* discussed in chapter 2. Decrying the parade of the players, a citizen cries, "How can the police tolerate such things?"

In Bergman, they do not tolerate them at all. Only the author's attitude toward the artistes has changed, for Bergman has no romantic illusions about the circus. Indeed, its wretchedness here fully contradicts Banville's glorifying. Bergman not only ignores any artistic skill the artists may have but also focuses his story on their human failings. Where Banville sees ultimate artistic striving, Bergman sees simply the misery of the human condition.

As a parallel to the professional shaming in these two scenes, the next two highlight the sexual humiliation presaged in the Frost sequence. Albert visits his ex-wife, who lives in the town, and Anne returns to the theater, surrendering to Frans. Bergman shows the reciprocity of the two actions by frequent intercuts of the women's faces close up. As each scene builds to its degrading climax for Anne and Albert, the two faces almost merge. (Here Bergman anticipates the fusing of the two personalities in *Persona.*)

This focus on the two-women-in-one shows that we are seeing the story from Albert's point of view. Ostensibly he goes to Agda, his ex-wife, to visit his two sons, but he really wants her to take him back. Anne has a similar purpose with Frans, with whom she hopes to escape the circus. Both ventures fail: Agda, now a successful tobacconist, rejects Albert, and Frans tricks Anne into submission with a worthless "jewel." Neither of the two lovers can enter the stable, safe, bourgeois world.

Albert, returning to the circus, sees Anne leaving a jewelers' shop, where she learns the true value of her seduction. Bergman echoes the sexual shame of the Frost flashback by shooting this scene in glaring sunlight. And

6. Screenplay quoted in Birgitta Steene, *Ingmar Bergman,* 80.

drumbeats again accompany a scene of humiliation. Back in their wagon, a violent fight erupts, with Albert brandishing a gun. Frost arrives to dispel the tension, which he and Albert dissipate by getting drunk. However, we know the gun will reappear, for Frost asks Albert to shoot Alma's pet, the bear, and, better yet, Alma too.

The climactic scene occurs in the circus ring. Not only the townspeople and the soldiers, but also the actors come to the show. So when Frans insults Anne on horseback and Albert incites him to a bloody fight, we see a composite jeering mob. As the lithe Frans ruthlessly beats the fat, sagging Albert, we again witness the martyr mocked by humanity. Bergman underlines the inevitable in this situation by prefacing the fight with a clown scene of perpetual slaps.

Albert staggers out of the tent into his wagon and tries to shoot himself. Instead he shoots his reflection in a mirror. Stumbling out again, he sees the bear cage, which he fixes with an agonized stare. Alma implores him; the aghast circus folk look on; Albert fires the gun, immediately releasing himself from the suicidal spell. With groans of pain and misery, he sinks down by his pet horse. Clinging to this ultimate bond of animal warmth, Albert begins to revive. He orders the tents packed up for departure.

At this point we grasp the full significance of the bear. He resembles Albert, another caged, heavy, panting animal who lives to entertain the mocking world. Both are sacrificial victims. But the symbolism goes further, since the bear serves as Alma's child. On an obvious level, Albert revenges his double, Frost, for Alma's betrayal. We see that Albert has symbolically shot not only his animal self but Alma too, for the camera shows the death of the bear only in her collapse along the cage bars. On a deeper level, Birgitta Steene links the bear with Albert's need for maternal security. "In Jungian studies of archetypal patterns, the killing of a bear signifies the murder of the mother: Alma's pet animal becomes a totem of motherhood, and its death relieves Albert of the suicidal impulses that prompted him to seek the passivity of Agda's world."[7]

Looking further in Bergman's work, we find an important image of a bear in *The Seventh Seal*. In a fearful scene of baiting and intimidation, a corrupt priest forces Jof, the innocent juggler, to imitate a dancing bear. Here again, a creature terrorized to dance connotes the cruelty of man. In the later film *The Rite* (1969), Bergman juxtaposes a circus poster of a bear with a close-up of an actor. Since this film concerns the public shaming of players, the bear again suggests ritual sacrifice.[8]

7. Ibid., 81.
8. Two literary parallels come to mind. In "Un Spectacle Interrompu," Mallarmé uses a dancing bear, "living cousin" of Heine's Atta Troll, to contrast the beast and the genius within every fairground performer. Heine's bear, like Bergman's, gets shot, but the mime of

The Naked Night ends as it began, with the wagons on the move. The allegorical circus setting may dictate this circular form. But it has further relevance, most obviously connoting the repetition and entrapment of the resigned players. On a deeper level, this cycle suggests a continuing journey of discovery. Anne and Albert have awakened to new insights in this day. Their various unmaskings make their circular movement not perfectly closed. Beyond resignation, they must now at least acknowledge their true motives. Self-knowledge gives the possibility of progress.

Katharina Knie, discussed in chapter 4, ends with a similar return to the circus road. Like Anne and Albert, Katharina awakens to herself through a painful experience of love. She thereby recognizes her innate calling, which brings an affirmation of the self. Anne and Albert find no such positive impetus, but acceptance of their shared plight may improve their lot.

In evaluating the relative pessimism here, most critics see the film as one of Bergman's bleakest. Indeed, this dark mood may help to explain its almost universal critical and financial failure in 1953. One reviewer called it "Bergman's latest vomit"; Pauline Kael quipped, "Powerful, alright, powerfully awful."[9] However, perceptive viewers see that *The Naked Night,* no less than *The Seventh Seal,* bespeaks that existential view of man as lost in a hostile universe that Kierkegaard, Kafka, Beckett, and Sartre had bequeathed to artists of the 1950s. From Sartre's *No Exit,* Bergman takes up the idea that "hell is other people"; like Sartre's Orestes, he seems to say that "human life begins beyond despair." Another writer helps us understand this film: Strindberg, whom Bergman claims as his deepest influence. In his own dramas of wretched marriage, Bergman always shows sex and love as a key problem. In *The Naked Night* we see first the painful burden of sex for Frost as a Crucifixion. Albert suffers comparably, for love—like the circus—imprisons him.

Finally, the two parallel couples, Anne-Albert and Frost-Alma, have learned to accept life as it is. To go on at all demands courage; Albert shows

---

acrobat and bear in Mallarmé does not deal with this traditional level of man-beast relation. Instead, the observing poet-persona sees in their play "the potential . . . sublimation of the animal—the spiritualisation of the bestial by art" (Ursula Franklin, *An Anatomy of Poesis,* 108). In *The Bound Man,* Aichinger has her protagonist shoot not a bear but a wolf. Albert achieves catharsis by killing the caged animal, but the bound man loses his identity by eliminating the wild one. His ability to perform agile feats while bound represents a superiority over the free animal. When he shoots the wolf instead of wrestling with it while bound, he loses that distinction. In this ironic parable of freedom, man liberates himself only by accepting, indeed transcending, his given limits.

9. Jorn Donner, *The Films of Ingmar Bergman,* trans. Holger Lundbergh, 96; Kael in Simon, *Bergman Directs,* 52.

not cowardice in refusing suicide, but the strength to tolerate the circus. Spurning the easy way out, he acquires a touch of heroism. Such courage typifies the existential figure.

For our context, the relevance of *The Naked Night* lies in the answers it gives for one of Bergman's most insistent questions, "Who is the artist?" From his earliest writing for the stage, *The Death of Punch* (1942), to his latest film, *After the Rehearsal* (1984), Bergman continues to probe the artist's nature. The circus player offers an image of the artist in exaggerated form: lonelier, poorer, more disreputable, more mocked by society, more childlike, and hence more prone to delusion.

This last trait, shown in Albert's desired return to passivity with his wife-mother, also marks Frost's dream that closes the film. As he and Albert depart the scene, Frost recounts his vision of Alma as the source of both life and death. Seeing his weariness, she invites him to creep into her belly and be rocked to sleep. As he does so, he becomes smaller and smaller, finally shrinking into a tiny seed and vanishing. Here Frost suggests not only the ambivalent power of woman, which some take as a principal theme of the film, but also the craving of the child for maternal union. For the adult who houses this child, such union means extinction of the self.

Bergman stresses this coerced squashing of the self, humiliation, as the prime factor in the artist's psychology. Based on his own reaction against a harsh Lutheran upbringing, he projects the fears of the debased child-artist onto all his creative figures. "If I've objected strongly to Christianity, it has been because Christianity is strongly branded by a very virulent humiliation motif. One of its main tenets is 'I, a miserable sinner, born in sin, who have sinned all my days, etc.' Our way of living and behaving under this punishment is completely atavistic."[10]

If we study the degrading scenes in *The Naked Night,* we find at the core an unmasking radical enough to connote nakedness. Albert echoes the initial undressing of Alma and Frost when he removes his coat at Agda's and in the ring to fight with Frans. So we note that the actor especially, a creature of masks, becomes vulnerable when undressed. The word *naked* in the American title seems apt in this regard, though critics have both praised and blamed it. Livingston finds this label meaningless, but Vernon Young sees its importance. (The Swedish title means *Evening of the Clowns,* which the British dilute as *Sawdust and Tinsel.* The French more properly call it *La Nuit des Forains.*)

The word *night* also suits the film, suggesting that dark night of the soul that it depicts. Daniel Dervin cites the circus wagon and bear cage as exam-

10. Bergman in Björkman, *Bergman,* 81.

ples of Bergman's typical image of the dark closet, his abiding memory of childhood punishment. Despite his Nordic fear of bright sunlight, Bergman finds not security but menace in the dark. Yet he exploits a sensuous range of shadows, especially in this mannered film. The subtitle, "a penny print," conveys the brownish Victorian aura of the popular milieu in 1900. Critics cannot find a single epithet for the style of this film, for it mixes Romantic mirrors and masks, brutal Naturalism, Expressionist melodrama, and surreal fantasy. Bergman defends such a mélange by referring to an admired master. "Listen to some piece of music by Stravinsky—other comparisons aside—and you'll hear reminiscences from the whole history of music. Though he mixes up everything, he has an idea, a vision of his own. He has something to say. And he uses whatever he likes to say it."[11]

Like Strindberg, Bergman develops "the chamber play." The small cast here, only six main characters, intensifies conflict. In such limitation we may find a classic quality, a restriction to basic themes. Indeed, Bergman treats the great problems of classic tragedy: self-knowledge, death, the relation of the sexes, an inscrutable god. However, most critics relate Bergman's limited scale to his precise, naturalistic rendering of milieu. Each setting plays its role, almost like a character: the soundless confinement of Agda's shop, the menacing illusions of Frans' bedroom. Accordingly, Bergman tracks his camera constantly, moving it around his characters to stress their enclosure in these determining spaces. Even the landscape, dominating the beginning and the end of the film, looms ominously relevant. Not surprisingly, this particular place in northern Sweden partly inspired the "demonic" quality of the film.[12]

Ultimately, Bergman relates the circus to film making. In *The Naked Night,* the theater represents art, the circus much less than art. As the director taunts Albert, "You offer tricks." Similarly, Bergman once called the stage his wife and film his mistress. (Hence Philip Mosley's subtitle *The Cinema as Mistress*.) This metaphor reveals the disrepute of film that Bergman senses. Echoing Banville remarkably, he also equates the daring of the aerialist with the risk of the film maker. "We are in the position of the artist who of his own free will performs a somersault high up beneath the big top in order to satisfy the spectators. We too have to risk our reputations in order to satisfy the needs of the cinema."[13]

11. Ibid., 93.

12. Donner, *Films,* 95.

13. Bergman quoted in Maria Bergom-Larsson, *Film in Sweden: Ingmar Bergman and Society,* trans. Barrie Selman, 49. Picasso, as exemplary as Stravinsky for Bergman, also relates artist to aerialist through their shared experience of risk. "Painting is freedom. . . . If you jump, you might land on the wrong side of the rope. But if you're not willing to take the

The Seventh Seal (1957)

The Seventh Seal shares much with *The Naked Night*. Again, a journey of self-discovery serves as a metaphor for human life; again, a play-within-a-play reveals larger meanings; and the prevailing tone again stems from an existential view of man tortured by moral questions in a godless world. However, the popular player here could hardly appear more different than before. Earlier, the artistes suffered every imaginable kind of physical and mental anguish; here they enjoy a seemingly blessed life free of any want or fear. How could Bergman's basic idea of the player have changed so radically in just four years?

First, we must consider *The Seventh Seal* as a religious parable whose characters we cannot take literally. Indeed, they appear not as characters at all in the modern psychological sense, but rather as symbols of various human conditions. Hence we cannot effectively compare them with the complex beings of 1900. Yet much in the life of the later players recalls their medieval forebears. The crowds remain as demanding, as suspicious, and as cruel toward their entertainers. Vagabonds still suffer the poverty of outcasts. But Bergman's preference for the theater of the Middle Ages helps to explain his positive view of its personnel. "Medieval actors still represent the sort of theater I love most of all: robust, direct, concrete, substantial, sensual."[14] Such a rejection of the decadent modern mode recalls Meyerhold's love for the medieval *cabotin* (see chapter 6).

Indeed, the three main players here—the Holy Family of Jof, Mia, and their infant, Mikael—represent the sole wholly positive element in this medieval landscape. Bergman indicts the Church for its corruption, its exploitation of human fear and ignorance, and its outright barbarism. The central episode of witch burning highlights, even symbolizes, the stark violence of that society. Moreover, the relentless intellectual probing by the virtuous knight also appears mistaken, especially in contrast to the graceful, fearless acceptance of life by the minstrels. So we must ask who these players are, and why they alone deserve salvation from the plague (see figure 30).

First let us summarize the plot. Antonius Block, a knight returning home to fourteenth-century Sweden from ten disillusioning years in the Holy Land, encounters Death. Challenging him to a chess match, Block wins a

---

risk of breaking your neck, what good is it? You don't jump at all. You have to wake people up. To revolutionize their way of identifying things. You've got to create images they won't accept. Make them foam at the mouth. Force them to understand that they're living in a pretty queer world. A world that's not reassuring. A world that's not what they think it is" (quoted in André Malraux, *Picasso's Masks*, trans. Jacques Guicharnaud, 110).
    14. Bergman quoted in Cowie, *Bergman*, 142.

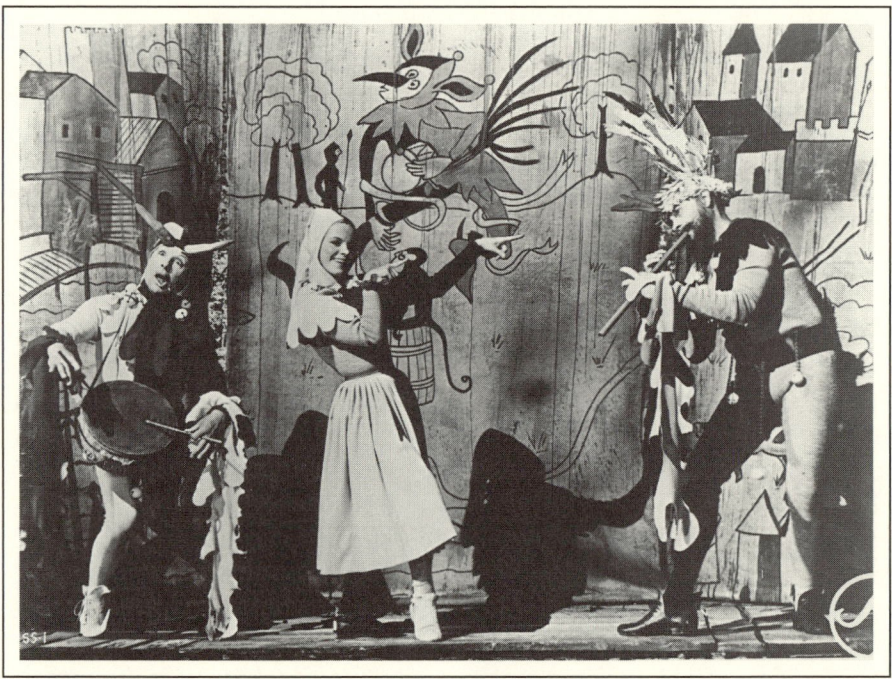

Figure 30. Ingmar Bergman, *The Seventh Seal,* Players Performing (1957). Courtesy of Janus Films.

respite. "And when he had opened the seventh seal, there was silence in heaven about the space of half an hour" (Rev. 8:1). The knight and his squire, Jons, meet a variety of people who believe that the raging bubonic plague signals the Last Judgment. Major dialogues occur among the two men and a church painter, who depicts the Dance of Death; an alleged witch en route to the stake for consorting with the devil; and the actor family, who share with Block a bowl of wild strawberries and milk representing the sacrament of divine love that the knight has long sought in vain. He finally accomplishes an act of true salvation at the chessboard, when he distracts Death from taking the troupers. However, he thus sacrifices himself, for Death checkmates the knight in his next move. When Block and his retinue return to his castle, Death comes to claim them all. Only the visionary Jof sees their Dance of Death across the horizon that closes the film.

Jof, Mia, and Mikael appear and reappear in the film from start to finish. The initial scenes show Block and Death on a desolate beach. As knight and squire travel through a forest, they meet one of Death's skeletal victims. In bright counterpoint to these shadowy confrontations, Jof jauntily greets a sunny morning from his circus wagon. Albert in *The Naked Night* also starts the film by emerging from his wagon at dawn, but with dread. And he further contrasts with the happy Jof in relating to his horse. Albert is constantly degraded by association with his animals; only in downfall can he find an instinctual link to the comfort of his pet horse.

But Jof immediately identifies with his horse in a comic sharing of privation. "Jof (talking to his scrawny old horse): Good morning. Have you had breakfast? I can't eat grass, worse luck. We're a little hard up. People aren't very interested in juggling in this part of the country."[15] As this scene vividly shows, the actors belong to both animal nature and the physical nature around them. Although Mia admits that summer is better than winter, they obviously live in harmony with their surroundings. This oneness with nature emerges most clearly in the climactic scene of the shared strawberries and milk.

Jof also contrasts with Albert in his relation to his son. Albert's sons ignore his circus, but Jof sees his baby son as a miraculous juggler. "Mikael will grow up to be a great acrobat—or a juggler who can do the one impossible trick. . . . To make one of the balls stand absolutely still in the air."[16] Here we find the first of many signs that these people represent divine grace. Not only their son suggests salvation, but also Mia appears as Virgin Mother to both Mikael and the childlike Jof. He undergoes a painful persecution at the tavern, where the villagers, seeking a scapegoat for the plague, force him at knife-point to imitate a bear dancing on a table. Bergman specifies the sacrificial nature of the innocent Jof by having him dance with arms outstretched, cross-like. We recall Frost's white costume in *The Naked Night*, stretched out on the ground as his emblem.

When the beaten, terrified juggler staggers out of the tavern into the arms of his soothing wife, we see him as a child. The same mothering relation emerged earlier, when Mia tenderly chided him for his visions and mocked his self-importance; here she actually cradles him. So we now have a complex of images characteristic not only of Bergman, but also of several other creators already discussed. Schiller, Baudelaire, Freud, Hofmannsthal, Kafka, Mann, Grass, and Böll all root the nature of the artist in the child within. Bergman belongs in this group, and so does Fellini. "Artists retain a strongly infantile streak; . . . the creative streak is so deeply tied up with a sort of infantility, or a leftover of the child's attitude to the world about him, that the artist also retains a lot of marginal behavior-traits."[17]

More specifically, Bergman has often referred to the "big child" quality he finds in the faces of geniuses such as Stravinsky and Picasso. We have already seen the importance of the humiliated inner child for the artistes in

15. Ingmar Bergman, *The Seventh Seal*, trans. Lars Malmström, 17.
16. Ibid., 19.
17. Bergman in Björkman, *Bergman*, 83.

The Naked Night. Jof adds to the miserable humbling of the tavern scene a transcendent purity and joy that the earlier players lack completely. If, as some reviewers believe, one film can "correct" a similar forebear, *The Seventh Seal* at least balances the anguish of the artiste with divine blessing.

Perhaps the players' main import for this film is their fearlessness. They alone treat Death as a mask, a cruel joke. Above all they do not fear it, as everyone else does. As the knight says, "In our fear we make an image, and that image we call God."[18] But the troupers, lacking fear, have only their love as God. They answer Block's fear-based quest. Moreover, their salvation has cathartic value for both Bergman himself and the nuclear age. He claims that this apocalyptic film freed him from his own fear of death. And, as many viewers have noted, the plague here represents nuclear holocaust.

The Silence (1963)

Bergman does not focus on circus players in this film. Yet part of our personnel—dwarves and puppets—reveal enough about the central ideas here to demand discussion. The subject, unconscious enmities in the nuclear age, may seem unrelated to our histrionic context. However, the boy Johan's puppet theater expresses the hostility of this psychological war. Furthermore, his bewildering encounter with some performing dwarves again externalizes a primary force in the story: the "monstrous powers" that overtake his dying aunt.

Two sisters, Anna and Ester, along with Anna's son Johan, arrive by train in a ghostly, forbidding city at war. They are traveling homeward, so that Ester, dying of tuberculosis, can rest. Not understanding the language here, they isolate themselves in two oppressive hotel rooms. (Bergman explains that he invented the few words spoken; the name of the place, Timoka, means "pertaining to the executioner" in Estonian.) Anna, desperate for some human comfort, picks up a waiter for an abandoned, animal kind of love. The disapproving Ester stays in bed, smokes, drinks, masturbates, and has a near-fatal attack.

Johan, partly bridging the hostility of the two women, suffers his own deep loneliness. His only encounters in the twenty-four-hour action involve an old hall porter and the mysterious dwarves, who take him into their room, dress him as a girl, and then abruptly dismiss him. On the next day, Johan and Anna depart by train; Ester stays behind to die, but she gives Johan a letter with some words in the foreign language. The screenplay ends with "this secret message."[19]

18. Bergman, *Seal*, 28.
19. Ingmar Bergman, *A Film Trilogy,* trans. Paul Austin, 143.

For our context, Johan is the pivotal figure. As the silent witness, he absorbs and reflects the terrors of this barren adult world. Bergman calls him the catalyst for the two opposing women, but he also has his own importance as the only way out of their terrible life. His fascination with the incomprehensible words bequeathed by Ester implies the curiosity, the ability to grow, that will make him transcend silence. "Johan's face is pale with the effort of trying to understand the strange language."[20] The silence of God still prevails, but the child can at least study the words he may some-day understand. One thinks of that enigmatic promise expressed by Kafka: "There is hope, but not for us."

What Johan reads in bed implies an ironic clue to his identity: Lermon-tov's *A Hero of Our Time*. Another piece of inherited culture especially dear to the musical Bergman provides a clearer definition for the boy: Ester listens to The *Goldberg Variations*. Peter Cowie notes the aptness of this particular music for the tortured woman, since Bach composed it to soothe the insomniac Goldberg. But Bach's relevance goes well beyond such hid-den meaning. First of all, he signifies for Bergman a pinnacle of aesthetic achievement. Apparently Bartók furnished the actual model for the rhyth-mic structure of this film, "the dull continuous note, then the sudden explo-sion."[21] Bergman also owes a general debt to baroque music, especially Mozart (*The Magic Flute*) and Bach (*A Passion*). In *The Silence,* Bach gives the only common language between Ester and the porter; both smile emphatically in repeating his name. By contrast, the composer also high-lights the animosity of the two sisters when Anna asks what music they are hearing, then impatiently switches it off.

Bach, a key symbol of European civilization, belongs in the baroque hotel, itself representing a remnant of that culture now menaced by a con-stant state of war. Hence the boy Johan may offer the same hope for civiliza-tion associated with the earlier Johann. Indeed, we may consider this boy a prototypical nascent artist, for Bergman links him quite literally with artist figures in other films. He uses the same young actor at the end of *Persona* (1966), his hand on the screen connecting the film maker with the spectator. In *The Hour of the Wolf* (1968) we meet a mature, albeit thoroughly neu-rotic creator, another Johan. The Johan preceding *The Silence,* a boy unbe-liever and aspiring astronaut in *Winter Light* (1962), suggests a defiant curiosity toward the world that also marks these other artist types.

Johan playing with his puppet theater recalls the budding creativity of Mann's artistes: Christian and Hanno Buddenbrook and the Bajazzo (see

20. Ibid.
21. Björkman, *Bergman,* 181.

chapter 4). However, Johan's brief Punch and Judy show bespeaks not so much the histrionic urge as the violence both inside and outside this hotel room. Its only action consists of the merciless beating of an old woman by Punch. The buffoon continues to rage after she promptly dies, for he doesn't know what else to do. Johan cannot explain to Ester what Punch says, as he speaks "a funny language, because he is frightened." And he is too angry to sing, as Ester requests. Naturally, Johan makes his puppets speak nonsense, for such sounds echo what he hears around him. Again, as in *The Seventh Seal,* a play-within-a-play reveals the actual condition of the characters.

The cutting that frames the puppet scene clarifies its ominous meaning particularly well. The sequence starts with Johan watching his mother and her new lover enter another room. From the corridor he hears her laugh, then cry out. The bewildered boy runs from this overheard primal noise into his own room, where Ester sleeps. From her window he observes a tank roll slowly into the street below. Suddenly all sound stops, everyone vanishes. Ester wakes and asks Johan, who feels "inexpressible anxiety," to read to her. Instead he offers the puppet show, which ends with him in tears, rushing from behind the bed-stage to embrace Ester. Closing the sequence, the camera returns to Anna and her lover.

In sum, this section of the film compresses its principal themes. The two opposing forces—Ester the male/intellectual type versus Anna the sensuous female—play out their hostility; they show their desperate need for love in a menacing, silent world; they confront man as mere object. Between the two sides of this terrible drama stands Johan, the innocent child, still healthy enough to seek solace for his fear but also projecting it through his puppets. The puppet show forms the center of the sequence.

More crucial to Johan's significance, and indeed to that of the whole story, are the dwarves. The confusion of critics over these figures emerges from two divergent views: Jorn Donner thinks their scenes are "just there," whereas Wood sees them as the heroes of the film. Surely this troupe of deformed little men represents the stunting, the corruption, of humanity. They bear an explicitly sexual symbolism throughout, which accords with "the sexual deformities" of the two women.[22]

Anna sees the dwarves onstage. They perform an aptly phallic number to accompany the brutish copulation that she watches nearby in the audience. When Johan finds this group of dwarves in their hotel room, one of them puts a dress he was sewing on the boy. Then another one rushes over to kiss

---

22. Robin Wood, *Ingmar Bergman,* 136; Daniel Dervin, *Through a Freudian Lens Deeply: A Psychoanalysis of Cinema,* 101.

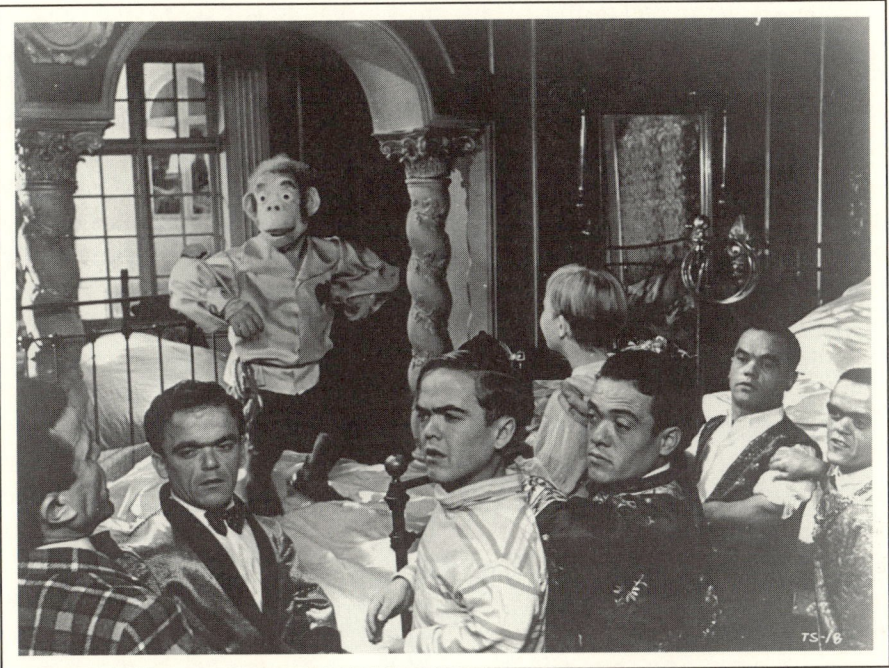

Figure 31. Ingmar Bergman, *The Silence,* Johan with Dwarves (1963). Courtesy of Janus Films.

him. Here the midgets play out Johan's inevitable confusion about the two largest areas of childhood anxiety: size and sex. As Leslie Fiedler notes, dwarves arouse adult curiosity about these same problems. But for the child identifying with such child-size adults, the question of adult sexuality looms especially troublesome (see figure 31).

Bergman introduces the midgets, as Grass does, to parallel the boy's reduced perspective. Like him, they see the normal adult world as outsiders. But their relevance in the film goes beyond identification for Johan. "Through the exploitation of their deformity as public spectacle, the dwarfs add another dimension to our awareness of Bergman's despair at the very concept of 'civilization'. . . . They evoke the sense of the messy and accidental nature of man's evolution, the radically un-Christian sense of human existence as a weird anomaly, that underlies the whole film."[23]

All three main characters see the dwarves. In their last appearance the dwarves march down the broad hotel corridor in costume and masks, a haunting tribute to Velasquez. Ester, having just seen Anna and the waiter in

23. Wood, *Bergman,* 132.

bed, stands in the hall as this bizarre troupe files slowly past. They start to sing and skip drunkenly, some giggle at Ester, others mockingly salute her. One man is dressed as a bride, and the last one wears a death mask. Do they perhaps mock her sterility? She reacts to this grotesque scene with an attack echoing the one that starts the film.

At both these moments, "a thin stream of blood runs quietly down over her chin, flecks her skirt and drips onto the carpet."[24] As in similar images by Antonioni in *La Notte* and *L'Eclisse* (1961, 1962), liquid trickling down connotes the draining of human forces. Here the juxtaposing of the dwarves with Ester's impending death suggests the fatal result of her own deformed, self-directed sexuality. In both scenes, blood staining her skirt explicitly points to the spiritual death of this sexually enclosed personality.

More generally, the all-male world of the dwarves contrasts with the female realm of the two main rooms. Surrealistically enough, the dwarves seem to be the only other hotel guests. All the other figures are men (albeit abnormal ones), and the city outside, with its tanks, soldiers, and ammunition, bespeaks the male climate of war. Bergman gives us a fully dichotomous humanity, for the film deals with the loss of unity implicit in the silence of God. The father the two women have lost represents just this dead authority; Bergman refers to a "collapse of ideology and a way of life."[25] Even the dwarves have their father figure, who sternly reproaches them for their drunken and transvestite play with Johan.

In this godless world, each woman represents only half a person, a problem to be resolved in *Persona*. Neither Ester nor Anna can find the human comfort she craves. Like the dwarves, the women are incomplete, arrested beings. Only Johan can integrate their two stunted personalities in his own life.

Fanny and Alexander (1982)

Twenty years later, Bergman again takes up the nascent artist, this time with clearly autobiographical overtones. Again a boy intently observes the strange sexual behavior of adults. Again the father's death plays a crucial role, for Alexander loses both Oscar, his own father, and a stepfather. Aptly enough, Oscar dies from a stroke suffered while rehearsing as Hamlet's ghost. And he returns as a ghost to haunt his son at decisive moments. Completing the father complex, the "remarkable" old Jew Isaak serves as surrogate father. Not only does he rescue the children from the sadistic

24. Bergman, *Trilogy,* 138.
25. Bergman in Björkman, *Bergman,* 181.

bishop; he also fuels Alexander's lively imagination by introducing him to the mysteries of his junkshop.

This stretto of father imagery in his personal farewell film shows conclusively that Bergman "has threaded his talent through the needle's eye of the father he regarded ambivalently."[26] However, some viewers have criticized the redundancy of so many fathers. Especially when Alexander's mother tells him not to play Hamlet, the film blatantly states what it has already suggested—several times. Yet we may also see here the necessary playing out of Bergman's own Oedipal drama, which does indeed echo the story of Hamlet. To regain his inheritance, Alexander must do battle with the false father.

Moreover, whether or not we accept the Hamletic equation, we must relate the father problem to Bergman's need to define creativity. We have already seen in *The Naked Night* that the child survives in the mature artist. *Fanny and Alexander* shows definitely that the father, having molded the child, also survives in the adult creator. Indeed, the relation of father to child forms the main axis in the artist's development. Naturally, Bergman sees in the father who created him the original Father. Hence the desolation of *The Silence,* where the whole idea of patriarchy has died. In bestowing several fathers on Alexander, Bergman gives him just the kind of security that his own childhood lacked. In fact, Kael thinks Bergman makes the boy ten years old in 1907 so that Alexander could be born, unlike Bergman himself, in the patriarchal nineteenth century. Completing the father-child link, Bergman the creator becomes a Father also.

Apparently recreating the scene of childhood anguish generates the creative process; the work of art springs from submission to the torturous womb of trauma. The artist may give birth in pain, but the "fantastic childbirth" bestows new power and reverses fears of masochistic submission. The child of his imagination becomes the scenario; the artist becomes the director; the original child replaces the father: "In the studio I am God. I say, 'Let there be light' and there is Light." Let there be a movie and there is an audience in the dark, being impregnated with his fertile imagery and giving birth to its own dreams and visions.[27]

The film begins with images of Alexander's puppet theater. Like him, these dolls gravely observe the spacious, ornate rooms of his grandmother's apartment. Thus we immediately see through the eyes of a child. Here Bergman best demonstrates that "to make a film is to plunge by its deepest

26. Dervin, *Freudian Lens,* 121.
27. Ibid.

roots down to the world of childhood."[28] Like Johan in *The Silence,* Alexander serves as a filter. From the floor where he sits we survey the stage where the story will occur. He even calls out the names of family members, as if to introduce the cast of characters.

Later on, the life-size puppets of Ismael, Isaak's androgynous nephew, suggest a deeper theater of mystery. (They may even signify Bergman's own life-size puppets, the actors.) Ismael, like Isaak and Aron, another nephew, represents that arcane world of fantasy that Alexander constantly seeks to enter. As he reveals most clearly in the lie that his mother has sold him to a circus, this scion of bourgeois prosperity must seek spiritual refuge among outsiders. Johan actually escapes from his difficult life through the dwarves; Alexander does so mentally as an imagined acrobat. This film mutes the blatant dualism of citizen vs. player in *The Naked Night,* for Alexander already belongs to a theatrical and truly histrionic family. To sharpen this conflict, Bergman exiles the children from their paradise to the brutal realm of the bishop.

The puppets connote art as a kind of magic. This equation lies at the core of Bergman's aesthetics. He has often spoken of that landmark in his childhood, the magic lantern that he, like Alexander, received as a gift. "This little rickety machine was my first conjuring set. And even today I remind myself that I am a conjuror, since cinematography is based on deception of the human eye. . . . I perform conjuring tricks with apparatus so expensive and so wonderful that any entertainer in history would have given anything to have it."[29]

Bergman explores the ambiguities of magic, especially its negative side, in *The Magician* (1958). He may partly identify with the magician-charlatan, but he claims to prefer Vergerus, the scientist who dreams of discovering the truth about magic. Like Freud, Bergman finds in creativity the sign of the most mysterious human urges. Although most of the artists considered here would agree, few would equate art with the anti-rational. Here lies one of the most troubling problems for the cerebral Bergman. Yet such a subversive aesthetics also produces his most challenging work.

FELLINI

La Strada (1954)

The most logical place to start with this film, its title, captures more than its obvious meaning. Fellini himself speaks of all his work as "a quest for the

28. Ibid., 98.
29. Bergman quoted in G. William Jones, ed., *Talking with Ingmar Bergman,* xii.

essential self, my own and others, along all the paths of life." Several critics echo his idea of film as a "spiritual odyssey"; Donald Costello even titles his book *Fellini's Road*.[30] Of course, artists often use the motif of the journey as a metaphor for the quest of life, as in Bergman's *The Naked Night* and *The Seventh Seal*. But their titles rarely encapsulate both the form and the significance of their stories as pointedly as this one does.

Viewers readily take the tragicomic Gelsomina as the focus of this story, although Fellini claims that her antagonist, the brutish Zampano, is his subject. "The point of departure . . . was the story of an enlightenment, of the shaking of a conscience, through the sacrifice of another creature."[31] However, his title points away from both characters toward the vehicle of their confrontation, the wandering road of the circus.

Zampano, seeking an "assistant" for his strongman routine, buys Gelsomina from her destitute mother for ten thousand lire. The two characters meet by the sea, where Gelsomina has been gathering twigs for the family fire. She bids a tearful but acquiescent farewell to her small siblings, then to the sea. From these first frames onward, we sense her attachment to the water, her most potent natural symbol. Later she will rush toward it on another beach, and she will die within sight of it. Now, departing from the sea of her origins, she ceremoniously kneels before it, in a consecration. The end of the film echoes this ritual moment: the anguished Zampano wades into the water, trying to retrieve the girl he has lost in her own element.

The first scenes of Gelsomina's "training" include a rehearsal of her drummed announcement of the act: "Zampano is here!" When she does not catch on quickly, he switches her legs. She must also cook a miserable soup for them and sleep with the master in their motorcycle-van. Her sole pleasure comes in trying on costumes, especially the black-brimmed hat that reminds critics of Chaplin. Right away this waif delights in the pretense of her role, which soon includes music and dancing. As their wanderings continue, Zampano and Gelsomina emerge as polar opposites. Just as the first frames set her against the sea and him against the land, so do the latter episodes contrast his cruelty with her gentleness, his pessimism with her innocence. He shows indifference toward everything outside his own appetites, while she eagerly opens herself to people and nature. She communes with a tree and plants tomatoes without hope of seeing them grow. Naturally, Zampano only laughs at such childishness.

Act 1, a classic exposition, introduces and develops the two main characters in a densely interdependent relation. Act 2 starts with the new impulse

30. Donald Costello, *Fellini's Road*, 6.
31. Fellini quoted in Edward Murray, *Fellini the Artist*, 62.

of outside influences on the couple. The pair perform at a peasant wedding. As usual, Gelsomina attracts children especially; they readily sense a mutual kinship. A group of them take her upstairs in the farmhouse to see the family wonder, a cretinous boy in bed, locked in a distant room. The children ask Gelsomina to make Oswaldo laugh, but she can only stare at him, awestruck. She feels a shock of recognition, for this ageless, sexless child embodies her own isolation. Gelsomina's mother has called her, like him, "different from the others." Here she senses the full measure of that apartness. Later that night, when her frustration with Zampano becomes intolerable, Gelsomina leaves him. With this first independent act, she announces her growing self-awareness, her first step on the road to possible fulfillment.

The next sequence introduces Gelsomina to the complex world of the communal spectacle. As she sits at the side of the road, three jaunty musicians appear from nowhere. Like some other figures in the film, especially an unexplained lone horse, these men have no clear bearing on the story. Charles Ketcham calls them the three Wise Men, but no one else labels them as anything but a transition. Gelsomina immediately responds to their happy tune and follows them into town. Here a religious procession overwhelms her in a typical Fellini scene: the bewildered individual succumbs to the mystery of public ritual.

One can speculate at length on the ambiguities that Fellini raises with this device, for his camera shows both awe and disgust for the vulgar pageant that entrances the faithful. However, for Gelsomina the meaning emerges clearly. Led from the secular parade to the sacred one, she moves joyously with the crowd, though it almost crushes her. To underline her role of willing innocent vessel, Fellini sets her against a sign reading "Madonna Immaculata."

Suddenly the crowd looks up, for a winged angel appears high above them. Il Matto, the fool, performs his aerial act between the cathedral and a building opposite. Illuminated by an altar-like flame, this acrobat not only walks the tightrope but also sits on the wire to eat spaghetti. Like the others, Gelsomina is dazzled by this man of the sky. Again, in juxtaposing the religious awe of the crowd with their wonder at the secular act, Fellini depicts piety ambiguously. At least we may conclude that the pagan carnival has equal value with the Christian parade; at most we may see in the former a satire on the latter.

Capping the religious spectacle, this fool seems holy indeed, for he suggests Christ. On the tightrope his balancing pole forms the horizontal piece of a cross. His round fool's hat frames his head like a halo. In contrast to Zampano's earthbound, banal routine, this lofty act inspires reverence.

Later scenes make this supernatural figure more clearly Christ-like: he rides a donkey, taunts his tormentor Zampano, and foresees his own death. Gelsomina becomes his ardent disciple, and his inevitable murder by Zampano occurs against the three trees of Golgotha.

Like his cognate image, Bergman's Frost in *The Naked Night,* the fool has sacrificial value. Frost gives up his human dignity when he undresses to rescue his humiliated wife; Il Matto sets Gelsomina on her path of self-sacrifice for Zampano. Moreover, he willingly gives up his life to the strongman, whom he has always mocked. Like Petrushka, the poet-clown, Il Matto must yield to the violence that rules the world. As for the link to Frost, Fellini's clown echoes his Crucifixion. The fool's cruciform corpse, dragged to burial by Zampano, recalls the end of the Frost flashback. There a blinding image shows us the fool's costume stretched out in a cross.

After the crowd disperses, Gelsomina sits alone by the town fountain. Zampano arrives in the cycle-van and, after a few slaps, takes her away. In the next scene they sign on with a large circus in Rome. Il Matto, already a member of the troupe, plays a tiny violin. He immediately taunts Zampano, and someone narrowly averts their fight. Later Il Matto teaches Gelsomina to play his theme song on the trumpet. Aroused to violent jealousy, Zampano draws a knife on the fool, and both men are fired and jailed. Late that night, with Zampano still in jail, the freed Il Matto talks earnestly to Gelsomina. He tells her a parable about a pebble he picks up. Convinced that even the stone serves some purpose, she resolves to fulfill her supposed purpose in staying with Zampano. So, although both Il Matto and the circus offer her refuge, she goes on with the strongman.

Act 3 begins in a new mood, for the fool has irrevocably changed the relationship of the wandering pair. Winter approaches, and they seek shelter in a convent. In an exchange with ironically biblical overtones, they learn that the house is full and they must sleep in the stable. After eating, Gelsomina plays her trumpet for the sisters, which inspires a remarkable change in Zampano. For the first time he shows actual emotion; her music, taught by the fool, touches him in spite of himself. Accordingly, he no longer mocks her performance and even offers, uncharacteristically, to help the women with washing up and chopping wood. The aura of contentment that the nuns radiate visibly effects Gelsomina. When one of them notes her envy, she asks if the girl would like to stay. Again, a concerned person offers a home, and again, Gelsomina refuses. She cannot waver in her sense of duty toward Zampano.

The next important scene brings the crisis of the action: they encounter Il Matto on the road, and Zampano unwittingly beats him to death. Gelsomina, as terrified witness, becomes hysterical. Crying, whimpering, she can only moan, "The Fool is hurt, the Fool is hurt." As they flee the murder and burial, Zampano shows increasingly complex emotions. He not only fears her distracted betrayal, but also displays his own guilt. Moreover, he shows some concern for her. He offers to take her home; he even asks if he may sleep with her in the van. Physically he imitates her movements, cringing in misery against a wall as she has often done. When she gets sick, he tries to take care of her. Falling asleep in the winter sun, Gelsomina murmurs her last pregnant words, "The fire's almost out." Once she is asleep, he abandons her. He makes a last, humanizing gesture, leaving her some money and, a tender afterthought, the trumpet.

This scene of abandonment, the emotional climax of the story, ends the third act. The few remaining scenes seem like epilogue, for years have passed and Gelsomina has vanished. Zampano, alone and surly as before, walks down the street of a seaside town where he is performing. Suddenly he hears a woman humming Gelsomina's song, the fool's music. Asking where she learned the tune, he hears how some people found Gelsomina on the beach. Although they too offered her shelter, she tacitly refused it by not eating. Soon she died, but her song survived with those who remember her.

A final scene, Zampano's collapse, forms a dénouement. Abandoning himself to years of pent-up grief and remorse, he staggers onto the beach and into the ocean. Finding no absolution in Gelsomina's sacramental water, he stumbles back onto the beach and prostrates himself. Clawing the sand as the dying fool did with the earth, he writhes and sobs. The last frames withdraw from the figure, now in the same fetal posture that Gelsomina took when he left her. The final shot broadens to include man, beach, sea, and sky.

This suggestion of elemental, even cosmic, resolution has not escaped the critics. In Zampano's baptismal bath and the two fetal poses, Costello sees the birth of new life out of despair: a parting message of hope. Gilbert Salachas thinks any remorse in a Fellini character cannot last. "By some mysterious alchemy, transformations . . . occur, a mind unfolds, a slumbering conscience is awakened. But take care: none of this is ever . . . definitive. Fellini carefully avoids the classic hypocrisy of spectacular, irreversible conversions."[32]

What, then, does this ending signify? Perhaps we should first tackle a more difficult question: "What is the film about?" As with most great stories, it seems impossible to make one definitive statement. On one level, *La Strada* deals with the tragedy of innocence in a graceless world. It also

---

32. Gilbert Salachas, *Federico Fellini*, trans. Rosalie Siegel, 58.

shows the spiritual triumph of the lowly, and it makes a tragicomic comment on the failure of human communication. The critics differ widely on where the stress lies among all such interpretations.

For Frank Burke, Zampano represents the intrusion of civilizing forces—discipline, routine, order—into Gelsomina's purely natural world. Hence he sees the film as showing that culture dominates and finally crushes nature. One problem with that view lies in the definition of Zampano as civilized, for he always bespeaks brute force. Moreover, Gelsomina's willing self-sacrifice arises not from her natural state, which would always seek self-preservation, but from the fool's influence. His idea that even a pebble serves a purpose rationalizes nature, which itself knows no aim. He imposes this Dostoevskian notion on Gelsomina, who then acts unnaturally.

Thus I cannot view *La Strada* in Burke's dualistic way. The film seems more complex, since both Zampano and Il Matto represent different forces intruding on Gelsomina's simplicity. Moreover, Zampano lives primarily by instinct, which she transcends in her spirituality. I find more satisfying Costello's "mythic triads": "The characters are three isolates: simpleton, brute and holy fool."[33] To resolve the inevitable conflict between Zampano and Gelsomina, Il Matto must inspire the girl's sacrifice. Beyond this tightly interwoven triad, Fellini also integrates sea, land, and sky as the symbols of each character.

For our context, *La Strada* plays a special role, since it provides our sole example of three popular players of equally large mythic import. Despite Fellini's valid claim that he treats mainly "the shaking of conscience" in Zampano, the film belongs also to the other two. However, Gelsomina's unique character highlights her; we have already met variants of Il Matto in Bergman's Frost and other holy fools in literature, ballet, and painting. Thus if she represents the quintessential clown for Fellini, as both he and his critics suggest, she tells us much of his view of the artiste.

Gelsomina's link to the sea expresses only one aspect of her naturalness. Her name means jasmine, a bush, and the first scenes show her carrying a bundle of twigs across her back. Gelsomina also communes with trees, imitating the design of their branches with her dance. Children and animals complete the complex of natural things that relate closely to her. Edward Murray suggests a whole subplot of dog imagery, from the way Zampano trains her to the dead dog a child mentions. Fellini explains that Gelsomina, hardly more than a child herself, represents his own "nostalgia for innocence." Here again we find the child-artist. Indeed, Fellini joins our other

33. Costello, *Road*, 6.

creators who see their pursuit as infantile. "An artist is a child always, and sees things with childlike wonder. That is what makes him an artist."[34]

Another feature of her innocence makes Gelsomina especially childlike: her sexlessness. As the scene with Oswaldo clarifies, Gelsomina stands apart from normal adulthood, although she is fully grown. Like the retarded boy imprisoned in his childhood, she will not develop sexually. In this light, her link with the Madonna in the procession scene makes sense. Although she submits physically to Zampano, Gelsomina still remains virginal. Those who see this story as a Christian parable speak of her as the vessel of grace, of faith, that saves Zampano. Peter Bondanella captures both this sacred aura and the earthiness of Gelsomina in calling her "a secular saint."[35]

This combination—childlike naturalness, asexuality, plus poverty and wandering—recalls our other outcast urchin players in Mallarmé, Picasso, and Apollinaire. Gelsomina's Christ-like innocent suffering and self-sacrifice relate especially to Mallarmé's *pauvre enfant pâle*. Both she and that waif offer redemption to those who reject them; their radiant spirits transcend their sordid surroundings. Her ambiguous sex reminds us of Picasso's androgynous adolescents. The girl in Picasso's *Girl Acrobat Balancing on the Ball* (1905) resembles a boy, and the youths in *Les Saltimbanques* have a female fragility. For Apollinaire, the comparable asexuality of the sprite in "Un Fantôme de Nuées" forms part of his otherworldly aura.

Fellini restrains his use of transcendent symbols for the girl, but he spares nothing for Il Matto. Her mystical connection with this literal Christ-figure emerges clearly when someone calls her *matta*. And Fellini makes the point visually by repeating the stripes on her jersey in the striped trousers of the fool. So we see that he completes her development. She needs his supernatural presence to release her full spirituality. On a more literal level, the fool introduces balance—after all, he is an acrobat—between Gelsomina and Zampano. And he also plays Pierrot to Zampano's Harlequin, although Gelsomina is no Columbine. In this light, he represents soul versus body (Zampano), fantasy versus reality, sky versus earth. Burke allegorically calls Gelsomina and Il Matto's relation Angel versus Beast.[36]

For our context, we may most tellingly compare Gelsomina and Il Matto with Zarathustra and his rope-dancer. Just as Nietzsche's aerialist falls yet lives on in Zarathustra, so does the fool bequeath his spirit to Gelsomina. The regenerated clown survives again in Chaplin's *Limelight*. There the

34. Murray, *Fellini,* 68; Keel and Strich, *Fellini,* 54; Fellini quoted in Murray, *Fellini,* epigraph.
35. Peter Bondanella, *Italian Cinema,* 133.
36. Frank Burke, *Federico Fellini,* 44.

dying Calvero, another Christ figure, finds living posterity in Teresa. The crucial difference between these examples and Gelsomina is her own withering after the clown's death. She, unlike Teresa and Zarathustra, lacks the mental strength to assume the identity of the martyred fool. In this difference we have a clue to the ultimate meaning of the film. Instead of depicting the triumph of the new spirit (*Zarathustra*) or the eternal life of the clown (*Limelight*), Fellini gives us a parable on the power of innocence. He concretes his metaphor with artistes because he finds innocence primarily among such performers.

Of all the characters Fellini has created, this trio—and Zampano especially—stands closest to him.[37] Unlike most critics, Young perceives that the brute contains, in nuce, the other two characters. He speaks of Zampano as "a spiritually abandoned savage" who has "rejected the Clown and destroyed the Fool in himself."[38] Young suggests a sort of determinism that accords with Fellini's fable-like narration. Zampano had to encounter his opposite self, Gelsomina, who also had to confront her heavenly alter ego, Il Matto. In killing the fool that he cannot tolerate within, Zampano moves toward his epiphany of self-recognition.

Two features of Zampano's life particularly characterize the stongman. From his first performances onward, he moves in a circle. Walking around the ring of spectators, he displays both his muscles and the heavy chain that he will burst with his chest (see figure 32). In a parallel way, the story shows us how he learns to burst the circle of his animal self. Fiedler echoes the solemn, static movement of the strongman routine: for him the film renders "the tragic circle of life."[39] In another scene offstage, Zampano again follows a circular pattern. After retrieving Gelsomina in the town square, he drives the van in a wide arc around the fountain.

Second, Zampano's unique van is an emblem of the wandering life. Both mobile and enclosed, it symbolizes Zampano's independence as neatly as does Father Knie's immaculate circus wagon (chapter 4) or Mother Courage's commercial truck. Although it lacks the melodramatic density of the caravan in *The Naked Night,* this vehicle still has deeply suggestive value. "This object, both unusual and banal, . . . attains . . . the force of concrete myth," claims André Bazin.[40] The phrase "both unusual and banal" recalls what Hoffmann called Callot's *Commedia* figures: "the strangely familiar."

37. Salachas, *Fellini,* 115.
38. Vernon Young, "La Strada: Cinematic Intersections," *On Film,* 67.
39. Leslie Fiedler, *Freaks,* 298.
40. Bondanella, *Federico Fellini,* 55.

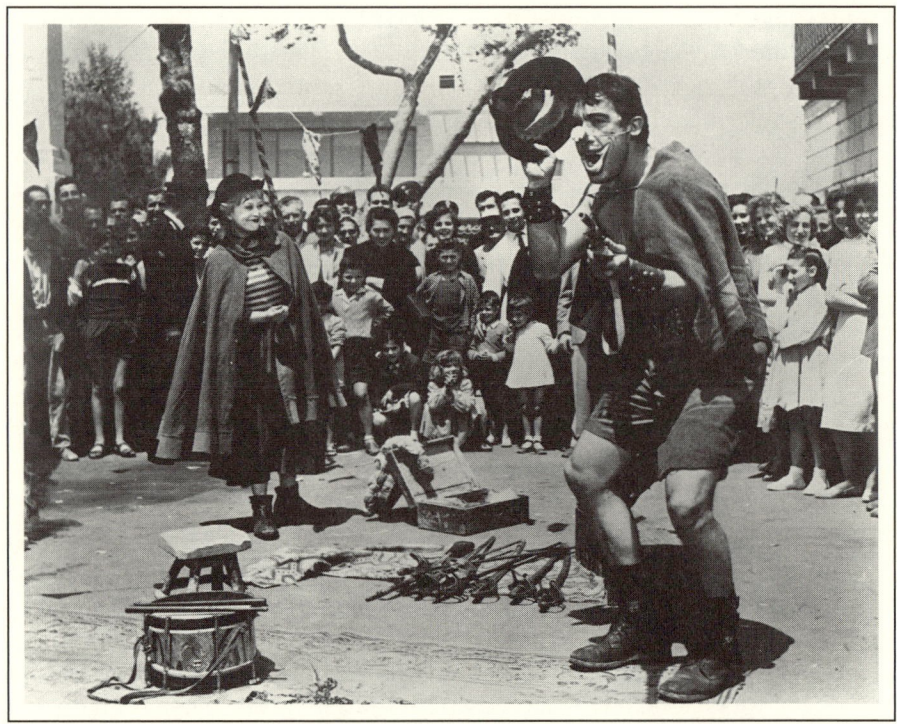

Figure 32. Federico Fellini, *La Strada,* The Circus of Zampano (1954). Courtesy of Janus Films.

Similarly, Mallarmé speaks of "the myth enclosed in all banality." Thus Zampano's van, like so much we have already seen of the circus, bespeaks something transcendental.

Not only the car's ingenious construction but also its decorations intrigue us. Mythological figures painted on its tarpaulin suggest the circus realm of fantasy. The owl and the mermaid may recall what Hugo says of Ursus' "wandering temple," "the chariot of his dreams," in *L'Homme qui Rit.* "A mythological frontispiece was useful for the traveling show."[41] Burke thinks these creatures refer to the dormant imagination of Zampano himself. I see the mermaid as an evocation of Gelsomina, his girl of the sea.

To sum up the significance of this film, we might start with the special status Fellini bestows on it. "The film I am most attached to is *La Strada.* Above all, because I feel that it is my most representative film, the one that is most autobiographical; . . . Gelsomina is, naturally, my favorite among all the characters." More specifically, Fellini says, "*La Strada* is really the com-

41. Victor Hugo, *L'Homme qui Rit,* ed. Marc Eigeldinger and Gerald Schaeffer, 1:371.

plete catalogue of my mythical world, a dangerous representation of my identity, undertaken without precautions."[42] Since he made this claim twelve years after the film appeared, we must note its importance.

Edouard De Laurot suggests Fellini's expiatory link to this material. Hence not only the affectionate portrait of his wife, Giulietta Masina as Gelsomina, explains the attachment; Fellini also works out his own redemption. He has often admitted inheriting a principal theme, the Christian striving for grace, from his teacher Rossellini. For them and other Italian Catholic directors, the need for salvation represents a general crisis of the era.[43] Here lies part of the quarrel with the so-called Marxist Neo-Realists: they cannot accept his depicted transcendence of the actual poverty of post-war Italy. In fact, this film deals movingly with just those social outcasts the Marxists think Fellini ignores. More perceptive critics see that *La Strada* combines his earlier naturalistic style with a new surrealism.

This film odyssey has a finally circular pattern. Starting and ending with the ocean, the story completes not the monotonous circle of the strongman routine but the cycle of birth, death, and rebirth. "The journey in *La Strada* is both literal and figurative; the literal journey leads from the sea back to the sea, while the figurative one leads Gelsomina from the state of childhood and innocence, through . . . knowledge, to death and a kind of apotheosis."[44]

This cyclical sense of the work compares readily to that in *The Naked Night*. There too we begin and end with the same imagery of the circus wagon on the move. And there too the characters have traveled a long psychic distance to arrive at self-knowledge. We may see both films as despairing views of the wanderers' wretched loneliness; they both document failed attempts at communication. On the other hand, both films, produced in 1953 and 1954, bespeak an existential hope. A central idea in Sartre may apply to both stories: life begins beyond despair. *La Strada* seems more tragic than *The Naked Night,* if only because no person dies in there. Only the slain bear represents a symbolic death for the child within Albert.

Fellini presents two deaths, with which we must identify emotionally. Yet his film prompts laughter, at least in its first half, while Bergman gives us hardly a smile. Perhaps the deepest kinship between the two films lies in their ultimate glimpse of redemption through suffering. To be sure, Bergman's film lacks the Catholic and supernatural dimension, for nothing in the

42. Fellini quoted in Salachas, *Fellini,* 107, and in Murray, *Fellini,* 62.
43. Mira Liehm, *Passion and Defiance: The Italian Cinema 1942 to the Present,* 153.
44. Suzanne Budgen, *Fellini,* 11.

action or characters alleviates the misery of his circus. For this reason *The Naked Night* creates more "difficult" viewing: we find nothing spiritual to uplift us, as Gelsomina does. Characteristically, even Bergman's clown act in the crisis scene shows mainly slapstick humiliation. Still, Albert and Anne have at least as much chance of renewal as Zampano does. So we may speak of fragile hope as the parting idea of both works.

The Clowns (1970)

Two related impulses gave birth to this film. First, Fellini wanted to make a documentary tribute to the old clowns he remembered from his youth. Second, he sought to integrate that filmed history into his own biography. As with most of his works, the personal element gives sharp focus to a subject that implies abstraction. In *La Strada,* Masina evokes, beyond the character of Gelsomina, some universal themes: art as magic, the conflict of nature with civilizing forces, the need to transcend ordinary life. In *The Clowns,* Fellini starts again with his own "nostalgia for innocence," but he produces something quite different from the lyric fable of *La Strada.* Instead he both laments the passing of a classic comic tradition and, paradoxically, rescues it from extinction.

This celebratory film itself immortalizes the clowns who have vanished, thus giving a "song of despair." As Penelope Gilliatt says of Beckett, style can make "a victorious retort" to material.[45] No one can witness the clown's spectacular funeral and circus regeneration closing this film and still believe the circus is dead. The spirit of the old buffoons that Fellini lovingly evokes survives in most of his films. Ultimately, instead of a documentary, *The Clowns* presents another treatment of the same themes animating *La Strada:* birth, death and rebirth.

We start with a specific memory of Fellini's childhood experience of the circus. One night, from his window above, the boy watches as a tent magically rises. The next day he sees the show, a parade of acts equally zany and grotesque. Robor, the masked strongman, endures a crushing weight; knives and cannibals' fire threaten the clowns; "Fakir Burma" descends underground, to fast forty days and forty nights. Fellini specifies the standard refrain for all such wondrous feats in a midget's parodied versions of these acts. And he repeatedly includes the audience as an active participant in the show. This midget first apes the weight-crushing and knife-throwing routines, then he races to the ringside to mimic the crowd's horror.

45. Barbara Price and Theodore Price, *Federico Fellini: An Annotated International Bibliography,* 232; Penelope Gilliatt, *Unholy Fools,* 299.

Similarly, the strongwoman Matilde, having eliminated a burly male wrestler, calls for a challenger from the audience. Such interplay between act and viewer climaxes when the ringmaster summons both boy/Fellini and camera to center ring, to admire his jar of Siamese-twin fetuses. A. J. Prats finds in this insistent volleying between ring and audience a parallel to the central dilemma posed implicitly by Fellini. Namely, how can the director objectively film the circus, which he also, subjectively, observes?

Suddenly a fanfare of trumpets heralds a fleet of clowns. Their phallic scatalogical and violent slapstick frighten the boy to the point of tears. His annoyed mother, echoing the blows in the ring, slaps him and takes him home: end of part 1. Fellini segues into the next part by telling us, in voice-over narration, why these clowns scared him. In particular, the "chalky faces," the "drunken, twisted masks," and the "atrocious jokes" reminded him of "other strange and troubled characters who roam around every country village."

Part 2: "The clowns are among us." Echoing the grotesques of the circus, the human oddities now surround the boy in daily life: Giudizio, the village idiot; the insane midget nun; the town drunk, whose Amazon wife hauls him off in a wheelbarrow. Perhaps the ruling irony of these scenes is their ambiguous link to part 1. How did the boy relate those circus buffoons to the everyday clowns in the street? Does art simply overlap life? For the mature director, the further question must arise: Is the clown a trained professional, as "ordinary" as the rest of us, or is he a true eccentric expressing himself?

Part 3 intends to answer such questions. Going in search of the old clowns of his youth, Fellini travels with his crew to Paris. There they visit film archives and interview famous old troupers. They turn clownish themselves in doing gags at the revered *Cirque d'Hiver,* lone survivor of those intimate arenas captured by Impressionist painters (see chapter 5). As visual punctuation for this largely verbal section, Fellini recreates clown acts that he hears described. Both these scenes and his conversations with circus researchers develop the polarity of two comic types: the Auguste and the white clown. These two categories overlap somewhat with our familiar *Commedia* duet of Pierrot and Harlequin, but Fellini broadens the definitions to embrace a whole psychology (see figure 33).

Four of the five clowning interludes—Jim Guillon's death, Antonet as pompous master chef, a competitive white clown fashion show, and the three Fratellinis' performances at public institutions—exemplify the two opposing kinds of clown character. In the two middle pieces, supreme white clowns exhibit their haughty, domineering nature. They exaggerate the superiority that Harlequin may have inherited from the First Slave of

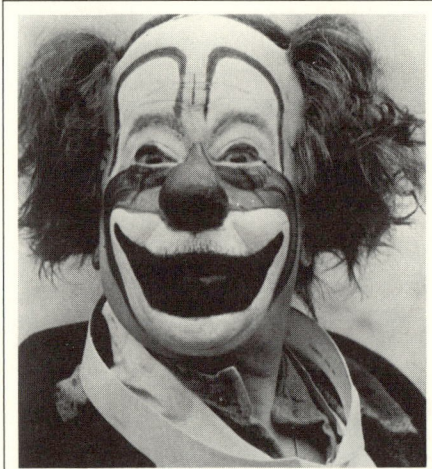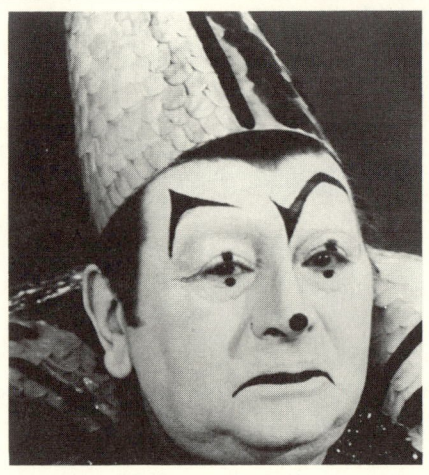

Figure 33. Federico Fellini, *The Clowns*, White Clown and Auguste (1970). Courtesy of Diogenes Verlag.

Roman comedy. Their fashion show gives a gorgeous mimed response to Fellini's question, addressed to the circus historian Tristan Rémy and a group of old clowns, about the origin of the white clowns' costumes. Accordingly, the parade echoes the utter disagreement among the experts, for the clowns also quarrel violently about who looks most handsome.

Jim Guillon, an ailing old Auguste, escapes from the hospital to see Footit and Chocolat, the adored pair of Parisian clowns drawn by Toulouse-Lautrec. The pathos of Guillon's devotion to his art emerges most palpably at the end of the vignette: the departing audience reveals the old Auguste, slumped dead but probably happy in his seat. (He may have died laughing.) Of these sequences, perhaps the tribute to the Fratellinis has the most memorable effect. We see the performance of these three zanies—one as a goofy, pig-tailed girl, the other two as butterflies cavorting on obvious wires in mid-air—in an insane asylum. The mere juxtaposing of their meticulous, crafted comedy with the dehumanized faces of the patients makes the scene unique in clown imagery. But we are particularly moved by the numb reaction of the inmates, hardly noticing yet another sign of irrationality in their mad world.

Rémy explicates the "theory" of the two clown types, which Fellini himself has developed and expanded in interviews.

The white clown stands for elegance, harmony, intelligence, lucidity, . . . Mother and Father, Schoolmaster, Artist, the Beautiful, in other words *what should be* done. . . . The Auguste is the child who dirties his pants, rebels against perfection, rolls about on the floor and puts up an endless resistance. This is the struggle between the proud cult of reason . . . and the freedom of instinct. The white clown and the Auguste are teacher and child, mother and small son, even the angel with the flaming sword and the sinner. In other words they are two psychological aspects of man: one which aims upward, the other which aims downward; two divided, separated instincts.[46]

Perhaps the concepts of superego and id suffice here, but Fellini does not acknowledge Freud. Indeed, he and some critics focus on Jung as his inspiration, at least for *8½* and *Juliet of the Spirits*. However, for Freudian readings of *The Clowns,* see Sylvie Pierre and Jean-Louis Comolli.

In any case, the dualism suggested by the white clown–Auguste scene recalls the alternation of elements already used in *La Strada*. Sea and land, day and night, comic and somber: in *The Clowns* Fellini compresses such oppositions into human character. Beyond the film, he catalogues many non-clowns in this way. "Pasolini is a white clown, Antonioni a speechless Auguste; Picasso a triumphant Auguste, brazen, without complexes, able to do anything; Einstein a dreamy Auguste, saying nothing but at the last moment . . . innocently [pulling] out of his bag the solution to the problem given by the white clown. Hitler a white clown, Mussolini an Auguste; Pope Pacelli a white clown, Pope Roncalli an Auguste; Freud a white clown, Jung an Auguste."[47]

This third section ends on a pessimistic note, for Rémy, the old clowns themselves, and even a taxi driver—voice of the people—have said that the circus is dead. "We felt disappointed. . . . Our journey had taken us nowhere. Perhaps Rémy is right. Maybe the clown really is dead." Here lies the impulse for part 4, a grandiose clown funeral.

The scene starts with a farcical eulogy for the departed clown Fischietto. Although he dies prematurely (at age two hundred), "we all mourn that he died now . . . instead of the moment he was born." We see the sobbing widow, with pillows as grotesque breasts, and the son, an ancient man with a floor-length white beard. The tears of one mourner spout a fountain of water into a bucket. Mocking death, the clowns indulge in an orgy of food and drink. Human horses draw the hearse around the ring at a frantic pace, until suddenly one beast rebels, withdrawing to sit in a chair at ringside. Complaining of overwork, he thus inspires in the English coachman a frenzy of white clown authority. "Go back to your places!" he keeps yelling.

But all the horses soon break free and start dancing together. As the many

46. Fellini in Keel and Strich, *Fellini,* 124.
47. Ibid., 130.

mourning clowns join the merriment, the whole ring erupts in a whirlwind of motion. This rebellion against death climaxes when Fischietto, whom several clowns cannot stuff into his coffin, explodes from a giant bottle of Martini aperitif. The company waltzes as the resurrected clown, high above the ring, swings through a mass of gaudy streamers, balloons, and fireworks. The scene ends as the coachman bows, and the camera winds down the hectic pace in slow motion. Fellini's voice announces: "It's over. Turn it off."

Like Rémy's pronouncing that the clown is dead at the end of part 3, the director now seems to close the film by confirming the loss of all that we have just seen. Yet the story has not ended; its visual and musical codas contradict the words that have challenged the film itself into being. After the funeral scene fades out, the lights come up on a single white clown in the ring's spotlight. He plays "Ebbtide" while the old clown Fumagalli tells Fellini of his routine. Echoing the vignette of Jim Guillon's dying at the circus, Fumagalli tells of a miraculous return from the grave.

We pretended that one of us was dead: sometimes me, sometimes Dario or Nello. The others were all crying, of course. . . . And then I'd go looking for him—looking for the dead man. I'd look round, like this, and say: "But where have you gone? Can you hear me? Even if you're dead, you're bound to be somewhere! Aren't you? A man can't just disappear! And then at the end I'd pick up my trumpet . . . (Bario picks up a trumpet). And, as if to try and cheer myself up, I'd start playing. It was as if I wanted to wave for the last time to my dead friend. . . . Like this . . . (Bario begins to play the trumpet. From high up, from some unspecified part of the big top, the sound of another trumpet answers him. Bario plays on. The other trumpet answers, slightly closer: little by little we come to see the other clown, who is youngish, with an expression of rather stupid contentment, playing the trumpet as he gradually approaches Bario, as if answering his call. Bario plays, and the other clown replies as he comes nearer. In the end, the two of them are standing in the ring, playing and walking slowly, still drawing closer together. Before they actually meet, darkness comes down on the ring, and the notes of the two trumpets die away.)[48] (See figure 34.)

In the film, Fellini changes the ending slightly. Standing together in the spotlight, the two clowns turn and slowly walk out together. The spotlight remains, yielding the image of an empty, silent circus: the same sight that greeted the boy in the beginning of the film. This empty ring leaves us with a characteristic Fellinian open ending. Indeed, it poses questions. What

48. Ibid., 128.

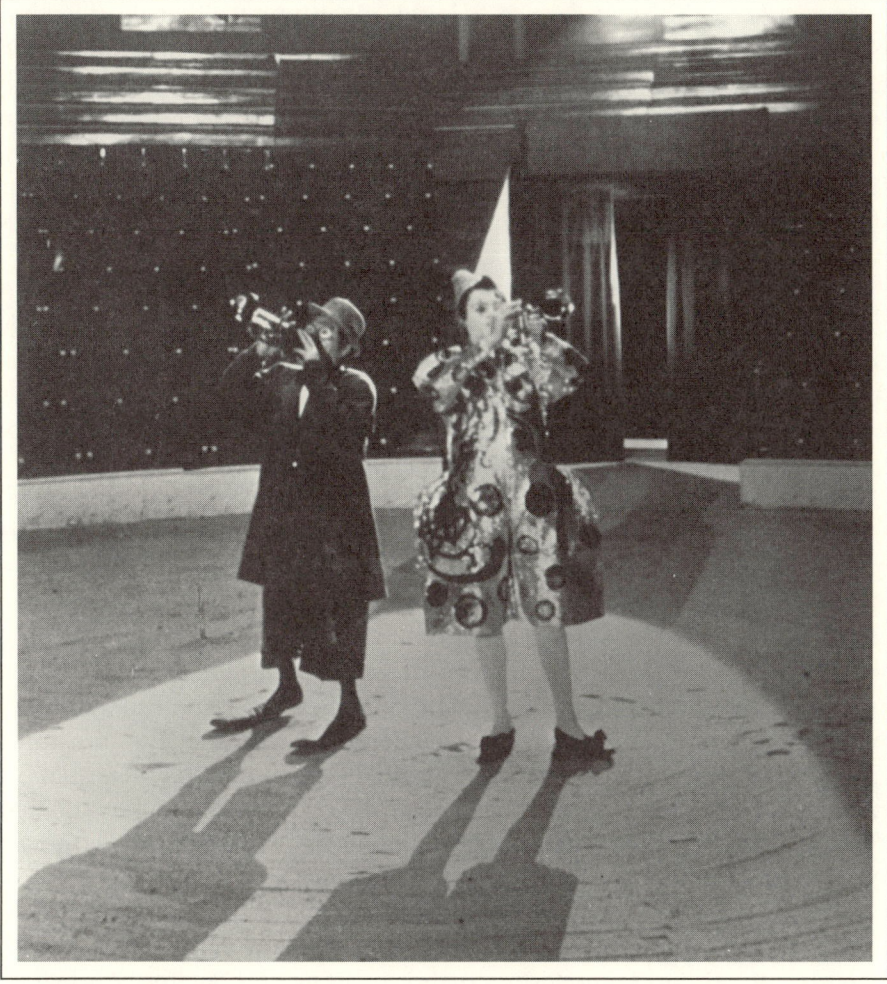

Figure 34. Federico Fellini, *The Clowns*. Courtesy of Diogenes Verlag.

does this elegiac farewell mean? Why not close, as the circus usually does, with laughter? What has really happened in this ring that spans the mind of Fellini? As usual, he lets us supply the answers.[49]

The classic interpretation of this coda, stated by Fellini himself, concerns

49. We noted another moving trumpet duet at the close of another clown drama: *Petrushka* (see chapter 6). "I wanted the dialogue for two trumpets at the end to show that [Petrushka's] ghost is still insulting the public" (Igor Stravinsky and Robert Craft, *Expositions and Developments*, 156). The echo of these two instruments in *The Clowns* probably comes from their association with circus players, especially for Fellini. Compare Gelsomina.

oneness. As with the ending of *8¹/₂,* the circle unites what the film has shown as psychic fragments. Here the union necessarily arises from the Fellinian dichotomy of the two clowns. "The two figures embody a myth which lies in the depths of each of us: the reconciliation of opposites, the unity of being."[50] The film could not end with the funeral extravaganza because there the rebellion of Auguste anarchy wins out. To integrate this vitality with white clown intellect, Fellini must bring back the rational partner and unite the two.

Several critics underline the relevance of this process for the director. In this light, the coda appears as a final synthesis that Fellini achieves for his own imagination. Accordingly, his retreat from verbal analysis liberates the last scene for its triumph of purely aesthetic harmony. Here Fellini "goes beyond words, beyond everything that has mediated, dissociated or abstracted his creative powers earlier in the film."[51]

For our context, this funeral and its redeeming coda have broad significance. On the specific level, they fully contradict what Gilliatt and others say of the film: Fellini shows us only that "he adores clowns."[52] On the deeper level of the clown canon in literature and the other arts, the ending is yet another variation on that immortal theme we have often confronted: the end of the clown. Think of Baudelaire's old *saltimbanque,* in whom the poet sees his own death; of the "heroic death" of his mime Fancioulle; of Nietzsche's rope-dancer, who must fall in order to survive in Zarathustra; of Daumier's moribund street folk; of Petrushka, the martyred "pitre châtié"; of Picasso's and Rilke's tumblers, already marked for death; of the crucified Frost; of Gelsomina, whose innocence dooms her. For these artists, the circus lives not under the sign of laughter but of death.

And so we have come full circle. We began with Baudelaire, whose old clown of 1861 announces this extended comedy of dying. More than a century later, Fellini reiterates the pathos of aging and decline. And again the author, often declaring himself a man of the ring, projects his anxiety onto the subject. Both "Le Vieux Saltimbanque" and *The Clowns* confer a double posterity on the clown. First, his spirit thrives in the artist who creates him; second, the work itself bestows immortality. Despite the perennial fears of the artist, his inner clown does not die.

Finally, we must ask what this arch-theme, the death of the clown, signifies. Who *is* this creature, and why does his passing matter to so many artists? Fellini defines the buffoons first as "ambassadors of my calling." In

50. Quoted in Keel and Strich, *Fellini,* 124.
51. A. J. Prats, "An Art of Joy, an Art of Life"; Frank Burke, "The Three-Phase Process and the White Clown-Auguste Relation in Fellini's *The Clowns,*" 136.
52. Gilliatt, *Fools,* 17.

their "apparition from my childhood" they gave "a prophecy, the annunciation made to Federico."[53] We note the air of sanctity surrounding both the clowns and the blessed director. On a broader level, Fellini sees in the clown pure irrationality, the instinct for anarchy that makes him a subversive figure. Fellini implies that such a force must survive in the healthy person. (Compare Lescek Kolakowski, *Marxism and Beyond:* society needs both priest and jester.) The disappearance of this element connotes a dearth of laughter, folly, in short: imagination. (Compare Tiepolo's *Punchinello* series.)

Relating *The Clowns* to works already discussed as circus tributes to fading traditions, we find in them all a new kind of creation born of nostalgia. *The Clowns* has drawn much critical attention, both positive and negative, for its unique form. John Russell Taylor calls it "an essay film"; others cite its combination of flashback, voice-over narration, documentary, and interview. *Petrushka* arose as a memorial to the *balagani* of Benois' fairground memories; from his nostalgia grew the complex mythic amalgam of the Christian-pagan poet-puppet. Picasso's *The Three Musicians,* another tribute to the enthusiasms of youth, also creates something new in the Cubist collage. And here too the artist muses on his own death.

Les Enfants du Paradis commemorates the *Funambules* and Deburau specifically, more generally the spirit of the French theater still vivid under Nazi occupation. In its novel merging of historical figures with fiction, this film relates closely to *The Clowns. Limelight,* Chaplin's last film, belongs in this group only because it too pays homage to a clown heritage: the English music hall. It does not offer anything formally new, but it compares readily with *The Clowns.* Chaplin does on the individual level what Fellini does for all clowns. *Limelight* compresses a lament for the old shows into the lonely Calvero, whose genius passes to Teresa, his surrogate daughter.

BERGMAN, FELLINI, AND THE CIRCUS

In conclusion, it seems useful to ask why circus figures loom so large in the human landscape of our two directors. For both these superbly visual artists, an obvious affinity lies in the primacy of mime and gesture at the circus. Both men usually excel at telling a story nonverbally; Fellini explains that dialogue does not matter for him.[54] In fact, his actors often say whatever occurs to them during filming, and he tapes the voices later. Here lies one reason for the scarcity of Fellini scripts. Bergman writes masterful screen-

53. Fellini in Keel and Strich, *Fellini,* 119, 121.
54. Ibid., 109.

plays, but his films often diverge from the printed text. Therefore the circus player, whose art consists largely in gestural expression, makes a natural aesthetic focus.

Second, both directors see themselves as brothers to the artiste. Fellini claims he would have become a circus impresario if he had not discovered film instead. *8½* ends with Guido, whip in hand, impelling his actors around a circus ring. We have amply documented the projection of Fellini's own "nostalgia for innocence" onto various clowns. Fellini also identifies with the danger of the circus. Its violence, its constant threat of death, remind him that the Roman circus displayed "blood on the sawdust."[55] Both he and Bergman translate the player's daring into the director's risk of failure. Of course, no one ever died from bad reviews or lack of funding, but these directors, like many artists, see their art as death-defying.

Bergman identifies mainly with the negative side of the wandering life: loneliness, the agony of outcasts. *The Seventh Seal* "corrects" the despairing view of *The Naked Night,* but there too the player suffers from a jeering, even menacing, public. Bergman expresses no nostalgia for the circus whose miseries he ruthlessly displays; but in *Fanny and Alexander* he shows the need of the bourgeois child for escape into a realm of fantasy. In this vein, both he and Fellini see themselves as child-artists.

Finally, both directors find something mysterious, even mystical, in the popular player. Frost, the dwarves in *The Silence,* Alexander's puppets, Gelsomina and Il Matto, the immortal clowns all introduce something beyond the human into ordinary life. They signify what the ballet dancer Jorge Donn calls the meaning of dance: "going beyond."

55. Ibid., 121.

9 CONCLUSIONS
The Spectacle as Metaphor and Myth

> The passionate desire to conclude is one of humanity's most pernicious and sterile manias.
> —**Flaubert**

> Don't tell them everything you know.
> —**Norbert Fuerst**

Trying to cap these seven chapters may invite exhaustion. Indeed, the reader must feel almost as relieved as I do to have finished this histrionic tour. However, a few summary words may help to integrate the seeming fragments into a whole. Like Fellini, I want to close with a complete circus ring. So let us start with the circle, which I have discussed in only a few works: "Un Fantôme de Nuées," *Les Saltimbanques,* "Auf der Galerie," *La Strada,* and *The Clowns.* Having surveyed the circus literature, we may now specify the metaphoric meaning of the actual shape of the show. I see three main areas of significance for the circle: holiness, morality, and freedom.

Various disciplines consider the circle the most basic and most ancient form. Children's first drawings usually emphasize circular shapes. Naturally, since he sees roundness everywhere, primitive man infers a divine imprint on stones, trees, the sun—even his own body. Ethnologists tell us of non-Western rites that envision the sacred in circles. Ring dances, probably imitating the sun, characterize worship in many African religions. According to Black Elk, "Everything an Indian does is in a circle, and that is because the power of the world always works in circles, and everything tries to be round."[1] We attribute "magic circles" to Agrippa, Cleopatra, and Solomon. Ever since Euclid (300 B.C.), mathematicians have represented infinity with spherical models. The circle connoted eternal, divine perfection long before Renaissance painters, echoing Dante, depicted paradise in rings of clouds. Georges Poulet starts his study of changing views of this unchanging shape with the old definition of God as "a sphere whose center is everywhere, whose circumference is nowhere."[2]

---

1. Quoted in J. Neihart, *Black Elk Speaks,* 198.
2. Georges Poulet, *Les Métamorphoses du Cercle,* 3.

Of course, the Romans had practical reasons for using arenas: wide visibility, freedom of movement, maximum audience capacity. Yet beyond this manipulation of space lie the roots of performance in ritual worship. However secular the intent of the Circus Maximus, a parade of colonial booty, it soon evolved into official homage to the divine ruler. A similar event occurs in modern Vienna. The architects of the *Ringstrasse* (1860) ostensibly designed a broad avenue for mobilizing the army, but they also created a spectacular stage for displaying the Emperor. Hence it should not surprise us that modern artists persist in seeing something beyond mere entertainment at the circus. Among our examples, Thomas Mann best evokes the circular stage as ritual in *Krull*. Contrasting the circus with the bullfight, he suggests the mythic dimension of both arenas.

In chapter 4 we saw the spectacle idealized as a moral example of wholeness, health. From Gautier through Wedekind, artists perceive in the circular form a corrective to modern fragmentation. They hope to merge prevailing dichotomies by the example of those "primitive" unities of mind and body, person and group, that they admire in the ring. However, Kafka cannot satisfy his "hunger for wholeness"; his circles evoke endless, passive futility. And Schnier, Böll's mime, can only collect moments. For him, both life and art consist of fragments. Accordingly, his story describes not a circle but a fall. Among contemporary artists—except for the painters—only Fellini uses the circle as a metaphor for wholeness. The closing of *8 1/2* in a vast arena, with Guido first directing and then joining the parade, symbolizes the psychic integration of Fellini himself.

For other artists, the circle signifies freedom. Fernand Léger asks: "Since the earth is round, how can you play square? . . . A circus is a rotation of volumes, people, animals and objects. The awkward, dry angle is not at home there. . . . Go to the circus! You leave behind your rectangles, your geometrical windows, and enter the land of circles in action. . . . The ring is freedom; it has neither beginning nor end."[3] Léger implies the lack of bounds that makes the circus especially dynamic. Other graphic artists—Gross, Chagall, Calder—find inspiration for their own work in the constant motion of the show.

Not only such unfettered movement but also other kinds of freedom appear in the ring. Aerialists suspend laws of gravity and probability; freaks defy our sense of size; and clowns destroy all expectations of decent behavior. In short, the spectacle subverts the civilized order: a sure appeal to the artist. On a less literal level, the wandering artiste's personal freedom attracts the creator. Wedekind, Zuckmayer, and Meyerhold lived briefly

---

3. Léger in Werner Schmalenbach, *Fernand Léger,* 154.

among showmen; Warhol simply adopted the deviant manners associated with the buffoon.

Yet these various liberties do not come unalloyed. Indeed, the counter-weight of death pulls strongly enough to form a dialectic with freedom in our circus canon. Perhaps the liberation these artists feel gains power from its very fragility. Because death lurks everywhere—in the trapeze, in the wild animals, in the hazardous life—one senses an extraordinary tension. This drama magnifies risk to an exhilarating degree.

Of all the themes touched by this study, two stand out as especially potent in our time: the canonizing of the clown-artist and the rejection of speech. Once artists identified with the highest ideals, they soon became god-like in their own eyes. As we saw with Jakob, the poor fiddler, playing "dear God" rather than Bach or Mozart meant playing himself. Put in the terms of Paul Robinson, the nineteenth century focused on the conflict of art and society, whereas the twentieth turns inward to the psyche.

To my mind, Freud plays only a minor role in this process, as the trend toward narcissism began long before he wrote. By now the performer himself appears god-like in the eyes of his audience. The cult of fame has so inflated such celebrities as Picasso and Chaplin that their private lives get as much attention as their work—in some circles, more. Often the artist himself manipulates the publicity. The wrappings by Christo (whose pseudonym captures his sense of self) would have little effect without the avid press he attracts.

And what can we conclude about silence, the mode of protest taken up by artists as diverse as Chekhov, Hofmannsthal, Beckett, and Syberberg? The post-Romantics had two reasons, aesthetic and political, for loving the *Funambules*. There they found both the liberation of fantasy and a needed link to the public. We have seen how their use of mime transformed the visual symbol from Baudelaire onward; by now muteness represents a model for all the arts.

At a moment in history loud with meanings and information, the choice of silence is a brave refusal to accept the world. It is not surprising, then, that sculpture has become "minimal," that directors speak of a "poor theater," "nonverbal language," and playwrights like Beckett and Pinter have reduced the conventional stage to a sparse and quiet dramatic moment. . . . Most modern art has eliminated the verbal correlative from its canvases. Often numbered rather than titled, they deal with abstract visual properties (surface, edge) which cannot be discussed. The viewer is denied not only his language but the one-point perspective of realism which puts him and the artist on the same comforting wavelength. The minimal object interrupts space, but does not fill it with noisy (and limited) explanations. Like silence, it is a specific fact, only appreciated on its own terms.[4]

Such minimal artists express a strong sense of that "indecency of speech" first noted by Hofmannsthal and Beckett. The less art says, the less it can lie. This urge to purify their statement recalls the old arguments about illusion, discussed in chapter 4. In Nietzsche's camp, art transcends, even redeems, life; Thomas Mann's camp condemns art as at least amoral. The latter group has a weakening factional aspect, for they see the causes of the problem variously. Despite his ambivalence, Baudelaire deplores the conditions imposed on art by a decadent public; Kafka decries neither art nor audience but the artist. Compare "La Muse Vénale," with its truly suffering poet, to the fraudulent hunger-artist. Kafka, like D. H. Lawrence, says to trust not the teller but the tale. Perhaps Wolf Lepenies best sums up the truth-telling of art in his "fool-function" for all literature. His idea of the fool as *Eulenspiegel*, gleefully unmasking hypocrisy, sharply contrasts with the utterly sober (and hence quite foolish) view of minimalists that art must not go beyond reality. In short, instead of healthily mocking life, art merely feeds on it.

Now for a summary evaluation of the spectacle. What does this study of artists' perceptions of it ultimately show? First let us consider the classic view, that famous root of "the anti-theatrical prejudice" in Juvenal. His tenth satire condemns popular culture as palliative: "panem et circenses."

> Ever since the time their votes were a drug on the market,
> The people don't give a damn anymore. Once they bestowed
> Legions, the symbols of power, all things, but now they are
>   cautious,
> Playing it safe, and now there are only two things they ask
>   for,
> Bread and the games.[5]

Attacking Roman indifference to the fate of the Empire, Juvenal labels the circus a mass tranquilizer. Modern interpreters have extended this demeaning notion of the popular stage along ideological lines. In the editorial "The Breadline and the Movies," Thorstein Veblen sees moviegoers as paying to be kept "under laughing gas."[6] And a more blatantly political bent emerges

4. John Lahr, *Up Against the Fourth Wall*, 54, 57.
5. Juvenal, *Satires*, trans. Rolfe Humphries, 124.
6. Quoted in Patrick Brantlinger, *Bread and Circuses*, 23.

from both the Left and the Right, all of whom oppose manipulation of the masses through entertainment.

Does the show offer mere pablum, then? Many of our post-Romantics favor instead the lies of illusion or the truth of the jester. My own view will probably frustrate the reader seeking one clear answer. For I must conclude that the entertainer gives us all three of these needed nourishments. First, we cannot dismiss "mere" entertainment as blithely as the satiric Juvenal does. "High" art draws on "low" amusement as metaphor and myth. Unlike the stern Roman moralist, Mallarmé perceives in the cheap show "the myth contained in all banality." Here we have seen such vulgar mysteries in the fragile distinction between man and beast, the fool as both Christian and pagan scapegoat, and the Romantic death of the clown.

As for truth versus lies, the artiste represents both: the double face of art. Picasso calls art a lie that reveals the truth. This concept extends Starobinski's "l'envol et la chute" (flight and fall) to embrace all the dualities of the spectacle. The circus especially joins the earthy and the ideal, the absurd and the sublime. Here we see both transcendent beauty and the misery of real life that it masks. Our archtext for such contradiction, Kafka's "Auf der Galerie," reveals both aspects of the show as permanent, even inevitable. This dichotomy between brutishness and grandeur typifies the post-Romantic artiste too. He both panders to vulgar taste and touches the deepest emotions evoked by art. But, as Baudelaire asks of two clashing images of one woman, "Which is the real one?" As long as artists find alter egos on the popular stage, the question remains open.

BIBLIOGRAPHY

Abbott, Berenice. *The World of Atget.* New York: Horizon, 1964.

Agel, Genevieve. *Les Chemins de Fellini.* Paris: Editions du Cerf, 1956.

Aichinger, Ilse. *Der Gefesselte.* Frankfurt: Fischer, 1958.

Anderson, Eleanor. "Max Beckmann's *Carnival* Triptych." *Art Journal* 29 (1965): 218–25.

Apollinaire, Guillaume. *Calligrammes.* Ed. and trans. Anne Hyde Greet and S. I. Lockerbie. Berkeley: University of California Press, 1980.

———. *Oeuvres Poétiques.* Ed. Marcel Adéma and Michel Décaudin. Paris: Gallimard, 1959.

———. *Selected Writings of Guillaume Apollinaire.* Ed. Roger Shattuck. New York: New Directions, 1971.

Arnott, Peter. *Plays Without People.* Bloomington: Indiana University Press, 1964.

Asaf'eyev, Boris. *A Book about Stravinsky.* Trans. Richard French. Ann Arbor: UMI Research Press, 1982.

Asker, D.B.D. "Vixens and Values: The Modern Metamorphoses of Garnett and Vercors." *Canadian Review of Comparative Literature* 10 (1983): 182–91.

Auerbach, Nina. *Woman and the Demon.* Cambridge: Harvard University Press, 1982.

The Authentic Librettos of the Italian Operas. New York: Crown, 1939.

Axsom, Richard. *"Parade": Cubism as Theater.* New York: Garland, 1979.

Bachelard, Gaston. *L'Air et les Songes.* Paris: Corti, 1959.

Baird, Bill. *The Art of the Puppet.* New York: Macmillan, 1965.

Bakhtin, Mikhail. *Problems in Dostoevski's Poetics.* Trans. R. W. Rotsel. Ann Arbor: Ardis, 1973.

———. *Rabelais and his World.* Trans. Helene Iswolsky. Cambridge: MIT Press, 1968.

Balakian, Anna. *The Symbolist Movement.* New York: Random House, l967.

Baldick, Robert, ed. and trans. *Pages from the Goncourts' Journal.* London: Oxford University Press, 1962.

Balzer, Bernd, ed. *Heinrich Böll: Werke, Interviews I (1965–1978).* Köln: Kiepenheuer und Witsch, 1979.

Bance, Alan. *The German Novel, 1945–1960.* Stuttgart: Heinz, 1980.

Banville, Théodore de. *Oeuvres,* vol. 1. Geneva: Slatkine Reprints, 1972.

———. *Pauvres Saltimbanques.* Paris: Michel Lévy, 1853.

Barish, Jonas. *The Antitheatrical Prejudice.* Berkeley: University of California Press, 1982.

Barr, Alfred. *Picasso: Fifty Years of his Art.* New York: MOMA, 1946.

Barrère, Jean-Bertrand. "Victor Hugo's Interest in the Grotesque in his Poetry and Drawings." In *French Nineteenth Century Painting and Literature,* ed. Ulrich Finke, 258–79. Manchester: Manchester University Press, 1972.

Baryshnikov, Mikhail. *Baryshnikov at Work*. Ed. Charles Angell France. New York: Knopf, 1978.

Bassermann, Dieter. *Der Späte Rilke*. München: Leibniz, 1947.

Bates, Scott. *Guillaume Apollinaire*. New York: Twayne, 1967.

Batterby, Kenneth. *Rilke and France*. London: Oxford University Press, 1966.

Baudelaire, Charles. *Oeuvres Complètes*. Ed. Claude Pichois. 2 vols. Paris: Gallimard, 1975.

————. *Petits Poèmes en Prose*. Ed. Robert Kopp. 2 vols. Paris: Corti, 1969.

————. *Petits Poèmes en Prose*. Ed. Henri Lemaitre. Paris: Garnier, 1962.

————. *Writings on Art and Artists*. Trans. and ed. P. E. Charvet. Cambridge: Cambridge University Press, 1981.

Beaumont, Cyril. *The History of Harlequin*. New York: Blom, 1967.

Beck, Evelyn. "A Feminist Critique of Böll's *Ansichten eines Clowns*." *University of Dayton Review* 12, no. 2 (1976): 19–24.

Benjamin, Walter. *Charles Baudelaire, Lyric Poet in the Era of High Capitalism*. Ed. and trans. Harry Zohn. London: NLB, 1973.

————. *Das Paris des Second Empire*. Ed. Rosemarie Heise. Berlin: Aufbau, 1971.

————. *Schriften*, vol. 1, pt. 2. Frankfurt: Suhrkamp, 1974.

Bennett, Virginia. "Russian *pagliacci*: Symbols of Profaned Love in Blok's *The Puppet Show*." In *Drama and Symbolism*, ed. James Redmond, 141–78. Cambridge: Cambridge University Press, 1982.

Benois, Alexandre. *Reminiscences of the Russian Ballet*. Trans. Mary Britnieva. London: Putnam, 1945.

Bentley, Eric. *The Life of the Drama*. New York: Atheneum, 1967.

Bergman, Ingmar. *Fanny and Alexander*. Trans. Alan Blair. New York: Pantheon, 1982.

————. *A Film Trilogy*. Trans. Paul Austin. New York: Orion, 1967.

————. *The Seventh Seal*. Trans. Lars Malmström. New York: Simon and Schuster, 1960.

Bergom-Larsson, Maria. *Film in Sweden: Ingmar Bergman and Society*. Trans. Barrie Selman. London: Tantivy, 1978.

Bergson, Henri. *Laughter*. In *Comedy*, ed. Wylie Sypher, 61–190. New York: Doubleday Anchor, 1956.

Bermel, Albert. *Farce*. New York: Simon and Schuster, 1982.

Bernard, Suzanne. *La Poème en Prose de Baudelaire à nos Jours*. Paris: Nizet, 1959.

Bernheimer, Charles. *Flaubert and Kafka*. New Haven: Yale University Press, 1982.

Bersani, Leo. *Baudelaire and Freud*. Berkeley: University of California Press, 1977.

————. *The Death of Stéphane Mallarmé*. Cambridge: Cambridge University Press, 1981.

Best, Alan. *Frank Wedekind*. London: Wolff, 1975.

Beutner, Barbara. *Musik und Einsamkeit bei Grillparzer, Kafka, del Castillo*. Köln: Ellenberg, 1975.

Binder, Hartmut. *Motiv und Gestaltung bei Franz Kafka*. Bonn: Bouvier, 1966.

————, ed. *Kafka-Handbuch in Zwei Bänden*. Stuttgart: Kröner, 1979.

Björkman, Stig, et al., eds. *Bergman on Bergman*. Trans. Paul Austin. London: Secker and Warburg, 1973.

Block, Haskell. *Mallarmé and the Symbolist Drama*. Detroit: Wayne State University Press, 1963.

Blöcker, Günther. "Der Letzte Mensch." In *Der Schriftsteller Heinrich Böll*, ed. Werner Lengning, 72–75. München: dtv, 1969.

Blume, Bernhard. *Existenz und Dichtung*. Ed. Egon Schwarz. Frankfurt: Insel, 1980.

Blunt, Anthony, and Phoebe Pool. *Picasso: The Formative Years*. New York: Graphic Society, 1962.

Boeschenstein, Hermann. *Deutsche Gefühlskultur*. 2 vols. Bern: Haupt, 1966.

Bohn, Willard. "Circular Poem-Paintings by Apollinaire and Carrà." *Comparative Literature* 31, no. 3 (1979): 246–71.

Böll, Heinrich. *Ansichten eines Clowns*. Köln: Kiepenheuer und Witsch, 1963.

Böll, Viktor, and Renate Matthei, eds. *Querschnitte*. Köln: Kiepenheuer und Witsch, 1958.

Bollnow, O. F. *Mensch und Raum*. Stuttgart: Kohlhammer, 1963.

Bondanella, Peter. *Italian Cinema*. New York: Ungar, 1983.

———, ed. *Federico Fellini, Essays in Criticism*. Oxford: Oxford University Press, 1978.

Bonitzer, Pierre. "Portrait de l'Artiste en Mythomane." *Cahiers du Cinéma* 346 (April 1983): 4–7.

Book-Senninger, Claude. *Théophile Gautier*. Paris: Nizet, 1972.

Bouissac, Paul. *Circus and Culture*. Bloomington: Indiana University Press, 1976.

Bovenschen, Sylvia. *Die Imaginierte Weiblichkeit*. Frankfurt: Suhrkamp, 1979.

Brantlinger, Patrick. *Bread and Circuses*. Ithaca: Cornell University Press, 1983.

Braun, Edward. *The Theater of Meyerhold*. New York: Drama Book Specialists, 1979.

———, ed. *Meyerhold on Theater*. New York: Hill and Wang, 1969.

Breunig, L. C., ed. *Apollinaire on Art*. Trans. Susan Suleiman. London: Thames and Hudson, 1972.

———, ed. *Chroniques d'Art*. Paris: Gallimard, 1960.

Brinkmann, Richard. *Wirklichkeit und Illusion*. Tübingen: Niemeyer, 1957.

Brombert, Victor. *Victor Hugo and the Visionary Novel*. Cambridge: Harvard University Press, 1984.

Brown, Frederick. *An Impersonation of Angels*. New York: Viking, 1968.

———. *Theater and Revolution: The Culture of the French Stage*. New York: Viking, 1980.

Brown, Marilyn. *Gypsies and Other Bohemians*. Ann Arbor: UMI Research Press, 1985.

Browning, Robert. "Language and the Fall from Grace in Grillparzer's *Der arme Spielmann*." *Seminar* 12, no. 4 (1976): 215–35.

Bryson, Norman. *Word and Image*. Cambridge: Cambridge University Press, 1981.

Buckberrough, Sherry. *Robert Delaunay: The Discovery of Simultaneity*. Ann Arbor: UMI Research Press, 1982.

Buckle, Richard. *Diaghilev*. New York: Atheneum, 1979.

———. *In the Wake of Diaghilev*. New York: Holt Reinhart, 1982.

———. *Nijinsky*. New York: Avon, 1975.

Budgen, Suzanne. *Fellini*. London: British Film Institute, 1966.

Burke, Frank. *Federico Fellini.* Boston: Twayne, 1984.

————. "The Three-Phase Process and the White Clown-Auguste Relation in Fellini's *The Clowns.*" *Film Studies Annual* 1 (1977): 124–41.

Burns, Edward, ed. *Gertrude Stein on Picasso.* New York: Liveright, 1970.

Byrom, Michael. *Punch and Judy: Its Origins and Evolution.* Aberdeen, Shiva, 1972.

Canetti, Elias. *Crowds and Power.* Trans. Carol Stewart. New York: Viking, 1963.

Caputi, Anthony. *Buffo!* Detroit: Wayne State University Press, 1978.

Carmean, E. A. *Picasso: Les Saltimbanques.* Washington: National Gallery, 1981.

Carter, Alan. *John Osborne.* Edinburgh: Oliver and Boyd, 1969.

Caws, Mary Ann, and Hermine Riffaterre. *The Prose-Poem in France: Theory and Practice.* New York: Columbia University Press, 1983.

Chambers, Ross. "The Artist as Performing Dog." *Comparative Literature* 23 (1971): 312–24.

————. "L'Art Sublime du Comédien." *Saggi e Ricerche di Letteratura Francese,* n.s. 11 (1971): 192–260.

————. "Frôler ceux qui rôdent: Le Paradoxe du Saltimbanque." *Revue des Sciences Humaines* 44, no. 167 (1977): 347–63.

Champsaur, Félicien. *Lulu, Pantomime en un acte.* Paris: Dentu, 1888.

Chan, Victor. "Watteau's *Les Comédiens Italiens* Once More." *Revue des Arts Canadiens* 5, no. 2 (1978–1979): 107–12.

Charney, Maurice. *Comedy High and Low.* New York: Oxford University Press, 1978.

————, ed. *Comedy: New Perspectives.* New York: New York Literary Forum, 1978.

Chartier, Armand. *Barbey d'Aurevilly.* Boston: Twayne, 1977.

Chevalier, Jean-Claude. *Alcools d'Apollinaire.* Paris: Minard, 1970.

Clark, T. J. *The Absolute Bourgeois.* London: Thames and Hudson, 1973.

Cocteau, Jean. "Le Numéro Barbette." *Nouvelle Revue Française* 18:257–63.

————. *Oeuvres Complètes.* 11 vols. Geneva: Margeurat, 1946–1951.

Cohn, Robert. *Toward the Poems of Mallarmé.* Berkeley: University of California Press, 1965.

Cole, Toby, ed. *Actors on Acting.* New York: Crown, 1970.

Comolli, Jean-Louis. "La Mort-Clown." *La Quinzaine Littéraire* 115 (April 1971): 28.

Cooper, Douglas. *Picasso Theatre.* New York: Harry Abrams, 1968.

Cope, Jackson. *Dramaturgy of the Demonic.* Baltimore: Johns Hopkins University Press, 1984.

Cornford, Francis. *The Origin of Attic Comedy.* New York: Doubleday, 1961.

Costello, Donald. *Fellini's Road.* Notre Dame: University of Notre Dame Press, 1983.

Cowie, Peter. *Ingmar Bergman.* New York: Scribners, 1983.

Cox, Harvey. *The Feast of Fools.* Cambridge: Harvard University Press, 1969.

Craig, Edward Gordon. "The Actor and the Über-Marionette." *The Mask* 1, no. 2 (April 1908): 3–15.

————, ed. *The Mask.* 1908–1929. Reissue. New York: Blom, 1966.

Crist, Judith. "Bergman's Rosetta Stone." *Saturday Review* (May–June 1983), 41–42.

Croce, Arlene. "Inside the Ballets Russes." *The New Yorker* (12 May 1980), 157–58.

Crosland, Margaret, ed. *Cocteau's World*. New York: Dodd Mead, 1972.

Cunliffe, Gordon. *Günter Grass*. New York: Twayne, 1969.

Daix, Pierre. *Picasso*. New York: Praeger, 1965.

Daniel, Howard. *The Commedia dell'Arte and Jacques Callot*. Sydney: Wentworth, 1965.

Daunicht, Richard. "Heinrich von Kleists Aufsatz als Satire betrachtet." *Euphorion* 67 (1973): 306–22.

Davies, Margaret. "Poetry as the Reconciliation of Opposites." In *Order and Adventure in Post-Romantic Poetry*, ed. E. M. Beaumont et al., 176–91. Oxford: Blackwell, 1973.

Davis, R. G. *The San Francisco Mime Theater*. Palo Alto: Ramparts, 1975.

Dédéyan, Charles. *Rilke et la France*. 4 vols. Paris: Sedes, 1963.

Deinert, Herbert. "Franz Kafka: Ein Hungerkünstler." *Wirkendes Wort* 12 (1963): 78–87.

De Laurot, Edouard. "La Strada, a Poem on Saintly Folly." *Film Culture* 2, no. 7 (1956): 11–14.

Delphendahl, Renate. *Grillparzer: Lüge und Wahrheit in Wort und Bild*. Bern: Haupt, 1975.

Denommé, Robert. *Leconte de Lisle*. New York: Twayne, 1976.

Dervin, Daniel. *Through a Freudian Lens Deeply: A Psychoanalysis of Cinema*. London: Analytic, 1985.

De Sugar, L. *Baudelaire and R.M. Rilke*. Paris: Nouvelles Editions Latines, 1954.

Diller, Edward. *A Mythic Journey*. Lexington: University of Kentucky Press, 1974.

Disher, M. Willson. *Clowns and Pantomime*. London: Constable, 1923.

Donner, Jorn. *The Films of Ingmar Bergman*. Trans. Holger Lundbergh. New York: Dover, 1972.

Dowson, Ernest. *The Letters of Ernest Dowson*. Ed. Desmond Flower and Henry Maas. London: Cassell, 1967.

———. *The Poetry of Ernest Dowson*. Ed. Desmond Flower. Cranbury, N.J.: Associated University Presses, 1970.

Duchartre, Pierre. *The Italian Comedians*. Trans. R. T. Weaver. New York: Dover, 1966.

Durzak, Manfred. *Der deutsche Roman der Gegenwart*. Stuttgart: Kohlhammer, 1973.

———. "Über das Marionettentheater von Heinrich von Kleist." *Jahrbuch des Freien Deutschen Hochstifts*, 308–29. Tübingen: Niemeyer, 1969.

Eagleton, Terry. *Walter Benjamin: Toward a Revolutionary Criticism*. London: Verso, 1981.

Edel, Edmund. "Zum Problem des Künstlers bei Franz Kafka." *Deutschunterricht* 15, no. 3 (1963): 9–31.

Eichendorff, Joseph von. *Werke in einem Band*. Ed. Wolfdietrich Rasch. München: Hanser, 1966.

Eitner, Lorenz. "The Open Window and the Storm-Tossed Boat." *Art Bulletin* 37 (1955): 281–90.

Elderfield, John. *European Master Paintings from Swiss Collections*. New York: MOMA, 1976.

Ellis, John. *Narration in the German Novelle*. London: Cambridge University Press, 1974.

Emrich, Wilhelm. *Franz Kafka, A Critical Study.* Trans. Sheema Buehne. New York: Ungar, 1968.

————. *Protest und Verheissung.* Frankfurt: Athenäum, 1960.

Esslin, Martin. *The Theater of the Absurd.* New York: Anchor, 1961.

Evans, G. L. "John Osborne and Naturalism." In *Modern British Dramatists: New Perspectives,* ed. John Russell Brown, 13–24. Englewood Cliffs, N.J.: Prentice-Hall, 1984.

Evans, Stuart. *The Function of the Fool.* London: Hutchinson, 1977.

Evréinov, Nikolai. *Life as Theater: Five Modern Plays.* Ed. and trans. Christopher Collins. Ann Arbor: Ardis, 1973.

Faber, Marion. *Angels of Daring.* Stuttgart: Heinz, 1979.

Fairlie, Alison. *Leconte de Lisle: Poems on the Barbarian Races.* Cambridge: Cambridge University Press, 1947.

Fava, Claudio, and Aldo Vigano. *The Films of Federico Fellini.* Secaucus, N.J.: Citadel, 1985.

Fedotov, G. P. *The Russian Religious Mind.* Cambridge: Harvard University Press, 1960.

Fehl, Philip. "A Farewell to Jokes: The Last Capricci of Domenico Tiepolo and the Tradition of Irony in Painting." *Critical Inquiry* 5, no. 4 (1979): 761–91.

Ferlinghetti, Lawrence. *A Coney Island of the Mind.* New York: New Directions, 1958.

Fetscher, Iring. "Menschlichkeit und Humor: Ansichten eines Clowns." In *In Sachen Böll,* ed. Marcel Reich-Ranicki, 275–84. Köln: Kiepenhauer und Witsch, 1968.

Fiedler, Leslie. *Freaks.* New York: Simon and Schuster, 1978.

Fingerhut, Karl-Heinz. *Die Funktion der Tierfiguren im Werke Franz Kafkas.* Bonn: Bouvier, 1969.

Finke, Ulrich, ed. *French Nineteenth Century Painting and Literature.* Manchester: Manchester University Press, 1972.

Fischer, Friedhelm. *Max Beckmann, Symbol und Weltbild.* München: Fink, 1972.

Flaubert, Gustave. *Correspondance.* Ed. Jean Bruneau. 2 vols. Paris: Gallimard, 1973–1980.

Flores, Angel. *Franz Kafka Today.* New York: Gordian, 1977.

Fokine, Mikhail. *Memoirs of a Russian Ballet Master.* Trans. Vitale Fokine. London: Constable, 1961.

Foulkes, A. P. "Auf der Galerie: Some Remarks Concerning Kafka's Concept and Portrayal of Reality." *Seminar* 2, no. 2 (1966): 34–42.

————. *The Reluctant Pessimist.* The Hague: Mouton, 1967.

Fowlie, Wallace. *The Age of Surrealism.* New York: Swallow, 1950.

————. *Jean Cocteau.* Bloomington: Indiana University Press, 1966.

————. *Love in Literature.* Bloomington: Indiana University Press, 1965.

————. *Mallarmé.* Chicago: University of Chicago Press, 1953.

————. "Swann and Hamlet: A Note on the Contemporary Hero." *Partisan Review* 9 (1942): 195–202.

Franklin, Ursula. *An Anatomy of Poesis.* Chapel Hill: North Carolina Studies in Romance Languages, 1976.

————. "The Saltimbanque in the Prose Poems of Baudelaire, Mallarmé and Rilke." *Comparative Literature Studies* 19, no. 3 (1982): 335–50.

Frazer, J. G. *The Illustrated Golden Bough.* New York: Doubleday, 1978.

Frenzel, Elisabeth. *Stoffe der Weltliteratur.* 5th ed. Stuttgart: Kröner, 1981.

Fried, Michael. *Absorption and Theatricality.* Princeton: Princeton University Press, 1980.

———. "Manet's Sources." *Artforum* 7 (1969): 28–79.

Friedrichsmeyer, Erhard. "Aspects of Myth, Parody and Obscenity in Günter Grass' *Blechtrommel* and *Katz und Maus.*" *Germanic Review* 40 (1965): 240–50.

Fritz, Horst. "Dämonisierung des Erotischen in der Literatur des Fin-de-Siècle." In *Fin-de-Siècle,* ed. Roger Bauer, 442–64. Frankfurt: Klostermann, 1977.

Frye, Norbert. *Fools of Time: Studies in Shakespearean Tragedy.* Toronto: University of Toronto Press, 1967.

Fuchs, Maximilian. *Théodore de Banville.* Geneva: Slatkine Reprints, 1972.

Fuerst, Norbert. *Die Offenen Geheimtüren Franz Kafkas.* Heidelberg: Rothe, 1956.

Füglister, Robert. "Baudelaire et le Thème des Bohémiens." *Études Baudelairiennes* 2 (1971): 99–143.

———. "Gaukler und Akrobat als Alter Ego des Künstlers." *Neue Zürcher Zeitung,* 15 Oktober 1967.

Furst, Lilian. *Contours of European Romanticism.* Lincoln: University of Nebraska Press, 1979.

———. *Romanticism.* London: Methuen, 1976.

———. *Romanticism in Perspective.* London: Macmillan, 1979.

Gandelman, Claude. "Max Beckmann's Triptychs and the Simultaneous Stage of the Twenties." In *Max Beckmann: The Triptychs,* ed. Nicholas Serota, 20–32. London: Whitechapel Art Gallery, 1980.

Gautier, Théophile. *Histoire de l'Art Dramatique en France depuis 25 Ans,* vol. 2. Paris: Hetzel, 1859.

———. *Histoire du Romantisme.* Paris: Charpentier, 1877.

———. *Souvenirs de Théâtre, de l'Art et de Critique.* Paris: Charpentier, 1883.

Gay, Peter. *Weimar Culture.* New York: Harper and Row, 1968.

Gedo, Mary. *Picasso: Art as Autobiography.* Chicago: University of Chicago Press, 1980.

Gelley, Alexander. "Art and Reality in *Die Blechtrommel.*" *Forum for Modern Language Studies* 2 (1967): 115–25.

George, Stefan. *Werke.* Düsseldorf: Kupper, 1968.

Gilliatt, Penelope. "Fellini Himself." *Unholy Fools,* 15–20. New York: Viking, 1973.

Giraud, Albert. *Héros et Pierrots.* Paris: Fischbacher, 1898.

Giraud, Raymond. *The Unheroic Hero in the Novels of Stendhal, Balzac and Flaubert.* New Brunswick: Rutgers University Press, 1957.

Gittleman, Sol. *Frank Wedekind.* New York: Twayne, 1969.

Glauert, Barbara, ed. *Carl Zuckmayer: Das Bühnenwerk im Spiegel der Kritik.* Frankfurt: Fischer, 1977.

Goethe, Johann Wolfgang. *Werke,* vols. 1, 3, 6, 7, 11, 12. Ed. Erich Trunz. München: Beck, 1981.

Goncourt, Edmond de. *Les Frères Zemganno.* Paris: Charpentier, n.d.

Goncourt, Edmond de, and Jules Goncourt. *Journal,* vol. 3. Ed. Robert Ricatte. Monaco: Imprimerie Nationale, 1956.

Graham, Ilse. *Heinrich von Kleist.* Berlin: DeGruyter, 1977.

Graña, Cesar. *Bohemian versus Bourgeois.* New York: Basic Books, 1964.

Grant, Richard. *The Goncourt Brothers.* New York: Twayne, 1972.

———. *The Perilous Quest.* Durham: Duke University Press, 1968.

———. *Théophile Gautier.* Boston: Twayne, 1975.

Grass, Günter. *Die Blechtrommel.* Berlin: Luchterhand, 1962.

———. "Vom mangelnden Selbstvertrauen schreibender Hofnarren unter Berücksichtigung nicht vorhandener Höfe." *Akzente* 13 (1966): 194–99.

Grasselli, Margaret, and Pierre Rosenberg. *Watteau.* Chicago: University of Chicago Press, 1984.

Greiner, Ulrich. *Der Tod des Nachsommers.* München: Hanser, 1979.

Grillparzer, Franz. *Sämtliche Werke,* vols. 3, 4. München: Hanser, 1965.

Guenther, Werner. *Weltinnenraum.* Bern: Haupt, 1943.

Guérard, Albert. *Art for Art's Sake.* New York: Lothrop Lee, 1936.

Guthke, Karl. *Modern Tragicomedy.* New York: Random House, 1966.

Hamburger, Michael. "Art as Second Nature: The Figures of the Actor and the Dancer in Hofmannsthal." In *Romantic Mythologies,* ed. Ian Fletcher, 225–42. London: Routledge and Kegan Paul, 1967.

Hamm, Charles, ed. *Petrushka: An Authoritative Score of the Original Version.* New York: Norton, 1967.

Hannemann, Bruno. "Zum Selbstverständnis des Dichters vor 1848: 'Der arme Spielmann.'" *Monatshefte* 69, no. 4 (1977): 337–90.

Hanson, Anne. *Manet and the Modern Tradition.* New Haven: Yale University Press, 1977.

Harms, Alvin. *Théodore de Banville.* New York: Twayne, 1983.

Harper, Paula. *Daumier's Clowns.* New York: Garland, 1981.

Harpham, Geoffrey. *On the Grotesque.* Princeton: Princeton University Press, 1982.

Harris, Edward. "Liberation of Flesh from Stone: Pygmalion in *Erdgeist*." *Germanic Review* 52 (1977): 44–56.

Haskell, Arnold. *Ballet Russe.* London: Weidenfeld and Nicolson, 1968.

———. *Diaghilev.* New York: Simon and Schuster, 1935.

Haskell, Francis. "The Sad Clown: Some Notes on a Nineteenth Century Myth." In *French Nineteenth Century Painting and Literature,* ed. Ulrich Finke, 2–16. Manchester: Manchester University Press, 1972.

Hassan, Ihab. *The Dismemberment of Orpheus: Toward a Post-Modern Literature.* Madison: University of Wisconsin Press, 1982.

———. *The Literature of Silence: Henry Miller and Samuel Beckett.* New York: Knopf, 1967.

Hatfield, Henry. "Günter Grass: The Artist as Satirist." In *The Contemporary Novel in German,* ed. Robert Heitner, 115–34. Austin: University of Texas Press, 1967.

———. "Mario and the Magician." In *The Stature of Thomas Mann,* ed. Charles Neider, 168–73. New York: New Directions, 1947.

Hauptmann, Gerhart. *Till Eulenspiegel.* Leipzig: Internationale Buchkunst, 1927.

Hedges, William. "Classics Revisited: Reaching for the Moon." *Film Quarterly* 12, no. 4 (1959): 27–34.

Heilman, Robert. "Variations on Picareque." In *Thomas Mann: A Collection of Critical Essays*, ed. Henry Hatfield, 133–54. Englewood Cliffs, N.J.: Prentice Hall, 1964.

Heller, Erich. *Thomas Mann, The Ironic German*. South Bend: Regnery, 1979.

Hellman, Hanna. "Über das Marionettentheater." In *Kleists Aufsatz über das Marionettentheater*, ed. Helmut Sembdner, 17–31. Berlin: Schmidt, 1967.

Henel, Ingeborg. "Ein Hungerkünstler." *DVLG* 38 (1964): 230–47.

Hermsdorf, Klaus. "Kunst und Künstler bei Franz Kafka." *Weimarer Beiträge* 10, no. 3 (1964): 404–12.

Heselhaus, Clemens. "Kafkas Erzählformen." *DVLG* 26 (1952): 353–76.

Hinchliffe, Arnold. *John Osborne*. Boston: Twayne, 1984.

Hoffmann, E.T.A. *Werke*, vol. 1. Ed. Herbert Kraft. Frankfurt: Insel, 1967.

Hofmannsthal, Hugo von. *Gesammelte Werke: Gedichte und Lyrische Dramen, Lustspiele 2, Prosa 1, 2, 3*. Ed. Herbert Steiner. Frankfurt: Fischer, 1946–1952.

Hollingdale, R. J. *Nietzsche, The Man and his Philosophy*. London: Routledge and Kegan Paul, 1965.

Holthusen, Hans Egon. *Der Unbehauste Mensch*. München: Piper, 1951.

Hoover, Marjorie. *Meyerhold: The Art of Conscious Theater*. Amherst: University of Massachusetts Press, 1974.

Houston, Beverle. "The Manifestation of Self in *The Silence*." *Film and Dreams*. Ed. Vlada Petric. New York: Redgrave, 1981.

Houston, John Porter. *Victor Hugo*. New York: Twayne, 1974.

Howarth, W. D. *Sublime and Grotesque: A Study of French Romantic Drama*. London: Harrap, 1975.

Hugo, Victor. *L'Homme qui Rit*. Ed. Marc Eigeldinger and Gerald Schaeffer. 2 vols. Paris: Flammarion, 1982.

———. *Théâtre Complet*, vol. 1. Ed. J.-J. Thierry and Josette Mélèze. Paris: Gallimard, 1963.

Huizinga, Johan. *Homo Ludens*. Boston: Beacon, 1955.

Ingold, Felix. *Literatur und Aviatik*. Frankfurt: Suhrkamp, 1980.

Irmer, Hans-Jochen. *Der Theaterdichter Frank Wedekind*. Berlin: Henschel, 1979.

Ivask, Ivar. Introduction to *The Poor Fiddler*, by Franz Grillparzer. New York: Ungar, 1967.

Jaeger, Hans. "Die Entstehung der Fünften Duineser Elegie." *Dichtung und Volkstum* 40 (1939): 213–36.

Janouch, Gustav. *Gespräche mit Kafka*. Frankfurt: Fischer, 1968.

Jendrowiak, Silke. *Günter Grass und die "Hybris" des Kleinbürgers*. Heidelberg: Winter, 1979.

Jensen, Dean. *Center Ring: The Artist*. Milwaukee: Art Museum, 1981.

John, Beynon. "Actor as Puppet: Variations on a Nineteenth-Century Theatrical Idea." In *Bernhardt and the Theater of her Time*, ed. Eric Salmon, 243–68. Westport: Greenwood, 1984.

Jonas, Ilsedore. "The Shattered Image: Rilke's Reaction to the Artists of Expressionism and to Some Works of Picasso." *Michigan Germanic Studies* 2 (1976): 121–32.

Jones, G. William, ed. *Talking with Ingmar Bergman*. Dallas: SMU Press, 1983.

Jones, Louisa. *Sad Clowns and Pale Pierrots*. Lexington: French Forum, 1984.

Jones, Robert. "Frank Wedekind: Circus Fan." *Monatshefte* 61, no. 2 (1969): 139–56.

Jürgensen, Manfred, ed. *Handke: Ansätze, Analyse, Anmerkungen.* Bern: Francke, 1979.

Juvenal. *Satires.* Trans. Rolfe Humphries. Bloomington: Indiana University Press, 1958.

Kael, Pauline. "Wrapping it Up." *The New Yorker* 59 (13 June 1983): 117–22.

Kafka, Franz. *Hochzeitsvorbereitungen auf dem Lande.* New York: Schocken, 1953.

———. *Sämtliche Erzählungen.* Ed. Paul Raabe. Frankfurt: Fischer, 1970.

Kahan, Gerald. *Jacques Callot, Artist of the Theater.* Athens: University of Georgia Press, 1976.

Kaiser, Walter. *Praisers of Folly: Erasmus, Rabelais, Shakespeare.* Cambridge: Harvard University Press, 1976.

Kaminsky, Stuart, ed. *Ingmar Bergman, Essays in Criticism.* London: Oxford University Press, 1975.

Kanfer, Stefan. "Pierrots and Augustos." *Time* (21 June 1971), 84.

Karsavina, Tamara. "Benois the Magician." *Ballet Annual* 15 (1961): 76–78.

Kauffmann, Stanley. "First Farewell." *The New Republic* (27 June 1983), 22–24.

Kaufman, Walter. *Nietzsche: Philosopher, Antichrist.* Princeton: Princeton University Press, 1968.

Kayser, Wolfgang. *The Grotesque in Art and Literature.* Trans. Ulrich Weisstein. Bloomington: Indiana University Press, 1963.

Keel, Anna, and Christian Strich. *Fellini on Fellini.* New York: Dell, 1976.

Keppler, C. F. *The Literature of the Second Self.* Tucson: Arizona University Press, 1972.

Kermode, Frank. "Poet and Dancer before Diaghilev." *Puzzles and Epiphanies.* London: Routledge and Kegan Paul, 1962.

Kern, Edith. *The Absolute Comic.* New York: Columbia University Press, 1980.

———. "The Modern Hero: Phoenix or Ashes?" In *The Hero in Literature,* ed. Victor Brombert, 265–77. New York: Fawcett, 1969.

Kessler, Charles. *Max Beckmann's Triptychs.* Cambridge: Harvard University Press, 1970.

Ketcham, Charles. *Federico Fellini.* New York: Paulist Press, 1986.

Kienlechner, Sabina. *Negativität der Erkenntnis im Werk Franz Kafkas.* Tübingen: Niemeyer, 1982.

Kierkegaard, Sören. *Repetition.* Ed. Walter Lowrie. Princeton: Princeton University Press, 1941.

King, Russell. "The Poet as Clown: Variations on a Theme." *Orbis Litterarum* 33 (1978): 238–52.

Kippenberg, Katharina. *Rainer Maria Rilkes Deutung des Daseins.* München: Kosel, 1953.

Kleist, Heinrich von. *Aufsätze und Essays.* Ed. Walter Müller-Seidel. Darmstadt: Wissenschaftliche Buchgesellschaft, 1973.

———. *Werke in einem Band.* Ed. Helmut Sembdner. München: Hanser, 1966.

Knapp, Bettina. *Maurice Maeterlinck.* Boston: Twayne, 1975.

Kobel, Erwin. *Hugo von Hofmannsthal.* Berlin: DeGruyter, 1970.

Kobs, Jürgen. *Kafka*. Bad Homburg: Athenäum, 1970.

Kolakowski, Lescek. *Marxism and Beyond*. London: Pall Mall, l969.

Koopmann, Helmut. "Der Faschismus des Kleinbürgers und was daraus wurde." In *Gegenwartsliteratur und Drittes Reich*, ed. Hans Wagener, 163–82. Stuttgart: Reclam, 1977.

Kott, Jan. *The Theater of Essence*. Evanston, Ill.: Northwestern University Press, 1984.

Kramer-Lauff, Dietgard. *Tanz und Tänzerisches in Rilkes Lyrik*. München: Fink, 1969.

Krasovskaya, Vera. *Nijinsky*. Trans. John Bowlt. New York: Schirmer, 1979.

Krotkoff, Hertha. "Über den Rahmen in Franz Grillparzer's Novelle 'Der arme Spielmann.'" *Modern Language Notes* 85 (1970): 345–66.

Kuhn, Reinhard. *Corruption in Paradise*. Hanover: New England University Presses, 1982.

Kutscher, Arthur. *Frank Wedekind*. München: List, 1964.

Kuzmin, Mikhail. *Selected Poetry and Prose*. Ed. and trans. Michael Green. Ann Arbor: Ardis, 1980.

Lackner, Stefan. *Max Beckmann: Die Neun Triptychen*. Berlin: Safari, 1965.

Ladendorf, Heinz. "Kafka und die Kunstgeschichte." *Wallraf-Richartz Jahrbuch* 23 (1961): 293–326.

Laforgue, Jules. *Poésies Complètes*. Ed. Pascal Pia. Paris: Gallimard, 1979.

Lahr, John. *Up Against the Fourth Wall*. New York: Grove, 1970.

Larkin, Oliver. *Daumier, Man of his Time*. Boston: Beacon, 1966.

Lea, Kathleen. *Italian Popular Comedy*. Oxford: Clarendon, 1934.

Leconte de Lisle. *Oeuvres*, vol. 2. Ed. Edgar Pich. Paris: Corti, 1966.

Lehmann, A. G. "Pierrot and Fin-de-Siècle." In *Romantic Mythologies*, ed. Ian Fletcher, 209–24. London: Routledge and Kegan Paul, 1967.

Leiris, Michel. *Manhood*. Trans. Richard Howard. London: Cape, 1968.

————. *L'Age d'Homme*. Paris: Gallimard, 1946.

Leonard, Irene. *Günter Grass*. Edinburgh: Oliver and Boyd, 1974.

Lepenies, Wolf. *Melancholie und Gesellschaft*. Frankfurt: Suhrkamp, 1972.

Lesko, Diane. *James Ensor*. Princeton: Princeton University Press, 1985.

Levin, Harry. "From Priam to Birotteau." *Yale French Studies* 6 (1950): 75–82.

————. "Thematics and Criticism." In *The Disciplines of Criticism*, ed. Peter Demetz et al., 125–45. New Haven: Yale University Press, 1968.

Leyreloup, Henri. "Baudelaire: Portrait du Poète en Saltimbanque." *Revue du Pacifique* 2 (1976): 33–41.

Liehm, Mira. *Passion and Defiance: The Italian Cinema 1942 to the Present*. Berkeley: University of California Press, 1984.

Lifar, Serge. *Diaghilev*. New York: Putnam, 1940.

Lipman, Jean. *Calder's Circus*. New York: Dutton, 1972.

Livingston, Paisley. *Ingmar Bergman and the Rituals of Art*. Ithaca: Cornell University Press, 1982.

Lockspeiser, Edward. *Music and Painting*. London: Cassell, 1973.

Loeffler, Peter. *Hanswurst*. Basel: Birkhaeuser, 1984.

Longaker, Mark. *Ernest Dowson*. London: Oxford University Press, 1944.

Lorenz, Dagmar. "Wedekind und die emanzipierte Frau: Eine Studie über Frauen und Sozialismus im Werke Frank Wedekinds." *Seminar* 12 (1976): 38–56.

Löwith, Karl. *From Hegel to Nietzsche.* Trans. David Green. New York: Holt Rinehart, 1964.

Luke, F. D. "Nietzsche and the Imagery of Height." In *Nietzsche: Imagery and Thought,* ed. Malcolm Pasley, 104–22. London: Methuen, 1978.

Lukens, Nancy. *Büchner's Valerio and the Theatrical Fool.* Stuttgart: Heinz, 1977.

McClelland, D. C. "The Harlequin Complex." In *The Study of Lives,* ed. R. W. White, 94–119. New York: Prentice Hall, 1963.

McClure, Michael. *Josephine: The Mouse-Singer.* New York: New Directions, 1980.

McCullagh, Janice. "The Tightrope Walker: An Expressionist Image." *Art Bulletin* 66, no. 4 (1984): 633–45.

Mackworth, Cecily. *Guillaume Apollinaire and the Cubist Life.* London: Murray, 1961.

MacLean, Hector. "The King and the Fool in Wedekind's *König Nicolo.*" *Seminar* 5 (1969): 21–35.

———. "Wedekind's *Der Marquis von Keith.*" *Germanic Review* 43, no. 3 (1968): 163–87.

Madden, David. *Harlequin's Stick, Charlie's Cane.* Bowling Green: Popular Press, 1975.

Majut, Rudolf. *Lebensbühne und Marionette.* Berlin: Ebering, 1931.

Makarova, Natalia. *A Dance Autobiography.* New York: Knopf, 1979.

Mallarmé, Stéphane. *Correspondance,* vol. 1. Ed. Henri Mondor. Paris Gallimard, 1959.

———. *Oeuvres Complètes.* Ed. Henri Mondor. Paris: Gallimard, 1945.

Malraux, André. *Picasso's Masks.* Trans. Jacques Guicharnaud. New York: Holt Rinehart, 1976.

———. *Voices of Silence.* Trans. Stuart Gilbert. Princeton: Princeton University Press, 1978.

Mann, Otto. *Der Dandy.* Heidelberg: Rothe, 1962.

Mann, Thomas. *Betrachtungen eines Unpolitischen.* Frankfurt: Fischer, 1918.

———. *Briefe.* Ed. Erika Mann. Frankfurt: Fischer, 1961.

———. *Gesammelte Werke,* vols. 1, 8, 9. Berlin: Aufbau, 1965.

———. *Letters, 1889–1955.* Ed. Richard Winston and Clara Winston. New York: Knopf, 1971.

Marshall, Herbert. *A Pictorial History of Russian Theater.* New York: Crown, 1977.

Martin, Marianne. "The Ballet *Parade:* A Dialogue between Cubism and the Future." *Art Quarterly,* n.s. 1 (1978): 85–111.

Martin-Méry, Gilberte, ed. *Les Arts du Théâtre de Watteau à Fragonard.* Bordeaux: Galerie des Beaux-Arts, 1980.

Mason, Ann. *The Skeptical Muse: A Study of Günter Grass' Conception of the Artist.* Bern: Lang, 1974.

Mason, Eudo. *Lebenshaltung und Symbolik bei Rainer Maria Rilke.* Weimar: Böhlaus Nachfolger, 1939.

———. *Rainer Maria Rilke, Sein Leben und Werk.* Göttingen: Vandenhoeck und Ruprecht, 1964.

Massine, Léonide. *My Life in Ballet.* London: Macmillan, 1968.

Mast, Gerald. *The Comic Mind.* Indianapolis: Bobbs Merrill, 1973.

Mauner, George. *Manet, Peintre-Philosophe*. University Park: Penn State University Press, 1975.

Mauron, Charles. *Le Dernier Baudelaire*. Paris: Corti, 1966.

Mauser, Wolfgang. "Bild und Gebärde in der Sprache Hofmannsthals." *Sitzungsberichte der Oesterreichischen Akademie der Wissenschaften*, 5–78. Wien: Böhlaus Nachfolger, 1961.

Mayer, Hans. *Das Geschehen und das Schweigen*. Frankfurt: Suhrkamp, 1969.

———. "Köln und Clown." In *In Sachen Böll*, ed. Marcel Reich-Ranicki, 21–26. Köln: Kiepenhauer und Witsch, 1968.

———. *Outsiders*. Trans. Dennis Sweet. Cambridge: MIT Press, 1982.

———. *Steppenwolf and Everyman*. Trans. Jack Zipes. New York: Crowell, 1971.

Melchinger, Christa. *Illusion und Wirklichkeit im dramatischen Werk Arthur Schnitzlers*. Heidelberg: Winter, 1968.

Mendel, Werner, ed. *A Celebration of Laughter*. Los Angeles: Mara Books, 1970.

Meyer, Herman. *Der Sonderling in der deutschen Dichtung*. München: Hanser, 1963.

———. "Die Verwandlung des Sichtbaren." *Zarte Empirie*, 287–336. Stuttgart: Metzler, 1963.

Michaelson, L. W. "Kafka's Hunger-Artist and Baudelaire's Old Clown." *Studies in Shorter Fiction* 5, no. 3 (1967): 293.

Miles, David. "Kafka's Hapless Pilgrims and Grass' Scurrilous Dwarves." *Monatshefte* 65 (1973): 341–50.

Miller, Henry. *The Smile at the Foot of the Ladder*. New York: Duell, Sloan and Pierce, 1948.

Moody, C. "Meyerhold and the Commedia dell'Arte." *Modern Language Review* 73 (1978): 859–69.

Mosley, Philip. *Ingmar Bergman: The Cinema as Mistress:* London: Marion Boyars, 1981.

Mouton, Janice. "Gnomes, Fairytale Heroes and Oskar Matzerath." *Germanic Review* 56 (1981): 28–33.

Mühlher, Robert. Introduction to *Nachtstücke*, by E.T.A. Hoffman. Hamburg: Rowohlt, 1964.

———. *Oesterreichische Dichter seit Grillparzer*. Wien: Braumuller, 1973.

———. "Der Poetenmantel." In *Eichendorff Heute*, ed. Paul Stöcklein, 180–203. Darmstadt: Wissenschaftliche Buchgesellschaft, 1966.

Müller, Joachim. *Franz Grillparzer*. Stuttgart: Metzler, 1966.

Munari, Bruno. *The Discovery of the Circle*. New York: Wittenborn, 1966.

Murray, Edward. *Fellini the Artist*. New York: Ungar, 1985.

Murray, Marian. *Circus: From Rome to Ringling*. Westport: Greenwood, 1973.

Musset, Alfred de. *Théâtre Complet*. Ed. Maurice Allem. Paris: Gallimard, 1958.

Nabokov, Vladimir. *Look at the Harlequins* New York: McGraw Hill, 1974.

Navarri, Roger. "Apollinaire: Poète du Déracinement." *Europe*, nos. 451–52 (1966): 133–41.

Neider, Charles. "The Artist as Bourgeois." In *The Stature of Thomas Mann*, ed. Charles Neider, 330–57. New York: New Directions, 1947.

———. "Two Notes on Kafka." *Rocky Mountain Review* 10, no. 2 (1946): 90–95.

Neihart, J. *Black Elk Speaks*. Lincoln: University of Nebraska Press, 1961.

Nemec, Friedrich. *Kafka-Kritik*. München: Fink, 1981.

Neumann, Gerhard. "Identifikation in der Gesellschaft." In *Kafka-Handbuch in Zwei Bänden,* ed. Hartmut Binder, 2:320–35. Stuttgart: Kröner, 1979.

Neumeister, Sebastian. *Der Dichter als Dandy.* München: Fink, 1973.

Newman-Gordon, Pauline *Le Rire en Pleurs: Corbière, Laforgue, Apollinaire.* Paris: Debresse, 1964.

Nicolai, Ralf. "Die Marionette als Interpretationsansatz zu Bölls *Ansichten eines Clowns.*" *University of Dayton Review* 12, no. 2 (1976): 25–32.

Nicoll, Allardyce. *Masks, Mimes and Miracles.* New York: Cooper Square, 1931.

———. *The World of Harlequin.* Cambridge: Cambridge University Press, 1976.

Nietzsche, Friedrich. *Der Fall Wagner.* Vol. 8 of *Nietzsches Werke.* 16 vols. Stuttgart: Kröner, 1903.

———. *Werke: Also Sprach Zarathustra, Die Fröhliche Wissenschaft, Geburt der Tragödie, Jenseits von Gut und Böse, Morgenröte.* Ed. Alfred Baeumler. Stuttgart: Kröner, 1953–1964.

Nijinsky, Romola, ed. *The Diary of Vaslav Nijinsky.* Berkeley: University of California Press, 1968.

Niklaus, Thelma. *Harlequin Phoenix.* London: Bodley Head, 1956.

Noble, Jeremy. "Igor Stravinsky." *The New Groves Dictionary of Music and Musicians.* London: Macmillan, 1980.

Nochlin, Linda. "Watteau: Some Questions of Interpretation." *Art in America* (January 1985), 68–87.

Ortmayer, Roger. "Fellini's Film Journey." In *Three European Directors,* ed. James Wall, 67–107. Grand Rapids: Eerdmans, 1973.

Osborne, John. *The Entertainer.* London: Faber, 1957.

Oxenhandler, Neal. *Scandal and Parade: The Theater of Jean Cocteau.* New Brunswick: Rutgers University Press, 1957.

Panofsky, Dora. "Gilles or Pierrot?" *Gazette des Beaux-Arts* 29 (1952): 319–40.

Pascal, Roy. *Kafka's Narrators.* Cambridge: Cambridge University Press, 1982.

Paulsen, Wolfgang. *Eichendorff und sein Taugenichts.* Bern: Francke, 1976.

———. "Der Gute Bürger Jakob." *Colloquia Germanica* 3 (1968): 272–98.

Pearce, Richard. *Stages of the Clown.* Carbondale: Southern Illinois University Press, 1970.

Penrose, Roland. *Picasso: His Life and Work.* New York: Harper and Row, 1973.

Perloff, Marjorie. *The Aesthetics of Indeterminacy.* Princeton: Princeton University Press, 1981.

Petrouchka: Scènes burlesques en quatre tableaux. (Piano Score, four hands.) Berlin: Editions Russes de Musique, 1911.

Philippi, Klaus Peter. *Reflexion und Wirklichkeit.* Tübingen: Niemeyer, 1966.

Pierre, Sylvie. "L'Homme aux Clowns." *Cahiers du Cinema* 229 (May-June 1971): 48–51.

Pilon, Edmond. *Paul et Victor Margeuritte.* Paris: Sansot, 1905.

Politzer, Heinz. *Franz Grillparzer, oder das Abgründige Biedermeier.* Wien: Fritz Molden, 1972.

———. *Franz Grillparzer's Der arme Spielmann.* Stuttgart: Metzler, 1967.

———. *Franz Kafka der Künstler.* Frankfurt: Fischer, 1965.

———. *Franz Kafka: Parable and Paradox.* Ithaca: Cornell University Press, 1962.

———. "Die Verwandlung des armen Spielmanns." *Jahrbuch der Grillparzer Gesellschaft* 3, Folge (1965): 55–64.

Pongs, Hermann. *Franz Kafka, Dichter des Labyrinths.* Heidelberg: Rothe, 1960.

Posner, Donald. *Antoine Watteau*. Ithaca: Cornell University Press, 1984.

———. "Jacques Callot and the Dances called Sfessania." *Art Bulletin* 59, no. 2 (1977): 203–16.

Poulet, Georges. *Les Métamorphoses du Cercle*. Paris: Plon, 1961.

Prats, A. J. "An Art of Joy, an Art of Life." *Film Studies Annual* 1 (1977): 143–60.

Praz, Mario. *The Romantic Agony*. New York: Oxford University Press, 1970.

Prévert, Jacques. *Children of Paradise*. Trans. Dinah Brooke. New York: Simon and Schuster, 1968.

Price, Barbara, and Theodore Price. *Federico Fellini: An Annotated International Bibliography*. Metuchen: Scarecrow, 1978.

Promies, Wolfgang. *Die Bürger und der Narr, oder das Risiko der Phantasie*. München: Hanser, 1966.

Pyman, Avril. *The Life of Alexander Blok*. New York: Oxford University Press, 1980.

Rajec, Elisabeth. *Namen und ihre Bedeutungen im Werke Franz Kafkas*. Bern: Peter Lang, 1977.

Rasch, Wolfdietrich. "Das Schicksal des Propheten." In *Viermal Wedekind*, ed. Karl Pestalozzi and Martin Stern, 60–73. Stuttgart: Klett, 1979.

———. "Tanz als Lebenssymbol im Drama um 1900." *Zur Deutschen Literatur seit der Jahrhundertwende*. Stuttgart: Metzler, 1967.

Ratcliff, Carter. "Odd Men Out." *Art in America* (Summer 1981), 110–12.

Raymond, Marcel. *De Baudelaire au Surrealisme*. Paris: Corti, 1947.

Reddick, John. *The Danzig Trilogy of Günter Grass*. London: Secker and Warburg, 1975.

Reeve, F. D. *Alexander Blok: Between Image and Idea*. New York: Columbia, 1962.

———, ed. *An Anthology of Russian Plays*, vol. 2. New York: Vintage, 1963.

Reff, Theodore. "Harlequins, Saltimbanques, Clowns and Fools." *Artforum* 10 (1971): 31–43.

———. "Manet's Sources." *Artforum* 8 (1969): 40–48.

———. "Picasso's *Three Musicians*: Maskers, Artists and Friends." *Art in America* (December 1980), 124–42.

———. "Themes of Love and Death in Picasso's Early Work." In *Picasso in Retrospect*, ed. Roland Penrose and John Golding, 11–47. New York: Praeger, 1973.

Rémy, Tristan. *Jean-Gaspard Deburau*. Paris: L'Arche, 1954.

Renaud, Philippe. "Ondes, ou les Métamorphoses de la Musique." *Apollinaire et la Musique*, 21–32. Stavelot: Les Amis de G. Apollinaire, 1967.

Richardson, Joanna. *Théophile Gautier, his Life and Times*. New York: Coward McCann, 1959.

Riggan, William. *Picaros, Madmen, Naifs and Clowns*. Norman: University of Oklahoma Press, 1981.

Rigoletto. Opera in Four Acts. Libretto by Francesco Piave. Trans. Ruth Martin and Thomas Martin. New York: Schirmer, 1957.

Rilke, Rainer Maria. *Sämtliche Werke*. Ed. Ernst Zinn. 6 vols. Frankfurt: Insel, 1966.

———. *Werke in drei Bänden*. Ed. Ernst Zinn. 3 vols. Frankfurt: Insel, 1966.

Rimbaud, Arthur. *Oeuvres*. Ed. Paterne Berrichon. Paris: Mercure, 1942.

Ritter, Naomi. "Apollinaire and Rilke: The Saltimbanque as Savior." *Yearbook of Comparative and General Literature* 30 (1981): 17–30.

———. *House and Individual*. Stuttgart: Heinz, 1977.

———. "Rilke, Picasso and the Street Circus." In *Rilke and the Visual Arts,* ed. Frank Baron, 78–95. Lawrence: Coronado, 1982.

———. "Up in the Gallery: Kafka and Prévert." *Modern Language Notes* (German Issue) 96, no. 3 (1981): 632–37.

Robert, Marthe. *Franz Kafka's Loneliness.* Trans. Ralph Manheim. London: Faber, 1982.

Roberts, David. "Aspects of Psychology and Mythology in *Die Blechtrommel.*" In *Grass: Kritik, Thesen, Analysen,* ed. Manfred Jürgensen, 45–74. Bern: Francke, 1973.

Robinson, Paul. *Opera and Ideas.* New York: Harper and Row, 1985.

Rosch, Ewald. *Komödien Hofmannsthals.* Marburg: Ewert, 1968.

Rosenthal, Stuart. *The Cinema of Federico Fellini.* New York: Barnes, 1976.

Roskill, Mark. *The Interpretation of Cubism.* Philadelphia: Art Alliance Press, 1985.

Rothe, Friedrich. *Frank Wedekinds Dramen.* Stuttgart: Metzler, 1968.

Rubenstein, William. "Ein Bericht für eine Akademie." In *Franz Kafka Today,* ed. Angel Flores, 55–60. New York: Gordian, 1977.

———. "Franz Kafka: A Hunger-Artist." *Monatshefte* 44, no. 1 (1952): 13–19.

Rubin, Vivienne. *Clowns in Nineteenth-Century French Literature.* Ann Arbor: University Microfilms, 1971.

Rubin, William. *Picasso in the Collection of the Modern Museum of Art.* New York: MOMA, 1972.

———. *"Primitivism" in Twentieth Century Art.* 2 vols. New York: MOMA, 1984.

Rudnitzki, Konstantin. *Meyerhold the Director.* Trans. George Petrov. Ann Arbor: Ardis, 1981.

Russell, John. "In Detail: Picasso's Three Musicians." *Portfolio* (June-July 1979): 12–18.

Ryan, Judith. *The Uncompleted Past.* Detroit: Wayne State University Press, 1983.

Sadoul, Georges. *Jacques Callot, Miroir de son Temps.* Paris: Gallimard, 1969.

St. Aubyn, F. C. *Mallarmé.* New York: Twayne, 1969.

Salachas, Gilbert. *Federico Fellini.* Trans. Rosalie Siegel. New York: Crown, 1970.

Salis, J. R. *Rilkes Schweizer Jahre.* Frankfurt: Suhrkamp, 1975.

Sand, Maurice. *Masques et Bouffons.* Paris: Lévy, 1862.

Sartre, Jean-Paul. *Les Séquestrés d'Altona.* Paris: Gallimard, 1960.

Sauer, Lieselotte. *Marionetten, Maschinen, Automaten.* Bonn: Bouvier, 1983.

Schiff, Gert. "Die Ikonographie der Triptychen." In *Munuscula Disciplinorum,* ed. Tilman Buddensieg, 265–85. Berlin: Hessling, 1968.

Schleifenbaum, Ingrid. *Guillaume Apollinaire: Ondes.* Bonn: Bouvier, 1972.

Schlöndorff, Völker. *Die Blechtrommel: Tagebuch einer Verfilmung.* Darmstadt: Luchterhand, 1979.

Schmalenbach, Werner. *Fernand Léger.* New York: Harry Abrams, 1976.

Schmidt, Henry. *Satire, Caricature, and Perspectivism in the Works of Georg Büchner.* The Hague: Mouton, 1970.

Schmidt, Paul, ed. and trans. *Meyerhold at Work.* Austin: University of Texas Press, 1980.

Schneider, Pierre. *The World of Watteau.* New York: Time, 1967.

Schnitzler, Arthur. *Gesammelte Werke. Die Dramatischen Werke,* vols. 1, 2. Frankfurt: Fischer, 1962.

Schoolfield, George. *The Figure of the Musician in German Literature.* Chapel Hill: University of North Carolina Press, 1956.

Schor, Naomi. *Zola's Crowds.* Baltimore: Hopkins, 1978.

Schorske, Carl. *Fin-de-Siècle Vienna.* New York: Knopf, 1980.

Schroder, Thomas. *Jacques Callot: das gesamte Werk.* München: Rogner und Bernhard, 1971.

Schulz-Hoffmann, Carla, and Judith Weiss, eds. *Max Beckmann Retrospective.* St. Louis: Art Museum, 1984.

Schwarz, Egon. *Josef von Eichendorff.* New York: Twayne, 1972.

Sebeok, Thomas, ed. *Carnival!* The Hague: Mouton, 1984.

Segel, Harold. *Twentieth-Century Russian Drama.* New York: Columbia University Press, 1979.

Seidlin, Oskar. "The Shroud of Silence." *Germanic Review* 28 (1953): 254–61.

Selz, Peter. *Max Beckmann.* New York: MOMA, 1964.

Sembdner, Helmut, ed. *Kleists Aufsatz über das Marionettentheater.* Berlin: Schmidt, 1967.

Seward, Barbara. *The Symbolic Rose.* New York: Columbia University Press, 1960.

Shattuck, Roger. *The Banquet Years.* New York: Vintage, 1968.

———. *The Innocent Eye.* New York: Farrar Straus, 1984.

Shroder, Maurice. *Icarus.* Cambridge: Harvard University Press, 1961.

Siclier, Jacques. *Ingmar Bergman.* Paris: Editions Universitaires, 1960.

Siegel, Marcia. *At the Vanishing Point.* New York: Saturday Review Press, 1972.

Silz, Walter. *Heinrich von Kleist.* Philadelphia: University of Pennsylvania Press, 1961.

Simmel, Georg. *Soziologie.* Leipzig: Duncker und Humblot, 1908.

Simon, John. "Farewell Symphony." *National Review* 35 (22 July 1983): 886–88.

———. *Ingmar Bergman Directs.* New York: Harcourt Brace, 1972.

———, ed. *Focus on the Seventh Seal.* Englewood Cliffs: Prentice-Hall, 1972.

Sitwell, Osbert. *Great Morning.* London: Macmillan, 1948.

Sjoman, Vilgot. *L136: A Diary with Ingmar Bergman.* Trans. Alan Blair. Ann Arbor: Karoma, 1978.

Slonim, Marc. *Russian Theater.* New York: Collier, 1962.

Sokel, Walter. "Demaskierung und Untergang wilhelminischer Repräsentanz." In *Herkommen und Erneuerung,* ed. Gerald Gillespie, 387–412. Tübingen: Niemeyer, 1976.

———. *Franz Kafka.* New York: Columbia University Press, 1966.

———. *Franz Kafka: Tragik und Ironie.* München: Langen, 1964.

———. "Perspective and Dualism in the Novels of Böll." In *The Contemporary Novel in German,* ed. Robert Heitner, 9–35. Austin: University of Texas Press, 1967.

Sontag, Susan. *A Susan Sontag Reader.* Ed. Elisabeth Hardwick. New York: Farrar Straus, 1982.

Spann, Meno. *Franz Kafka.* Boston: Twayne, 1976.

———. "Franz Kafka's Leopard." *Germanic Review* 34 (1959): 85–104.

Staiger, Emil. *Meisterwerke deutscher Sprache.* Zürich: Atlantis, 1961.

Stamelman, Richard. *The Drama of Self in Guillaume Apollinaire's Alcools.* Chapel Hill: North Carolina Studies in Romance Languages, 1976.

Stammler, Wolfgang. *Frau Welt, eine mittelalterliche Allegorie*. Freiburg (Schweiz): Universitätsverlag, 1959.

Stark, John. *the literature of exhaustion*. Durham: Duke University Press, 1974.

Starobinski, Jean. "Note sur le Bouffon Romantique." *Cahiers du Sud,* nos. 287–388 (1966), 270–75.

———. *Portrait de l'Artiste en Saltimbanque*. Geneva: Skira, 1970.

———. "Sur Quelques Répondants Allégoriques du Poète." *Revue d'Histoire Littéraire de la France* (April-June 1967): 402–12.

Starr, Sandra. *Joseph Cornell and the Ballet*. New York: Castelli, Feigen, Corcoran, 1983.

Steegmuller, Francis. *Apollinaire, Poet among the Painters*. New York: Farrar Straus, 1963.

———. *Cocteau, A Biography*. London: Macmillan, 1970.

Steene, Birgitta. *Ingmar Bergman*. New York: Twayne, 1968.

Steffen, Hans. *Das deutsche Lustspiel*. Göttingen: Vandenhoeck und Ruprecht, 1969.

Stein, Gertrude. *Picasso*. Paris: Floury, 1938.

Steiner, George. *Language and Silence*. New York: Atheneum, 1967.

Steiner, Jacob. *Rilkes Duineser Elegien*. Bern: Francke, 1969.

Steinhauer, Harry. "Hunger Artist or Artist of Hunger?" *Criticism* 4 (1962): 28–43.

Stephens, Anthony. *Rilke's Gedichte an die Nacht*. Cambridge: Cambridge University Press, 1972.

Stern, J. P. *A Study of Nietzsche*. Cambridge: Cambridge University Press, 1979.

Storey, Robert. "The Pantomime of Jean-Gaspard Deburau at the Théâtre des Funambules." *Theater Survey* 23, no. 1 (1982): 1–29.

———. *Pierrot: A Critical History of a Mask*. Princeton: Princeton University Press, 1978.

———. *Pierrots on the Stage of Desire*. Princeton: Princeton University Press, 1985.

———. "Verlaine's Pierrots." *Romance Notes* 20, no. 2 (1979): 223–30.

Strauss, Walter. *Descent and Return: The Orphic Theme in Modern Literature*. Cambridge: Harvard University Press, 1971.

———. "The Reconciliation of Opposites in Orphic Poetry: Rilke and Mallarmé." *Centennial Review* 10 (1966): 214–36.

Stravinsky, Igor, and Robert Craft. *Expositions and Developments*. New York: Doubleday, 1962.

Stravinsky, Vera, and Robert Craft, eds. *Stravinsky in Pictures and Documents*. New York: Simon and Schuster, 1978.

Swain, Virginia. "The Legitimation Crisis: Event and Meaning in Baudelaire's 'Le Vieux Saltimbanque' and 'Une Mort Héroique.'" *Romanic Review* 73, no. 4 (1982): 452–62.

Swales, Martin. *Arthur Schnitzler, A Critical Study*. Oxford: Clarendon, 1971.

———. *The German Novelle*. Princeton: Princeton University Press, 1977.

Symons, James. *Meyerhold's Theater of the Grotesque*. Coral Gables: University of Miami Press, 1971.

Sypher, Wylie, ed. *Comedy*. New York: Doubleday Anchor, 1956.

Szarkowski, John, ed. *The Works of Atget*, vol. 4. New York: MOMA, 1985.

Tank, Kurt. *Günter Grass*. Berlin: Colloquium, 1965.

Tarachow, Sidney. "Circuses and Clowns." In *Psychoanalysis and the Social Sciences,* ed. Geza Roheim. New York: International Universities Press, 1951.

Tauber, Herbert. *Franz Kafka.* London: Secker and Warburg, 1948.

Taylor, John Russell. *Cinema Eye, Cinema Ear.* London: Methuen, 1964.

Tetel, Marcel. *Rabelais.* New York: Twayne, 1967.

Thomalla, Ariane. *Die "femme fragile": Ein literarischer Frauentypus der Jahrhundertwende.* Düsseldorf: Bertelsmann, 1972.

Thompson, Ewa. "The Archetype of the Fool in Russian Literature." *Canadian Slavonic Papers* 15, no. 3 (1973): 245–73.

Tierney, Neil. *The Unknown Country.* London: Hale, 1977.

Tobias, Toby. "Four by Fokine." *Program Notes* (Ballet Theater), 1977.

Towsen, John. *Clowns.* New York: Hawthorn, 1976.

Trottenberg, Arthur, ed. *A Vision of Paris: The Photographs of Atget, the Words of Proust.* New York: Macmillan, 1963.

Trousson, Raymond. *Un Problème de littérature comparée.* Paris: Minard, 1965.

Trudgian, Helen. *Les Idées Esthétiques de J. K. Huysmans.* Paris: Conard, 1934.

Turk, Edward. "The Birth of *Children of Paradise.*" *American Film* 4, no. 9 (1979): 42–49.

Ubersfeld, Anni. *Le Roi et le Bouffon.* Paris: Corti, 1974.

Ugrinsky, Alexey, ed. *Heinrich von Kleist Studies.* New York: AMS Press, 1980.

Urbach, Reinhard. *Arthur Schnitzler.* Trans. Donald Daviau. New York: Ungar, 1973.

———. *Schnitzler-Kommentar.* München: Winkler, 1974.

Vaget, Hans Rudolf. "Der Asket und der Komödiant: Die Brüder Buddenbrook." *Modern Language Notes* 97 (1982): 656–70.

van Caspel, J. "Josephine und Jeremias." *Neophilologus* 37, no. 4 (1953): 241–45.

van der Will, Wilfried. *Pikaro Heute.* Stuttgart: Kohlhammer, 1967.

Verlaine, Paul. *Oeuvres Poétiques.* Ed. Jacques Robichez. Paris: Garnier, 1969.

Vetrocq, Marcia, and Adelheid Gealt. *Domenico Tiepolo's Punchinello Drawings.* Bloomington: Indiana University Art Museum, 1979.

Vigée, Claude. "Les Artistes de la Faim." *Comparative Literature* 9, no. 2 (1957): 97–117.

Vincent, Howard. *Daumier and his World.* Evanston: Northwestern University Press, 1968.

Vlad, Roman. *Igor Stravinsky.* London: Oxford University Press, 1978.

Vogt, Jurgen. *Heinrich Böll.* München: Beck, 1978.

von Boehn, Max. *Dolls and Puppets.* London: Harrap, 1932.

von Wiese, Benno. *Die Deutsche Novelle.* 2 vols. Düsseldorf: Bagel, 1956, 1968.

Vos, Melvin. *The Drama of Comedy: Victim and Victor.* Richmond: Knox, 1966.

———. *For God's Sake Laugh!* Richmond: Knox, 1967.

Wager, Walter, ed. *The Playwrights Speak.* London: Longmans Green, 1969.

Waidson, H. M. "Starvation-Artist and Leopard." *Germanic Review* 35, no. 4 (1960): 262–69.

Waldeck, Peter. *The Split Self from Goethe to Broch.* Lewisburg: Bucknell University Press, 1979.

Wechsler, Judith. *A Human Comedy.* Chicago: University of Chicago Press, 1982.

Wedekind, Frank. *Gesammelte Werke,* vols. 3, 4, 9. München: Müller, 1924.

Wedekind, Tilly. *Lulu, die Rolle meines Lebens.* München: Rutten und Loening, 1969.

Weinberg, Kurt. *Kafka's Dichtungen.* Bern: Francke, 1963.

Welsford, Enid. *The Fool.* Gloucester: Peter Smith, 1966.

White, Eric Walter. *Igor Stravinsky.* Berkeley: University of California Press, 1979.

Wiles, Timothy. *The Theater Event.* Chicago: University of Chicago Press, 1980.

Willeford, William. *The Fool and his Scepter.* Evanston: Northwestern University Press, 1978.

Willeke, Audrone. "Frank Wedekind and the 'Frauenfrage.'" *Monatshefte* 72 (1980): 26–38.

———. "The Tightrope-Walker and the Marionette: Images of Harmony in Wedekind and Kleist." *Proceedings* (Mountain Interstate Foreign Language Conference, 1977), 89–95.

Wilson, A. Leslie. "The Grotesque Everyman in Günter Grass' *Die Blechtrommel.*" *Monatshefte* 58 (1966): 131–38.

Wittmann, Horst. "Hofmannsthals *Der Schwierige:* Die Potentialität des Leichten." *Seminar* 10 (1974): 274–97.

Wood, Robin. *Ingmar Bergman.* London: Studio Vista, 1969.

Woodring, Carl. "Josephine the Singer." In *Franz Kafka Today,* ed. Angel Flores, 71–75. New York: Gordian, 1977.

Woodward, James. *Leonid Andreyev, A Study.* Oxford: Clarendon, 1969.

Wysling, Hans. *Narzissmus und Illusionäre Existenzform.* Bern: Francke, 1982.

Yates, W. E. *Franz Grillparzer, A Critical Introduction.* Cambridge: Cambridge University Press, 1972.

Young, Vernon. *Cinema Borealis: Ingmar Bergman and the Swedish Ethos.* New York: Lewis, 1971.

———. "La Strada: Cinematic Intersections." *On Film,* 59–67. Chicago: Quadrangle, 1972.

Zguta, Russell. *Russian Minstrels.* Philadelphia: University of Pennsylvania Press, 1978.

Ziolkowski, Theodore. "The Author as Advocatus Dei in Heinrich Böll's *Group Portrait with Lady.*" *University of Dayton Review* 12, no. 2 (1976): 7–17.

———. *Disenchanted Images.* Princeton: Princeton University Press, 1977.

———. *Varieties of Literary Thematics.* Princeton: Princeton University Press, 1983.

———. "Vom Verrückten zum Clown." In *In Sachen Böll,* ed. Marcel Reich-Ranicki, 345–57. Köln: Kiepenhauer und Witsch, 1970.

Zohn, Harry. *Karl Kraus.* New York: Twayne, 1971.

Zuckmayer, Carl. *Meisterdramen.* Frankfurt: Fischer, 1968.

INDEX